DR. JANET WILLIAMS —

TO A GREAT American —
with Appreciation for
"Adding value to America";
with your innovative
work in Rural Emergency
medicine —

God Bless,

John Blennan

CALL OUT THE GUARD!

The Story of Lieutenant General John B. Conaway and the Modern Day National Guard.

Lt. Gen John B. Conaway
and
Jeff Nelligan

TURNER PUBLISHING COMPANY

TURNER PUBLISHING COMPANY
412 Broadway • P.O. Box 3101
Paducah, KY 42002-3101
Phone: (502) 443-0121

Turner Publishing Company Staff:
Publishing Consultant: Douglas W. Sikes
Production Coordinator: John Mark Jackson
Designer: Heather R. Warren

ISBN: 1-56311-372-4
Library of Congress Catalog Card Number:
97-60384

TABLE OF CONTENTS

THIS BOOK IS DEDICATED TO THE

MEN AND WOMEN

WHO ARE THE NATIONAL GUARD

PAST, PRESENT, AND FUTURE.

FOREWORD

The famous U.S. Senator Wendell Ford, D-KY, as our special guest at the annual National Guard Bureau Dining-in. He was the Governor of Kentucky who appointed me Commander of the Kentucky Air National Guard in 1972. Senator Ford is the Co-Chairman with Senator Kit Bond, R-MO, of the Senate National Guard Caucus.

For me, this book is a homecoming of sorts because I've known the principals — John Conaway and the National Guard — for many, many years.

First off, John and myself share a similar history. We are both born and bred West Kentuckians and our lives have been shaped by that great region of that even greater state. We've both spent many years in Washington in public service, the only difference being John wore three stars and I wore the title of "U.S. Senator."

And last and most importantly, we both believe deeply in the National Guard.

In 1972, I appointed John the Commander of the Air National Guard in Kentucky. Back then, I recognized his potential and knew he had a future that would take him far beyond Standiford Field in Louisville. Nearly three decades later, it's pretty clear that my confidence in him was truly justified. And it was his journey as a Guardsman from Henderson, Kentucky to the Pentagon that forms the backdrop of this magnificent book. How appropriate, as well, that Turner Publishing, located in Paducuh, Kentucky, should be its publisher.

This book tells a story I've seen up close and personal. I served in the Guard for 14 years and was involved in several call-ups. As Governor of the Commonwealth of Kentucky from 1971 to 1974, I mobilized the Kentucky National Guard on many occasions to help protect the people and property of our state.

And as a U.S. Senator since 1974, I've made it a point to closely monitor Guard issues. Indeed, I currently serve as the co-chairman of the Senate's National Guard Caucus.

The story that John and Jeff Nelligan have laid out in a detailed, readable fashion is one that should resonate not only with Guard members and their families, but with all Americans.

The Guard has always been there for America, fulfilling a role that no other agency or government entity could perform. I imagine that many folks wish that other aspects of our state and federal government would function as efficiently and selflessly as the National Guard.

America's National Guard is truly a success story — and this book is gratifying to all of us who, over the years, have seen this incredible story unfold.

Senator Wendell Ford of Kentucky

FOREWORD

Linda and I with our good friend, Chairman G.V. "Sonny" Montgomery in the Hall of Heros, the Pentagon.

This magnificent book comes at an ideal time, a time when the Guard is more prominent in America than at any time in its 360-year history.

Having said that, let me discuss several things in the interest of full disclosure.

First, I was a member of the Guard for more than three decades, rising from 2nd Lieutenant to Major General. I've seen the Guard up close, beginning as a platoon commander in Company A, 198th Tank Battalion, MSARNG. I was mobilized for the Korean War and called-out many times during the civil rights protests in the South during the late 1950s and early 1960s.

Second, as a Member of Congress for three decades, I did everything in my power to improve and enhance the Guard and I consider myself one of the strongest advocates the modern Guard had on Capitol Hill.

Third, John Conaway is and has been a close friend of mine for many years. And, like many folks in Washington and out there in real America, I believe he was absolutely the right leader at the right time as the modern day Guard evolved.

All of which is to say, I've had a birds-eye view of this subject for decades. And having read this book, I can tell you that Conaway and Nelligan cover the subject about as well as it can be covered.

There are many aspects of today's Guard that, given my history with the force, I find astonishing. But what really sticks in my mind is that today's American military establishment — the most powerful on the planet — cannot make a commitment, whether it be Panama, Somalia, Bosnia, Haiti, or the Persian Gulf, without the direct and heavy involvement of the Guard.

This is an absolutely amazing development — and three decades ago it was utterly unforeseen.

As upbeat as I am about the Guard, my greatest fear is that the Guard is too often taken for granted because its units are quick to respond, do not elicit a lot of fanfare, and fade right back into the communities from where they came.

Given this, when the subject of cuts in the Guard comes up, I am always quick to ask Members and others: What would happen if we didn't have the Guard?

Who would pick up the pieces — literally — after entire communities are washed away by floods, or by hurricanes? What law enforcement agency in the land could instantly mobilize hundreds of personnel to help in a search for a missing child? What group, in a matter of hours, could provide water, food and shelter for tens of thousands? What military component can provide the nitty-gritty combat support for large deployments of troops halfway around the world?

In fact, no group or organization can do any of this. That's why I've always said that this nation would be nearly paralyzed by various crises if the Guard did not exist.

The Guard remains one of America's most valued institutions, part of the fabric of virtually every community in the nation.

And this book is not only a book for those in the National Guard. It is also a book for every American citizen who wants to know about their community-based defense force.

Over the past three-and-a-half decades, the Guard has emerged as one of the things in this nation that works and works well. And to sum it up simply, Conaway and Nelligan tell the story of how that came to be.

Congressman G.V. "Sonny" Montgomery of Mississippi

PROLOGUE

26 January 1968

I'm walking across the floor of a vast hangar at Standiford Field in Louisville, the home of the Kentucky Air National Guard. From a loudspeaker comes the words, "Attention all personnel. This morning, President Lyndon Johnson announced in Washington that he is mobilizing units of the National Guard and Reserves in response to North Korea's seizure of the U.S.S. Pueblo. I repeat..."

Twenty-two years later, a similar call would echo throughout hangers and armories across the United States. This time, mobilization of the Guard came not in response to seizure of a ship, but to the seizure of an entire country. In 1968, with what became known as the "Pueblo Crisis," as in 1990 with Desert Shield, the call-up would serve as an immediate and dramatic statement of American resolve.

The Pueblo incident prompted the Guard's fourth mobilization since the eve of World War II. It was the decision of a President fighting one land war in Asia and attempting to avoid fighting another. It was a reassuring signal to our South Korean allies that we would defend them. And it was a belated acknowledgement that the U.S. was unable to fulfill its global defense commitments because a minor "action" in Vietnam had irretrievably become a major war.

The failures of the Johnson Administration were lessons learned well by President George Bush and his civilian leaders and military commanders. In 1990, the mobilization announcement came just 21 days after advance elements of the 82nd Airborne Division dug in on the Saudi Arabian border facing Kuwait. There was not yet a comprehensive, over-arching strategic or tactical military plan for responding to Iraqi aggression. But the Administration understood clearly and quickly that an overseas deployment of virtually any size or duration required Guard and Reserve support.

A fact perhaps under-appreciated at the time was that by calling out the Guard, President George Bush was summoning forth not only one of the world's oldest continually operating military organizations, dating from 1636, but also one of the modern world's most powerful military forces. In August of 1990, the Guard boasted the world's 4th largest air force, and the world's eighth largest army. Most Guard units had first-rate equipment and training, and 50 percent had been prior service — that is, had served in the active duty military.

The National Guard, both Air and Army, is one of two elements of America's Total Force, which is comprised of five separate active forces and seven separate reserve components. Together, these services comprise the most powerful military legion, measured by any standards — lethality, reach, training, equipment — in the history of the world.

The National Guard's genesis was as a militia regiment first mustered and recognized in the Bay Colony, Massachusetts in 1636. The militia system that developed in the early Colonies and which continues today as the National Guard is a product of America's origins.

It was in 1637 that militia units fought the Pequot Indians in the Pequot War, recognized today as the first military engagement in the New World by European settlers.

In colonial and later frontier times, it was agreed that every man owed a duty to the state in time of need as a member of the militia. By 1787, threats of foreign wars were on the minds of the Founding Fathers. As they debated the sections of their proposed Constitution that dealt with military matters, many of the Philadelphia statesmen drew on their own military experiences from the Revolution. They knew, based on General George Washington's difficulty in fielding an effective national army, that a well-regulated militia — ready for the call to provide national defense — was vital to the survival of their young nation.

The Constitution's Militia Clause was the result of that decision making process two centuries ago. Like much of the Constitution, the words of the Militia Clause developed by the Founding Fathers have proved sufficiently flexible to have a modern adaptation. Indeed, the dual status of the National Guard in the modern era derives from this clause. Based on the National Defense Act of 1934, this duality is represented by the National Guard of the individual states (and the three Territories and the District of Columbia) in pure organized Militia status — the state force — and the National Guard of the United States in organized units — the federal force. This is the structural centerpiece of Guard units of the National Guard in their peacetime, state-controlled status. These are the same units that are part of the National Guard of the United States which train and are prepared for assimilation into the U.S. Army and U.S. Air Force upon a Presidential mobilization.

The state-organized militias envisioned in the Constitution were later named the "National Guard" in the 1820s. As the French are fond of pointing out, it was a Frenchman, Marquis de Lafayette who when trooping the line of the New York Militia in August of 1824, noted that they reminded him of his own "Garde Nacional," the French National Guard troops of Paris. Not long thereafter, the militia took the name "National Guard."

The Guard has participated in every conflict America has entered — the Revolutionary War, the War of 1812, and the Indian Wars. National Guard units fought on both sides of the Civil War, and following that, along the Southwest border. Moreover, it was a Guard unit that took part in the famous, if reckless, charge up San Juan Hill.

It's also little known that in the fifty years prior to World War I, the National Guard served as the primary military land force in defense of the United States. In World War I, the Guard sent 208,000 troops to

Europe and Guardsmen were the first soldiers to see combat in France. World War II brought full mobilization of the Guard, accounting for 377,000 men. All of the 18 Guard divisions in existence in December of 1941 were sent overseas. It was the Guardsmen of the 29th Infantry Division who first set foot on the Normandy beaches of France on D-Day, June 6th, 1944. Moreover, the Army units involved in General of the Army Douglas MacArthur's war in the Pacific were almost exclusively Guard units.

America's post-war emergence as a superpower required that a large, well-trained reserve force was imperative if our global responsibilities were to be met. And in fact, the largest mobilization in the history of the Guard was the 382,900-personnel call-up for Korea.

The construction of the Berlin Wall in August of 1961 prompted a 65,000 Guard mobilization; the Pueblo crisis inspired a 33,000 man call-up. Guard men and women, both Air and Army, undertook missions in the Grenada and Panama operations and the 1985 attack against Libya. Finally, nearly 80,000 Guard men and women were mobilized for Operations Desert Shield and Desert Storm, a superb snapshot of the modern Guard's capability.

But it was not only conflict that brought the Guard into the global arena. Throughout the 1980s, the Guard participated in nation-building exercises in Central America, in NATO exercises in Europe, and Team Spirit in South Korea. In the post-Cold War world, Guard personnel have played a role in humanitarian interventions in Bosnia, Somalia, Rwanda, Nigeria, the Dominican Republic, Honduras, El Salvador, and many other countries. The Guard has been the lead player in military exchanges with the forces of the Central European, Eastern European, and Baltic nations and other emerging democracies. At any time of day throughout the year, Guard soldiers and airmen are deployed along side their active duty counterparts, in the remote corners and main streets of nations around the world.

And yet, despite this global reach and many years of overseas achievement, the National Guard is an anomaly among the world's armies and air forces. It is a force that until federalized, is directed by the Governors of the 50 states and three territories of America. As such, it fulfills a diverse range of missions — responding to floods, hurricanes, volcanoes, blizzards, tornadoes, forest fires, missing persons, industrial accidents, civil disturbances, and any other missions ordered by a Governor.

As time changes, society's concerns change; and thus, so do missions. A 360-year-old institution rooted in American communities must respond to local difficulties. In its earliest days, the militia responded to Indian raids. Today, the challenges are as acute.

And that's why today's Guard — in addition to disaster relief and overseas missions — provides medical assistance to under-served areas, patrols high-crime areas, combats narcotics smuggling, works to improve destitute urban neighborhoods, and runs boot camps to help turn around errant teenagers.

It's important to emphasize that the National Guard is playing a significant role in both the external and internal matters of the United States. At any given moment, the Guard is a visible, positive presence in 4,200 communities across America. Twice a day on average, a Governor somewhere is mobilizing a Guard unit to respond to some type of emergency.

The Guard is America's community-based defense force, a familiar face to residents of towns and cities in rural and urban America. And at the same time, the Guard provides the active military with the added punch and support needed to operate, fight, and win anywhere in the world.

The Guard has assumed a prominence in America unimaginable when I first joined the force more than 35 years ago. Little did I know then what changes I would witness and little did I imagine that I would help guide them along.

This is the story of just four decades in the National Guard's 360-year history. But these four decades provide a magnificent prism through which to glimpse the Guard. It remains one of the oldest institutions in American life and the spirit animating the citizen-soldier and citizen-airmen has not changed during those many, many years. It is a principle of simplicity, and yet of endurance — service to community, service to country.

Moreover, it is a principle on display every day as towns and statehouses and even the corridors of Congress echo with the refrain heard when disaster strikes or the country is threatened:

"Call out the Guard!"

Section I. "In The Field"

CHAPTER ONE

"PRELUDE TO THE STORM"

"Make no mistake, our Total Force Policy is alive and well. This has been clearly demonstrated during Desert Storm and Desert Shield. The Guard and Reserve were critical to the success of the mission. We simply couldn't have done it without them."
General of the Joint Chiefs of Staff, Colin Powell
May 26, 1991

Later, as a report from the famous RAND think tank would state: "Even before the decision was made to send military forces into Saudi Arabia, it was clear that the reserve forces of certain kinds would be needed quickly. For the Air Force, 64 percent of the tactical airlift and half of the strategic airlift reside in the Reserve Components ....the Army Guard and Reserve include 71 percent of the military police companies and 69 percent of the military intelligence units. Water purification and communications skills are found principally in the reserves. All of these skills were needed in August to help deploy active units."

Secretary of Defense Dick Cheney, Chairman of the Joint Chiefs of Staff, General Colin Powell, and Commander-in-Chief of Central Command, General Norman Schwartzkopf knew this in August of 1990. So did I.

What follows is a brief chronology of key events leading up to the largest Presidential mobilization of Guard and Reserve forces in four decades, an event that would demonstrate once and for all the wisdom of the Total Force policy.

2 August 1990

Iraq attacks Kuwait at 0100 on 02 August 90, Eastern Standard Time. Iraqi forces quickly overrun the tiny Persian Gulf nation.

3 August 1990

Iraq masses troops on the border of Saudi Arabia. Early this morning, I met Major General Billy Navas, Vice Chief of the National Guard Bureau; Major General Phil Killey and Brigadier General Don Sheppard, the Director and Deputy Directors of the Air National Guard; and Major General Don Burdick, Director of the Army National Guard — to discuss how the U.S. might respond to the Iraqi invasion and what role the Guard would play. After much discussion, a consensus emerges that if the actives become involved in the region, the Guard would be — and should be —right behind. We also agreed to offer immediately any forces the Army or Air Force needed on a volunteer basis to help in the U.S. or in the Persian Gulf theater until a mobilization decision was made. I personally carried this message to the Joint Chiefs and to the Army and Air Force leadership.

6 August 1990

Secretary of Defense Dick Cheney meets with Saudi leaders in Riyadh and, not surprisingly, they ask for an immediate deployment of U.S. forces to Saudi Arabia. One day later, units of the 82nd Airborne Division are ordered to move to the Saudi-Kuwait border.

7 August 1990

A briefing paper is prepared for Major General Navas and Major General Burdick and for "Reasons for a 200K Call-up." Looking back, this document was emblematic of the forward-looking, pro-active thinking that had been a hallmark of the Guard during the last decade.

The major thrust of this memorandum was that with 70 percent of the combat support and combat service support capability in the Guard and Reserves, and with the distant location of the Persian Gulf theater, any contingency lasting a month or longer would require substantial use of the Reserve components. (Contrastingly, such a self-sustaining capability did exist in the European theater. As the backbone of NATO, the U.S. had stockpiled equipment and supplies there for decades. Much of this material was subsequently sent to the Gulf.)

Second, the paper asserted that a call-up would demonstrate national will. Movement toward the Guard and Reserve was almost tantamount to placing the nation on a high military alert. Finally, a mobilization would demonstrate that the Total Force policy was a guiding principle of the American military establishment, and not an empty slogan.

Even as this paper began circulating, Mississippi's 172nd Military Airlift Group was flying into the theater, the first ANG unit to do so. ANG KC-135 air refueling tankers were assigned to Tanker Task Force locations at bases in Bangor, Maine; Pease, New Hampshire; Phoenix, Arizona; and, Forbes, Kansas, for support of the airlift to Saudi Arabia. The morning of the next day, August 8th, ANG planes begin ferrying combat troops and equipment to Saudi Arabia. And later that same day, several members of the 228th Signal Brigade from South Carolina become the first ARNG personnel to enter Southwest Asia.

9 August 90

President Bush, in a televised nationwide address from the Oval Office, outlines the U.S. response to the Iraqi invasion of Kuwait. He gives the operation a code-name: "Desert Shield."

Lead elements of the 82nd Airborne Division reach Saudi Arabia.

It is almost universally agreed, by both proponents and opponents, that President Bush's reaction to events in the Gulf has been unusually quick and decisive. It's clear that he is way out in front of American public opinion; indeed, many Americans probably couldn't have located Kuwait on a map.

The deployment of units of the elite, well-known 82nd Airborne is a major policy and political decision. By stationing these highly regarded soldiers at the edge of the Saudi border with Kuwait and Iraq, the President is quite literally drawing a line in the sand. Then as now, I and many other senior military commanders believed that if Iraq had plunged across the border with its heavy armor, the lead battalions of the 82nd would have suffered heavy casualties, relying for their very survival on the intervention of massive U.S. air power.

It is also at this point, that both Secretary Cheney and General Powell are, with the help of senior staff throughout the Pentagon, formulating a single critical war plan: Defending against and ultimately halting an Iraqi thrust into Saudi Arabia.

Central to any defensive plan was the immediate deployment of the Army's premier units the so-called "fast movers." This was the famed 18th Airborne Corps, the Army's primary contingency force. The 82nd was already in the theater, and to follow were the 1st Cavalry Division from Fort Hood, Texas; the 24th Infantry Division (Mechanized) from Fort Stewart, Georgia; the 101st Airborne Division (Air Assault) from Fort Campbell, Kentucky; and the 1st Armored Division, based in Germany.

As stated earlier, the Guard and Reserve Components held the bulk of the Army's combat support and combat service support, which supplied, in that memorable phrase, the beans and bullets for the frontline combat troops and airmen. This meant, yes, haulers of beans and bullets, and also clerks, computer operators, electricians, water purifiers, mechanics, even postal and laundry units.

In addition, there was also a need to replace, or "backfill," those active troops in CONUS (Continental United States) and in other theaters who were deploying to Desert Shield.

We accomplished this in many instances through volunteerism, a subject explored in an in-depth study of the war by the RAND Corporation (an acronym which stands for Research and Development.) As the RAND study noted, "The large number of reserves who tried to volunteer for active duty in Operation Desert Shield was unprecedented and unanticipated. Guard units across the country reported that their phones were busy with offers from Guard members who wanted to support the military action."

"In the Air Guard and Air Force Reserve components from early August of 1990 to October 31, 1990, the number of those willing to volunteer was about 25,000, double the number allowed to volunteer for active duty (12,000). By August 22nd, 10,500 Guard and Reserve volunteers were serving on active duty. They flew 42 percent of the strategic airlift and 33 percent of the refueling missions. These volunteers moved 7 million tons of cargo and 8,150 passengers."

Moreover, the report added, "Many Army Guard personnel simply showed up at units to help with tasks necessary to ready the unit for mobilization. Reserve volunteers opened ports, received and shipped equipment, and even deployed to help establish strategic communications as well as to provide other needs, such as water purification specialists and Arabic linguists."

The heavy volume of volunteers, besides helping with critical tasks in the deployments, demonstrated something else: that Guard and Reserve personnel were eager to serve their country. Later, as I scrutinized the Guard units committed to Desert Shield purely because they'd had almost universal volunteerism of both enlisted and officer personnel, I recalled what an oldtimer had said to me when I was called up in 1968: "Everyone trains for the big game and when it finally comes, they want to be there, no matter what. That's the nature of the military; that's the nature of those of us who wear the uniform."

10 August 90

At my direction, the NGB staff closely reviews the mobilization process with the active duty components.

The Army Guard staff begins work with Forces Command (FORSCOM) in Atlanta on a computer model which identifies the conditions and types of Guard and Reserve soldiers needed in the Gulf. This list ultimately tops 88,000, which raises concerns among senior Army officials, including the Secretary of the Army, Michael P. Stone. The general feeling is that the 88,000 number is simply too high; another problem is that some units are designed for offensive combat action. It's decided the list must be thinned out.

The criteria for any Guard and Reserve unit on the FORSCOM force list is that it has to be a unit needed by General Schwartzkopf; it had to meet readiness standards, which were determined by the unit's C-rating; and, if possible, the unit should be matched with its CAPSTONE partner (CAPSTONE was the program under which Guard and Reserve units were aligned directly to commands, i.e. in Europe or Korea, to which they would be assigned under contingency plans when mobilized.) Given Secretary Stone's wishes, the list is ultimately cut to 48,800 personnel, of which approximately 25,000 are Army Guard.

Not a single soldier from the ARNG round-out brigades — the 48th Infantry Brigade (Mechanized) (GA), the 155th Armored Brigade (MS), and the 256th Infantry Brigade (Mechanized) (LA) — were on the list, although the gaining active component Divisions that the 48th and 155th were part of were being deployed. Roundout units provided the missing pieces to purposely under-structured active divisions and were trained, equipped, and programmed for mobilization and deployment with their gaining command. Because of their status, all of these roundout brigades were tested and met the mobilization readiness standards prescribed by the Army.

The Air National Guard and Air Force Reserve handled things a bit differently. Senior Air Force officials asked the different Air Force commands, i.e. tankers, fighters, bombers, transport, combat communications, reconnaissance, logistics, and air refueling — what their most compelling needs were. The Air National Guard officers assigned to each command could then brief the actives on what Air Guard units could best fit the particular requirements of each active command. In addition to this close liaison, the Guard credibility is aided by the fact that nearly every Air Guard component unit was rated either C-1 or C-2, the highest levels of readiness, and hence ready for deployment in a maximum of 72 hours. Because of this system, the Air Force is willing to use the Air Guard and Reserve in virtually all endeavours.

12 August 90

In mid-morning, I receive a draft message from the Secretary of the Army entitled "Alert Order for Presidential Call-up of Selected Reserves to Active Federal Duty." The machinery of mobilization is slowly moving forward.

14 August 90

An issue that would cast a long shadow over the Desert Shield/Storm deployment is triggered at this point. The Department of the Army asks that those Guard combat units identified for deployment to Saudi Arabia — which could only mean our three round-out brigades — be certified by a training readiness evaluation conducted at the National Training Center (NTC) in California.

The round-out concept was a fundamental part of the Total Force policy, an ingenious way to unite the active and reserve components. It was the brainchild of the legendary General Creighton Abrams, Chief of Staff of the Army, who felt that the reluctance to call up the reserves during the Vietnam War was a tragic mistake, ultimately costing the U.S. military the popular support needed to prosecute the war effectively and successfully.

Under the Total Force, in order to bring cohesion to the active and reserve forces, selected active divisions (consisting of three brigades) would have two active brigades and a Guard brigade as the third brigade in the divisional structure. The 24th Infantry Division (Mechanized), for example, had two active brigades and was rounded out by the 48th Mechanized Infantry Brigade, Georgia Army National Guard, headquartered at Fort Stewart, Georgia, home of the 24th. The 155th Armored Brigade, Mississippi Army National Guard, was assigned to the 1st Cavalry Division, stationed at Fort Hood, Texas. The 256th Infantry Brigade (Mechanized), Louisiana Army National Guard, at Fort Polk, Louisiana rounded out the 5th Infantry Division,

These Round Out brigades trained with the active brigades and had first-rate equipment — M-1 Abrams tanks, Bradley Fighting Vehicles, first-rate artillery, HUM-VEES and top-flight communications gear. The Round Out brigade soldiers had access to all the Army schools and not surprisingly, these brigades had a high degree of readiness and morale. No less than General Norman Schwartzkopf had bestowed praise upon the 48th when he commanded the 24th ID.

Given the longstanding Total Force policy and the demonstrated abilities of the Round Out brigades, those of us in the Guard Bureau, were puzzled by the Army's sudden requirement of NTC certification. The NTC is the huge, desert warfare school in Southeastern California. It features a tough "opfor" (opposition force) and a computer-monitored battlefield stretching over dozens of square miles. In fact, a number of ARNG units, including battalions of both the 48th and 156th, had successfully completed rotations at the NTC. NTC certification had never been a readiness requirement for the round-out brigade nor for active Army units. Why should it be so now?

The next day, August 15th, something more ominous occurred. The Chiefs of Staff of the 24th Infantry Division and the 1st Calvary Division were promoted to Brigadier General and assigned to the Assistant Division Commander positions formerly occupied by the Army Guard officers commanding the 48th and 155th Round Out brigades.

On August 16th, Forces Command reported that the 82nd Airborne Division was 40 percent deployed in Saudi Arabia, the 2nd Brigade of the 24th ID was steaming toward the Gulf, and the 101st Airborne Division was enroute to U.S. ports of departure for the Gulf.

At the same time, the 24th ID Commander, Major General Barry MacCaffrey, told Vice-Chief of Staff of the Army, General Gordon Sullivan, that both the commander of the 48th Brigade, Brigadier General Al Holland, and the Georgia Adjutant General, Major General Joe Griffin, declare the 48th is ready to go to war.

17 August 90

For the first time in its history, the Stage 1 Civil Reserve Air Fleet (CRAF) is activated. The CRAF contracts with DOD to haul troops to theaters when the Air Force simply doesn't have the transport capacity. This activation was a little-noticed indication of just how large this contingency, only two weeks old, was becoming.

In the Pentagon and in the Administration, there is intense focus on possible use of the President's call up authority under Section 673(b). Initially, this would be a 90-day call-up, with the option of an additional 90-day extension. This provided a 180-day period in which the President did not need Congressional approval for mobilization.

There is little question that there was a compelling need for a call-up. And I wasn't the only one who understood the capabilities of the reserve components. Indeed, in his book, It Doesn't Take a Hero, General Schwartzkopf stated "The President's next move was to call up the reserves. He had the authority to activate up to 200,000 reserves for up to 180 days without asking Congress, and by doing so, he gave a powerful signal to the people of the United State that we had a job to do as a nation. I was in favor of this move. I'd always been convinced that one of the terrible mistakes we'd made during the Vietnam War was not mobilizing — Washington sent our soldiers into battle without calling on the American people to support them."

General Schwartzkopf continued: "I knew precisely what we needed: Truck drivers, stevedores, ammunition handlers, telephone installers, mechanics — workers to take on the nitty-gritty tasks of supporting a deployment in a combat zone." Needless to say, his beliefs were shared by many, many senior active officers.

In addition to sentiments expressed by the actives, Congressional pressure for a call-up was also rising. Congressman Sonny Montgomery, Chairman of the House Veterans Affairs Committee; Congressman Les Aspin, Chairman of the House Armed Services Committee; Congressman Floyd Spence, Ranking Republican Member of Armed Services; Congressman John Murtha, Chairman of the Subcommittee on Defense Appropriations; Senator Sam Nunn, Chairman of the Senate Armed Services Committee; Senator Daniel Inouye, Chairman of the Senate Defense Appropriations Subcommittee; and, Senator Ted Stevens, Ranking Republican Member of that Subcommittee — all were adamant that the President and the DOD adhere to the Total Force policy doctrine and mobilize the Guard and Reserves.

There were several powerful precedents for a call-up. First, the Guard and Reserve had been used in past contingencies. Why in the current emergency (whose size offered compelling reasons for a call-up), should there be a cause for departure from Total Force? Second, it was precisely the kind of action contemplated in the Gulf — an action requiring extensive combat support and combat service support — for which the Guard had been trained and equipped. Third, force levels were coming down and future contingencies would be conducted with a smaller active force supported by a larger reserve component, just as they had done throughout history until Vietnam. This was an ideal situation in which to test these evolving new roles. And, a good way to test the mobilization system.

Last, and perhaps most compelling, was the argument that if the Administration wanted to build public support for a fight halfway around the world in which direct U.S. interests were not involved, it was critical to gain public support in America's communities. The sole use of the active duty components is not sufficient to building broad-based public support for a conflict. The only way to do this is with the Guard and Reserve. No less than the senior commander on the ground, General Norman Schwartzkopf, knew this.

Others in the active components, however, did not see a need for Guard and Reserve combat troops — the so-called 'trigger pullers.' And more importantly, the Administration was concerned that a call-up at this early stage would lead to a skeptical reaction by the American people, possibly undermining what was already a delicate situation.

On August 21st, I personally told General Powell that the Guard was ready and willing to give him all the manpower he needed. I told him we had Adjutants' General with their hands in the air, offering up support. We had thousands of volunteers already in active duty roles. We had more sophisticated equipment, training, and expertise than almost any other professional standing army in the world. But we couldn't move units if we didn't have a call-up.

20 August 90

The National Guard Bureau's Army Directorate develops a memorandum, the subject of which is "Order to Active Federal Service Sequence."

22 August 90

President Bush signs Executive Order 12727, implementing Section 673(b) for the first time ever, almost 50 years to the week in which President Franklin Delano Roosevelt signed the 1940 call-up in response to events in Europe. As a result of President Bush's action today, a total of 48,800 reservists are authorized for activation, including 25,000 from the Army National Guard and U.S. Army Reserve, 14,500 from the Air National Guard and Air Force Reserve, 6,300 from the U.S. Navy Reserve, and 3,000 from the U.S. Marine Corps Reserve.

Nearly 80,000 Army and Air Guard personnel would eventually be federalized. And ultimately President Bush's action would become the largest Guard and Reserve call-up since the Korean War.

At the press conference in Kennebunkport, Maine, at which Mr. Cheney and General Powell are also present, President Bush notes, "We are activating those special categories of Reservists that are essential to completing our mission. As our forces continue to arrive, they can look forward to the support of the finest Reserve components in the world."

24 August 90

As the Chief of the National Guard Bureau, I send this message to the states: "Subject: Alert Order #1 for Presidential Callup of Selected Reserve," which alerts 69 Army National Guard units for federalization in support of Operation Desert Shield. The Air National Guard orders are soon to follow.

The Guard has become part of the shield in the Saudi Arabian desert.

CHAPTER TWO

"GATEWAY TO THE AIR FORCE"

A kid born and raised during the 1930s and 40s was likely to have a childhood suffused by turmoil and by war. I was such a child, born in 1934 in Henderson, Kentucky, and raised in Evansville, Indiana, a mid-size city on the Ohio River across from Henderson. These were quiet communities in a quiet region. But as World War II approached, towns close to the big rivers draining the Middle West became key points for war material production and shipment.

Even prior to Pearl Harbor, nearby Camp Breckinridge, KY was alive with troop processing and training — ironically, many of them were National Guard troops mobilized in August of 1940. But it was really after December 7, 1941 that virtually every aspect of daily life involved, in that imposing phrase, "the war effort."

My father tried to join the Army, failed the entrance physical and was categorized as a 4-F. He went to work for Sunbeam Corporation making artillery shells. My grandmother worked in a factory producing rifle grenades and .45 calibre ammunition. Less than five miles from our house was a riverside plant making LSTs — Landing Ship, Tank — and at the Evansville Airport, Republic Aviation produced the P-47 Thunderbolt. My father transferred to Republic during the war and helped produce the P-47s. Homes in the area were crowded with the wives and children of troops stationed at Breckinridge. All my buddies played war games in the woods with BB guns, while news of the war played at all the movie theatres.

World War II was total war, a concept exceedingly hard to comprehend by people today who did not live through this period. The sheer magnitude of the war effort couldn't fail to leave an impression on those who lived through it. Indeed, one of my most unsettling memories as a child took place at the Henderson train station one evening when I saw railroad workers straining to unload dozens of wooden coffins, hurriedly putting flags on each one as they walked them to trucks. It wasn't long after this that my family learned that two of our cousins had been killed in the opening days of the Battle of the Bulge.

The frantic celebrations following V-E and V-J days only momentarily ended the wartime edge of my childhood. Veterans came back home to Evansville, and with them, stories of the fighting. Some vets enrolled at nearby Evansville College. The brick National Guard Armory, one of the largest in the state, was located two blocks from my home and became a central gathering place for returned soldiers and younger folks like me, full of awe for men who had beaten the German and Japanese war machines.

Then, in 1948, our erstwhile allies, the Soviets, blockaded the Western portions of Berlin. The famed airlift began and remained a staple of daily news until the Soviet Union backed down in 1949. Less than 20 months later, North Korea drove across the un-aptly named Demilitarized Zone into South Korea and once again, America was at war.

Although teenagers are rarely coherent or systematic observers of their time, there was a definite sense among my peers and me that conflict was America's natural state of affairs; the country at peace was glimpsed only briefly.

By the start of my senior year at Bosse High School in the fall of 1951, I'd done well enough to attend a first-rate college out of town. However, my parents didn't have that kind of money and so the next autumn I enrolled at Evansville College. At the same time, I joined the U.S. Air Force Reserve Officers Training Corps (ROTC).

I joined ROTC because I felt it was the right thing to do. I could have skipped ROTC and simply used college to secure a four-year deferment from military service. Yet, there was a war going on and I wanted to be part of it. Besides, I'd had a fascination with aircraft ever since I was a child, when my father would take me to watch the test flights of the P-47s at the Evansville Airport.

Moreover, Evansville College only had one ROTC program — that's right — Air Force. As an independent military component, the U.S. Air Force was only five years old. It was so new that it didn't yet have the blue uniforms by which it would be known later. Instead, we had a khaki outfit that was a lighter color than the Army's; hence, our uniform nickname, the "Silver Tans."

The ROTC units met at the National Guard armory right next to campus. A senior NCO trained us endlessly in drill and ceremony. We marched over every inch of the armory's concrete parade ground during our four years of college. At first, none of us understood the need for this constant shuffling around in the hot sun and cold wind. Later, we realized that marching the group in formation helped build a sense of cohesion, discipline, and pride among the various personalities in the unit. It was a valuable lesson in the intangible but sustaining rituals of military life, one I will never forget.

Colonel Taylor was our senior Air Force officer at Evansville

College and instructed us in military science and strategy. Equally important, he taught us how to maintain a trouser crease and how to make a shoe shine stick.

But the greatest gift the ROTC gave us was the opportunity to fly. Guys in the unit would drive over to Scott Air Force Base in Bellevue, Illinois with Colonel Taylor and go up in old C-47s, the "Gooney Bird," and the C-119, "Ole Shaky." As I look back, I marvel at our excitement at being strapped into jump seats as we trembled and shivered and shouted above the deafening prop noise during the entire flight. We were uncomfortable as hell, but we loved every minute of it.

My most memorable rides came in the famed B-25, the World War II bomber with the huge glass nose. A tube ran from the cockpit back through to the bombardier, with other tight passages going all the way back to the rear gunner. The night flights would last for hours and we'd spend the entire time crawling around the plane, inside the tube, over the empty bomb racks to the gunners and back to the cockpit. When we weren't crawling around, we'd gaze out of the glass nose at the lights of Chicago and other towns below.

We revered the pilots and crewman, most of whom were combat veterans of World War II. They were superb role models and genuinely liked to have us along. We were curious about every aspect of the aircraft and we asked endless questions about everything. I think the pilots understood and took a great deal of pride in the realization that they were passing along their expertise to the next generation of Air Force pilots.

Another rite of passage occurred between my junior and senior year: ROTC summer camp at Bergstrom Air Force Base in Austin, Texas. It was four intense weeks of marching and stern guidance on how to pass uniform and gear inspection. In addition to this solid advice on finding success in the Air Force, I also received my first jet ride.

Active duty pilots were assigned to take cadets up in the T-33 in order to give them a feel for jet flight, and perhaps, weed out those who thought they wanted to fly, but didn't have the stomach for it. I'm sure the unstated aim of every pilot was to terrorize and ultimately sicken his passenger. I can still remember how pale and nervous we were as we stood in line inside one of the Bergstrom hangers, watching each T-33 taxi toward us after finishing a flight with one of our fellows.

When my turn came, I watched as my predecessor climbed slowly out of the back cockpit, his flight suit streaked with the remains of his undigested breakfast. He stiffly turned around to make a few wobbly attempts at wiping off the speckled control panel in the backseat. Then he teetered down the ladder and staggered towards me as the pilot sat on the edge of the cockpit, flight helmet in hand and feet on the wing, grinning and motioning for his next victim — me. What an introduction to jets. As I look back on it, my ride was exhilarating beyond belief and scary as hell at the same time.

But it was more than that. It was a turning point in my life. When I got down from that cockpit after that flight, I was convinced that I would do what ever was necessary to become a jet pilot.

I had married my college sweetheart, Rosemary Mohr, on August 13, 1955 and we lived in the Rotherwood Apartments, just a block from the Armory. On June 4th, 1956, we both received our baccalaureate degrees, Rosemary's in Education and mine in Business Administration. One hour later, in a separate ceremony, I was commissioned a 2nd Lieutenant in the United States Air Force. We were both on pins and needles as to our future until I received orders to report to Lackland Air Force Base in San Antonio, Texas.

And so one day late in June, with money borrowed from our parents, Rosemary and I climbed into our brand new 1956, two-tone blue Chevrolet Bel Air, and pointed it south on Highway 41. We were two green beans from southern Indiana headed to God-knows-what — and Rosemary was four months pregnant. Except for my brief stint at Bergstrom, neither of us had been more than 50 miles from Evansville. One thousand miles later on June 30th, we drove into Lackland AFB, passing under a huge sign over the main entrance that read: "Gateway to the United States Air Force."

Though only nine years old in 1956, the Air Force was already on an equal footing with the other services. To the great chagrin of the venerable Army and Navy, the Air Force was the prominent force in the brand-new nuclear age and the thunderbolt in its quiver was SAC — the Strategic Air Command.

SAC bombers carried nuclear weapons, doomsday devices to counter the offensive designs of the Soviet Union. SAC was the leviathan that kept the peace. The SAC motto, "Peace Is Our Profession," said it all. The SAC Commander-in-Chief was General Curtis LeMay, an enigmatic cold warrior and the high priest of air power. With Lemay at the helm, the USAF was full of swagger and convinced of its total superiority.

Air Force personnel, many of them wide-eyed kids like Rosemary and me, streamed into Lackland by the thousands, the human ingredient in the immense American military establishment. Lackland was the processing base for all Air Force personnel, a perpetual motion machine of paper and people.

For all arrivals to the service, the first few months are an unceasing, confusing whirlwind. You must first learn to live with the herd concept; you and an endless mob of other shaved heads are moved from building to building, room to room, clutching reams of forms, each of which must be inspected, signed, stamped, and processed. If it seems like you spend all your time in lines, it's because you do. They stretch for hundreds of feet and countless hours. There are tests for everything — eyesight, hearing, blood, strength, fractured bones, swelled ligaments. If you are from a small community like me, it's your first assimilation into a large bureaucratic institution and you find it chaotic and unsettling.

My monthly base salary was all of $222.30. With this, I had to buy uniforms and various gear, make a deposit and pay rent on an apartment in Billy Mitchell Village, secure insurance, and use whatever was left to buy groceries at the commissary. Needless to say, there wasn't a lot of money left for food so our first phone call was to our folks to borrow more money.

All the while, I was going through modified boot camp and preflight training, learning that there was only one way to do things and that was the Air Force way. After about one month of this frenzy, we were both relieved to see the Lackland main gate disappear in our rear view mirror. We were on our way to our next home — Bartow Air Base near Winterhaven, Florida, a pilot training base.

Three days later on Saturday, as we pulled into the base, we witnessed a rather poignant sight. We arrived right in the middle of a huge airshow and as we drove onto the base, the elite Air Force Thunderbirds did a fly over in their brand new F-100 Super Sabres. It was an awesome display of power and symbolic of the total dominance of the jet engine in the Air Force.

The last event of the show was equally powerful. It was a fly away of the T-6 trainer. This plane had helped prepare the great Army Air Corps and Navy pilots of World War II, heroic men who had unflinchingly carried the war to the German and Japanese armies and cities. The T-6 before us was the last in the U.S. inventory and as it disappeared into the clouds on its way to Washington, D.C. (and the Smithsonian, where it's still on display today), I suddenly realized that the era of prop driven, tail wheel aviation was near an end.

"Damnit, Conaway, you aren't worth a damn as a pilot. You ain't never gonna make it. I don't know why in the world you're here anyway."

Gilbert Field, Winterhaven, Florida. Garner Aviation was the Air Force's civilian contractor for Primary Pilot Instruction. Garner was a company composed almost entirely of ex-World War II veterans all of whom looked as though they were straight out of Hollywood central casting. Talk about your role models. They wore dark aviator glasses, Ike jackets, leather hats and scarves. They smoked hand-rolled cigarettes, cursed like crazy. And man, they could make a plane dance.

The aforementioned words of encouragement had just been shouted after my problem-plagued eighth flight, which included four or five bounces down on the runway during landing. Although the day before I'd handled the plane pretty well, my instructor Mr. Wilson was livid.

"Conaway!" he screamed.

"Yessir."

"What's the matter with you. Yesterday, your were fine. Today, you scaring the &*%$#!@ out of me! What in the hell did you and your wife do last night?" These guys were experts at getting under your skin.

I was taxiing to the hanger, reaching down to turn off the engines. "Don't shut this damned thing down!"Wilson bellowed from the back of the plane as I glimpsed at him removing his flight helmet.

"You stay here! Keep your butt in that seat!" Wilson was still yelling. Then he opened the canopy, climbed out on the wing and turned back. I thought he was going to get back in but he reached in to strap the seatbelts down so they wouldn't flop around. Then he said with less fierceness, "I know you can fly this thing better than you just did. Now go do it."

He clambered off the wing and walked toward the hangar without looking back and I was alone in the cockpit.

I was trembling, fighting a range of emotions from embarrassment, anger, to sheer terror. After I pulled myself together, I slowly rolled down to the end of the runway. As I turned the plane around and looked down the one mile of concrete, I took a deep breath and opened the throttle.

Let me tell you, nothing compares with the experience of your first take off in a plane without the instructor back there yelling in your headphones, and ready to save your butt if you screw up.

I was up for 30 minutes — which is a short flight. I just stayed in the traffic pattern, did a few touch-and-go's on the runway, and then came in for a full-stop landing. I'll never forget climbing out on the wing of that plane, grinning like mad, young, proud, and full of myself — and dammed lucky to be alive. Then I was introduced to a great Air Force tradition: I got hosed down by the laughing maintenance crew. That day remains one of the happiest and most memorable days of my life.*

The flight training at Bartow continued for seven months, from August of 1956 to March of the next year. The Air Force refused to let its young officers stand still. After Primary Pilot Instruction we were off to Basic Pilot Training. Because I was ranked in the upper third of my class of 60, I was selected to learn to fly jets at Greenville

*(One of the other proud moments soon thereafter was the birth of our first child, Ellen Rosemary, born at MacDill AFB on 23 November 1956. As my only daughter, I've always held her exceedingly close to my heart. Today, Ellen and her family live in Lawrenceburg, Kentucky.)

Air Force Base in Mississippi. The quarters weren't exactly palatial. We lived in a duplex with a washer on the back porch. And Rosemary was pregnant again.

Mississippi was scorching hot and muggy this time of year and from dawn to dusk the community was serenaded by the sound of jet trainers, their throttles inexpertly opened and idled. And always in the ears of pilots rang the sweet sound of instructors yelling and cajoling their charges.

I became a part of the Class 57 Victor in the T-33 jet trainer, the same aircraft I had my only jet flight orientation in during ROTC summer camp. Class rankings, then as now, were extremely important and were a combination of continual tests in class and cockpit expertise. Competition between pilot trainees was essentially friendly but there was always an undercurrent of survival. If you finished low in the class or washed out, the Air Force would decide what kind of support position you would occupy during your next three years in uniform. I worked hard and soloed in my first jet at Indianwood, Mississippi, in June of 1957.

Finally, in September 1957, after more than a year of instruction came the reward — a set of silver wings. After 14 months and 240 hours of flying time, I was elated and ready. I had no ribbons or badges on my uniform, just a name tag and my new wings. As funny as it sounds, to get something above that left pocket was incredibly rewarding.

Slowly I was beginning to act like a pilot. I didn't have a swagger yet, but I was gaining an appreciation of what it took to be an aviator. I ranked seventh in a class of about 70 graduates. And when it came time to choose my next assignment, my thoughts returned to my first flight at Bergstrom. I knew what I wanted — fighters.

I was fortunate that I was high enough in class rank to choose any plane I wanted — fighters, transports, bombers, tankers, you name it. As you neared the middle of the class, the open assignments were generally B-47 and B-52 bombers, which were just starting to come into the inventory. Those at the bottom would have to take what was left — the old propeller transports, C-119s, the "Flying Boxcar."

In those days, the bomber guys ran the air force. But the newest pilots all wanted the glamour of flying fighters even though some of the bomber bases were better duty stations. For one thing, you weren't gone as much. You got stationed at places like Forbes Air Force Base near Topeka, Kansas, or Fairchild Air Force Base in Spokane, Washington and you could settle down with your family. You'd fly long missions, maybe around the world, but you would recover right back at the home base with many days off. While the fighter guys, hell, they were gone much of the time.

Also at that time, the saying in the Air Force was, 'If you want to get anywhere, you gotta go SAC,' i.e. the Strategic Air Command. The same people would also say, 'Fighters are more fun. But bombers are more important.' That was probably true because the bomber guys certainly moved up into the Air Force hierarchy faster than everybody else in those days.

But some of us didn't appreciate that back then. We were young and full of vinegar and we thought we could handle a T-bird pretty well in training. So we forgot bombers. When you're ranked high in your class, you want to go into fighters unless there's some special reason not to — if you have a special skill or you want to follow in the footsteps of someone you've always admired.

Well, I choose the F-86s at Perrin Air Force Base, Texas. The F-86 was what we called, "Sierra Hotel" — a hot machine — and the Air Defense Command had a crucial mission then. There were over 100 Air Defense units in the USAF, responsible for protecting U.S. borders against attack, as well as units watching territorial borders in Europe and Korea.

Of the 92 flying units of the Air National Guard at that time, over half, 69 squadrons, were air defense. The Air Force also had approximately 40 such Air Defense units. Although it sounds farfetched these days, we were really expecting the world's greatest invasion from the Soviet Union back then. The Soviets had just shut down Hungary for good, they were making threatening noises all over Europe, and the U.S. wasn't taking any chances. It was truly the height of the Cold War.

Everywhere you turned, there were air defense squadrons. There was even one as far south as Knoxville, Tennessee, in the middle of the country.

To guard borders, you need eyes and ears. Radars are of only limited value. So the F-86 satisfied two interests for me. I wanted to fly fighters. And, I thought interceptors would be interesting and allow me to be based in the continental U.S. Many of those who flew fighters went overseas to assignments in Japan, France, Germany, Korea, and elsewhere.

If a pilot wanted air defense and wanted to fly fighters, he was either sent to a training assignment at Perrin Air Force Base in Sherman, Texas, or Moody Air Force base, in Valdosta, Georgia. Rosemary and I were sent to Perrin.

The first class at Perrin was Advanced Instrument Training in the T-33. Unlike day fighters, which ran home at the first indication of bad conditions, air defense was an all-weather assignment. That meant you had to fly by instruments in the worst of weather. In order to acclimate ourselves to flying blind, a white cloth was stretched over the inside of the back-seat canopy. The front-seat training instructor prevented the plane from crashing if the trainee was about to make a serious mistake. We flew by instruments only, at night, during the day, in all kinds of weather. It was nerve-wracking work but I can honestly say it saved my life at least a dozen times during real world missions throughout the rest of my military career.

Following my "40 hours under the hood", as we called the shroud, I stepped into my first combat aircraft, the single seat F-86. I had trained in a simulator but at that time, such equipment was rather primitive. Black and white screens, little depth in the scope, and no sensations or vertigo. The real thing felt so strange.

Flying that F-86 for the first time was a true rite of passage because there were no two-seat trainer versions of the plane. This was solo flight from the git-go. Which was why the simulator, despite its limitations, was so important.

Plus, this was my first experience with an afterburner. Rolling down the runway, I lit the afterburner and got a kick in the butt like I'd never felt in an aircraft up to that time. The plane was about 2,000 feet off the deck and my brain was still back on the runway.

A perfect one-hour flight was the final test — flying to a traffic pattern at another facility, the execution of low approaches, performance of an instrument approach, and a few touch-and-go's. This flight test was yet another hurdle to get over. Because if you blew it, you could say goodbye to fighters. Thank goodness I didn't blow it.

At Perrin I began to appreciate that the essence of military life is upheaval, or to put it gently, change. And I think this holds true for all services, ranks, and military occupations. A career in the service builds as much personal durability and maturity as does the actual military training. That's because a career is a succession of new bases, new quarters, new assignments, new equipment, new surroundings, and most of all, new people. You are continually adapting to new situations and, just as you grow comfortable with one place, you are invariably forced to leave it for another.

If you've got a family, the constant transition is doubly difficult. I've heard people describe their childhood as spent being a "service brat." The term is thrown off casually, even dismissively. But it disguises a truly arduous time — kids yanked in and out of schools, torn away from friends, spouses exiting a peer group and trying to enter a new one.

Then there is the melancholy of life on base — the worn-out housing, thin carpets and small rooms and scuffed walls, furniture chipped and scarred from past moves, garages stacked with boxes that no one wants to unpack because another move is imminent. Bases were hot, dusty, and listless in the summer, and cold, windy and remote in winter. And there was always the scramble for money. I remember General Colin Powell remarking in his retirement speech that he and Alma, his wife, had lived in 24 different houses during his 32 years of service. His words resonated deeply with many military folks, a simple and straightforward comment on the lifestyle of service life. Even in peacetime, the sacrifice of those associated with the military is never truly appreciated.

After six months of advanced training, I ended up third in my class of 13. And it was time to select a new assignment — this one to an operational unit. Finally, after 18 months, I was getting out of the Training Command. We'd been at four bases in those 18 months and Rosemary had just delivered our second child, David. David was born on 25 January 1958 at the Sherman Hospital, Sherman, Texas.*

I looked around at my options. The F-102 — the infamous Delta Dagger — had just entered the Air Force inventory; it was definitely state-of-the-art. A brand new century series fighter that everyone wanted to fly. I was fortunate enough to land an F-102 assignment.

We even got to select our own location. We chose Kinross AFB in Sault St. Marie, Michigan. Rosemary and I thought at the time, "Hey, it's the next state up from Indiana." Our naivete was complete. Not only was the Michigan border 300 miles from Evansville, Kinross was located in one of the northern-most regions of the United States, and was one of the coldest installations in CONUS. (Later, the base name would be changed to Kinchloe Air Force Base, in honor of a Michigan test pilot killed in a F-104 in the California desert.)

Kinross was somewhat remote. The closest town, Sault St. Marie, was 15 miles away and the base itself consisted of only a few buildings and a runway. Deer and other wild animals were every-where and would often stray onto the runway. The surrounding forests seemed to stretch to the horizon, and the vast, foreboding Lake Superior routinely wrapped the place in fog. Nonetheless, it was a beautiful setting.

Of course, nothing about our fifth move in 18 months was going to be easy. When we got to Kinross after an exhausting three-day drive, I went to sign in at the orderly room. The Tech Sergeant looked at my orders, looked up at me, and said, "Sir, that unit ain't here."

Due to runway repair at Kinross, the 438th Fighter Interceptor Squadron had just been moved to K.I. Sawyer Air Force Base, 125 miles due west, but still in the Upper Peninsula of Michigan. So we piled into the Chevy and drove to K.I. Sawyer in Marquette, Michigan to live for six months. When that time was up, we had yet another move.

As envisioned by the U. S. Air Defense Command, the principle threat to the United States was a mass attack of Russian bombers coming over the North Pole. The Distant Early Warning, or DEW Line, stretched across the rim of northern Canada. Little known to

---

(Today, he is a Navy Commander flying F-18s in VFA-195 on the USS Independence at Atsugi, Japan. He and his family presently reside in Orange Park, Florida.)

the public was that a second line of air defense — developed in anticipation of a ferocious Soviet attack breaching the DEW line — was established in southern Canada near the U.S. border and was known as the Pine Tree Line.

The 438th was part of the 30th Air Division, whose cone of defense began in Knoxville, Tennessee, with the sides of the cone stretching to the west through Chicago, and to the east through Detroit. The 438th was tasked with a threefold mission: intercept, identify, and then destroy invading enemy bombers.

We used to practice our tactics with SAC. A huge fleet of SAC bombers would sweep down from Canada simulating a mass attack. As soon as the klaxon went off at our alert barn, we'd jump in our planes and streak out to intercept them. We had a 5-minute alert across the border, which meant we had to be airborne five minutes after the horn announced the first sighting of planes. During these exercises, the SAC crews would try every trick in the book, including chaff and electronic countermeasures, to throw us off.

It's difficult for many people today to grasp the Cold War gestalt. Irrespective of the pathos of Russia and the former Soviet Union today, a Soviet bomber attack on the continental United States was a huge concern of U.S. decision makers in the mid-1950s Indeed, it remained so, in varying degrees, right up until the Soviet Union ceased to exist. It was only in May of 1991 that President Bush stood down the bomber and tanker alert.

Most of our flying was done over the vast waters of Lake Superior, which even when you were at 35,000 feet, stretched into the horizon in every direction. It was always a little unnerving to fly over the lake, even in daytime. At night, it was ghostly and I never failed to notice that the engine always sounded funny just as I left land and began to fly out over the lake. It was just north of Superior one day that I witnessed a gruesome mid-air collision which took the lives of my good friend, F-102 pilot Gaylord True, and the crew of a B-47 bomber, during one of those big SAC training exercises.

As 1959 ended, it was decision time. My date of separation, (DOS), from the Air Force was 31 March 1960. The options were clear: I could extend my term of service indefinitely or enter the civilian world. Several things persuaded me that it was time to leave the Air Force.

First, it looked like the fighter interceptor role was slowly shrinking. We still had a bomber-heavy force, the essence of power projection. Second, it was becoming increasingly apparent that missiles, both intercontinental and tactical, were the weapons of the future — relatively accurate, unmanned, and devastatingly powerful.

Finally, there was a great likelihood that if I decided to stay, my next assignment would be to a remote post farther north along the

DEW Line. It would probably be a non-flying assignment, pulling duty as an air traffic controller, in other words, a "scope dope." It was an important job — we relied heavily on these guys — but it was just not for me.

Perhaps most compelling was that although Rosemary was a great trooper, she was tired of the constant moves. We'd just had our third child in four years with the birth of Daniel in Sault Ste. Marie.*

We'd already lived at six different bases, and we'd be packing for a seventh if I extended. To Rosemary and me, it seemed as though we'd spent the last four years stumbling around drab installations, bare-foot, pregnant, bleary-eyed and poor. It was time to settle down.

On the morning of March 31, 1960, I walked down the front steps of our base house at Kincheloe, got into the car with Rosemary and the rest of the Conaway brood, turned south on Highway 270 and never looked back. We did what young people always do when confronted with change: we went home to mom and dad.

Three weeks later in Evansville, I landed a civilian job — as a sales representative for Mead Johnson. Four weeks after that, I was the new Mead Johnson sales representative for West Virginia, traveling the state and visiting doctors, hospitals, and pharmacies. My job was to sell boxcars of baby formula — Pablum, Enfamil — and a brand new diet product called Metracal. Selling came easy for me and before long, I was at the top of the Company sales charts.

Late that summer, I drove over to Kanawha Airport outside Charleston, parked the car and aimlessly poked around the field and hangars. I met a technician in an oil-stained jump suit, a Lieutenant by the name of Stu Stewart, who invited me to have a cup of coffee with him and a few other guys who flew for the West Virginia Air National Guard. It turned out to be one helluva important cup of coffee.

CHAPTER THREE

"CIVILIAN LIFE"

15 December 1960.

A Democrat, John F. Kennedy, had just been elected President during a campaign in which he decried a missile gap with the Soviet Union. A Republican was soon to give his famous address on the military industrial complex threatening America. But I really wasn't paying much attention to national news. Free of the 24-hour rigors of active duty, I was enjoying life in a way I'd never known. We were living in a new home in Dunbar, West Virginia, just outside Charleston. Rosemary and the three kids were happy. And Metracal was making every Mead Johnson salesman look very good.

Best of all, I was flying again. Because on December 15, 1960, I had joined the West Virginia Air National Guard. And so began the next 33 years of my life with the National Guard.

It hadn't been easy.

The 130th Special Operations Group hauled around active and Guard paratroopers, the former based at Fort Bragg, the latter at Parkersburg, West Virginia. The unit's aircraft was the SA-16, affectionately known as the "Flying Albatross" because of its big, awkward appearance. It was a strong bird, capable of landing on water, in open fields, and on any kind of unimproved runways. The mission demanded superb flying skills and exceptional competency in night flying.

Beginning with that first cup of coffee at Kanawha, I had gradually become a familiar face around the airfield, always stopping by to say hello and talk flying with anyone who would listen. Then one day I inquired about joining the 130th. The officers scoffed. Colonel Ralph Cowgill, the commander, told me, "John, all you've got is single engine fighter time. We need pilots who can fly multi-engine." It was easy to see their point. But I figured I could learn to fly anything and began to pester Cowgill and even the state Assistant Adjutant General for Air, Brigadier General Kemp McLaughlin. After a few months of this gentle persuasion, I either persuaded them of my flying skills or else they decided the only way to get rid of me was to take me in. So I became a member of the unit.

From a pilot's perspective, it was a big change. The lumbering ole Albatross, even with the throttle wide open, maxed out at 180 knots. The F-102 I'd been flying didn't even lift of the runway until you hit 170 knots. But I was flying again and that was all that mattered. And I got some good advice on learning to fly the Albatross. Some came from 1st Lieutenant Stu Stewart, who was still giving me good advice 30 years later when he worked for me in the Pentagon. Another source of instruction about the plane and about everything Air Force came from General Mclaughlin himself, a highly decorated veteran of World War II and a survivor of "Black Thursday," the 1944 raid over the Ploesti oil refineries which resulted in the greatest single-day loss of men and aircraft ever suffered by the Army Air Corps.

I spent two years flying with the 130th, becoming combat ready in amphibious landings, both inland and open sea. We would pick up troops in a remote field in the middle of the night and then take them to a jump site. Then we'd fly around and land on a nearby lake and suddenly, from out of nowhere, these guys would come paddling up to us in rafts. We'd throw them a gangplank, they'd clamber onto the plane, and we'd take off and head for home. It was really a lot of fun.

I went to my first Annual Training at Alpena, Michigan, in June of 1961. It was hardly the Ritz; all I recall was an open-bay barracks with 120 very loud sleepers and an old clapboard latrine that must have been built during the Civil War.

It was during the summer of 1961 that East Germany began construction of a concrete and steel wall dividing Berlin into two cities, East and West. All along the East German border, barricades and control point security was increased to limit movement of peoples between free Germany in the West and the Soviet-controlled Germany in the East. As this new threat to freedom in Europe developed, President John F. Kennedy reacted by mobilizing US forces and preparing for a potential conflict should it become necessary.

Over 150,000 Army National Guard (ARNG) and U.S. Army Reserve (USAR) men and women were mobilized and sent to Active Component installations to train up in preparation for their augmentation to the Active Forces.

The state of Kentucky, later to become my home state, mobilized two ARNG Armored Battalions. The two battalions, 2-123d Armor headquartered in Owensboro, Kentucky and the 3-123d Armor, headquartered in Bowling Green, Kentucky were called to active duty on 1 October 1961. The 2d battalion was moved to Fort Stewart, Georgia while the 3d battalion was moved to Fort Knox, Kentucky.

Looked at it in an unscientific fashion, many stories from the experiences of these two units tell of the good and the not-so-good treatment that Guardsmen and Reservists receive when called to Federal Service. The most glaring report I heard of was the treatment of the men of the 3d

Battalion, who upon arrival at Fort Knox, were treated the same as new enlistees, even though many had prior service, including wartime service, and all had completed basic training. Although physicals had already been administered at home station before movement to Fort Knox, they had to be retaken. The men also had to retake a battery of written tests normally administered when first enlisted and all had to retake most of the basic training tasks regardless of their rank and past experiences. Mobilization plans maintained prior to mobilization were discarded and the Command was instructed that the battalion would respond to the Commander, Fort Knox. The battalion was assigned to the School Brigade, U.S. Army Armor School, a peacetime command and control organization whose mission was to provide support to the School and its students. But the battalion's real mission was to train for potential deployment - possibly Europe.

Problems often occurred when Guardsmen attempted to get medical treatment for minor ailments. Except for emergencies, these soldiers were often turned away with only aspirin and returned to duty, though some were too ill to perform. The perception was given that the Guardsmen were only there for a short time, similar to their normal annual training, and were not treated as "green ID" carrying federalized soldiers.

When mobilized the 3d battalion had only the M47 tank on hand although authorized the newer M48. The battalion received the M48 tank upon arrival at Fort Knox; however, the tanks received were towed from their location at Boatwright Field Maintenance facility, Fort Knox and were in a great state of disrepair. Only a small number of the tanks received were in operational condition, and tremendous pressure was placed on the battalion to make them operational. The post commanding general, Major General Bastion whose staff car was a black Cadillac provided by the local (on post) taxi company, was frequently in the Battalion's motor park with his swagger stick poked into the stomach of the battalion's maintenance officer demanding an explanation of why all the tanks were not operational.

The motor park consisted of a gravel base with very little hardstand. Driving in the park caused gravel and gravel dust to cover the sides and roof of the maintenance and office buildings. Once when the Post was visited by President Kennedy, the battalion was ordered to clean the sides and roofs of these buildings facing the approach of the Presidents route on the Post.

After several months of intensive training and conditioning of equipment, the battalion successfully completed its training requirements and was pronounced combat ready. The battalion successfully completed a battalion-level Army Training Test (which, was the precursor to the current Army ARTEP - Army training and evaluation program) and was rated as having achieved the highest scores ever recorded at Fort Knox.

The battalion was prepared, highly motivated, and ready for any mission it might be given. However, in the summer of 1962, tensions eased in Europe and began to heat up in Cuba. The battalions were released from federal service and returned to home stations in August of 1962.

These two National Guard combat-ready battalions were well prepared for callup as Vietnam loomed as the next major hot spot. However, neither were called during the Vietnam conflict and many hard-earned skills were lost as individuals left the Guard. Some volunteered and entered on active duty as individuals, while some left the Guard altogether because of a lack of faith in the system. Within one year following the mobilization, the battalion had experienced an approximate 50% turnover of personnel. It was a lesson to have an eerie resonance nearly three decades later.

A few days after erection of the Berlin Wall on August 12th, 1961, the 130th was initially alerted. We were then told to stand down because the Albatross didn't have enough airlift capacity.

On August 30, 1961, President John F. Kennedy ordered 146,000 Guardsmen and Reservists to active duty in response to Soviet moves to cut off Allied access to Berlin. The Air Guard's share of that mobilization was 21,067 individuals; and the units mobilized two months later in October included 18 tactical fighter squadrons, four tactical reconnaissance squadrons, six air transport squadrons, and one tactical control group. On November 1 the Air Force mobilized three ANG fighter interceptor squadrons.

It was in late October and early November that eight of the tactical fighter units flew to Europe with their 216 aircraft in "Operation Stair Step," the largest jet deployment in the Air Guard's history. Because they were not trained and equipped for aerial refueling, the pilots island-hopped across the Atlantic Ocean, with all arriving safely without a single accident or aircraft loss. Because of their short range, 60 Air Guard F-104 interceptors were airlifted to Europe in late November. The F-104 units called up included the 134th Fighter Group (FG) and the 151st Tactical Fighter Squadron (TFS) from McGee-Tyson Air Base in Tennessee; the 169th FG and 157th TFS from Columbia, SC; the 161st FG and 197th TFS from Harbor, AZ; and the 102nd FG from Boston, MA. Many of the units headed to Europe had been trained to deliver tactical nuclear weapons, not conventional bombs, and so the pilots had to be retrained for conventional missions once they arrived on the continent.

The majority of the mobilized Air Guard personnel remained in the Continental United States, flying airlift missions and undergoing preparation as a follow-on force in case the Berlin crisis escalated into war.

In 1962, the 130th was called up by Governor W.W. Barron to assist with storm damage right in Charleston. The entire area, including Kanawha Airfield, was devastated by heavy rain and flooding and three people were killed. Even though our role lasted only a few days, the operation made a great impression on me. We trained year-round in tough conditions to meet an enemy whom might never materialize. All the while we were on alert for a real-world mission. We had to be ready to use our skills and equipment at a moment's notice to help our neighbors at home. That state call-up gave me my first insight into the importance of the Guard in directly assisting America and Americans. It was an experience that would affect my thinking for the rest of my Guard career.

At the same time, I was doing very well in my civilian job. 1962 had been an outstanding year for Mead-Johnson. The firm's gross profits had doubled in just 12 months, thanks to Metracal. West Virginia had the largest percentage growth in profits of any state in the country.

So, in February of 1963, Mead asked me to transfer to Louisville. Rosemary and I were overjoyed at the chance to get closer to home, which in our minds was still Evansville. We moved in March of 1963 and I was able to transfer from the West Virginia Guard to the Kentucky Guard without a break in service, thanks to a phone call from Colonel Cogwill to Colonel Vern Yahne, the Base Commander of the 123rd Tactical Reconnaissance Wing. Colonel Yahne, Colonels McClure and Kinnaird and other great Kentuckians took me in as a fellow Kentuckian and made me feel right at home.

We flew the B-57 at Standiford Field, a twin-engine jet Canberra reconnaissance bomber made by Martin in Baltimore. It was an easy transition to the B-57 from the Albatross and in time, I was flying five to eight times a month, participating in exercises at Alpena; Savannah, Georgia; and Gulfport, Mississippi.

In addition to working for Mead and flying in the Guard, I began attending night school at the University of Louisville in the fall of 1963. To continue rising within Mead, I figured I needed an MBA. It was while in class that I became friends with some fellows from AT&T. At that time, AT&T owned the Southern Bell Company. When I told these guys about my brief career with Mead, they urged me to go to work for AT&T. I didn't think much about it until the spring of 1964, when Mead decided to transfer me to Oakland, California, to become a district manager.

The idea of another big move, this one 1,700 miles away, floored Rosemary and me. We decided pretty quickly that we simply weren't going to do it. So, I said goodbye to my employer of almost four years and joined Southern Bell as a marketing executive. Of course, as luck would have it, within months, they also asked me to move, this time to Winchester, near Lexington. At that time, Kentucky had only one Air Guard unit and that was at Standiford. Commuting to Louisville for drill and flight time gave me a lifetime appreciation for Guard personnel who travel long distances to serve with their units. Despite the 100-mile drive, I was having a ball with the unit. Rosemary and the kids were happy. And the job with Southern Bell was going well.

Perhaps too well. Because my performance in 1964 led Southern Bell execs in the spring of 1965 to offer me the post of state account executive for Kentucky. It was a big promotion, carrying vast responsibilities for the entire state-wide telephone network of government offices. It would necessitate another move but I felt as though I had no choice but to take it.

Then one day in March, even as Rosemary and I were a few days away from signing a contract for a new house in Frankfort in anticipation of the new job, I got a call from Colonel Yahne. The wing needed a full-time flying training instructor and he wanted to know if I was interested. I told him about the new post with Southern Bell and he said, "Don't do anything until we can talk." We met and he offered me the job.

Imagine the dilemma — the Bell position was a plum, a huge career boost and a stepping stone into the corporate hierarchy. But I was beginning to realize — perhaps too late, perhaps just in time — that something was at work here. Transfers with the private sector were coming as fast as they did with the military. In fact, if you did well in marketing, you were going to move a lot. Hell, we'd left the Air Force in order to settle down. And now we were preparing for our fourth move in just five years.

I weighed all the advantages and disadvantages and decided that everything came down to two things: Rosemary and I liked Louisville and I wanted to fly.

I called Colonel Yahne and told him I'd take the job. Then, because all officer positions in Kentucky at that time required the approval of the Adjutant General, I met with Major General A.Y. "Arthur" Lloyd, a dignified senior officer who calmly smoked a pipe and nodded as I sat across from him and answered some brief questions.

And that was it. One day I was an executive carrying a briefcase, the next day I was in a flightsuit toting a helmet bag.

And so on March 15, 1965, almost five years to the day after leaving active duty, I was back in military, as an NGC-12, full-time technician. I'd had a five-year hitch of civilian life. Now I was a Captain in the Kentucky Air National Guard, wholly prepared to spend the rest of my life in Louisville and be with the Air Guard flying whatever planes they had. My office was in the hangar and I wore a a flight suit spattered with fuel while the sound of jet engines roared in my ears.

I wore three hats at Standiford Field — instructor pilot, test pilot, and flight examiner. I checked out pilots in my old friend, the T-33, as well as in the B-57. Then in the fall of 1965, the unit was assigned the century series fighter, the RF-101 — the infamous "Voodoo" — and I discovered that I was the only pilot in Kentucky Air Guard who had what we called "Century Series" fighter time.

We received surplus F-101 A's and C's from U.S. units in England and then modified them to RF-101 G's and H's by fitting them with cameras, cockpit sensor controls, panoramic screens on the bottom of the plane, and light flare launchers on the fuselage. We also had to install a cable and arresting gear at each end of the Standiford runway for emergency stopping, if necessary. We flew out of Knoxville, Tennessee for six months while this construction was done.

In addition to performing my flight instructor duties, I learned how to perform air-to-air refueling. It's quite a test of pilot skills and I remember my first experience behind that lumbering old KC-97 quite vividly.

The basket swung down from the tanker and moved erratically all over the sky as I chased it. The old pros told me to look right through the basket at the tanker and when plugging in, to hold the power to kink the hose. This kept pressure on the gas nozzle holding it tight against my intake valve. Then the tanker boom operator poured on the gas to me. Somehow I lost a little power and backed away far enough for the kink to come out of the hose, which disconnected, sending a blast of jet fuel spray on my canopy, momentarily blinding me.

Today, the probe plugs into a receptacle behind the canopy. You fly in formation with other aircraft and do as the boom operator says, "up two, forward three, right one." It's a lot faster than it used to be but you still have to be a superb formation flyer to stay plugged into that big ole gas station in the sky

During this time, I was getting a closer look at the Guard. I'd been a traditional Guardsman for five years; now my full-time position made me appreciate the importance of the technicians responsible for keeping the Guard units ready. Maintenance was particularly important with Air Guard wings, which have a lot of sophisticated equipment requiring constant attention.

I also found, from first-hand experience, that the uniformed full-time Guardsmen provided a visible, positive, everyday military presence in their locales. I was convinced this presence was important for its public relations in instilling confidence in our communities, i.e. the citizens of Louisville knew that we were there to serve them.

The Hunting Creek Country Club sits outside Louisville and was the site of the annual squadron Christmas party in 1967. Spirits were high and were also being liberally consumed. As usually occurs at these types of gatherings, the military camaraderie leads to singing. We had quite a few World War II and Korean vets in the squadron and soon we began to belt out the 1940s hit made famous by Arthur Godfrey — "Itazuke Tower." This song was named after an installation on the south island of Kyushu, Japan. A Japanese base during World War II, it was used extensively by the U.S. during the Korean War.

The song and the place were famous throughout the Air Force. And every pilot knew the words:

"Itazuke tower, This is Air Force 801
I'm turning on my downwind leg
My prop is overrun
My coulant's overheated, the guage says 1-2-1
You better call the crash crew, and get them on the run.

Air Force 801, this is Itazuke tower
I can not call the crash crew
`Cause this is coffee hour
Your not cleared in the pattern
Now that is plain to see
So take it on around again, we have some VIP

Itazuke tower, this is Air Force 801
I'm turning on the down wind leg, I see your biscuit gun
My engine's runnin' rough, and the coulant's gonna blow
I'm gonna be a Mustang, so look out down below... "

I sang along with everybody else, looking over two generations of American pilots, many of whom had intimately known that famous tower. What I didn't know was that the song presaged my own rendezvous with that famous place.

CHAPTER FOUR

"CALL-UP!"

The U.S.S. Pueblo was steaming in the Sea of Japan when it was seized by naval forces of North Korea on January 23, 1968. Two days later, President Lyndon Johnson issued Executive Order 11392, mobilizing 9,343 Air Guardsman. Hearing that news as I walked across the hangar floor at Standiford, I instantly thought, "Oh man, we're in for it now." You automatically think that you — Joe Snuffy — are going to be the one mobilized whenever a call-up is announced, no matter where it is or what it's for.

Why the mobilization? First, it was intended as a signal to the North Koreans, whose brazenness in seizing the Pueblo must be answered immediately. At the same time, the call-up was short of a Tonkin-Gulf style declaration of hostilities.

Second, the call-up was intended as a means of reassuring South Korea, which was concerned that North Korean belligerency would ultimately erupt in an invasion. Fearing this, South Korea had already told President Johnson they were pulling their forces out of Vietnam to provide maximum defense of their homeland. To prevent this rupture in Southeast Asia, Johnson's move was to shift aviation resources to Korea.

And so from bases all over the globe, 267 tactical aircraft were dispatched to South Korea, which created a need for pilots and aircraft to fill the gaps.

Third, the Tet Offensive occurred less than a week after President Johnson's announcement. This prompted him to ask for even more Guard units, both Army and Air as backfill throughout the world, and demonstrated the fragility and vulnerability of his Vietnam manpower strategy.

To many of the participants and observers alike, the mobilization almost seemed as if the President and his Administration treated the call-up as a belated acknowledgment of an action they should have taken earlier in war. Now, it was too little too late.

This was the second call up in six years, the fourth in 27 years.

Approximately 33,000 personnel — 23,000 Guard and 10,000 Reserve — were called up for the Pueblo crisis in a period extending from January to June of 1968.

Actually, it was a relatively small mobilization, given that only 13,000 were called from the 80,000-strong Air Guard and only 10,000 sought from the 300,000-man Army Guard. Not many, to be sure, but as an enlisted man would tell me during the Gulf War 23 years later, "When you're the one called, it might as well be a one-hundred percent call-up."

The Korean theater commander needed three RF-101 squadrons, and our 123rd Tactical Reconnaissance Wing at Louisville, which included Little Rock's 189th Tactical Reconnaissance Group and Louisville's 165th Tactical Reconnaissance Squadron, and Reno's 152nd Tactical Reconnaissance Group were chosen for the call-up. Suddenly, in terms of equipment and training, the 123rd went from a Priority Four to a Priority One unit. Top-of-the-line reconnaissance equipment started coming to us and advanced training was scheduled.

An unusual event occurred at this time, one which would indirectly affect my career. I had met a promotion board in December of 1967 for elevation to Major and my paperwork was somewhere in the dark void of processing for federal recognition. Immediately after the call-up, the Chief of the National Guard Bureau, Major General Winston P. "Wimpy" Wilson, announced that pending promotions for those personnel mobilized were to be approved effectively on the date of the call-up.

So, I went on active duty as a Major. It was a field-grade position and the timing, in terms of dates in time in grade, proved to be crucial, as later events would show.

We went to post-mobilization and its ever-present administrative dance — physicals, eye-tests, family ID cards, insurance, update of personnel files, briefings, and finally, the issuance of the green identi-fication cards for all personnel on active duty.

Back then, there were two types of call-ups — partial mobilization, which was up to one million personnel for two years, and full mobili-zation, which was for all personnel for a time period, in that memorable phrase, "for the duration plus six months." Congressional authoriza-tion was needed for both.

For some, mobilization was a significant interference with their civilian life. Dick Frymire was a Major in the Air Guard and a close friend of mine in the unit. He was also Majority Leader of the Kentucky State Senate and a practicing attorney in Madisonville, Kentucky. Another close friend was Major Fred Arnold, a veternarian in Lexing-ton. There was also Fred Bradley, a prominent Frankfort lawyer. They all could have claimed hardship and been excused but they put duty ahead of self-interest. For Frymire, that was pretty much the end of his elected political career. I have always greatly admired these superb warriors for their citizen-airmen sacrifices for our country.

Our post-mobilization training included sea survival, conducted out of Homestead Air Force Base near Miami, and flight tactics and advanced training at Shaw Air Force Base at Sumter, South Carolina. At the time, we were still not sure whether we were going to Korea or Vietnam.

Finally, in June of 1968, the wing was given assignments which were to be rotated among the three squadrons. The Louisville and Reno units were first assigned to Richards-Gebaur Air Force Base near Kansas City. We then rotated to Howard Air Force Base in Panama and had reconnaissance responsibility for Central America. We also deployed to Elmendorf Air Force Base in Anchorage and responsible for photographing and mapping portions of Alaska as well as keeping an eye on the North Pacific. And in July, the Little Rock, Arkansas unit, true to the song of last December, was sent to Itazuke Air Base in Japan. Ultimately, all three units would rotate to Itazuke and fly daily missions over Korea.

My job at the beginning of the deployment, as the Wing's Chief of Standardization and Evaluation, was responsibility for rating aircrews and their procedures as they flew their various missions at the overseas sites around the world.

Our first mission occurred in August of 1968 and was the deployment of part of the Louisville unit from Richards-Gebaur to Elmendorf. It would be the first ever long-range deployment for the Kentucky Air Guard utilizing air refueling tankers. After several planes had to abort and return to the home base upon take-off, I ended up leading the remaining formation.

After we all arrived safely in Alaska, we set out to photograph basically every square inch of the state. Remember, there was no high-resolution satellite imagery then, and Alaska was not only the newest state, but also the most remote and the largest. If you went down in Alaska, your chances of being rescued were pretty slim. After this mission, I returned to Richards-Gebaur and in October of '68, flew down to Panama where Major Fred Bradley was task force commander of the aircraft assigned there to pull reconnaissance duty for Central America. The Air Force wanted a jet aircraft presence in the region as a check against communist forays into some of the more unstable governments. I'll never forget the reaction of the folks there as they watched our flying. Many of them had never even seen many prop planes, much less a jet streaking by at 500 miles per hour. We would occasionally do a slight acrobatic maneuver to impress people, a high performance afterburner climbout, frankly, as much a thrill for them as for us.

In January of 1969, the irony of the Christmas party chorus came full circle as I found myself looking over at Itazuke Tower, making my final approach on the field to evaluate the Reno unit. One month later, the Kentucky unit arrived for their rotation. Our first task was to perform a theater check, a two-and-a-half-hour mission. After taking off from Itazuke, we'd follow the east coast of South Korea, turn left at the Demilitarized Zone (DMZ), fly just south of the 38th parallel and then begin our reconnaissance mission. At the western-most point of the DMZ, we'd turn south and land at Osan Air Base, download the mission film, refuel, and then head back to good ol' Itazuke Tower and our base.

We flew the same mission several times every day in order to ascertain what, if any, preparations the North Koreans were making for offensive war. More than a few times, we'd see MIGs shadowing us just north of the DMZ. Sometimes, North Korean radar operators would try to lure us off course, using decoy signals to bend our navigation pointer by as much as 45 degrees off course. A slow right would then take you over the DMZ into North Korean territory, which might result in a formal complaint or even a shootdown, and further exacerbate an already bad situation. An Air Force RF-4C had been lured over the parallel and subsequently shot down before our arrival in theater.

While at Itazuke, I was asked to pilot a battle-damaged RF-101 from Clark Air Force Base in the Philippines to McClelland Air Force Base in California. They wanted an experienced instructor test pilot because the plane had been flown pretty hard in combat over North Vietnam. I volunteered because of the challenge, knowing that anything could go wrong with the aircraft and, if there was a problem, I wouldn't have much time to correct it. As well, I was one of the high time F-101 pilots in the Air Force.

Lord, what an interminable trip. The drill then was that a K-135 tanker would lead a flight of several aircraft, either from the states to Vietnam, or from Vietnam to the states. Each aircraft, called a "chick," would have its gas tank topped off every hour or so by the "mother hen" so that if the tanker plane suddenly malfunctioned, we had almost a full load of fuel on which to find a runway in the Pacific. I got in behind a KC-135 tanker, which was flowing eastward toward the states, and began regular refueling after we left Clark.

We flew to Guam and spent the night and then on the second day we overflew Wake Island on our way to Hawaii. About two hours from Hawaii, five hours into the trip, after seeing nothing but sea, my body began cramping up, I started nodding off at the stick and dimly realized it was time to pop a "go" pill.

These were amphetamines, devised to keep pilots awake on long flights. You were told to take one when you felt drowsy. However, there was a slight problem. They got you on such a high that you'd begin to think everything was fine, even when it wasn't. The plane could be experiencing serious problems and you wouldn't care. Your landing gear wouldn't be down and you would think it was. I hadn't taken a pill before and haven't since but in that situation, I had no other choice. It worked fine. Indeed, I was so awake and paranoid before we landed at Hickam that I checked everything — including the landing gear — about ten times.

As we began our approach to Hickam, I heard the airmen in the tanker talking over their own intercom. The tanker guys seemingly spent their entire service escorting jets to and from Vietnam when they weren't on their tour in the theater. Their biggest fear was that when they started their flow back to United States, they'd get stopped somewhere and have to fly back to Vietnam.

Hawaii was the last stop before the states, and it was the critical leg of the trip where the crews got the most nervous. They wanted to make sure they had some fighters to take back to the mainland. And so over the radio you could hear them say, "Hope we don't get turned around. I gotta see my wife. There's got to be some chicks (fighters) at Hickam, man. At least two."

As luck would have it, this particular crew did get turned around at Hickam. And I got to spend four days on the beach in Hawaii waiting for another mother hen to take me the final leg back to McClelland Air Force Base in Sacramento, California.

In the spring of 1969, a U.S. aircraft near the DMZ was shot down by North Korea. The Louisville unit was then at Itazuke and preparing to return to the states. But for the moment, all our hopes about a transfer home were dashed. And the inevitable happened, which occurs any time you get two or more guys in uniform together: the rumor mill cranks up. And it was cooking now. We were never going home; we were getting transferred to Vietnam; a new Korean war was about to break out; we were needed in the Philippines; Congress was going to extend the two-year mobilization. Amazingly, the situation resolved itself without further incidents.

Our squadron was soon cleared to leave Itazuke and after we arrived home, we were deactivated with a large ceremony in Louisville on June 5th, 1969.

During that 18-month period, Colonel Vern Yahne, the Base Detachment Commander, stayed with a skeleton crew as a caretaker at Standiford. When I returned to the states, House Resolution 2, the National Guard Technician Act, was in effect. This act shifted all National Guard technicians into federal civil service status. We became U.S Code Title 32 employees with all of the rights, retirement, and health care benefits other federal employees enjoyed. However, we still worked for the Governor and the Adjutant General. This switch in designation was a big step for the National Guard and helped improve the quality and morale of the technician program.

The lessons of the call up were pretty clear cut. Although there were glitches, the mobilization proved you could put together a competent, combat-ready force from your Guard and Reserves in a rapid fashion. The training and equipping of crews went much smoother than it had just seven years earlier during the Berlin Wall call-up.

The success of the Pueblo call-up must have been a bittersweet victory for the Administration. The final deactivation occurred in June of 1969, two-and-a-half agonizing years before the U.S. left Vietnam. What would have happened if a larger, more comprehensive call-up had been made earlier than 1968? It's a question that senior leaders from that period wrestled with for years. One, General Creighton Abrams, as discussed later, took it to heart and later would ensure that there would be greater involvement by the Guard and Reserve in foreign conflicts.

And if we hadn't noticed it before, it was clear by the time we got home from our deployment that a lot of things had changed in America.

In the spring of 1970, I became operations officer of the squadron and simultaneously was elected Vice-President of the National Guard Association of Kentucky. In the spring of 1971, I was elected President of the organization.

In November of 1971, Wendell Ford was elected Governor of Kentucky. His campaign was co-chaired by Dee Huddleston and by my friend Dick Frymire, who had returned from the Pueblo call-up to his Madisonville law practice. Two weeks after the election, Ford offered the post of Adjutant General, a two-star billet, to Frymire, who was a Lieutenant Colonel at the time. When Frymire accepted, Ford, in front of some of Frymire's key staff, presented him with a pair of pajamas with two stars pinned to each shoulder. Dick Frymire took some good ribbing over this for years to come.

Under one of the older and more unusual tenets of Kentucky law, the first act of the new Governor following inauguration must be the swearing in of his Adjutant General so that the state is "protected." And so less than 20 minutes after taking the oath of office in December of 1971, Ford swore in Dick Frymire.

Frymire's youth and overnight ascendancy from O-5 to O-8 (Lieutenant Colonel to Major General) presaged his startling affect on the Kentucky Guard. Indeed, his leadership was key to surviving some of the rocky times ahead.

First, because he'd been in the field as a traditional Guardsman, he had a good feel for the concerns and gripes and interests of the enlisted personnel and officers.

Second, as a longtime Guardsman, Frymire knew that a subtle shift of power from the World War II and Korean War-era vets to a younger crew of commanders was taking place; he wanted to make this transition as graceful as possible.

Third, he was closely aware of what was happening to American society because of the catharsis caused by Vietnam. He knew what this meant for the future of the military, both in Kentucky and the rest of the nation.

Last, he was selfless in helping his troops, both officers and enlisted, advance their careers, as I was soon fortunate to discover.

In February of 1972, I was the operations officer of the 123rd. Colonel Yahne was the full-time wing commander, the Base Detachment Commander (BDC), and Air Commander of the Kentucky National Guard. He'd been BDC since 1956 and had done a superb job in leading the Kentucky unit into the high reconnaissance jet age. His service time was up in October, when, by law, he would have to retire and the BDC appointment was to be Frymire's first major Air Guard decision as TAG.

One day in June of 1972, Frymire called me into the TAG office in Frankfort. And he got right to the point.

Dick and I had been close professionally and personally for a long time and I assumed he was giving me a heads-up on who I was going to have to work with as the new BDC for the next few years.

"Colonel Yahne will be leaving in October and I want you to replace him."

I was stunned. I never thought I'd be considered for the post — I'd been a Lieutenant Colonel for less than a year and there were at least a half a dozen more senior people in the wing. It was exactly because of this that there might be a problem. Frymire was way ahead of me. "It might not be easy sometimes," he said. "You've got several of them older than you and some of them are going to be upset. You'll outrank them civilian-wise," remarked Dick — because as BDC I would be a GS-14 and they were GS-13s or below — "but from a military sense and on drill weekends, you'll still be a Lieutenant Colonel and some of them will be senior to you." Frymire went on to say the announcement would be made in July, so I could begin a 60-day understudy period with Yahne.

What a confluence of events — the move to Louisville with Mead Johnson, Colonel Yahne's offer of a full-time slot, the call-up and instant promotion, Ford's election, Frymire's selection, and now this. At 37, I would be the youngest Air Commander in the country at that time.

Ultimately, by selecting me, Ford and Frymire really did me a huge favor. It was tough sometimes because even though I had experience in running an installation and managing people, I wasn't as experienced in all things military as some of the senior colonels there.

In addition to obtaining the leadership experience, the position and Frymire's patronage would introduce me to the various tangible and intangible aspects of the Guard — the not-so-hidden agendas of the Adjutants' General, the characteristics of each state organization, the role of the governors, the strength and weaknesses of the Guard Bureau, the nature of the Guard's political clout, and the personalities involved thoughout the Guard structure.

In short, I would no longer just keep my vision focused on the flight line at Standiford; I'd get a glimpse of the big picture. I didn't know it then, but Frymire's decision was the first step on the long road to Chief, National Guard Bureau.

CHAPTER FIVE

"A TIME OF TURMOIL"

I became Base Detachment Commander at a turbulent time in modern American history. The Vietnam War, social unrest, and an almost self-destructive youth culture unleashed a wave of disenchantment against most American institutions; probably none was more reviled than the military.

The 1960s were a period in which young people tore into mainstream values and attitudes; amazingly, their assault went unchallenged by an older generation who should have known better. This upheaval had its political impact as the Nixon Administration scrambled for a plan to end U.S. involvement in the Vietnam War.

President Nixon's policy of "Vietnamization" began in 1970. By 1972, the sole focus of administration was its almost desperate negotiations with the North Vietnamese communists in Paris. By late 1972, Henry Kissinger would announce that "peace is at hand." It wasn't but that didn't stop him from winning a Nobel Prize in 1973 for a war ending in 1975.

Of course, I don't mean to say the 1960s were an utterly bleak period. Civil rights and greater equality for blacks and women emerged from this period as well, social milestones that — I might add — were immediately taken to heart in the Guard. Beyond these two noteworthy achievements, however, the effects of the 1960s were hardly positive.

As a husband and father, I saw disturbing cultural trends take root during these times: the increase of astonishing poverty despite massive government intervention; a persistent disrespect for authority; an ebbing of self-discipline; increased promiscuity and its consequence — illegitimacy; the devaluing of marriage and the dissolution of families; the decline of urban areas and the rise of almost pathological violence and drug use.

How ironic then, that a generation later, I would see the Guard dealing on a daily and direct basis with many of the consequences of the 60's meltdown.

Two months after I assumed command of the unit, the U.S. undertook an air campaign of unprecedented ferocity against Hanoi in an effort to force the communists to negotiate an end to the war. The bombing did just that. Yes, unfortunately, civilians were killed.

But the results — the North Vietnamese hustling back to the Paris peace talks — were undeniable. The short two-week campaign lent credence to the idea that a total war against the North, spear-headed by relentless air power, might have resulted in a different outcome. Moreover, the resort to similar sanction if the Paris peace agreements were not honored following U.S. withdrawal might have saved the South Vietnamese from their nightmare.

As the first and last great American air offensive of the war ended and the bulk of U.S. combat forces departed in mid-1973, they came home to a military — including the Guard — in an unparalleled state of disarray and shock from events of the previous decade.

The Guard had a singular role in this chaos. As Vietnam grew longer and more complex, the anti-war movements also grew and spread, often becoming violent. The Guard became a political scape-goat for failure on the part of the Johnson and then Nixon administra-tions to totally commit to mobilizing for the war.

Participation in the Reserve Components (RC) exempted individu-als from being drafted for the war. Therefore many young men opted to fill RC units rather than face the potential of serving in Vietnam. The Guard has always been a volunteer organization, where patriotic men and women may serve their state and nation with the expectation that when needed, they will be called to war. During the 60's that proud heritage was stained. The Guard as an institution wanted to participate; after all, that's what it had traditionally done throughout history. But, it was not to be until the administration was convinced in 1968, follow-ing the Pueblo incident, to call up Guard and Reserve units.

I've already spoken about the Air Guard contribution during this period. Seventy-six Army Guard and Reserve units totaling 20,034 personnel were mobilized and served either as units or were used as individual fillers for service in Vietnam. These personnel served with distinction, fighting and dying in Vietnam with their active duty counterparts.

But there was an additional opprobrium to which the Guard was subjected. First, the Guard was perceived by the anti-war activists as part of the hated military establishment and Guard personnel were badly treated in some instances by militant protesters. Second, there were those Guard members who had entered the Guard solely to escape the draft, had anti-war sentiments, and often times made life miserable for Guard commanders. And last, there were many in the active Army who looked down on the Guard as a haven for draft dodgers and an incompetent group of individuals. We simply couldn't win.

Unfortunately, even today there remains some ill feelings among active Army individuals who had served tours of duty in Vietnam, while ARNG units and individuals did not serve. Some, inexplicably, blame the Guard and believe that had the Guard participated, there would have been fewer active duty troops needed for that unpopular conflict. It was and remains a tragic misunderstanding.

Moreover, against the backdrop of this malaise throughout America was its affect on the increasing internal unrest within the Guard. Because when the U.S. began to disengage from Vietnam, the draft was terminated by President Nixon and the Guard went through a complete metamorphosis.

I have often unsettled audiences by flatly declaring that the Guard during these times, really up until 1977, was mostly an all white, male, draft-motivated force. Minorities and women accounted for less than two percent of the combined Army and Air Guard in 1972. The few females the Air Guard had were mostly nurses. And one reason we had only a handful of minority troops, however blunt this may sound, is because they lacked the contacts to join the Guard or Reserve during the draft era.

Overall, despite this external and internal buffeting, the Guard was ironically, a rather effective force during this time — it had high-calibre recruits (a remarkably high percentage were college students or college grads) and most executed their duties smartly. Why? Troops knew that absenteeism, non-performance, or a bad attitude was the surest way to get kicked out of the Guard and into an active duty billet. Most of our units were above 100 percent strength because there were always plenty of folks clambering to get in.

However, as soon as the draft ended in January of 1973, we began to feel a slackening in numbers of qualified personnel.

It was like a daisy chain — the U.S. role in the Vietnam War ended, and so did the draft. There was not a lot of affinity for the service in the first place and then all of a sudden, the main reason for military service ends.

Then came the flowering of the disgruntlement factor. A good portion of our troops hadn't really wanted to join the Guard — or any military service for that matter. But it was an alternative to the draft and active duty, so many grudgingly joined and did an adequate job while in uniform.

Now that the draft had disappeared, these guys were suddenly faced with three, four, or five years of Guard enlistment and they were furious. That's when the difficulties began.

The worst was attendance — some soldiers and airmen just gave up coming to drill. Or, they were chronically late. Or, they came to drill under the influence of drugs or alcohol. Or, they refused to work when at drill. Or, they refused to follow the proper forms of military courtesy and respect. Such attitudes acted like a cancer inasmuch as unit cohesion depends upon certain rituals and protocols and can be undone by the behavior of even a few members.

Major W. Stu Stewart, later my chief of staff in the Bureau, recalled a visit of active duty inspectors to his Charleston, West Virginia air base, where I'd been stationed a decade previous. The inspection team got off the plane in Class A uniforms and were going to drive into town for dinner. They immediately asked where they could change into civilian clothes. Stewart and his Air Guard colleagues asked why? They replied, "Well, you said we're going to dinner off base and we never wear our uniforms around civilians."

Stu told them, "Wait a minute, folks. You're in West-by-God Virginia." Further discussion revealed that these men had actually been verbally and physically attacked in another state when they wore their uniforms.

From my vantage point, I'd have to say that the overall social acceptance of the military was good in Kentucky. The state had a long and distinguished military heritage; the political winds were moderate to conservative. And, the vast Army installations, Fort Knox and Fort Campbell, were big employers and good neighbors.

Elsewhere, however, as the experience with Stu Stewart demonstrated, citizens lobbied members of Congress in attempts to have Guard units transferred away from their communities. We had our list of "problem airports" where the Air Guard was harassed. These included Chicago, Detroit, Van Nuys (California), and Westchester County, New York to name just a few.

There was also a serious problem at this time with technicians and full-timers who didn't want to wear military uniforms to their armories and air bases. Their complaints were so loud that the U.S. Civil Service Commission, which handled personnel issues at that time, told the Guard that we had to come up with a "compelling need" for why these personnel had to wear uniforms in which to perform their duties. It was so bad that even in the nation's capital, both officer and enlisted personnel would report to the Pentagon in civilian clothes.

In my own unscientific way, I periodically measured the quality of my unit during these difficult times, as I imagine other commanders did with their units. In the 123rd Wing, of approximately 1,100 personnel, we had about 250 non-traditional Guardsman who performed full-time work at Standiford maintaining the aircraft and the facilities. These were considered good jobs in Louisville and these key personnel formed a core which helped hold the unit together over the roller-coaster 1970s.

Of the remaining 850 traditional Guard members, I would say that about 650 were squared-away personnel who showed up to drill on time, performed their jobs well, and were solid representatives of the National Guard.

The other 200 were not so good; in fact, in an earlier time, when strength was not an issue, many would have been kicked out with dishonorable discharges. This group ebbed and flowed — some would leave, and others would take their place. Few of them were willing to do more than the minimum to get by. They were late or absent from drill and openly disdainful of the rigid aspects of military life.

For me, the breakdown was symbolized most graphically by an

incident in 1974. Our unit was assembled for an annual inspection by a team from the active duty unit we backed up. This was an important affair inasmuch as it demonstrated your unit's overall readiness and fitness to your parent unit. It was usually performed by no-nonsense officers and NCOs who looked closely to find weak areas in a unit and then recommend corrective action.

As the entire, 1,100-man unit stood in formation, there was a disturbance in front of the formation. A car drove up and out jumped an airmen who had nothing on but his hat.

Painted on his body, front, back, and sides, was a detailed airmen's uniform, complete with the white t-shirt showing at the neck, a collar, name tag, buttons, sleeves, trousers, creases, even the eyelets and laces for boots were painted on his ankles. He stepped to attention in front of the formation and the inspectors with this silly grin on his face.

We immediately had him arrested, sent him to the hospital for a sobriety test and then to a psychiatrist. I was shocked — the incident was humiliating for the entire unit. Moreover, what were the actives going to say about this?

In fact, far from being incensed, the inspectors proved to be understanding — they said they'd seen this type of shenanigans on active duty bases. I have no doubt that many commanders during this period have similar tales.

Guys like this exhibitionist just didn't want to be in the service. But unlike their counterparts of 30 years ago, some of whom undoubtably felt the same way about the service, these recruits of the late 1960s and 70s were defiant. Instead of simply serving their enlistment time going to drills — which was hardly comparable to the sacrifice of combat troops in Vietnam — they challenged the principles of national service that had been honored for more than 200 years. This behavior by so many individuals was a poor reflection on that generation and has endured even to this day. And it stands in stark contrast to the dedication of those who served overseas.

Unfortunately, we had little recourse in preventing breakdowns of this kind. Just a year before, when the draft was in force, the command reaction to a recalcitrant would be his immediate assignment to the active duty force. But now, the Army and the Air Force didn't want problem children — they had plenty of their own. And, they were under the gun to down-size their force structure. Without the active-duty hammer, our sanctions in the Guard were very limited.

Moreover, we couldn't just start minting dishonorable discharges, military prison terms, or court-martials reports for absenteeism and unsatisfactory attitudes, though I would have loved to have made a few examples out of some of our worst soliders and airmen. My concern was, like that of other field commanders, I dreaded the long, drawn-out spectacles, bad press, and even legal entanglements. I was also concerned about the reaction of elected officials and consequent Congressional scrutiny because some home-town clown or his parents complained loud and long enough.

The bottom line was, the Guard and Reserve were stuck with a lot of people who wanted out. So, finally, simply to get rid of the biggest troublemakers, we began issuing Administrative Discharges, which carried none of the opprobrium of a Dishonorable Discharge. Only if the troop had committed a serious crime, like assault or burglary, would we give him a dishonorable discharge and only in the worst cases would we conduct court-marital hearings.

And if all this wasn't enough to try the patience of even the most forbearing Guard leader, in addition to the steady problems with discipline, the loss of the draft, and the general disdain for military service, the services were beginning the transition to All-Volunteer Force (AVF). This was a concept and an eventual achievement which I don't believe has ever been adequately appreciated by the American public.

Military historian John Keegan has written that in the past, the hallmark of the modern nation-state was the creation of a large conscripted army. It was only by constructing a force geographically and demographically diverse that a country could muster the necessary will to defend and advance its interests.

In a sense, the AVF ran completely counter to that concept. Instead, under the AVF, America's national defense would consist of volunteers, lured to arms by attractive pay, good benefits, and the promise of learning a trade useful in the civilian world.

Given the social currents at the time, the AVF would have been a daring experiment in any Western nation during the 1970s; recall that many of our NATO allies, for example, operated under conscription and still do. In America, defender of the free world however blooded from Vietnam, the All Volunteer Force was a watershed event. And it meant that all components, active and reserve, were engaged in a mad scramble for recruits.

In the fierce competition for the best recruits, young men and women were simply not going to stand in line outside our armories waiting to enlist. We had to sell them on the Guard, going head-to-head with civilian employers. In this new environment we had to train a cadre-of full-time recruiters and establish recruiting offices throughout each state.

It was an utterly staggering idea.

In the past, the Guard would just designate a corner of an armory as an enlistment office, which always had a willing group of able-bodied men, many of them one-step ahead of the draft. No selling was involved. Now, we had to teach our own people to sing our praises, in sweeter tones than any of the other components.

Today, recruiting is done with splashy ads, snappy music, displays of fast-charging tanks, ships, helicopters and planes, and promises of superb benefits, PX privileges, pensions, skill training, and the Montgomery G.I. bill! I hate to say it, but back then, at its inception, recruiting was little more than primitive arm-twisting.

In the 123rd, I had great support in my recruiting efforts from Colonel Carl Black, Major John Smith, Major Joe Kottak, Captain Bill Lesley, and my chief of maintenance, Major John Greene, all of whom would later become commanders themselves. They were well-known in the community and well-liked by the troops. Recruiting in Kentucky was probably easier than in other states because of the state's military tradition. Plus, the 123rd was not only the sole Air Guard unit in the state, it was also the state's only Air Force unit, active or Guard, or reserve. Any young man or woman interested in aviation would end up hearing our pitch.

Another major reform taking place during this period, as if the end of the draft and creation of the AVF weren't enough for field commanders, was the formation by Secretary of Defense Melvin Laird of one of the most far-reaching ideas in the history of peacetime U.S. military strategy — the Total Force concept.

Initially proposed in 1970, the Total Force policy was prompted by the manpower and force structure debacle of Vietnam — the heavy reliance on an inequitable draft, reluctant and piecemeal use of Guard and reserve forces, and the intense pressures of maintaining a global military presence. Assisting Laird was a sharp Pentagon strategist, Dr. Ted Marrs, himself an Air Guardsman of many years.

The Total Force Policy envisioned the integrated use of all the active forces — Army, Navy, Air Force, Marines, and Coast Guard, as well as their reserve components — the Army National Guard and the Air National Guard, the Army Reserve and Air Force Reserve, the Naval Reserve, Marine Corps Reserve, and the Coast Guard Reserve. These 12 separate components and the tremendous manpower and training they represented were only tenuously linked together in terms of an overarching U.S. military strategy.

Under the Total Force Policy, these components would be considered collectively in any planning for wars or contingencies.

The reserve forces would be integrated into the war plans and force structure of the active duty forces, giving planners the ability to quickly utilize any single individual in uniform, active, Guard, or reserve. Moreover, Secretary Laird envisioned that reserve forces would be used in ongoing, real-world missions heretofore performed only by active duty forces.

The Total Force Policy promised increased roles and responsibility for Guard and Reserve units. It acknowledged the past errors of Vietnam. It was a welcome and long-overdue recognition that Guard and Reserve were vital to the military structure and strategy of the United States.

As Lewis Sorley has written in his classic biography of General Creighton Abrams:

"One of the most fateful decisions of the war in Vietnam had been Lyndon Johnson's refusal to call up the [Guard and] reserves. All the

Joint Chiefs, but especially General Harold K. Johnson, the Army Chief of Staff, had found this a very traumatic thing, with General Johnson even coming close to resigning in protest — and at the end of his life, describing the failure to do so as his greatest regret."

"Abrams, as Vice-Chief of Staff during the buildup for Vietnam, had to cope with the disabilities induced by the lack of mobilization. Now, as Chief of Staff, he appeared determined to ensure that never again would a President be able to send the Army to war without the National Guard and reserves maintained for such a contingency. The vehicle for doing this was revised force structure that integrated reserve and active forces elements so closely as to make the reserves virtually inextricable from the whole."

General Abrams' committment to Total Force policy became a decisive part of U.S. military thinking.

In 1973, Secretary of Defense James Schlesinger made Total Force policy the official policy of the Department of Defense and specified that "Reserve forces would be the initial and primary augmentation of active forces and any military response would involve the integrated use of all the forces available, including active, reserve, civilian, and allied."

As one of ninety-one Base Detachment Commanders, I had a unique vantage point from which to view these Washington-based reforms flowing down to the individual units and leaders in the field. Like it or not, it was the senior officers and enlisted at each installation — and this was true for all services — who would live or die with these changes.

I was fortunate to serve under an Adjutant General who best exemplified the critical role of Guard leadership at the state level. The fact is, Major General Dick Frymire was one of the best things that ever happened to the Kentucky Guard. He was a favorite with the enlisted troops; he was well-liked by members of both parties in the Frankfort legislative chambers. He had the ear of the Governor and the respect of his commanders. He took Kentucky Guard personnel all over the country to various Guard events to introduce us to our counterparts, observe their operations, and listen to their concerns. He was energetic and far-sighted and, fortunately for me, politically savvy and well-connected.

Because of General Frymire's patronage, I met and got to know many of the key senior National Guard leaders. These were truly the legends of the Guard — Major Generals Frank Gerard of New Jersey, Frank Bailey of Arkansas, Charlie DuBois of Missouri, Bill Sefton of Indiana, John Dolny of Minnesota, Pete Phillipi of Pennsylvania, and Ed Fry of Kansas, to name a few.

These men were the corporate memory of the Guard. Fifteen to 20 years older, most were combat veterans, had been through as many as four call-ups, and all had served through the agonies of Vietnam and the difficult peacetime periods. These men were institutions in the Air Guard and all were my mentors.

In 1972, Major General I.G. Brown, the legendary Air Guard Director, and his deputy, Brigadier General John Pesch, appointed me to serve on a national panel, the Dubois Committee, later the Phillipi Committee, which set out to restructure the Air Guard at the unit level. Of course, as a new Lieutenant Colonel, I had no illusions about my own status at any of the meetings of these general officers and in many instances, my main function was to serve as a glorified recorder of the proceedings.

One of our big problems at that time was that we had Base Detachment Commanders who were not aviators. Hence, when we were mobilized, as for the Pueblo crisis, these BDCs could not go with their units. It was an unacceptable situation inasmuch as it is imperative that a unit commander in charge of the training and leadership of his troops accompany them to war in the event of mobilization.

And so, in addition to other reforms, the Phillipi Committee redesignated the BDC as the "Air Commander," with the requirement that he or she have wings, either as a pilot or a navigator and that they be assigned to a mobilization position. This long overdue change insured the unit commander would be mobilized along with his troops.

In addition to knowing most of the Adjutant Generals, General Frymire was also on good terms with the National Guard Bureau folks in Washington. Through him, I was fortunate to meet and spend time with Major General LaVerne Weber, the Director of the Army National Guard, and Major General Francis Greenlief, Chief of the National Guard Bureau at that time. I met Major General Weber when he was Frymire's personal guest at the 1972 Kentucky Derby and also got together with him for other functions during this time. Little did I know that my association with General Weber would dramatically affect my own future.

Because of General Frymire's activities and visibility, I had a unique perspective on the many ways in which Guard matters were handled. For example, in February of 1972, the Air Guard Deputy Director John Pesch notified General Frymire that the 123rd was going to "change missions," a term guaranteed to put any commander into a cold sweat.

General Pesch said that we were going to trade in our RF-101s for A-37s, a small, armed attack fighter. I was not particularly alarmed; it was always a challenge to learn the ins and outs of a new aircraft.

But there was a catch. In accepting the new plane and the new mission, the unit strength would drop from 1,050 to 700, while the number of full-timers would be cut in half, from 250 to approximately 125.

General Frymire hit the ceiling when General Pesch gave him the news. "For God's sake, John, Ford's been in office only a month and you're going to cut us in half? I can't take that news home with me." The loss in numbers, particularly full-timers, was unacceptable to an administration just getting off the ground. General Frymire worked the issue expertly and ultimately, the entire wing was re-structured by General Pesch. We retained our RF-101s and personnel, dropped the Little Rock squadron (which received KC-135 tankers), and rounded the wing out by picking up a squadron in Boise, Idaho.

In February of 1975, General Frymire promoted me to full Colonel after I'd spent the minimum time in grade as Lieutenant Colonel. I was 40 years old and had followed an unusual promotion pattern, to say the least. It had taken me 12 years, from the ages of 21 to 33, to move from Second Lieutenant to Captain but it had taken me only seven years to go from Captain to Colonel.

The next year, in 1976, the squadron was given RF-4s to replace our RF-101s, which after 11 years in our unit, had become an outdated aircraft platform. The Air Force was taking its RF-4s out of Europe and cutting back on tactical reconnaissance world wide. At this time, there were only two reconnaissance wings in the Guard, ours and the 117th based out of Birmingham, Alabama, which was complemented by squadrons in Mississippi and Nebraska.

In Louisville, Brigadier General Fred Bradley, a traditional Guardsman on weekends, was the wing commander (he would also become a state senator). I was the everyday commander, the number-one civilian in charge during the week and the number two military officer on drill weekends.

The RF-4 was a Rolls Royce compared to our outdated RF-101s; a definite "Sierra Hotel" that could hit mach 2 speed if necesary. It was also a two-seater. Believe, me, the weapons system operator/navigator in the back sure made the pilot's job a lot easier. In the RF-101s, you were constantly looking outside and around you while reading a map stuck to a clipboard balanced on your knee. This flying method got a bit dangerous at high speeds and low levels. But it was the only way to get the job done in an aircraft with one seat.

The RF-4 had a forward-looking radar, infra-red sensors with a day and night capability. In the old RF-101, we had to shoot flares out and then take pictures, using the flare as a kind of flash bulb. It was pretty unsophisticated at the very least and frankly, damn dangerous in hostile territory. Because, if there was an enemy down there, all he had to do was just shoot ahead of the flares and he'd have a good chance to hit the aircraft.

In 1975, Kentucky elected a new governor, Julian Carroll, to replace Governor Ford, who had been elected to the United States Senate. General Frymire's reputation was so good that Governor Carroll asked him to stay on as the Adjutant General. General Frymire was slowly but doggedly making his vision for the future of the Kentucky Guard a reality. He was determined to make the Kentucky Army and Air Guard one of the premier organizations in the nation. The officer corps was strong, with the right mix of age and youth, manpower levels were steady, and despite the social turbulence, morale was high.

Training and checking out crews in the RC-4s took up almost all of 1976. No conversion is ever easy but they do provide you with new training opportunities and a real sense of accomplishment as the pilots, maintenance, and support personnel get up to speed. As one of the senior ranking blue-suiters in the only Air Guard unit in the state, I discovered a new-found prominence in the many military and civilian functions that took place throughout Kentucky. I was a regular invitee to all sorts of events at Fort Knox and Fort Campbell. And, because I ran the state's only military air base, I regularly hosted dignitaries such as General Creighton Abrams and General William Westmoreland, when they flew into Kentucky.

Even though we had not quite exited from the social and cultural turmoil convulsing the country during the 1970s, I knew that ultimately, we'd win back respect for the uniform. The military was just too vital to American life to be down too long.

Our family had settled in well in Louisville. We had our fourth child, Bolyn, born in 1967 in Lousiville, and Rosemary and I reveled in our children and our stable, comfortable lifestyle. We often spoke as though we'd be in Louisville for the rest of our lives. We were very active in school and community life as well as our church, Watkins Memorial United Methodist.

Then in December 1976, a message came down from Washington.

In late 1976, Air Guard Director Major General John Pesch announced his retirement and his deputy, Brigadier General John Guice was named to replace him, leaving open the post of Deputy Director for Air.

Now, many commanders in the field felt the Pentagon was the last place they wanted to go. But we also knew there was pressure to have some of the field commanders nominated for key billets. It was common knowledge that there were folks in the Department of Defense who were aware of the need for a fresh field perspective in the Bureau.

So when it came time to fill the Deputy Director billet, it wasn't going to be business-as-usual. What the leadership was looking for was new blood, candidates who had first-hand experience with the changes taking place in the field, where the rubber meets the road.

I never knew when the vacancy for Deputy Director was announced. General Frymire called me in one day, told me about the opening, and suggested that I submit my name. I was working hard on the conversion at that time and promptly let the whole matter drop.

Then, on the last day before the vacancy was closed, General Frymire got a call from the Chief of the National Guard Bureau, Major General Weber, in Washington. After saying goodbye to Weber, Frymire phoned me immediately.

"John, I just got off the phone with General Weber about the Deputy Director opening and he said he'd really like see your name get submitted. I don't want to lose you, but I think you should consider this." General Frymire went on to say that Kentucky had never had a candidate for a senior Bureau post before and that an application now would be a good base for a candidacy if I wanted to throw my hat in the ring for the Adjutant General in four years.

So with General Frymire's full support, I agreed to apply. Frymire then had Governor Carroll formally nominate me hours before the announcement closed in Washington.

All of the nominations and the accompanying personnel packages went to a five-member board, composed of active and senior Guard officers, which met in January 1977. The members examined the credentials of each applicant — command experience, education, ROTC or Academy, combat service, state and federal mobilization experience, overseas assignments, and a range of other criteria.

Then, in late January, I was stunned to learn that I was one of three finalists, the others being Colonel Alex McDonald from the North Dakota Air Guard at Fargo, and Colonel Bill Berry, from the Georgia Air Guard in Atlanta.

The three of us flew to Washington for interviews. Officially, the Deputy Director was an appointment made by the Secretary of the Air Force. But it was actually made in close coordination with the selection board, the Air Guard Director, General Guice; the Chief of the Bureau, Major General Weber; and the Chief of Staff of the Air Force, the legendary General David Jones.

I first met with General William McBride, the four-star Vice Chief of Staff of the Air Force. I can still remember how anxious I was as I sat stiffly right beside his desk in a huge office in the E-ring of the Pentagon.

General McBride got right to the point. "John, you're a young colonel. You'll be the wing commander at Louisville and get a star within a year. Jeez, I know how those posts operate — you're a big man down there. Why do want to come here, uproot your family and get involved with all this craziness?"

Well, he woke me up. Because I hadn't thought of it that way. I was sitting here in this office primarily because other people had wanted me to apply and because it would be good for the Kentucky Guard and the field commanders. I figured I was too young and too inexperienced for a management position in Washington. I already thought, quite sincerely, that I had the best job in America — commander of the Kentucky Air Guard.

McBride was right. I was a big fish in the small pond of Louisville — hell, I might as well have a couple of stars. Every morning, I'd pull directly in front of the Main Headquarters building at the airfield and walk 20 feet to my office. If I wanted to fly that day, I'd drive to the flight line, park in the number-one spot reserved for the top full-time guy, get in my jet fighter and fly pretty much all I wanted. These were things only full generals got to do on big bases and here I was doing it as a colonel.

It was like my own little kingdom, really. I was master of my job and my fate and I was going to give it all up to come to Washington? Rosemary and I had talked about how it was nice to stay in one place for awhile. Besides, I'd just put a year into the new plane and I wanted to see the results.

So I said to General McBride, "To tell you the truth, General, I really wasn't sure I wanted to be a candidate but I had my name submitted anyway. Now that I've made it this far, I want to win — not for me because it would be a big upheaval for my family. But because I want to be able to help the commanders in the field. I think there's a feeling that some folks in the building don't understand what's been going on in the units, be that right or wrong. Having a field guy in a senior position might change that perception."

My final interview was with the Air Force Chief of Staff, General David Jones. He was a superb leader and we had a great meeting.

I came back convinced that I hadn't made an impression on anyone I'd spoken with in the Pentagon, particularly General McBride. But it didn't matter because I came back to Louisville and the job I really enjoyed.

Six weeks later, General Weber called General Frymire, and told him I'd been selected.

It turned out, I had just the kind of experience they were looking for — I'd served on active duty, flown several different types of aircraft and missions, I'd been in two state National Guards, participated in a call-up, and I'd commanded troops during the post-Vietnam upheaval.

As soon as the news got out, calls started coming in from around the country: it seemed all the different Air Commanders were pleased they'd have someone in the Pentagon who had come from their ranks.

It was decided my start date would be 1 April 1977. On March 29th, my nomination to Brigadier General was confirmed by the U.S. Senate.

But even before the confirmation, Rosemary and I squeezed into our Chevy Vega and drove to Washington. We stayed in Wainwright Hall at Ft. Myer and I was briefed on my new job while she went house-hunting. Once again we were on the move.

General Weber, with General Frymire and Rosemary in attendance, conducted my swearing-in and promotion in the conference room off Minuteman Hall in the Pentagon. I was 42, the youngest general in the Pentagon at that time. And as I got out of my beat-up Vega in Row 17 of the South Parking Lot and gazed in the distance at the Pentagon, I felt as though I was closer to the flight line at Standiford than I was to my new office.

SECTION II. "PENTAGON DAYS"

CHAPTER SIX

"THE YOUNGEST GENERAL"

It's one thing to pass through a big city and marvel, maybe a bit uneasily, at the traffic, the opulence, the tempo, the determined-looking inhabitants. And then leave all of this behind in your rear-view mirror.

It's quite different to roll into such a maelstrom knowing you're going to stay there and actually deal with everthing.

Which was the emotional jolt Rosemary and I encountered when first arriving in the nation's capital.

On top of that, we had the same experience shared by every couple that comes in from the field to headquarters. It occurs no matter how much you prepare for it — price shock. It's an old story, to be sure, but during the course of my career, I saw it learned anew every time a military family came to Washington to settle down for the first time.

Everywhere we went, from restaurants to supermarkets, furniture dealers to gas stations, department stores to real estate agents, we were absolutely stunned by the prices for everything. The cost of living was and remains the biggest problem for those of us from Hometown U.S.A. who are given the honor of spending a period of time in the Pentagon. Frankly, it's also the main reason a lot of folks never go back there.

In Louisville, Rosemary and I had been accustomed to living in a nice home near work, school, stores, and the downtown. Naively, we approached house-hunting that same way in Washington. However, after spending several hours one morning with a real estate agent, it finally sunk in that we were deluding ourselves.

In fact, for the home we eventually bought out in Virginia, we were forced to sell our splendid home and property in Louisville, our beautiful lakeside cabin, even my treasured World War II Jeep. Despite this sacrifice, we were still to struggle with the house payments on our home in Springfield for years to come.

My first 30 days as Deputy Director were, appropriately, emblematic of the pace of the Washington military establishment. One week after my swearing-in ceremony, my secretary buzzed me and said that the Director of the Air Guard, Major General John Guice was on the line, calling from his home. "John," he said. "Yes, sir," I answered, wondering what this was all about. "Here's your first mission. You're hosting next week's conference."

I was floored. He was talking about the senior Air Guard Commander's conference in Memphis. It was held on an annual basis as a way of bringing the field and the Bureau into synch. General Guice then filled me in. He had severe leg and back problems from his flying days; sometimes it became so painful that he could not sit up, much less travel. It was only later that I realized how many times General Guice uncomplainingly came to work, despite his pain. Obviously, things must have been pretty bad for him to cancel out of this annual command performance.

And so in place of the seasoned Director, the greenest Brigadier General in the Air Guard was now going to host a group of the some of the most experienced officers in the entire Air Force. Immediately, Colonel Bill Muir and Lientenant Colonel Don Price, General Guice's assistants, brought me up to speed on the Guard Bureau issues. The next week in Memphis, I received an affectionate welcome; after all, only two weeks before, I'd been one of them, a field commander with all the usual biases — distrustful of Washington, despairing of headquarters understanding our problems, and quick to note the self-important attitude of Pentagon officers. Now here I was standing before them, giving the Bureau line!

The Conference went smoothly and ultimately, General Guice was able to fly down and back on one of the days and speak to the Commanders.

Upon my return from Memphis, I packed and accompanied General Verne Weber, Chief of the National Guard Bureau, to the ceremonies in Europe officially ending "Operation Creek Party."

This was the most significant Air Guard deployment up to that time, a sizable operation that functioned wholly on volunteers. During the mid-1960s, most of the Air Force's new KC-135 tanker fleet was facing the Pacific Theater to provide air- refueling for aircraft in Vietnam and for planes shuttling back and forth from Vietnam, Korea, and Hawaii to the continental United States. The Pacific is a vast ocean, three times the size of the Atlantic, a distance requiring then and now a lot of tankers and a major refueling effort.

Consequently, other regions were left wanting. Europe, theoretically the critical arena for air operations against a potential Soviet attack, was desperately thin in tanker support for fighters, interceptors, and reconnaissance jets. So, in 1967, the Air Force made a decision that would have enormous and far-reaching ramifications: to involve the Air Guard in a continuous, active duty rotation <u>without using a Presidential call-up or mobilization.</u>

The resulting operation became known as "Creek Party."

At any one time, anywhere from six to ten Air Guard KC-97 aerial tankers were based at Rhein Mein Air Base in Frankfurt, Germany. These planes flew round the clock, assisting the active Air Force in refueling over the skies of Europe. What began as a temporary assignment in 1967 to assist an Air Force stretched too thin became the most successful, long-term, continuous reserve rotation in the history of America's reserve forces at that time.

"Creek Party" was the benchmark for today's many Air Guard deployments — 24 hours-a-day, 365 days-a-year — with the active forces. When the Air Force's KC-135 tanker fleet eventually balanced out in all theaters after the Vietnam War, "Creek Party" finally came to an end.

To skeptics and supporters alike, the operation demonstrated three things: First, the Air Force could not possibly meet all of its global commitments if engaged in a sizable conflict and therefore, would have to employ the Air Guard; second, Air Guard crews and aircraft were qualified and capable of carrying out an active duty mission; and third, the deployment of what were ostensibly part-time troops could be conducted over a sustained period of time through a series of organized rotations. Operation "Creek Party" preceded articulation of Secretary of Defense Melvin Laird's Total Force Policy, and yet in many ways, came to symbolize the spirit and the intent of the new policy. "Creek Party" remains a huge milestone for the modern day Guard.

When I returned from Europe, the first thing I did was put together a list of things I wanted to accomplish as Deputy Director. My primary goal was to make sure we got plenty of input from the field; after all, that's why I had been chosen. Even though my address was the Pentagon, I wanted to remain close to the commanders. These were the leaders who really made the Air Guard go. They were the commanders, in this era, making things happen, keeping these units together, struggling to keep morale stable despite the muted — and sometimes not-so-muted — anti-military tenor of the times.

It was in the first few months that I became acclimated to the "Building," which is what the Washington crowd calls the Pentagon, the world's largest office building. I was also beginning to get a fuller picture of the Guard, its relations with the active Air Force, the responsibilities of the Army and Air Guard leaders, the role of the budget, the political landscape on the Hill, and the other tangible and intangible matters.

It didn't take me long to figure out that the most important issue of this period came down to two words: unit strength.

The Chief's Annual Review for FY 1977 contained this simple and straightforward understatement: "The emphasis on maintaining strength can not be overemphasized. It is the most critical and the number one program in the Guard."

For any military organization, all roads lead to manpower. From the start of the All Volunteer Force, strength was a particularly acute concern. The 1977 Army Guard budget, for example, stipulated a beginning year strength of 380,000, an average monthly strength of 390,000, and a programmed end strength of 400,000.

Unfortunately, the Army Guard was not able to increase by 20,000 troops. In fact, it actually lost troops, ending the fiscal year 37,000 below target, at 363,000. Worse, the decline in manpower reached 355,721 in July 1977, only 85 percent of authorized strength. This set off alarm bells in the Bureau. Not since August 1963 had the federally recognized strength dropped to less than 90 percent of authorized. Only a major recruiting push in the last two months of the fiscal year brought the end strength up.

As the Chief's report noted, "NGB believes that the decline in strength is primarily due to the loss of those who joined the Guard as a legal alternative to the draft in the early 1970s...and are now reaching the end of their service obligation."

It was clear to everyone: Without the draft gun pointed at their heads, young men had no desire to join the Guard.

The strength picture was a little better in the Air Guard, where our personnel numbered 92,500 on October 1, 1977, or 99.8 percent of programmed end strength. In fact, the Air Guard had the highest retention and enlistment rate of all the services, active and reserve, mostly because the pilot and maintenance skills were so closely interchangeable with the civilian world. Even so, just standing still in terms of manpower was not good enough.

Although this situation was alarming to everyone in the Guard — from those in the field trying to maintain units to those of us in Washington answering Congress and the active leaders — these numbers would have been far worse without the frenzied recruiting efforts by both services.

Our recruiting folks were just getting their sea legs at this point. They'd been hurriedly authorized and trained to replace the thousands of days of part-time effort that had been the mainstay of Guard recruiting in the past.

The first step was easy. The Army Guard hired 1,750 full time recruiters. They then assigned them at active installations to corral those soldiers about "to ETS," that is, leave the military on the date of their "Expiration of Term of Service." The Army also studied ways to improve the success rate of those new enlistees who couldn't seem to hack the initial entry basic training and were discharged out.

The Air Guard had 340 nationwide full-time recruiters during this time. We were not only competing directly with the actives for personnel, we were also asking for their help.

The Air Guard vigorously sought out active duty Air Force separatees under the "Palace Front" program. Under this, ANG recruiters visited air bases several times each month to talk with airmen and women about to separate. The "Palace Chase" early release program was also instrumental in getting prior service airmen to join the Air Guard. It was a good deal for us because it allowed individuals to join the Air Guard by signing up for two years with the Guard for every one year they had left with the active Air Force.

You see, every service was in a frenzy over strength. Even though the Air Force needed the Guard to get some key missions done, some commanders resented the fact that we were taking airmen and women from them through the "Palace Chase" program.

During this turbulent era, the top leaders in the Bureau — General Weber, General Charles Ott and General Mickey Walker of the Army Guard, General Guice and myself — met frequently to figure out ways to increase strength. We'd also convene conferences all over the country to draw upon the expertise in the Guard. Bob Ensslin, for example, was director of a large ad agency in Florida. He was also a Brigadier General in the Florida Army Guard and you can bet we went to him for advice on marketing. Dan Donohue, Chief of the Public Affairs for the National Guard, was very helpful in overseeing our marketing and advertising campaign.

Simple manning levels were not only a problem at this point. There was also shortages of folks in particular skills. (The Air Force vocations fall under the AFSC, the Air Force Specialty Code while the Army uses the term MOS, Military Occupational Specialty.) Sure, everyone wants to be a pilot. But who wants to be the maintenance guy turning wrenches in the hangar, or the guy doing the paperwork for the guy turning wrenches? And yet those critical support personnel were the ones we had to not only recruit but also retain in order to get the job done.

General Guice and I attended many meetings with our active duty counterparts on the issue of strength. Everyone was having problems making the All Volunteer Force work and many active component commanders were somewhat antagonistic toward the Guard because they were convinced that our recruiting efforts were somehow, some-way, taking people away from them.

The Air Guard had another problem, too. The same Air Force officers would scan lists of under-strength Guard units without suffi-cient crews to keep all of their aircraft in the air. Under the "Gaining Command" concept, some of these undermanned units were required to perform missions with the active forces in the event of war. Then, General Guice and I would sit there as a three-star would ask us, "When is such-and- such unit going to get well?" i.e. up to strength with the correct mix of skills. Sometimes we had an answer; at other times we didn't.

It seemed as if the strength problem would never go away.

After two years of major efforts, 18 months of which I'd seen up close in the Pentagon, the 1978 Chief's Report dourly noted, "The maintenance of strength continued to be major objective of the Army and Air National Guard."

Throughout this time, our public affairs departments were frantically working with various ad agencies in an effort to craft a persuasive recruiting strategy. An intensive national advertising campaign, centered around the phrase "Get Your Guard Up" was launched in 1977 and proved quite effective; nearly 27,000 individuals joined the Guard in a two-month period after the campaign got underway. Other promotions featured mail-back coupons attached to magazine ads, billboard posters, brochures, television advertisements with national celebrities (for example, in the 1980s, we used actor Tom Selleck, an Army Guardsman), bumper stickers, and radio ads.

Another campaign included use of the phrase, "The Different Guards," which emphasized the distinctive contributions the Guard made to various geographic locations — urban, suburban, small town, and rural. Other slogans, along with "Get Your Guard Up," included "The Guard of Opportunity", "Help Somebody, Including Yourself", and "We Guard America's Skies."

We did everything we could to make the Guard an interesting and attractive organization young people would want to join. Yet, by August of 1978, Army Guard strength had declined to 82 percent of authorized strength, the lowest ever. Indeed, the Army Guard finished the fiscal year at 347,000, a drop of 63,000 in just four years.

In his Annual Report for 1978, the Chief tersely summarized that the ARNG "continues to recruit in a no-draft environment with no enlistment incentives, the national unemployment rate has dropped to its lowest level in five years, and the pool of available prior service personnel keeps shrinking..." And the Air Guard, instead of climbing, had fallen slightly as well, from 91,840 in 1977 to 91,674 in 1978, despite our most frantic recruiting efforts.

It seemed that nothing was working. Our ANG retention, the envy of the other components, dropped from 59 percent in FY 1976 to 49 percent in FY 78.

Given the breadth of the force and the great variety between regions and states, we got into almost comic situations on the manpower issue. We'd tell units, "If you can go to 120 percent strength, do it" because we knew a similar unit somewhere else wouldn't get above 80 percent, no matter what they did.

For example, when I was Deputy Director and then later as Director, I could always count on the North Dakota and Alabama Air Guard units to hit 115-120 percent strength. It seemed that whenever we sent the word out for volunteers, these two great states always had their hands up.

By the time I had been in the Pentagon for nearly a year, I realized that recruiting and retention were taking the bulk of everyone's time. It was though maintaining strength had become an end in itself, while training and equipping had become peripheral issues.

Despite the all-consuming nature of the strength issue, we managed to make progress on other fronts. Generals Weber, Ott and, Walker, no doubt aware of the close cooperation between the Air Force and Air Guard, were determined to guide the Army Guard toward a "One Army" Total Force role in spite of the current, (no doubt, transitory) manpower problems.

Gradually, over time, combat readiness became the rallying cry of the Guard. In 1978, NATO reserve force units in Europe and National Guard units in CONUS (Continental United States) exchanged training sites. At about the same time, the Army developed the ARTEP, the Army Training and Evaluation Program, which to this day remains an effective way in which to measure unit readiness.

Skill Qualification testing, which is also used today, was also instituted during this time, testing individual soldier proficiency in their MOS (Military Occupational Specialty).

During Annual Training in 1978, Army Guard units went to the field with active components in exercises "Brave Shield", "Empire Glacier", "Bold Eagle," and "Foal Eagle." Moreover, Army Guard units took part in the large-scale "Reforger '78" NATO exercise in Europe. In conjunction with these pioneering field training exercises, the Army also solidified its "Gaining Command" concept. This philosophy was similar to that of the Air Force in which Army Guard units worked closely with and developed command relationships among the active units they would deploy with in time of war.

The Army devoted a great deal of time and effort to MOBEX 78, the largest mobilization exercise since World War II. Tens of thousands of Guard troops in armories across the nation walked through the procedures that would be required in the event of a mass mobilization for a national emergency or war.

It was at this time that my close friend and aide, Colonel Frank Van Fleet, co-chaired a study in concert with the National Guard Bureau and FORSCOM at Fort Stewart Georgia, which evaluated the potential for direct deployment from the U.S. of mobilized units. This study, which looked at the 53rd Brigade's capability to mobilize and deploy directly was done as an adjunct to MOBEX '78. Many issues were raised and brought to the attention of the Chain of Command. Although not proven conclusive, it was determined that the potential was there for selected units to deploy directly, thus expediting their employment in theater.

The Guard was also evaluating programs that had been undertaken in the past. During the 1960's, for example, the Army recognized the need for a selected group of Reserve Component units that would be well trained and equipped and could mobilize very early in the event of an emergency.

Those selected units were designated as the Selected Reserve Force (SRF) and were provided funding for additional training days to meet more strenuous training requirements.

The SRF program was short lived due to many reasons, not the least of which was failure to motivate individuals of the need for the additional training requirements and lack of support from the active Army. The SRF experience showed that in order for individuals to respond to programs such as these, there must be an intense involvement of the active component to integrate the Reserve Component units into the Army team.

It wasn't until 1973, after General Creighton Abrams became the Chief of Staff of the Army, that recognition was given to the need for better integration of the Reserve components into the Army structure. Several studies had been done before and others were commissioned to look at how this might be accomplished.

From those studies came what was known in 1973 as the Steadfast program. Then Lieutenant General Jack Vessey was the Deputy Chief of Staff, US Army, and it was under his guidance that Steadfast was initiated and brought to fruition. (Later, General Vessey was to be named Chairman, Joint Chiefs of Staff.) Prior to Steadfast, there existed on the Army Staff a three-star directorate known as the Chief of Reserve Components (CORC). CORC level staff provided the link between the Chief, National Guard Bureau and the Chief, Army Reserve, with the Chief of Staff Army.

Steadfast went a long way toward integrating the Reserve Components into the Army by eliminating CORC and reducing the overhead at the Department of Army level. Today, the Chief of the National Guard Bureau deals directly with the Army Chief of Staff and his functional staff offices.

Steadfast further reduced or eliminated other barriers and added Active Army elements, whose sole purpose was to assist, support and evaluate the training of the Army Guard and Reserve units. It further provided for the addition of Guard and Reserve personnel to be assigned to Army commands for the purpose of bringing Reserve Component experience and coordination of Reserve Component activities to the active Army.

This new program, which became known later as the Active Guard and Reserve Program (AGR), was to become one of the most significant readiness enhancers devised to support training improvements in the Reserve Components and maintain a closeness to the actives.

Some training programs that grew from Steadfast include the Affiliation Program, which matched Active Component Divisions with Reserve Component Combat Units for the purpose of providing training support and assistance. FORSCOM's ABSAT (Active Battalion Support to Annual Training) designated selected Active Component Divisions which were responsible for providing Battalion task force teams to support a partner National Guard Division or Brigade. The program provided support to the Divisions of the Army National Guard which were not receiving dedicated Active Army support under the Affiliation Program.

In 1975, the Affiliation Program produced the Roundout program, which as discussed earlier, assigned a National Guard brigade or battalion as a "filler" organization which replaced a comparable active organization that had been deleted from the Active Division's force structure. These roundout units were to be supported, assisted, evaluated and when mobilized, employed as a part of the active division to which assigned. Unfortunately, when brought to the test in 1990 during Desert Shield/Storm, the Army opted not to take advantage of the years of training and integration that had so greatly improved the readiness and capability of these roundout units.

It was also during this time that the Department of Defense began looking into how we mobilize the Reserve Components and the problems associated with bringing large numbers of "civilians" into the Active forces at one time. So began a series of bi-annual exercises to test mobilization procedures and to seek improvements. Many changes have been made over the years to improve and make less cumbersome this process. These exercises were highly effective in teaching all the components the complexities of the then current systems and also to use common sense along with new technology in overcoming such problems. We have come a long way in improving the mobilization process — a good example of which was Desert Shield/Storm system.

We also used this time to bulk up the Air Guard. We undertook eight unit aircraft conversions, retired the venerable KC-97C tanker and the F-100 fighter, and had ANG units participate in seven Joint Chiefs of Staff exercises. Most significantly, at the end of FY 1978, ten ANG units were placed on the Strategic Air Command's Single Integrated Operations Plan (SIOP) alert. The SIOP was the master plan for responding to a Soviet strike against the continental U.S. It was a complex mix of bombers, fighters, and missiles into which the ANG was to provide refueling tankers. This was another significant step, a realization by the actives that the Air Guard could be relied upon around-the-clock for this extraordinarily important mission.

Another milestone, unnoticed but significant, passed in FY 78: the Bureau issued 2,784 letters of eligibility for retired pay for those turning 60. This represented a downward trend and "indicated that the bulk of individuals who entered during the Korean era and shortly afterward have completed their 20 years of qualifying service." Slowly but steadily, the Guard was passing into the hands of a new generation.

The strength issue was also closely related to two other huge changes affecting both the Guard and the active military. In writing about these changes, Air Force historian Dr. Joseph Gross has pointed out that the ANG "became a racially integrated organization because of growing pressure to admit blacks and the need to secure additional sources of manpower once the draft ended..." Dr. Gross added that a "second major change in the 1970s was inclusion of women on a significant scale."

From the start, both the Air and Army Guard were resolute in trying to do the right thing in recruiting and welcoming minorities and women to their ranks. I know — I saw it in the field and later at the Pentagon.

In 1970, minority participation in the combined National Guard, Army and Air, was 1.1 percent. By 1973, we had raised that to 3.4 percent. By 1980, minorities made up 26 percent of the Army Guard and 14 percent of the Air Guard, an unprecedented and remarkable turnaround.

The story was only a little different with women. In 1972, there were exactly 56 women in the 368,738-person Army Guard, one year later, there were nine times as many. To be fair, throughout the 1970s, the primary Military Occupational Specialties (MOS) in the Army Guard were combat or combat service, in which women were prevented from serving. There simply wasn't a role for females in the Army Guard at that time. Nonetheless, by 1980, women made up 4.5 percent of the Army Guard; by 1994 as the number of MOS's multiplied, that figure was nearly 20 percent.

Less than one percent of the Air Guard was female in 1970. By 1980, that figure had risen to seven percent. I distinctly remember a photo in the Chief's 1975 report of four women in flight suits with the caption underneath, "The `Happy Hooligans' of the North Dakota Air National Guard provided the only All Girl Weapons Load Team in the 1975 William Tell Air Defense Interceptor competition." The Guard was changing — and we all knew it.

As well, social currents on the outside of the Building were managing to filter inside. We now had an "Office of Human Resources," no longer just plain old "Personnel." Our senior officers attended national conventions of major minority organizations. Indeed, years later, I was priveleged to attend several NAACP national conventions and was awarded the Roy Wilkins award for the gains in minority strength in the Guard.

In early 1978, non-prior service women under the age of 26 years became eligible for a six-year term of enlistment, the same as men. But our women made even more important progress that year. Because on August 28th, 1978, the new National Guard-wide personnel regulations read: "The involuntary order to active duty for unsatisfactory participation" — in other words, a dose of full-time military for those whose Guard performance was found lacking — became applicable to women.

Even with the daily fretting over strength during these lean years, the Air Guard was being more fully integrated into the active force with each day. The Air Guard's outstanding performance in "Creek Party" did not go unnoticed and led to more and more assignments.

In October 1977, we undertook "Operation Volant Oak," a six-month rotation between Guard and Reserve C-130 units at Howard Air Force Base in Panama. "Volant Oak", as Air Force historian Gary Gault points out, involved 110 people of which approximately half, given the proximity of Panama to CONUS, rotated in and out every two weeks.

"Volant Oak" aircraft flew regularly scheduled missions, known as "channel flights," throughout Central and South America, supporting embassies with food, mail, equipment, and other supplies.

Some of the air and maintenance crews would stay on longer at Howard and overlap with a new unit. But the beauty of the operation was that each participating unit knew their rotation period a year ahead of time.

One year later, we launched "Operation Coronet Cove." In this operation, we based A-7D Corsair II aircraft at Howard to provide for the defense of the Panama Canal while giving the Southern Commander-in-Chief jet fighter capabilities in the region. This also gave the U.S. an aerial presence in the Canal Zone and gave the A-7Ds the opportunity to work with the Army on air-to-ground operations. The Guard had 14 A-7 units at the time and the operation's rotation period was for 30 days. So, everyone knew where they stood for scheduling purposes and we always had a unit in the barrel with a backup for any given month.

In the late 1970s, the U.S. Southern Command, under which the "Volant Oak" and "Coronet Cove" deployments fell, was not a high priority command (a situation that would turn around almost overnight during the presidency of Ronald Reagan). The assistance we provided was critical at that time because the bulk of U.S. resources and attention were going to the Central Front in Europe and the Middle East during that period of the Cold War.

The senior SOUTHCOM officers were imaginative. They knew they weren't going to get much more than a minimum of help from Washington so they scrounged anywhere and everywhere for personnel and equipment in order to provide a U.S. presence in the region. When they came to the National Guard, we were more than happy to supply whatever was needed.

After all, someone had to provide a presence down there and the mission was a natural for us. Besides, Central America was close to home and didn't necessitate the long-distance flights required in the European Atlantic or Pacific theaters. We didn't know it at the time, but our presence in the region would later propel us into a legal wrangle ending up in the United States Supreme Court.

Permanent rotations such as "Creek Party," "Volant Oak" and "Coronet Cove," were of great benefit to the Guard, particularly OCONUS (Outside the Continental United States) operations. These deployments built morale and unit pride because Guardsmen knew they were contributing to an essential, real world mission. It was also good for unit cohesion: People in the participating units got plenty of advance warning about deployments and thus could plan their employment schedules. Finally, the deployments beat the heck out of repetitive, mind-numbing drills back at the home installation.

Even though I was a green one-star during all of this activity, it didn't take me long to find out what most of the people in the Pentagon spend most of their time doing: they attend meetings.

Whenever I called someone on the phone, or dropped by their office, they were always in a meeting. It didn't matter where or with whom. Everyone was in a meeting somewhere. And if they weren't in a meeting, they were on their way to one. Or preparing for one. Meetings seemed to chew up all the available time of every clock on the wall.

In fact, the meeting runaround was particularly crazy for those of us in the Guard Bureau. We had so few flag officers compared to the active component forces and there was no end to these gatherings at which Guard general officers were expected or required.

First, there were the weekly internal meetings with Bureau staff, which we all had to attend. Then there were the daily (later twice-weekly) meetings with the Air Force staff, chaired by the Air Force Chief of Staff, to which the Director of the Air Guard was invited. If General Guice couldn't make it, I had to fill in. These meetings were always held in the same room — a room in which it seemed I would spend a considerable part of my military career: BD927, the Air Force tank.

This was the secure Air Force facility in the Pentagon and most of the budget meetings were held in this room. It was a wide, high-ceiling room with a huge screen covering one entire wall; there was a long stage with a briefing podium at each end. There was also a semi-circular table for the three-stars and four- stars and three rows of theater seating for the one and two stars, which is where I sat.

Beginning as a one-star, I would come to spend thousands of hours in there, helping craft the Air Force budget. The budget drill is probably the most arcane yet vital process the services engage in. There are hundreds of steps involved and the staff work that goes into the process is in my estimation, some of the finest analytical thinking that takes place in this town.

Three steps in the process stand out. The first involves the deliberations undertaken by the Program Review Committee (PRC). This forum is attended by colonels from all the components of the Air Force. This is the level at which the sparring over various programs takes place. Next, is the Air Staff Board, presided over by the Deputy Chief of Staff for Programs and Plans (at that time the incomparable Lieutenant General Abbott Greenleaf). The Air Staff Board is attended by the one- star and two-star ranks and is where programs developed at the PRC level are further refined.

The next step is the Air Force Council, led by the Air Force Vice-Chief of Staff. Each component Deputy Chief of Staff is present and this is where the hard numbers for each account are hammered out. Then they are presented to the Air Force Secretary and the Chief of Staff.

Finally, the whole thing is further honed by the Joint Chiefs and the Secretary of Defense before the completed package is presented to the President to send to Congress as part of his overall budget.

Most of the process takes place in good ole BD927 in the basement of the Pentagon, which is physically and literally, the womb of the Air Force.

But there are not only endless meetings inside the building. The dance card is also filled with the innumerable events outside the Pentagon.

Conferences, conventions, seminars, trade shows, association gatherings — there are dozens and dozens of these kinds of functions annually. Even a partial list is exhausting. For example, there are commander conferences at least once a year for the various commands such as SAC (Strategic Air Command), MAC (Military Airlift Command), TAC (Tactical Air Command) and others. Then there were conferences for the numbered Air Forces, the First, Eighth, Ninth, Twelfth, and Fifteenth. On top of that, there are the conferences for the various theaters. There are 50 states, three territories, and the District of Columbia, all of whom have an air component that requests the presence of a member from the Washington establishment. On top of that, there are governor's conferences and the various association conferences. And of course, you have to make sure you make time for CORONA, the senior Air Force Commanders conference. Keep in mind, too, that the conferences are not confined to the Air Force and Air Guard; the Army Guard has at least as many functions, if not more, given their larger force.

General Guice had done a great deal of traveling and I knew early on that he wouldn't hesitate to call on me to attend an event if he was unable to go himself. In fact, in my car for last minute engagements, I always kept an overnight bag with a change of uniform and a change of civilian clothes. And I often had use for it.

In 1979, there was a structural change within the Bureau — the Chief's post went from the rank of Major General to Lieutenant General, from two stars to three. This was an important and long overdue change. The Chief routinely attended meetings in the Building at which three-star and four-star generals were making the decisions. At these meetings, the measure of your input was directly related to the number of stars you wore on your shoulder.

Moreover, within and without the Pentagon, there is a big break between the ranks of Brigadier and Major General on the one hand, and Lieutenant General and full general on the other. Three- and four-star generals must secure Senate confirmation for the position they are assuming and confirmation for elevation to their new rank.

While General Weber and the rest of us were gratified that the Guard was being recognized as an important part of the U.S. military establishment, this was not the most popular move with the active Army in the Building. All the Army and Air Guard General officers were assigned to Title 10 active duty general officer billets. This meant General Weber's promotion would mean one less Lieutenant General slot for the active duty Army and no-one wanted to give up that three-star position.

But Congress, and more importantly, the Administration had decided it was the right thing to do. President Carter had been a military man, a governor, and had also been close to his adjutant General in Georgia, Major General Joel B. Paris III. He was well aware of the reach and usefulness of the Guard at the community, state and national levels and it was his support for the elevation of the Chief's position that proved crucial.

There was another good reason for a three-star Chief. At this time, there were 52 National Guard entities in the field, the majority of which were headed by a federally recognized two-star Adjutant General. It didn't make sense that the person who headed the National Guard and controlled the purse strings should be the same rank as the adjutants General in the states and territories.

Finally, General Weber, despite all the Guard's momentary strength concerns, was still overseeing one of the largest forces in the entire U.S. military establishment. In many ways, the three-star level for Chief was long overdue.

In 1978, the Air Guard attained the highest overall combat ready status in its history — 97 percent. The main reason for our outstanding performance was our success with the Operational Readiness Inspection (ORI). The ORI was a comprehensive test of a unit's combat readiness in a simulated real-world environment which the Air Force provided. It was a great test of skills.

I had several ORIs while at Standiford and they commonly worked like this:

As a unit commander, you'd receive a preliminary notice that within the next three months, you could expect an ORI.

Suddenly one day, an Air Force ORI team composed of between 25 and 40 persons would land at your airfield. These were the teams from the numbered Air Forces. These folks were the undisputed experts in every element of air operations — tactics, maintenance, air and ground safety, ordnance, logistics, personnel, supply, and administration.

The team leader would march immediately to the unit commander's office, hand him a sealed envelope containing an operations order, and say something like, "You have 36 hours in which to prepare your squadron for deployment to West Germany."

Then all hell broke loose for the next five days.

The first phase of ORI was <u>mobilization</u>. You began by composing an operations plan for your unit. Then you'd go through your alert roster, alert your people, and hope they'd all reach the mobilization station on time. Then you'd have to move them through the administrative processing procedures at the station. While all of that was going on, you readied your aircraft and palletized your equipment and spares.

The next phase of ORI was <u>deployment</u>. During this aspect of the inspection, you'd have to fly your combat aircraft as well as your transports loaded with your equipment — usually not 100 percent — to a permanent Air Guard training site such as Gulfport, Mississippi, or Savannah, Georgia, or Volk Field, Wisconsin or some active Air Force base and simulate going overseas. You'd have a requirement to perform air-to-air refueling on the way.

Then you moved into the <u>employment</u> phase. This was when you demonstrated that you could put the steel on target. You'd receive fragmentary orders to perform a specific mission under simulated conditions. Typically, the fighter squadrons would go to gunnery ranges, put ordnance down, and be scored on their hits and misses. Reconnaissance would receive targets for pre-strike assessment and post-strike bomb damage assessment. Often, the mission would require tankers for air-refueling somewhere along the way. The airlift and tanker units would do similar exercises to see if they were ready.

Finally, there was a <u>re-deployment</u> phase. Most of the excitement was over by then. But you couldn't let down because you were still begin graded until you returned to home station and unpacked everything. It was typically a five-day exercise, usually running from Friday to Tuesday, with a comprehensive debrief at the end.

During the debriefing, you were graded on each of the different stages, mobilization, deployment, employment, and then re-deployment. If you reported, for example, that you were at a C-1 level — that is, combat ready, fully equipped, manned, and trained — then you'd be expected to meet all the standards for C-1. If any one element of the four-stage test didn't measure up, you'd be graded C-2 or C-3 or C-4, and your whole unit would be classified at that level.

These ORIs were tough but they put us on a level playing field with the active Air Force. Our guys and gals loved the competition and most often rose to the challenge. The ORI spurred the Air Guard to the highest level of readiness any reserve component has ever achieved. In 1979, the Air Guard pass rate in ORIs was 100 percent, for the second year in a row. That kind of sustained demonstrated performance gave the actives great confidence in the Air National Guard.

Two years earlier, near the end of 1976, the Air Force notified Congress that they had decided not to purchase any more C-130 Hercules transports. By then, the C-130 was recognized world wide as the turbo-prop, modern-day "Gooney Bird," for inter- and intra-theater transport. In short, it was the backbone and workhorse of air forces around the world. The Air Force made the decision to concentrate on bringing more of the larger C-141 Starlifter and C-5 Galaxy jet transports into their inventory.

The imminent loss of this long-time buyer prompted Lockheed to contemplate shutting down it's Hercules production line in Marrieta, Georgia. Congress, particularly members of the Georgia delegation, balked and decided that if the Air Force didn't want the plane, then the Air Guard would get them. Sure, politics got involved. But no one can dispute that the C-130 is the perfect platform for the community, state and national mission and the Air Guard absolutely needed this plane to carry out core missions. And the fact is, nations around the globe all want the C-130.

So in the fall of 1977, the Air Guard received a brand new set of eight C-130H aircraft which went directly to Will Rogers Field in Oklahoma City, Oklahoma.

This unexpected windfall in 1977 became the start of the modernization the Air Guard needed. Because since that first delivery, the Air Guard has received at least one set of eight brand new C-130s every year. In some years, we've obtained 12, 16, or even 20 planes. Over the course of 18 years, the Air Guard has secured between 150 and 180 brand new C-130Hs. The Air Force Reserve, Navy Reserve, Marine Corps Reserve and the active forces have also been modernized with new C-130s.

This delivery has immeasurably enhanced readiness and allowed the Air Guard to participate in dozens of real world active duty deployments. Ironically, the C-130H was a big star in Desert Shield and Desert Storm because of its suitability for intra-theater operations.

I've often said, fighters, reconnaissance aircraft, and interceptors may be a more fun mission to fly. But the C-130 is the most important weapons system the National Guard has in support of state, community and federal mission. Whether dropping hay to starving livestock stranded in winter storms or floods, taking our modular fire fighting units to forest blazes, airlifting civilians out of harm's way, performing the EC-130's special operations electronics mission, or landing in snow in Alaska or on ice caps in the Arctic or Antarctica — you name it — the Herc is an incredibly versatile aircraft.

Even as we received the C-130s, we also were acquiring other modern aircraft. Our good fortune was partially a result of the end of the Vietnam War and the consequent downsizing of the Air Force. President Carter's decision to cancel the B-1 bomber also helped us inasmuch as it freed up a huge appropriation for other weapons procurement. During the late 1970s and into the early 80s, the Air Force transferred to us KC-135A tankers, RF-4Cs (like the one I'd flown), F-4C Phantom fighters, and the A-7D ground attack support fighter. At the same time, we were shedding old aircraft — the bulbous nosed KC-97L tanker, the F-100D, and the RF 101s.

In 1979, we received another new aircraft directly from the production line — the A-10 ground attack jet. Nicknamed the "Warthog" because of its ungainly appearance, it was equipped with a 30-millimeter rapid fire gattling gun, complete with uranium-depleted rounds designed to destroy Soviet armor that attempted to advance across the Central Plain of Europe. The Air Force was not particularly fond of this plane; it was sub-sonic, was solely a ground support aircraft, and was just plain ugly.

However, we were more than happy to modernize with the A-10. Twelve years after it entered the Air Guard inventory, the A-10s flown by units of the Maryland Air National Guard proved to be an armor killer without parallel in the Persian Gulf War.

It's important to clarify the Air Guard's relationship with the Air Force at this time. Yes, we had our differences at times. But we always had a firm and mutual respect for each other. It is to the great credit of the Air Force that they accepted the Air Guard as an equal partner and tasked us with a multitude of missions during this the decade of the 1970s, certainly a decade of great change. By 1980, we had two permanent rotations at Howard AFB in Panama. More than 50 Air Guard units were participating in JCS exercises and 85 ANG Civil Engineering Units were deployed in support of projects at U.S. Air Force bases, ANG bases, and Army Guard installations.

We had KC-135 tanker task forces in Europe, Guam, and Alaska in support of the Strategic Air Command. These aircraft had only entered the Guard inventory in 1975 and yet, just six years later, we had 13 units equipped, trained, and combat ready in support of the SAC SIOP. This innovative rotation scheme was the brainchild of the SAC commander, General Russell P. Dougherty. In the mid-1970s, he was a strong supporter of the B-1 bomber and the KC-10 tanker, both of which had big price tags. In order to make room in the Air Force budget for these two aircraft, he realized it was to his advantage to ask the Air Guard to take some of the tanker mission — and its cost — away from the active tanker force. Perhaps this was not the most selfless thinking, but it certainly provided a huge boost to the Air Guard. I believe General Dougherty, a fellow Kentuckian, is one of the Air Force's all-time great leaders. His son-in-law, General Joe Ralston, also a fellow Kentuckian, is currently the Vice-Chairman of the Joint Chiefs of Staff.

The increasing responsibility was clear affirmation of our standing with the active Air Force. We had shed, once and for all, our reputation as a weekend flying club. The active duty ORI inspection teams gave us tougher and tougher scrutiny — the kind of evaluations which would have been unheard of in the 1960s and early 70s. It was clear they were trying to help us by bringing us up to the standards of their active duty units. And they did. Sure there were times the Air Guard leaders didn't like it, but as I look back, it was a critical turning point in our relationship with the Air Force and the rest of the Reserve and active component forces.

By the end of FY 78, our authorized end strength was 92,900 and we had 93,379 personnel on board. One year later, the ANG celebrated its highest strength ever. So, even as 1978 came to an end, we in the Air Guard were starting to breathe easier. We knew intuitively that we were turning things around.

Try as it might, however, the Army Guard wasn't. The ARNG strength hit rock bottom in 1979, at 346,974, 82 percent of authorized strength. "Maintenance of strength continued to be of prime concern and the foremost program in the ARNG during FY 1979," wrote Weber in the 1979 Chief's Report to Congress.

But the focus on strength generated masked some positive initiatives in the Army Guard.

The "One Army Policy," the inter-Army interpretation of Total Force, got a big boost in 1979. Numerous Army Guard units participated in OCONUS training as part of the Affiliation and Active Component Support to Annual Training Program. This forged a Guard working relationship with the active units they'd join in a mobilization.

In 1979, the Army also reviewed closely the Air Force gaining command program and had determined a need to further integrate the Reserve Components by assigning the Reserve Component units to an active Command in peacetime for implementation in wartime. The then-Commander of Forces Command, General Robert Shumaker had his staff look even further into developing a program that he named CAPSTONE.

CAPSTONE went beyond the gaining command concept by actually assigning the RC units with their AC units against a wartime mission. These units were then to train together in peacetime, assisted by their active component chain of wartime command and to employ with them when federalized. CAPSTONE was perhaps the most effective and far reaching program developed to actually meet the goal for integration of the Army components. It was effectively used for mobilizing and employing selected RC units under Desert Shield/Storm within the Seventh Corps. However, following Desert Storm, the Army unfortunately opted to do away with the program.

In December of 1978, the Army implemented the new Selected Reserve Incentive Program (SRIP) as a test and then in the following year it became a permanent program. This included a reenlistment bonus, split training options which allowed recruits to break up extended school training periods so as to make it easier for them to keep their jobs or continue their college education.

Despite these improvements, a high rate of non-ETS losses — soldiers who washed out of basic training or went AWOL from drill — continued to hurt the Army Guard. This chronic problem prompted the chief to set up an NGB/ARNG Attrition Management Working Group under general officer chairmanship, to find ways to reduce the non-ETS attrition rate.

Although the non-ETS loss was still a nagging concern, the Army and the Army Guard were getting higher quality recruits. The Armed Services Vocational Aptitude Battery (ASVAB) is a four-part test (general topics, administration, electronics, and mechanics) given to all enlistees; it yields scores which rank recruits in Categories I through IV, with IV containing the lowest scorers. Obviously, the Army, as well as the other services, didn't particularly covet Category IV recruits but still needed a few to meet recruiting goals.

In April of 1975, the Department of the Army set a standard of not enlisting more than 18 percent of Category IV recruits and no more than 45 percent of non-high school graduates.

Non-prior service accessions, those enlistees who had never been in the military before, made up 9.9 percent of the ARNG Category IV

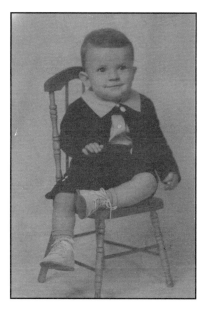

(Above Left) Mother always liked to dress me in shorts. Here on my first birthday in Henderson, KY.

(Above Right) In Evansville, Indiana, at age eleven years old on my first bicycle, just after WW II was over.

(Below Left) In 1946 at twelve years old, playing coronet in the Washington Elementary School Band.

(Below Right) High school graduation, Bosse High School at seventeen years old in Evansville, Indiana

(Above Left) I knew I wanted to be a fighter pilot. In 1955 at Kentucky Lake. Rosemary and I were on our honeymoon.

(Above Right) Rosemary and I on graduation day, June 4, 1956, from the University of Evansville.

(Below Left) June 1956-leaving for the Air Force right after graduation from Evansville College.

(Below Right) First official photograph as a new 2nd Lt. at Lackland AFB, Texas in summer, 1956.

(Above) *August 1956, soloing at Bartow AB, Florida in T-34.*

(Above Right) *In my first Air Force uniform, the silver tan in 1957 as a 2nd Lt. just after receiving my pilots wings from USAF pilot training.*

(Middle) *Jet Pilot training, Greenille AFB, Mississippi, 1957. I am second from right. Our Instructor, Capt. James Clark is second from left.*

Here with Rosemary, Dave, Dan, and Ellen in our home in Dunbar, WV in 1960. I had just joined the WV Air National Guard.

Annual training, summer 1963, Alpena, Michigan. Here I am debriefing a mission I have just returned from in my RB-57 Canberra. I was now in the KY Air National Guard.

1967. KY ANG annual training at Savannah, GA. I am fourth from right standing with all our pilots. Our units RF-101 in background.

Arrival in Washington from Kentucky, 1 April 1977. Here Chief, National Guard Bureau, Lt. Gen La Vern Weber and Rosemary pinning on my first star and starting my 17 years as a General in the Pentagon.

Kentucky Generals-1977 (L to R) Brig Gen Bill Gast; BGen Larry Quebbeman; MGen Richard L. Frymire, Adj Gen; BrigGen Fred Bradley, 123rd Wing Commander and myself as new Deputy Director of the Air National Guard.

Here in the late 70s as Deputy Director returning to West Virginia for a National Guard dinner honoring the famous Senator Jennings Randolph, WV, second from left. Also (L to R), CMSgt Lynn Alexander, Senior Enlisted Advisor for the ANG, Brigader General Kemp McLaughlin, Asst Adj Gen of WV and famous WW II flying hero; MGen Robert L. Childers, Adj Gen of WV, and myself.

March 1981, presenting Maj Gen John Guice, Director, Air National Guard, a "This is your life" book at his retirement dinner. He was a superb boss.

April 1, 1981, after my promotion to Maj Gen and Director, Air National Guard. L to R - brother-n-law Owen Barnett; Mother; Dad; daughter, Ellen; myself; Rosemary; son, Bolyn; Uncle Stanley Hoffman; and sister, Carolyn.

With son, David when he received his pilot "Gold" Wings in the Navy.

Our team in the early eighties overseeing the Air National Guard. Here Rosemary and I with my most able Deputy Director, Brig Gen Wess Chambers and his wife Bonnie.

(Above Left) In the mid-80s with the legendary Gen Jimmie Doolittle at the gala dinner at the National Air & Space Museum, where he was honored by President & Mrs. Reagan
(Above Right) Total Air Force leadership picture on the cover of Air Force Magazine in 1984. With me is MajGen Sloan R. Gill, Chief, Air Force Reserve and Gen Charles Gabriel, Chief of Staff, U.S. Air Force. Gen Gabriel was legendary from his flying days in Korea & Vietnam. He was a big help in modernizing the ANG in F - 15s & F - 16s.
(Below) As Director of the Air National Guard in the 80's in the Oval Office as we presented President Reagan the Harry S. Truman Award. He was a great friend of the Guard and knew us well as Governor.

88

At the Professional
Military Education
Center, commissioning a
new class of ANG Sec-
ond Lieutenants.

Brig Gen (Ret) Chuck Yeager as I
was presenting him our Air National Guard top award. He was a
good friend of the Guard and flew
with several of our units, primarily, the Nevada Air Guard. "Mr.
Right Stuff" is one of our heroes,
and spoke often to our airmen.

Trying to imitate son, Bo, who was Tri -
State Body - Building Champion in Evansville, Indianaa

Here relaxing on the farm in Evansville, Indiana.

With famous U.S. Senator Barry Goldwater, a former Guardsman, at a Guard function.

Son Dave Conaway checking Dad out in his F-18 Hornet. I don't have the skills he has to fly off those aircraft carriers and I have the utmost respect for all who do.

Going down the alert pole at one of our Air Defense fighter units. I was proud of the 24 hour-a-day commitment and the selfless service of these Guard men and women.

With then USAF Chief of Staff, Gen Larry Welch, presenting me with the Air Forces top award for flying safety for the Air National Guard, at the Air Force "Corona" Commanders Conference in 1986.

Son Lt. Commander David Conaway transferred from the Marine Corps to the U.S. Navy and Squadron VFA-83 still flying F-18 aboard the U.S.S. Saratoga. Left is youngest son Bolyn James of Evansville, Indiana and on right is middle son Daniel Bolyn of Lebanon, Ohio.

Here at Air Force Commanders Conference with the "King," Arnold Palmer.

With MSgt Edwin Barbosa in Puerto Rico.

Linda and I in the late eighties with our good friends, the Secretary of the Air Force "Pete" Aldrich and his wife, Jody.

At the 45th Anniversary of D-Day at Normandy in 1989 with U.S. Congressman Sam Gibbons, D-FL, a paratrooper in the D-Day invasion and Maj Gen Charles Kiefner, the Adjutant General of Missouri.

92

At the National Guard Memorial at Normandy with the Mayor of Vierville.

In a relaxing moment after a round of golf.

With Air Force Asst. Secretary Gary Cooper (second from right and today the Ambassador to Jamaica.) In the center is the famous Lt. Gen Benjamin O. Davis, the commander and leader of the original Tuskegee Airmen.

Visiting with President Bush as Vice Chief, National Guard Bureau. President Bush appointed me Chief, National Guard Bureau and nominated me for my third star in January 1990. A great American, patriot, and warrior.

Here in Guatemala with the Executive Leadership Council visiting our neighbors and the National Guard in training.

The Aviators in the family. Here with Lt. (now Capt.) Bill Barnett, nephew and pilot with the D.C. Air National Guard and son David (now commander, USN.)

The clan after my pinning to 3-star & swearing in as Chief, National Guard Bureau in Feb 1990 - sitting L to R - Mother, Dad, & Linda's mom Dorothy. Standing L to R - nephew Capt. Bill Barnett & his wife, Tody; son-in-law, Greg Williams; son, Dave; daughter, Ellen; daughter-in-law Cathy; myself; Linda; son, Dan; Nick and his wife, sister-in-law Dorothy; sister, Mary Ann; niece, Christine; brother-in-law, Bob; daughter-in-law Julie, and son Bo.

One of the recent photos with our four children, Lieutenant Commander Dave, Bo, Ellen, and Dan at my pinning to 3-stars.

Linda and I with our good friend and mentor, Maj Gen (Ret) John J. Pesch, former Director, Air National Guard.

Here presenting a National Guard heritage painting to my fellow Kentuckian General (Ret) Russell Dougherty. Gen Dougherty retired as Commander-in-Chief, Strategic Air Command. He was a role model, mentor, and sponsor to me and played a major role in my move from Kentucky to the Pentagon.

In September, 1990, on front lawn of the Pentagon as the Guard hosts the official WWII 50th anniversary celebration of the total mobilization of the National Guard. With me are four former chiefs.

At the retirement dinner in New Jersey for my lifelong friend and National Guard legend, Maj Gen Frank Gerard. Frank was Adjutant General of New Jersey, a former fighter wing commander and WW II fighter ace.

Here in 1990 as Chief, with my senior Generals in the Pentagon and the Adjutants' General of the 50 States and 4 Territories.

Dancing with Rosemary's mother, Amanda Mohr, she is now 95, and still living on the farm in Evansville, Indiana.

recruits in 1979. That was the lowest number of Category IVs since 9.5 percent in FY 72, when the Guard was still receiving draft-motivated recruits. Even better, there was an increase in the number of high school seniors entering the Guard and a corresponding decrease in the number of non-high school graduates (NHSG).

At long last, there was a ray of sunshine on the bleak ARNG recruiting landscape. High school seniors and high school graduates combined made up 63 percent of the Army National Guard recruits in 1979, an eight percent rise over FY 1978. And, for the first time since FY 74, enlisted losses were below programmed objectives.

It was the full-time recruiting force created in response to declining manpower that kept the Army Guard afloat during this difficult period and contributed to the resurgence. In addition, by 1980, the Army, just like the Air Guard in 1979, showed signs that things were finally turning around. A great deal of credit goes to the late General Maxwell Thurman and his commitment to fashioning a strong, effective recruiting message.

By the end of 1979, the National Guard Bureau staff totaled 179 military and 378 civilian personnel. These professionals were some of the most capable, innovative, and resilient individuals I've ever served with. They had to be, given the erratic series of events taking place. The continuing drama over strength, the fits and starts of the All-Volunteer Force, the relationship with the actives, and the social currents at the time made for an emotional and professional roller coaster.

I can't say enough about the Director of the Air National Guard at this time, Major General John Guice. He was my immediate boss and one of the finest leaders I ever met during my service career. He was the only West Point graduate to occupy the positions of Deputy Director and Director of the Air Guard. General Guice got his wings as an air cadet during World War II, then went to West Point, and graduated as an aviator in 1947. He served on active duty with the U.S. Air Force throughout the Korean War and was a statutory tour officer who came to the Bureau in the 1960s where he worked for Generals Winston P. "Wimpy" Wilson, and I.G. Brown and John Pesch.

General Guice had served as the executive officer to two Chiefs — Major General Wilson and Major General Francis Greenlief. He moved over to Deputy Director for Air in 1974 under Major General Pesch, then became Director in 1977. General Guice had a lot of friends on the senior Air Staff because a host of the senior officers there at the time were West Point grads. At that time, the Air Force Academy graduates had not yet begun moving up the ladder to the senior officer slots.

With the time he'd spent at the Office of the Secretary of Defense, in the active Air Force and the National Guard Bureau, General Guice was known as a great administrator, well-respected by top Pentagon officers of all services and the Department of Defense. In the Pentagon, he was known as "Mr. Inside" and he allowed me to become "Mr.

Outside;" that is, concentrating on the concerns of the field commanders. He was a superb boss and a great friend; his retirement in 1981
marked the end of an era.

General Guice had a peculiar sense of humor, which is one reason
he introduced me to one of the legendary events in the Building, "The
5:30 Vespers."

At that time, Lieutenant General Abbot Greenleaf was Air Force
Deputy Chief of Staff for Programs and Plans and he considered himself
quite the visionary thinker. Late in the afternoon several times a week,
he'd call down to the Bureau asking for "Big Juice," a phonetic twist on
the spelling of John Guice's name. The message would come down that
"Big Juice" was needed immediately for a meeting in DCS for Plans and
Programs, Greenleaf's office.

Over time, these meetings became known as the "5:30 Vespers" —
and as General Guice rapidly found out, these were hours-long skull
sessions dominated by General Greenleaf, featuring his theories on Air
Force reorganization.

Time meant nothing to General Greenleaf, who would stride around
his office swatting at charts with a pointer in his hand. After General
Guice went to a few of these assemblies, he became mysteriously absent
whenever General Greenleaf phoned in the late afternoon.

The phone in our office would ring and the General would yell over
the line, "Is Big Juice there?!" I'd say "no" and General Greenleaf,
who'd begun calling me, the Deputy, "Little Juice," would say, "Little
Juice! Get your butt up here!" and I'd high tail it up to his office. There
I'd be, a young one-star in a roomful of senior two- and three-star
Generals. The force structure discussion would go around and around
and when it came to the Guard, I'd have to explain to them why this or
that would or wouldn't work. Then a day or two later, the phone would
ring at 5:00 or 5:15 p.m. and General Greenleaf would yell for Little
Juice, and I'd soon be on my way up there again.

Lieutenant General LaVern Weber, our Chief, helped build a superb
Bureau, with folks like Brigadier General Mickey Walker, Deputy
Director for Army. And there was also an Army Colonel named Herb
Temple from California, who sat across the hall from my office working
in the Bureau's Policy and Liaison shop.

In 1978, General Walker was promoted to Major General and
became Director, ARNG. Then Herb Temple was promoted to Brigadier and became Deputy Director. These were two smart moves for the
Army Guard and as the years passed, Generals Walker and Temple
would precede me as Chief.

The Bureau was an organization of extremely competent and dedicated individuals, a magnificent group of mentors for a generation of
Guard officers. Their leadership during these chaotic times was invaluable.

And although we didn't know it at the time, the Guard had weath-
ered its severest test in decades. A great resurgence lay ahead.

CHAPTER SEVEN

"THE REAGAN YEARS"

Not even the most optimistic of military leaders could foresee what the November 1980 election of Ronald Reagan would mean for the U.S. military establishment. President Reagan's campaign was predicated on a stronger military and a more activist foreign policy. But I don't think many people realized, least of all, our Soviet adversaries, what a dramatic effect Reagan would have on personnel and procurement. From his first budget, Reagan was the tribune of a defense renaissance that resulted in the creation of the most powerful military force in the history of world. It was a revolution of technology, training, and equipment. And the results of this renewal were graphically displayed in the desert almost ten years later to the day of his Inauguration in January of 1981.

I and many of my Guard colleagues were delighted with Reagan's election — just as we had been with the election of Jimmy Carter four years earlier. Remember, whether Democrat or Republican, these two men had been governors. They understood the Guard and they had relied on the Guard for help in their states. They appreciated our skills and strengths as a community-based national defense force. It was Jimmy Carter who supported the third-star promotion for the Chief; it was his administration, working with Congress, that had consistently increased Guard budgets and upgraded our equipment and training throughout the doldrums of the mid- to late-1970s. Now we were about to see what President Reagan and his administration had in mind for us.

By the end of FY 1980, Army Guard strength had finally began an upward trend, reaching 368,000, for a net gain of 20,000 over FY 1979. The Army Guard's first recruiting force, fielded in FY 1978, had hit its stride. The retention programs were beginning to take hold. With this expansion, 75 percent of the enlisted structure became eligible for enlistment bonuses while 63 percent of the enlisted structure became eligible for retention bonuses.

By 1980, "Total Force Policy" had become a reality with the partnership the Air Guard and the Air Force had forged. In November of 1980, Air Guard A-7s from the 150th Tactical Fighter Group in New Mexico participated in "Bright Star," the Rapid Deployment Joint Task Force exercise in Egypt. This was where the unit, the 150th TFG, was "checkered flagged" to; in other words, where they trained and were scheduled to deploy to in the event of hostilities or a contingency. (The Rapid Deployment Force was operating out of McDill Air force Base in Florida, which has since become Central Command.)

Also in 1980, the Tactical Air Command re-instituted the William Tell air-to-air weapons competition. The California Air Guard's 194th Fighter Interceptor Squadron was ready for the challenge and won the event that year in competition with the active Air Force. We had a record 98 percent combat-ready status at the end of 1980. Moreover, after setting a record in 1979 for the highest ever overall strength in the Air Guard, we exceeded it again in 1980, going from 93,379 to more than 96,000. We were on top of the world in terms of our morale and spirit.

It was at this time that the Guard public affairs officials, along with our public relations consultants, hit upon a slogan which we felt communicated perfectly the Guard's distinct military service identity in a message reaching out to all target audiences: "The Guard Is America At Its Best." Along with a similar phrase, "Americans At Their Best," these themes really resonated well with the public.

Other ad campaigns were established around such slogans as "When You're Responsible For 60 million Miles Of Sky, You Don't Do It Alone," "We Guard America's Skies," "Command Respect In The Job Market — Take Command in the Army Guard," "Get A Summer Job Worth Taking Back to School," "Be One Of The New Minutemen," and "The Most Important Part-Time Job In America." We even aired radio spots with fast-paced, rock music, all with the theme that each individual Guard member was an important part of his or her community.

My own place in the Guard hierarchy changed at this time —John Guice was retiring, leaving the Air Director's billet open.

Just as with my initial decision to come to Washington, the choice of whether to stay in Washington or go back home was not going to be easy. Even though Rosemary and I had bought a home in Springfield, Virginia, Ellen and David had graduated from the University of Kentucky. Ellen was now in Washington working on Capitol Hill and David was a Marine aviator in pilot training in jets at Beeville Naval Air Station, Texas. Dan was a student at the University of Kentucky and our youngest, Bo, was in Virginia with us starting high school at West Springfield.

Rosemary and I had always entertained thoughts of going back to Louisville after my Pentagon tour. I figured I could go back to the Kentucky Air National Guard, perhaps take over the Wing, a one-star billet, and maybe even become the Adjutant General some day.

But General Weber and General Guice urged me to apply for the Director's job. They felt I was the best person for the position because

I'd been in the Building for some time and had a good handle on the system. To be sure, the first year in the Pentagon was tough. The learning curve was almost straight up. I was just hanging on as they threw the material at me — getting to know the Pentagon, the budget process, force structure, the active components and leaders, the Hill, and the committee system.

During the second year, I started feeling more comfortable, which meant I had just enough knowledge to be dangerous. Everyone went through this process. Indeed, I firmly believe it took two years of on-the-job training to get the necessary "Building smarts" to be effective in the Pentagon as well as in Washington.

I felt that with all the turbulence I'd seen and been through, I wanted to stay here and see some of the things through that we'd started. In January of 1981, Kentucky Governor John Y. Brown nominated me for the position of Director. The Secretary of the Air Force and the Air Force Chief of Staff, General Lew Allen, appointed me and on March 31, 1981, I received my second star and became Director of the Air Guard.

As Director, I had three simple goals. First, I wanted to take care of the people already in the Air Guard so that we could retain the highest possible number of troops and at the same time, continue to attract good new recruits. Second, I wanted to keep on modernizing the force so that the Air Force would continue to utilize and depend on us. Third, I wanted to improve our Air Guard bases and installations nationwide.

When I took over, the Air Guard had units assigned to the seven major gaining commands of the Air Force. Our inventory was enhanced by the acquisition in 1981 of 54 A-7S, 43 F-4Ds, 11 A-7Ks, and 10 A-10s. That brought our total ANG aircraft inventory to more than 1,600, which made us one of the largest air forces in the world.

We were a superb force. As the Chief's report noted in 1981, "The Total Force policy has had a dramatic impact on the Air National Guard. This policy directs that the ANG be manned, trained, and equipped the same as the active force. This, plus emphasis on realistic exercises and training, enables the ANG units to maintain a level of combat readiness that gives credibility to the Total Force concept."

Our tactical deployments in '81 provide a sense of the global, Total Force player we had become. "Black Hawk" in Panama; "Coronet Sail" in Germany; "Coronet Mast" in Norway; "Cape Thunder" in Philippines; "Coronet Canvass" in United Kingdom; "Coronet Cruise" in Ireland; and, "Coronet Rig" in Italy. In addition, we'd been in on the large-scale "Team Spirit" exercise in Korea, "Reforger" in Europe, "CRISIX 81" in Spain, "Ocean Venture 81" in the Caribbean, and "WINTEX 81" in Europe.

It was becoming increasingly clear that the National Guard had finally become a player and partner in the Total Force. For example, in 1981, the Army Guard contained 46 percent of the Army's combat forces and 37 percent of its support forces. Of the combined active and reserve component Air Force, the Air Guard had 66 percent of the interceptor force, 54 percent of the reconnaissance aircraft, 32 percent of the tactical airlift, and 27 percent of the fighter aircraft.

This huge inventory of equipment and installations could not be maintained by solely traditional Guardsmen at weekend drills. Behind it all was a highly trained group of technicians and Active Guard and Reserve (AGR) personnel. Today, they are even more indispensable with the increased role of the Guard throughout the nation.

The National Guard military technician and AGR full-time support programs have gradually evolved through three distinct phases. The first phase was what was called the "caretaker phase." A caretaker was a member of a Guard unit in a local armory. He or she tended to such routine administrative and logistical concerns as were required between training assemblies, which at that time were held one evening a week.

By the 1960s, the program had evolved to the administrative-supply technician (AST) phase. One AST was provided for the first 100 personnel in a unit and one more for each additional 50 members. ASTs could be any enlisted rank; frequently the senior person was the first sergeant, at the E-8 level. Prior to the National Guard Technicians Act of 1968, all were state employees. Most entered excepted federal civil service in 1968, although some remained in a state status because of retirement benefits. In a two-AST armory, the senior individual was a GS-7, the junior a GS-5 at that time.

By the late 1970s, as the federal civilian workforce was being trimmed, Congress took action to prevent a similar reduction in the Guard's full-time force. As a result, the Active Guard and Reserve program was created in 1979 as part of the Department of Defense Authorization bill. These soldiers and airmen were to be "full-time active duty for the purpose of organizing, administering, recruiting, instructing or training the reserve components."

The AGR were to provide a military full-time support force who were members of the unit and not subject to civilian reductions in force. It was subsequently decided that the successful miliary technician force should not be converted to AGR members. So, Congress established a floor on the authorized level of technicians each year to ensure that they weren't converted to an AGR status. Since that time, most of the full-time growth has been in the AGR program. As a result, both AGR and military technicians often work side-by-side in Guard units. It may be a little cumbersome at times but it is no overstatement to say that the Guard could simply not function without these skilled personnel to keep the day-to-day administration of units on track.

During my seven years as Director of the Air Guard, one success I'm most proud of was probably one of the least glamorous. And that was the re-engining the KC-135 tanker.

The KC-135 was a workhorse of the Air Force. But the older models the Air Guard possessed needed modernizing. Their engines were extremely loud and were awful polluters, problems which were sore points with the communities in which our KC-135s were based. The KC-135A had the J-57 water-injection engine. It was extremely ineffective because it required hundreds of gallons of distilled water to generate adequate takeoff thrust when the plane was fully loaded.

This meant we had to haul thousands of gallons of distilled water to wherever we were operating. I flew out of Mildenhall Air Force Base in Germany several times in the "A" model and we'd start on one end of the runway, really pour the power on, and we'd barely lift off at the other end. Just one trip down that runway was enough to convince me that we needed to get rid of these antiquated J-57s and find a newer engine for our fleet as soon as possible.

I brought it up with numerous senior active Air Force officers but I usually got the same answer. They all wanted us to follow the Air Force modernization program, which would have meant going on a waiting list for the newer CFM-56 engine and conversion of the plane to the "R" model. This would take at least fifteen years. I was extremely concerned because I was convinced that if we went with the Air Force program, the delays would lead to conflict with the actives. Plus, we could never be sure that the Air Force wouldn't terminate the program before our entire KC-135 fleet was completely re-engined.

So we came up with another idea. At this time, I knew that the commercial airlines were retiring a lot of their old Boeing 707s, which was using one of finest aircraft engines on the market at that time — the JT3D fan-jet. We figured we could take the JT3Ds off of the retired 707s and put them on our KC-135s. This process would move a lot faster than waiting a decade to re-engine our fleet. Moreover, Congress would probably support the idea because it would be a lot less expensive and provide an unforeseen boost for the airlines. Congressional staffers Sean O'Keefe (later Secretary of the Navy), and Steven Cortese (now staff director for the Senate Appropiations Committee) were very interested in the success of this cost-effective program.

What followed was legislation backed by Senators Barry Goldwater, Howard Baker, Ted Stevens, Jake Garn, John Glenn, and Robert Dole which established the JT3D re-engine program. (Of course, it didn't hurt that Goldwater, Garn, and Glenn were all former aviators.) The retired 707s were taken to Davis-Monthan Air Force Base in Arizona. The engines and the tail section were removed and the brake system was disassembled. The JT3Ds were shipped to Boeing's Wichita facility, zero-timed, and then put on the Air Guard KC-135s.

These changes made the KC-135s a modern-day tanker with greater fuel carrying load, quieter operating take-offs at municipal airports, and a reverse thrust capability for operating in bad weather areas like Alaska, Canada, and Iceland. Involving 128 aircraft, this program amounted to only $4 million per plane. When completed, it turned out the be one of the most cost-effective, fast-payback programs in readiness efficiency ever undertaken by any of the military components.

Best of all, we did all of the re-engineering in just under four years, which allowed us to participate in the Grenada operation, the bombing of Libya, the Panama invasion, and most importantly, Operations Desert Shield and Desert Storm. Although several of the senior generals in the active Air Force were not exactly pleased with the Guard on this issue, I had support from Secretary of the Air Force Vernon Orr, the Air Force Chief of Staff, General Charlie Gabriel, and Deputy Chief of Staff for Plans and Programs, Lieutenant General Larry Welch.

Ultimately, as it turned out, my concerns about delays in the Air Force modernization program were ultimately borne out. It was not until 1993 that we started receiving the "R" models of the KC-135 from the program begun by the Air Force in 1982! And the only reason we received them in '93 was because the Air Force was down-sizing, not because "our turn" in line had come. The Air National Guard, fifteen years later, is still flying with the KC-135E model with the JT3D engine on many of their aircraft.

This kind of minor friction, however, was the exception rather than the rule. Active-Guard relations were exceptionally positive for the most part due to the tone that was set by the top Air Force leadership. General David B. Jones, Chief of Staff of the Air Force from 1974 to 1978 and then Chairman of the Joint Chiefs of Staff until 1982, was a great proponent of the Air Guard and of the Total Force. When he became Chairman, he was succeeded as Chief of Staff by General Lew Allen, who served in that position from 1978 to 1982. I believe General Allen was one of the brightest men ever to work in the Pentagon; he was also a great advocate for Guard deployments overseas and participation with the actives.

Following General Allen as Chief of Staff was General Charlie Gabriel, a highly decorated hero of the Korean War and a former commander of U.S. Air Forces Europe. He too was a great supporter of the Air Guard and he went out of his way to attend and speak at many of our conferences. He was famous for his congeniality. Sometimes, when bearing bad news, he was so pleasant about it that you found it difficult to get upset about what you were hearing. General Gabriel played a central role in Guard modernization and we could not have made the KC-135 re-engining initiative work without his help. Our acquisition of F-15s and F-16s also sped up under his watch.

Another good friend of the Guard was General Wilbur Creech, Commander of the Tactical Air Command (TAC) during the early 1980s. During his tenure, he set the tone for accelerated modernization and combat capability. He kept a close eye on the readiness and equipment inspection teams and was extremely fair. He never tried to sabotage our efforts or make us look foolish.

In 1982, as the Reagan defense build-up got into full swing, the Bureau bid farewell to one of its stalwarts, Lieutenant General Verne

Weber, who'd been Chief since 1974. Simply put, General Weber is a legend and will always remain a key figure in the history of the modern National Guard.

A Marine Corps officer during World War II, a combat veteran of Korea, the Adjutant General of Oklahoma, a Director of the Army National Guard, General Weber was Chief during a time of tremendous change and upheaval. His leadership was what held the Guard together during the post-draft, All Volunteer Force era when our strength and morale was sinking. He was the first Chief to wear three stars and the first to wear the famous Army General Staff "liver patch" which was originally designed by a General Douglas MacArthur when he was Chief of Staff of the Army. The Army General Staff badge was worn on the right pocket, a symbol of recognition and as General Weber once put it, "a license to practice in the Building."

General Weber had a real feel for the Guard in small town and rural America and believed that the Guard should be woven into the fabric of every community. He'd grown up in good ole Idabell, Oklahoma and had served in the Oklahoma Guard when it contained a high percentage of Native Americans. Indeed, he once told me that when he was a company commander in the early 1950s, a majority of his troops were American Indians.

His experience with troops other than white males would serve him well as Chief. General Weber, along with the prior Chief, General Francis Greenlief, enthusiastically endorsed and oversaw the initial efforts to recruit more minorities and women into the Guard. Indeed, General Weber felt that the most momentous American cultural event of this century was the integration of the U.S. military. He more than anyone else deserves the credit for making the Guard truly representative of the communities we serve and his service to the Guard in tough times can never be overstated.

After leaving the Bureau, General Weber went to Forces Command in Atlanta as Deputy Commanding General. This was the first-ever peacetime assignment of a Guard general to an active command and served as a bellwether of things to come.

When General Weber prepared to depart, I'd been Director of the Air Guard for one year and was just getting the hang of the job. Nevertheless, General Gabriel took it upon himself to persuade me to enter the competition for Chief. He was convinced that I was the strongest Air Guard candidate. Other Guard officers were nominated for the post by their Governors, including Major General Mickey Walker from Mississippi, the Director of the Army National Guard. I considered my candidacy just a formality inasmuch as I knew I lacked the experience for the position. Besides, the Chief's position had traditionally gone to a green-suiter because of the larger Army Guard operation, a four-to-one-ratio at the time over the ANG.

Hence, I wasn't surprised when Major General Walker was

appointed Chief in July, 1982 by President Reagan. He was eminently qualified and did a superb job during his tenure.

Shortly after General Walker took over as Chief, Congress established a separate appropriation for National Guard and Reserve equipment. The separate budget line authority was the result of concern over the rate of modernization of Army and Air Guard equipment.

The prime movers behind this proposal were Congressmen Sonny Montgomery, John Murtha, Bill Chappell, Joe Addabbo, Sam Stratton, and Les Aspin, and Senators Daniel Inouye, Ted Stevens, and Sam Nunn. Of course, the National Guard Association (NGAUS) was heavily involved, as it had been in every major Guard legislative initiative for more than 100 years.

This was a singular achievement for the Guard — it gave us Congressional approval to speed our modernization. Through this legislation, we were able to buy Blackhawk helicopters, Abrams tanks, Bradley Fighting Vehicles, new upgraded trucks for our transportation companies, communications equipment, and forward-looking infrared radars for our aviation assets.

The C-130s that were part of the Air Force procurement account up until 1982 were now put in the Guard procurement account along with some F-16s. We received support aircraft such as the C-12 and the C-26, and much-needed avionics and radio upgrades to our equipment. We were also able to acquire the funding necessary to modernize the 201st Airlift Squadron, also known as Detachment #1 of the District of Columbia Air National Guard, with used Boeing 727s and new Lear 35s, which enabled the Bureau leadership and senior staff to get out to the states on a more frequent basis as well as support the Guard worldwide. Overall, this account has been very useful for the readiness of the Guard.

Along with the new account came bigger budgets. From the first Reagan budget onward, funding for the Guard more than doubled from $1.02 billion for the ANG and $1.9 billion for the ARNG in FY 1981 to $2.9 billion for the ANG and $5.36 billion in for the ARNG in FY 1986, the decade's peak year before military budgets began to decline.

In 1982, the Army Guard was operating from 2,806 armories and 2,104 non-armory facilities and camps. More importantly, the ARNG reached a manpower milestone: more than 400,000 personnel.

As Director of the Air National Guard, I was obviously pleased by the new dollars. It was money our expanding force desperately needed. By 1982, the Air Guard reached a benchmark of our own — we went over 100,000 personnel — and we had a big celebration with Secretary Orr and General Gabriel. Indeed, by the end of 1982, the Air Guard had 1,054 units, 24 wings, 67 groups, 91 squadrons, 650 support units, 106 communications-electronic units, and 116 miscellaneous units. We had 86 flying bases and 110 non-flying installations and our total aircraft inventory was a whopping 1,630. We had blossomed into an extremely powerful, effective, and far-flung force.

Given our flush state, it was tempting to expand the force above 91 squadrons, a number which had stayed steady since 1975. However, we in the Air Directorate knew that, as attractive as these budgets were right now, they wouldn't last forever. Why expand unnecessarily? We didn't want to be faced in future years with the thankless task of having to deactivate units, fire personnel, close installations, and consequently raise the ire of communities across the nation.

Indeed, towns and cities everywhere were clamoring for Army and Air Guard personnel and installations. What a turnaround from even four years ago, when more than a few communities wanted to eliminate these Guard units!

In light of the sea-change that had taken place in attitudes and funding, it was hard for those of us in the Bureau not to be pleased as 1983 moved underway. Virtually everyone of us had endured firsthand the disappointments of the late 1970s; now things had turned around 180 degrees.

But the big budgets and new equipment were not merely the Bureau's triumph alone.

Certainly the Guard had solid allies within the local governments, state houses, and a presence in every one of the 435 Congressional districts. But the group that was absolutely crucial to our success and which played a pivotal role in all Guard matters was the National Guard Association of the United States (NGAUS), headquartered at One Massachusetts Avenue, a literal window on Capitol Hill.

The association was conceived in 1878 at a banquet in St. Louis that was the first constructive meeting of officers from the North and South following Reconstruction. The purpose of the organization was to provide united National Guard representation before Congress, with the goal of obtaining better equipment and standardized training.

At the beginning of the 19th Century, President Thomas Jefferson had urged Congress to appropriate $200,000 for the militia. Seventy years later, the annual appropriation was <u>still $200,000</u>, despite the fact that the nation had grown three times in area, ten times in population, and had problems of vastly greater complexity.

Four decades after is formation, NGAUS could proudly point to the fact that the annual appropriation had increased ten-fold to $2 million.

At the turn of the 20th Century, NGAUS had an energized membership and even a greater asset: Major General Charles F. Dick of the Ohio Militia. He was not only a U.S. Congressman, he was Chairman of the House Militia Committee. In 1903, he expertly shepherded the Dick Act through Congress. The Act gave the militia national recognition, a more clearly defined state role, a program of training from the Regular Army, and a new "Militia Bureau" in the War Department. (Later, in 1933, the Militia Bureau was renamed the National Guard Bureau.)

The key provision of the second Dick Act in 1908 was that it established the Guard as a federal force that could, when mobilized, be sent outside of the country. The importance of this edict cannot be overestimated; it has allowed the President and the Congress to use the Guard immediately in conflicts ranging from World War I to Desert Storm.

The 1908 Dick Act prompted great controversy. The anti-Guard faction in Washington, which included many active duty commanders, insisted that the Guard could not be mobilized as units and deployed except by the awkward process of requiring all the individual members to volunteer. Guard commanders argued that under this scheme individual volunteers would be split out and used as back fills for active duty units. And the Guard, thanks once again to NGAUS, prevailed.

The NGAUS legacy is splendidly outlined by longtime Guard historians Colonel Alan G. Crist and Colonel W. D. McGlasson:

"The handful of Civil War veterans who set out to make something of the Guard at the 1879 meetings in St. Louis never in their wildest dreams could have anticipated the enormity, variety, and complexity of the issues that crowded in on their successors after World War II. In almost every instance, the Association was at or somewhere near the center of the action, seeking more resources for the Guard, pressing for improvements in administration and training, prodding Washington officialdom for the policies and assets that would produce a more effective military force, and defending the Guard against attack." And at the center of these relentless efforts was the famed, red-bordered "Action Gram", sent out to key individuals throughout the nation when matters of compelling interest to the Guard are being considered in Washington.

The list of legislative achievements spurred by NGAUS covers every major and minor victory secured by the Guard on Capitol Hill. They include obtaining a clearly defined status for civilian technicians; incorporating the technician structure into the federal Civil Service system; keeping the pay of Guard personnel equal with that of active duty troops; preserving military paid leave for federal employees who served in the Guard; medical care while on duty less than 30 days for training; military post exchange privileges; full-time Serviceman's Group Life Insurance; the Montgomery GI Bill, the first GI Bill to encompass Guard and Reserve participants; the Montgomery Amendments which protected National Guard participation in OCONUS training; year-round commissary shopping privileges; dedicated equipment procurement funding for the Army and Air National Guard beginning in 1981; creation of the position of Assistant Secretary of Defense for Reserve Affairs, a position designed to promote the interests of the Guard and Reserves at highest levels of the Pentagon; Selected Reserve Inventive Program (SRIP), which involves various bonuses and other incentives for Guard and Reserve enlistment and re-enlistment; protection of Guardsmen during duty by the Federal Tort Claims for actions in official status; portal-to-portal medical coverage of Guard personnel during drill weekends; and many other benefits.

In addition to these many successes NGAUS has become an institution in Washington, home to the Edward Martin Library, the most extensive collection of Guard historical publications and documents in the nation.

Over the years, there have been many fine NGAUS Executive Directors. One of the best was the peerless Major General Greenlief, former Chief of the National Guard Bureau from 1971-1974. His ten-year reign from 1974 to 1984 helped give NGAUS its reputation today as the most influential military associations in Washington and one of the most powerful voices in a city crowded with groups clamoring for support on Capitol Hill.

General Weber succeeded General Greenlief and served as Executive Director from 1984 to 1993. He continued the great work and also moved the Association into the new National Guard Memorial Building at 1 Massachusetts Avenue, N.W. Weber was succeeded by retired Major General Robert Ensslin, former Adjutant General of Florida and President of the Association. He was succeeded in turn by retired Major General Edward Philbin. Ed was a traditional Guardsmen who also served in public positions as Deputy Assistant Secretary of Defense for Reserve Affairs; U.S. Federal Maritime Commissioner, and Chairman, Interstate Commerce Commission.

These are all dedicated Guardsmen who continue to lead the association as a strong voice for a ready National Guard

Indeed, Martin Binkin of the famed Brookings Institution, when writing in The Washington Monthly on the most effective lobbying organizations in Washington, said of NGAUS, "These guys make the NRA (National Rifle Association) look like amatuers." Perhaps no higher compliment is possible.

While my professional life was satisfying, 1983 was a tumultuous year for me and the family.

My wife of twenty-eight years, Rosemary, contracted cancer and spent much of the year at Walter Reed Hospital. She fought a gallant fight but died on October 31, 1983 at Walter Reed. She was a great wife, mother, and first lady of the Air National Guard who was always there to help any member of our large Guard family in need.

Ellen and the youngest son, Bo, were in Washington and served as an inspiration to me during this extraordinarily difficult period. David was a jet instructor pilot at Beeville in Texas and Dan was a student at the University of Kentucky. Obviously, we all stayed in close touch during this time.

At a time like this, the entire Guard family stepped forward, providing great support to me and the family.

My Deputy Director at the time, Brigadier General Wes Chambers and his wife Bonnie, were a tremendous help. They stepped in and picked up the slack in helping oversee the Air Guard during these trying personal times. I will always be grateful to Wes and Bonnie as well as our Chief, General Walker and his wife, Tuta.

On October 23, 1983, the United States invaded the Caribbean island of Grenada. The operation involved personnel from every component, including the Air National Guard.

Several Guard tankers and the EC-130 Special Operations Group from Harrisburg, Pennsylvania participated in the conflict. While the forces arrayed against the United States were negligible and combat operations lasted only three days, the use of the Guard in hostilities on a voluntary basis, without a call-up, was the beginning of a historic trend. Like "Creek Party" in 1967, it was an omen of what would occur later in the raid on Libya, "Operation Just Cause" in Panama, Desert Shield, and in Haiti. The use of Guard aircraft in Grenada was also affirmation of something else — U.S. operations in a military conflict, even as one as relatively small as Grenada, required the Guard.

If the Air Guard had seen its fortunes begin to rise in 1979 and 1980, then similar pivotal years for the Army Guard were probably 1982 and 1983. The upward trend in strength from 1980 to '82 had not been transitory; Army Guard manpower was 417,000 in 1983, the highest since the draft-driven year of 1967. Mobilization readiness was at its highest level ever and Army Guard units had become fixtures at JCS exercise, including the important "Reforger '83," in Europe and "Team Spirit" in Korea, as well as "Brim Frost," "Display Determination," "Bold Eagle," "Gallant Knight," and "Flintlock."

This was also a period of major restructuring for the Army National Guard. The round-out brigade of the 24th Infantry Division (Mechanized), the 48th Infantry Brigade from Georgia, was reorganized. In addition, the Guard's 35th Infantry Division (Mechanized) from Nebraska, Kansas, Missouri, and Kentucky was reactivated while the first Roland Air Defense battalion in the Army was activated in New Mexico, as was a mountaineering school in Vermont to provided specialized training in mountain warfare.

The "Captains to Europe Program," under which Army Guard captains were attached to active units in U.S. forces in NATO, was expanded to include both Panama and Korea. This was a great program for both the Army Guard and the Active Army. In fact, in Europe, a Guard captain developed the USAREUR counter-terrorist program and another developed the M1 Abrams Tank fielding program. The 30th Infantry Brigade (Mechanized), from the North Carolina Guard participated in Overseas Development Training in Italy with its own gear. This was the first time an Army Guard unit had ever shipped its equipment overseas for an exercise. The top-of-the-line M1 Abram tank was issued to the 1st Battalion, 252nd Armor, North Carolina, a round-out unit to the 2nd Armored Division. Another battalion, the 1/108th Armor, participated in training with the 24th ID (M) at the National Training Center in California. And finally, during FY 83, each of the 54 state headquarters organizations were reorganized into State Area

Commands or STARCs, establishing an organization which would be more effective for mobilization.

Not only was the training improving, so was the quality of entering personnel. Only six percent of non-prior service accessions were in Test Category IV, the lowest percentage ever in this group. Almost two-thirds (sixty-one percent) of the new ARNG recruits had high school diplomas or were seniors in high school. (In fact, the Army Guard had become so sophisticated about recruiting that the ARNG film, "America at its Best" won the CINE Golden Eagle Award as the 1982 outstanding non-theatrical documentary film.)

Equally encouraging was that minority strength in the Guard approached population parity, with blacks, Hispanics, Asians and other minorities making up 26 percent of the force.

Large and small, all of these signs demonstrated that the Army Guard, under the solid leadership of its Director, Major General Mickey Walker, and Deputy Director, Brigadier General Herb Temple, had managed to ride out and rise above the rough years. Probably no reserve component had been so severely buffeted during the 1970s. And yet, by October of 1984 the Army Guard had raised its strength to 434,700, an increase of 88,000 personnel in just six years, a phenomenal achievement, a testament to General Walker and General Temple's leadership and to the high morale and volunteer spirit of Army Guard men and women and their commanders.

By the end of 1984, the Air Guard's manpower was up to 106,000, once again exceeding our programmed end strength. The combined Army and Air Guard now totaled 540,000, which made us as large as the other five reserve components combined, with 2,851 armories, 2,344 non-armory facilities, and 86 flying bases. It was hard for even the active component personnel to understand how any Army and Air Force of this size could be run from Washington by a National Guard Bureau consisting of only 193 military personnel and 256 civilians. But it just goes to show that a bigger headquarters staff is not always a better staff.

My term as Director of the Air Guard was up in early 1985 and I was asked by senior Air Force and Guard officers to compete for a second term. We'd reached an unprecedented prominence, budgets were increasing, and first-rate equipment and training were plentiful. The field commanders were behind me and I had the experience that comes from spending eight straight years in the Pentagon. After that much time in the puzzle palace, I had a handle on things.

However, there are always those folks who view such longevity as a liability. Unfortunately, one of those people was Vernon Orr, Secretary of the Air Force. He asked me to meet with him after he received my re-appointment documents, which had been approved by General Gabriel.

I went up to his huge E-ring office without a clue of what was coming. After greetings and small talk, he went straight to the point.

He said, gesturing at my paper work on his desk, "I'm not sure I want to sign off on your package, John."

Needless to say, I was stunned. I was aware that Secretary Orr had a strict policy he exercised with senior Air Force commanders. He expected Air Force personnel to spend a maximum of four years in the Pentagon and then have them return to a position in the field. He reasoned that any officer who stayed longer than four years in the Washington milieu would get corrupted by the Beltway Culture, lose touch with the troops, and never recover his or her military edge. I'd thought that Secretary Orr's practice didn't apply to the Guard, but it was apparent it did.

"This appointment runs counter to my policy," he said as I cringed inwardly. "You've already got eight years here and I think that's four years too many. Now you're asking me to sign you on for four more. I think you've done a great job as Director. But let me ask you, what options do I have?"

"Sir," I said, "I guess you could turn me down, even though I was a unanimous selection. Then you'd have to go back to the field for nominations."

"How would that play?" Secretary Orr asked.

"Well, sir, I don't want to appear self-centered but I don't think it would play well at all because there was no competition except for the two favorite-son state nominees who are about to retire anyway. And the states, the Hill and Air Force folks all the way up to your level support me." We talked for a little while about the other candidates and then he said the strong support for my candidacy placed him in a bit of a dilemma. "What else could we do with you? Do you have anything back in Kentucky?" No, I told him, the Adjutant General position was filled and besides, that was the governor's call.

"Can we assign you somewhere else in the system?" Even though we were talking about my career at this point, I figured that Secretary Orr was going to do what he was going to do, regardless of any pleadings on my part.

"The Army has done that in the past, sir."

"What'd they do?"

"Well, sir, when General Weber finished up his second tour as Chief he didn't have enough time for retirement — like him, I'm about five years short myself. Although he was a three-star whereas I'm a two-star, the Army and Army Guard appointed him to Forces Command as the deputy commander, which is the gaining command for all Army Guard and reserve units during a mobilization."

"That's great" said Secretary Orr, who was now getting enthused, "What would be the FORSCOM equivalent in the Air Force?"

"I guess, sir, that would be like you sending me down to TAC [Tactical Air Command headquarters] where most Air Guard forces are gained in a mobilization, and make me vice-commander for TAC, which is a three-star billet."

"That's a superb idea," said the Secretary.

What I'd described sounded good but there were some major problems. "If I may say, sir, that's what the equivalent would be. You and the Air Force have been good about including the Guard in your major air commands. But as good as you've been to us, I don't think many of the senior staff are ready for this type of move. They have their own flow of active generals they are working to fill the various active duty positions. If I went down as vice-commander, I'd be moving one of the active senior officers out of the pattern."

Orr just nodded, and I plunged on.

"Sir, I think the idea is ahead of its time. If you assigned me as vice-commander now, you'd upset the Air Force. In about five or ten years this kind of move will probably happen because the Air Force will see the need for it. So instead of leaving the Bureau at this point, I think I can be of more use to you and General Gabriel and the Guard if I stay as your Director."

In our discussion, I also told Secretary Orr that I had a lot of friends on the Hill, which could be useful to the Air Force and the Guard. I'd been testifying and working with Congress for eight years. Both the Members and their staffs knew to call me if they needed anything and I'd immediately work with them. I'd learned the crucial importance of good legislative ties under Dick Frymire back when he taught me how to deal effectively with the Kentucky legislature.

There's no way around it: The National Guard is a part political entity and at least 50 percent of what you do at the Bureau is related to Capitol Hill. The better your communications with Congress, the more you can accomplish for the total military. In fact, I've always thought that many of the military's conflicts with Congress could have been defused if general officers spent more time educating and discussing their key programs with Congress.

After I left Secretary Orr's office, I made sure I told General Gabriel about my meeting with the Secretary. General Gabriel agreed with my assessment of the situation. A short time later, Orr signed off on my package and I was reappointed Director of the Air National Guard. (In January of 1994, General Tony McPeak, Chief of Staff of the Air Force appointed Major General Phil Killey, Director of the Air National Guard, to be commander of the First Air Force. This was an unprecedented move — but one which Secretary Orr and I had discussed years earlier.)

The good relations we established with the Hill helped the Guard, particularly with regard to equipment acquisition. And therein lies a story about how equipment is distributed throughout the Guard. I call it the "Hill Audit Trail."

In July of 1983, the Air Guard's first F-16s were given to the 169th Tactical Fighter Group at McIntire Air National Guard Base in South Carolina.

Ten years earlier, they'd been the first unit to receive brand new A-7s right off the factory production line. The 169th was and still is a top-notch fighter unit, always at C-1 ratings and always with a

hand up to volunteer for whatever exercises or real world contingency surfaced.

But the reason they got the A-7s and later the F-16s was that the South
Carolina Congressional delegation took a genuine interest in the unit.

One day back in 1981, I met with Senator Strom Thurmond.
During our meeting, he made sure there was no doubt in my
military mind that he was willing to do whatever it took in the
various Senate committees to secure the F-16s for the 169th. The
same held true on the House side with Congressmen Floyd Spence.
He was 100 percent behind the effort to assign F-16s to the South
Carolina Guard.

That's the "Hill audit trail." If you do your homework, you'll
find an audit trail that leads to those Members who have worked the
issue from the start right through to completion of the acquisition.

Another example of the "Trail" took place with the top of the
line C-5A Galaxy. The first C-5As we bought were assigned to the
105th Tactical Air Group at Stewart Air National Guard Base, New
York. Congressman Joseph Addabbo took a personal interest in the
C-5A and was determined to get that aircraft for the New York
Guard. In this case, it wasn't only the plane he was interested in —
he also wanted funding for the construction of a new strategic
airbase on the East Coast. So we closed down an older base in
Westchester and with the help of Congressman Addabbo and the
rest of the powerful New York delegation, funding was approved for
both the new plane and the new base.

Our close link with every Member of Congress through the Guard's
vast nationwide network of individuals and installations is the corner-
stone of the Guard's support on Capitol Hill. And we make the most of
the money we get from Congress. Members realize that appropriations
for the Guard always go further than other federal money disbursed to
the states.

When I'm asked how the Guard manages to get so much bang
for the buck, I point out the two main advantages the Guard has over
the active component forces. First, the Guard truly adds value to
America's communities, whether they be Sioux City or New York
City, Evansville, Indiana or Jacksonville, Florida. A municipality
with a Guard unit has a competent, tested organization available for
immediate use in any kind of emergency. We're on call and available anywhere from one-tenth to one-fourth the cost of a full-time
active duty unit. Moreover, active forces aren't always available
when communities need them because by statute, federal forces are
restricted from playing a role in many types of local contingencies.

Second, there is an ingenious federal-state formula for the funding of armories and other types of Guard installations. The state
provides the land upon which the facility is to be built. The state
then contributes 25 percent of the cost of construction and the
federal government appropriates the remaining 75 percent. Follow-

ing completion of the project, the federal government licenses the building to the state, which is then permanently responsible for maintaining the facility. It's an ideal partnership that benefits the unit, the surrounding community, the state, and the nation.

The state can rent out the armory to various organizations for events as a means of generating revenue for the upkeep. So, the neighborhoods in which the armory is located have a terrific resource in the building for a wide range of activities, from civic functions to pick-up basketball games.

More than that, however, armories become a prominent feature of everyday community life. In many instances, particularly in small town and rural America, they provide a central gathering spot.

One small anecdote tells the story. Later in my career, when I became Chief, I tried to inactivate a unit in New Jersey which would have resulted in the closing of an armory. Before I knew it, the local community was up in arms because a Catholic high school rented the armory for basketball practices and games. Without that armory, the school didn't have access to a decent — or safe — gym in the area. This became a huge issue with both state and federal elected officials and ultimately we were able to leave the armory open.

This state-federal partnership and the importance of armories as a true community magnet are a primary reasons why it doesn't make a lot of financial sense for the federal government to close armories for fiscal savings. These armories are fully supported and maintained by state funds until it is time to replace them. They are an inexpensive, reassuring presence in communities across America.

Yet another development at this time was the rapidly increasing reliance on the Guard by the state governors.

In 1977, the first year I came to Washington, the Guard responded 229 times to emergency conditions in 46 states and territories. This included everything from tornadoes, floods, hurricanes, and forest fires to water hauls, search and rescue, air crashes and industrial accidents. Two years later, the Guard responded 330 times to contingencies in 48 states and territories; in 1981, there were 347 individual state callups; 511 in 1983; and, 614 in 1985.

Inexplicably, the number of state call-ups kept rising. Great swings in weather patterns, cyclical and unexplainable, were one reason. Chief Mickey Walker and later Chief Herb Temple also attributed the rise in state mobilizations to two other factors. First, state governors, mindful of budgets, were increasingly using the relatively inexpensive but highly effective Guard men and women for emergencies instead of utilizing state employees with their overtime salaries. Second, the Guard was increasingly called upon to assist various federal and state agencies with programs related to national security and law enforcement.

And, after 1984, a large number of call-ups were associated with drug interdiction and eradication. For example, by 1986, nineteen states and territories had participated in 230 drug support missions, resulting in $1.06 billion in illegal drugs being eradicated or confiscated.

As I entered my second tour as Director, I had the great fortune to be surrounded by superb staff. Brigadier General Wess Chambers, formerly commander of the Air Guard Fighter Weapons school house in Tucson, served as my Deputy Director from 1981 to 1985. He was perfect for the job, a vigorous, independent deputy whom I could rely on without question, whether I was in the building or traveling in the field.

Despite my appeals, he left in 1985 to become the Air Guard Assistant to the U.S. Pacific Air Force and subsequent promotion to Major General. Brigadier Gneral John McMerty replaced him in 1985, heading east from the ANG Fighter Training School in Wichita, Kansas. John and his wife Joan did a superb job for the Guard and retired to Costa Rica in 1989.

It was also at this time that I was presented with one of my most treasured awards. In April of 1985, I had the distinct honor of becoming a recipient of the "Order of the Sword." This presentation was made to me by the Air Guard Non-Commissioned Officers (NCOs) at their annual national conference in Louisville. Few of the awards I've been fortunate to receive over the years mean more to me than this one. I consider it the ultimate honor for an officer to be recognized by the enlisted men and women under his command. The elegant trophy I received is mounted on the wall of my den — a silver sword with an engraved gold handle.

It was also during this period that the Air Guard narrowly avoided an unneeded battle with the active Air Force over the Northrup F-20 Tigershark fighter.

In 1985, as the Air Force began looking for a new fighter, Congress mandated competition between the General Dynamics F-16 and Northrop's F-20 prototype. At the time, the Air Force believed, correctly, that some Air Guard wing commanders were intent on securing their very own new aircraft instead of relying on the cascading of aircraft the Guard usually got from the active Air Force. These Air Guard commanders feared that there wouldn't be enough F-16s leaving the Air Force inventory to equip the Guard in the 1990s. They reasoned the F-20, cheaper than the F-16, would fill this expected shortfall.

At the time, the F-16 didn't have the necessary air defense capability to carry the AIM-7 missile. The F-20 was built to carry all the AIM missiles (as was the F-18). Northrop wanted to get the F-20 production line up and moving and a U.S. government buy would make it happen. At the same time, another group of folks in the Pentagon knew that the new plane would enhance our foreign military sales capability. In fact, it probably would have replaced the F-5 around the world.

Unfortunately, Northrop had two very untimely F-20 accidents around this period and that hurt the aircraft's chances with many Members on Capitol Hill as well as with the Pentagon. Ultimately, the Secretary of the Air Force, Pete Aldrich, selected the F-16. When the decision was made, the Air Guard saluted smartly. I could have lived with either decision at the time.

But in hindsight the best decision was made. After five straight years of growth, the defense budget was poised to head down after 1986 and it was better not to have too many different kinds of fighters to take care of logistically. Today, the Air Force basically has the F-15 and F-16 to maintain. Both planes, with upgrades, are superb aircraft and capable of performing the whole range of Air Force missions.

In late 1985, General Mickey Walker announced his intention to retire as Chief of the National Guard Bureau. In a mirror image of four years ago, the two leading candidates to replace him were the Directors of the Army and Air Guard — General Herb Temple and myself.

For many years, the Chief's selection was barely noticed by the rest of the Building. This time, things were different. The Guard had quietly over time become one of the largest, most visible organizations in the Pentagon. Our soldiers and airmen were also winning consistent praise for their performance while serving alongside their active component counterparts.

Commensurate with this newfound respect was a change in the composition of the Chief's selection board. The selection boards for the Chief and the Directors and Deputy Directors were assembled by the two civilian service secretaries and the Chiefs of Staff of each service. In 1978, the board selecting the CNGB had been chaired by an Army three-star general. In 1982, the board was chaired by an Air Force three-star and was composed of one other Air Force three-star, a two-star Air Guard Adjutant General, an Army three-star general and a two-star Army Guard adjutant. That year, despite the 3-2 Air Force edge, the board had recommended General Walker, the green-suiter, which was clearly the correct decision given General Walker's experience.

In 1986, we learned that the board would be chaired by an Army four-star general and rounded out with Army and Air Force three-stars, an Army Guard two-star Adjutant General, and an Air Guard two-star Adjutant General.

The Chief's billet was a Presidential appointment, one of only several such military positions in the Pentagon. It had been a virtual photo finish between Herb and myself. We were equally qualified candidates in terms of our Bureau experience, field, and command experience. Moreover, we were good friends.

Because the competition was so close, instead of just one package being forwarded to the White House from the Secretary of Defense for the President's decision, both names were sent to the President. It was at the White House that Herb pulled ahead of me.

Herb was a Californian, a Korean War combat veteran with the Golden State's famed 40th Infantry Division. As a Guardsman during the late 1960s, he served as military assistant to then Governor Ronald Reagan and his wife Nancy. Herb was by far the best qualified Army

Guard officer at the time. And that July, President Reagan selected Herb as Chief.

Though disappointed, I was not in the least embittered by Herb's good fortune. In fact, when the official announcement was made in Washington, I was at Wright-Paterson Air Force Base outside Dayton, Ohio. From there, I immediately called Herb and his wife Pat in Washington to congratulate them. We'd been great friends before and we continue to be friends to this day. Moreover, we worked very well together as the senior Army and Air officers in the National Guard.

Deep down, I knew that Herb's elevation would be good for the Guard, particularly because of his relationship with the President and First Lady. Frankly, it had been strenuous to go through this process, sitting on the bubble of a presidential appointment, and I was glad to have the whole process behind me and to get with Herb and get on with our important work.

I enjoyed immensely my tenure with General Temple and he did an extraordinary job in enhancing the Guard's readiness and performance during the military renaissance of the Reagan years.

CHAPTER EIGHT

"TURNING IT AROUND"

In 1986, the Guard celebrated its 350th anniversary as a military force and our advertising slogan for the year was simply "Citizens. Soldiers. Patriots."

But even as we carried on the militia tradition of the citizen-soldier from three centuries past, we were also closely engaged in the social currents of contemporary America.

We had determinedly undertaken efforts to bring minorities into our ranks. In just a decade, the Army Guard had risen from 18 percent minority to nearly 25 percent in 1986; the Army Guard officer corps was 10 percent minority, up from 2 percent in 1976. The Air Guard had also made impressive gains in this area. In 1976, the Air Guard had 6 percent minority representation. By 1986, that figure had risen to 14 percent, with minorities composing 7 percent of the officer corps.

During the 1970s, we also pulled out all the stops in an effort to include more women in the Guard. In the Air Guard, which as late as 1972 had fewer than one percent females in its ranks (all of them nurses), women grew to compose 11.6 percent of the force in 1986, with 7.5 percent of the officer corps composed of females. In the ARNG by 1986, women accounted for 5.3 percent of the enlisted ranks and 5.6 percent of the officer corps.

Increased minority and female Guard participation were two of my primary goals, from the day I became Deputy Director of the Air Guard to the day I retired as Chief. I felt then as now, that even more than the active force, it was critical that the Guard reflect America and the communities we serve.

As the force changed its composition throughout the 1980s, our state missions also increased. Chief among these was the slow but steady war on drugs and the Guard was rapidly becoming a daily presence on the front lines. Two state Guards claim the distinction of being the first to undertake the fight against narcotics. The Georgia Guard asserts that a 1982 marijuana detection and eradication mission was the first Guard effort in this area. However, the Hawaii Army

National Guard claims that a 1977 joint Army Guard-state police operation code-named "Green Leaf" — to find cultivated marijuana — was the first drug detection and eradication mission.

In any case, the mission grew fast. Of 531 call ups in 1986, 230 involved narcotics eradication and confiscation. The war against drugs had begun and in 1986 alone, Guard operations resulted in more than $1 billion dollars worth of drugs destroyed or seized.

During the next six years, the Guard would become a major player in the nation's counterdrug program. And because of the state aspects of the mission, the Guard Bureau put together a state-by-state plan in late 1988.

Less than six months later, newly installed Secretary of Defense Cheney was pushed by various Administration officials, including drug czar Bill Bennett, and Congress, to provide a DOD anti-drug plan. Into the Secretary's office came Assistant Secretary for Reserve Affairs Steve Duncan, with our 1988 comprehensive 50-state National Guard plan. This unforseen deliverance was long-remembered by the Secretary. He signed off on the Guard document and DOD was off and running in the drug war.

During FY 1991, the National Guard counter-drug mission operated in all 54 states and territories, with ground and aerial surveillance in 45 states and container searches in 42 states. In May of 1991, the California Guard assisted the U.S. Customs Service in a warehouse seizure of white heroin — 1,100 pounds worth an estimated $2 billion. A year later, the Guard provided well over one million man-days/workdays in support of local, state and federal law enforcement agencies responsible for narcotics control.

Ultimately, in 1992, the Guard participated in operations that yielded impressive results: more than $61.7 million in cash confiscated and 83 million marijuana plants eradicated; seizures including 445,000 pounds of processed marijuana, 165,000 pounds of cocaine, 1,000 pounds of heroin, 631 pounds of opium, 165,000 pounds of hashish, 5,100 vehicles and hundreds of weapons seized; and, over 22,000 arrests made.

In other arenas, 1986 was a great year for the Guard. The Army and Air were once again at record strength levels with a combined force of 560,000 personnel. Readiness and mobilization were also at the highest levels ever and we had daily, worldwide responsibilities.

Never had so many ARNG formations deployed to so many different places. More than 30,000 Army Guard personnel trained overseas in 35 nations in 1986; 7,600 of those troops participated in SOUTHCOM exercises in Central America. From 1978 to 1984, the Army had added 100,000 troops, an astonishing increase in manpower. The Army Guard also received its first High Mobility, Multi-purpose Wheeled Vehicle (HMMVE), the famous "HUM-VEE" which was to become the backbone of the Army Guard's vehicle fleet.

The Air Guard had a phenomenal re-enlistment rate of 92 percent and an FY 86 budget of $2.9 billion. And we'd undertaken an important real world operation in Europe. "Operation Creek Klaxon" lasted from April 1986 to March 1987 and involved the participation of 22 Air Guard F-4 units. These planes flew air defense alert out of Ramstein Air Force Base in Germany while the Air Force units normally responsible for this duty transitioned to the F-16.

The Air Guard, for the second time this decade, also supported a combat operation. This time it was the bombing of Libya following a bomb explosion at a German nightclub frequented by American soldiers. These and other acts of terrorism finally persuaded President Reagan to launch a punitive attack against Moamoar Quaddafi. An Air Guard tanker unit, the 141st Air Refueling Group of Washington, refueled some of the U.S. planes that bombed Tripoli in 1985.

It was also during 1986 that the influential Goldwater-Nichols Department of Defense Reorganization Act was passed and signed into law. The authors said it best: "The purpose of this bill is to improve and enhance the role of professional military advice...ensure that senior civilian decision-makers receive the full range of divergent military advice, strengthen the representation of the joint military perspective and improve the performance of joint military duties."

This bill was the product of the most comprehensive examination of the U.S. defense establishment since the National Security Act of 1947. It had two principal objectives:

First, it strengthened the Chairman of the Joint Chiefs of Staff, ensuring that the Defense Department spoke with one voice to the President. And secondly, it institutionalized the concept of "jointness" — a collegial cooperation among all the services as opposed to the destructive and harmful inter-service bickering that took place in the past.

The legislation transferred "to the JCS Chairman the principal duties now performed by the corporate JCS..." The Chairman no longer needed the support of the Joint Chiefs to make a recommendation to the President or the Secretary of Defense. The position of a Vice-Chairman of the JCS was also created. The intent was to make the position the alter ego to the Chairman and the person in charge whenever the Chairman was absent. The result was less domination of the JCS by the individual services, which heretofore could veto almost any proposed JCS action.

Goldwater-Nichols also emphasized the idea of jointness among the services in structure, operation, training, and basing. The commanders-in-chief of the different combatant commands and theaters who were formerly too weak to settle service rivalries, saw their authority and prerogatives strengthened. The bill was designed to force the Department of Defense to develop military officers "capable of effectively performing the responsibilities of the joint duty assignments." As a result, joint duty assignments became coveted career moves on the ladder up to flag rank.

The legislation also recognized that the interests and pursuits of the four services created a potentially harmful imbalance and that "the predominance of service perspectives in DOD decision making results from three basic problems; OSD [Office of the Secretary of Defense] is not able to integrate service capabilities..., [the] JCS system [is] dominated by the services...and unified combatant commands are dominated by the strength and independence of the service component commanders within those commands and constraints are placed upon the authority of the unified combatant commanders."

Moreover, "unified combatant commands remain a loose confederation of single-service forces which are often unable to provide effective unified action across the spectrum of military missions."

Under Goldwater-Nichols, the CINCs were now able to directly request support from the Pentagon, instead of asking the various services within the command. More important, the CINCs could bypass the active component commanders and come directly to the Guard and reserve and request troops and equipment. For our part, we in the Bureau made sure that the individual Adjutant Generals began to think in terms of providing resources, Army and Air, that would be attractive to the various CINCs. The legislation also mandated that a Roles and Missions report be compiled every three years. Admiral Crowe put together the 1989-92 report, General Powell delivered his in May of 1993. The most recent report was developed under the direction of Dr. John White, now the Deputy Secretary of Defense.

For the Guard, Goldwater-Nichols sent a clean and concise message to all the services: jointness was in. And this was with no small amount of irony. Because probably the one organization within the Pentagon (outside the Joint Chiefs of Staff) most representative of jointness in 1986 was the National Guard Bureau. We had been joint since the Air National Guard was created in 1947 and had been the model of the joint directorate at work ever since. In fact, the first joint Air Guard-Army Guard mission was carried out in 1958, when Utah Army Guard troops were flown to Puerto Rico in Utah Air Guard planes. Indeed, our 54 Adjutant Generals, with their joint commands of Air and Army units, were classic examples of the Guard's jointness at the working command level in every state and territory.

Goldwater-Nichols was a revolution for the services. The two main elements of the bill — the emphasis on jointness and the creation of powerful Vice-Chairman under the Chairman — gave impetus to an idea that we in the Bureau had been discussing for years: creation of a "Vice-Chief" position in the Bureau, a member of the opposite service as the Chief. We felt this would accomplish several goals.

First, such a post would provide a long needed back-up for the Chief. The Chief of the National Guard Bureau was a joint-duty assignment because he oversaw two service components. And yet, he had no deputy to fill in for him when he was either swamped with work or absent from the Building and unable to weigh in on critical issues.

The Chief was generally on the road at least half the time. As I described earlier, there are all sorts of meetings, functions and major conferences which require his attendance — joint staff and OSD meetings; Congressional hearings; national governors conferences; regional governors conference; state association meetings; Adjutant General meetings; visiting units all over the world; visiting at the major commands of the Army, the Air Force; NGAUS meetings, senior commanders conferences, conferences on logistics, procurement, management, and everything else it takes to run a 550,000 personnel force. The Chief simply could not appear at every function. What generally happened was that he would go to one of the two directors and ask, "Could you cover this for me?" Often, the directors would have to hastily revise their own schedules to attend in the boss's stead.

Clearly the new position would take pressure off the five National Guard Bureau generals. It was a tremendous commitment for general officers at meetings inside and outside of the United States. We were overseeing a $10 billion organization and had more than half a million men and women in the field — with only five general officers at headquarters level. It was so bad that we couldn't get sick or take leave. The Army's Deputy Chief for Operations, for example, had 13 conferences alone; we were forced to send Majors to represent us at some of these meetings!

Finally, a Vice-Chief of the opposite service would balance out the perennial disparity in Guard generals — with an Army Chief, we always had three Army generals and two Air Force generals in the Bureau.

I found it troubling that the Bureau was operating with fewer general officers than there were in most of the Deputy Chief of Staff (DCS) offices in the Army and Air Force. For example, there would be five to seven generals each in the DCS commands such as Operations, Personnel, and Logistics.

After Goldwater-Nichols, General Temple began talking about creating a Vice-Chief within the National Guard Bureau. We outlined a job description in 1987: a Vice-Chief of the opposite service, with the same three-star grade because he would be at the same management level as the Chief. We figured that when the Chief was on the road, the Vice-Chief would be there to oversee the staff and work on major issues with all the powers that were vested in the Chief. By the same token, when the Chief was in town, the Vice-Chief could be on the road attending the meetings requiring a senior Guard presence.

We knew from our discussions with staff and Members on Capitol Hill that Congress was in favor of the position.

So we sent the proposal forward for consideration by the Army and Air Force. They approved it and then it went to the Joint Chiefs. The Chairman at that time, Admiral William Crowe, his Director of the Joint Staff, Lieutenant General Robert Riscassi, and Secretary of Defense Frank Carlucci, both gave full approval to the position.

But soon thereafter, General Temple called me to his office and said, "John we got the position. But only as a two-star." Temple explained that the Joint Staff was unwilling to give up one of their precious three-star billets and would only authorize the post at the level of Major General, not Lieutenant General. I was concerned because a two-star would not have the authority of a three-star. Temple asked me, "What do you think? Should we take it?"

Just getting the post was a milestone, so I told General Temple we ought to agree to the position with the idea of trying to secure the proper grade in the future. So we did.

Not long after, Temple said, "You know, you're the senior ranking major general around here." As I later found out, I was not only the senior ranking major general in the Bureau, I was the senior two-star in the whole Pentagon. General Temple continued, "How'd you like to be the first Vice-Chief?"

As the senior blue-suiter, I was honored to serve as Herb's Vice-Chief and, as the first Vice-Chief of the Bureau.

So Temple put in for a concurrence by the Army, the Air Force, the Office of the Secretary of Defense (OSD), and the JCS to laterally move me from Director of the Air Guard to Vice-Chief. It was approved and in the summer of 1988 I became the first Vice-Chief of the National Guard Bureau.

It was in 1987, after being widowed four years, that I was married to Linda Narcavage and not only did I fall in love with her, so did my children and grandchildren.

I could not have carried out my increased responsibilities of Vice-Chief and later Chief without her by my side. She was also a tremendous supporter in helping our large, growing family and has had tireless energy and love for the National Guard.

My most important responsibility, now that I was on the Joint Staff of the National Guard Bureau, was to make sure that the Staff was providing the services needed to both the Air and Army Directorates. In addition, I was also to assume responsibility for all of the United States Property and Fiscal Officers in the states and to cover for General Temple whenever he was away.

I immediately began a schedule of frequent visits to Army National Guard units and installations to get a greater feel for the green-suit side of the National Guard. I became knowledgeable about the non-traditional roles and missions that the Guard was performing and got heavily involved in the Guard's counterdrug and drug demand reduction efforts. I worked closely with many of the disaster call-ups taking place and threw my efforts into international training missions and started the total quality management process in the Guard. I also attended the Joint Chiefs of Staff joint exercises known as "Reforger '88" in Europe, "Team Spirit" in Korea, and traveled to see the newly formed Guam National Guard.

My schedule was linked with General Temple's so at least one of us was at the Bureau every day. The Chief-Vice Chief set up provided continuity for the Bureau and took a lot of the day-to-day management matters off the Chief's plate. With less of Bureau administration to worry about, he was free to concentrate more on the macro issues inside the Pentagon, the Administration, and the Hill. General Temple and I worked extremely well together; he placed enormous trust in me and knew that I was firmly committed to advancing his interests as well as those of the Bureau.

During my first two months as Vice-Chief, I was also acting Director for Air and impatient for a successor. When the board got underway in August 1988, the two top candidates were the Adjutant General of South Dakota, Major General Phil Killey, who had also served as a field commander, and Brigadier General John McMerty, the current Deputy for Air. Both men were extremely qualified but the Air Directorate had not had an Adjutant General in recent years at Headquarters. I think that ultimately helped General Killey get the post.

When I learned that Phil had been selected, I took John McMurty out to lunch at the Army-Navy Country Club before the official announcement. I broke the news to him there and he handled it like the gentleman he is. A year later he retired, which opened up the Deputy Director's job. It was filled by Colonel Donald W. Shepperd, the commander of the 102nd Fighter Interceptor Wing at Otis Air National Guard Base in Massachusetts. They just don't get any better than Don. He was a 1962 USAF Academy grad, recipient of the prestigious Commander's Award, and a combat veteran of the Vietnam War. Here was history in the making with our first Air Force Academy graduate ascending to one of the top posts in the National Guard Bureau.

Another important if little-noticed move in 1987 was an increase in the Presidential call-up authority from 100,000 to 200,000 in non-war and emergency situations, a result of Congressional legislation crafted by Senate Armed Services Chairman Sam Nunn and Congressman G.V. "Sonny" Montgomery.

And in keeping with the currents of the times, we had Equal Opportunity Training at the Bureau, Sexual Harassment seminars, and Discrimination Complaint Management training. The Air Guard was randomly drug testing up to 2 percent of the troops annually. HIV testing had begun two years earlier with a Guard-wide average of 1 in 1,000 testing positive for the AIDS virus.

In 1988, the first Apache attack helicopter was fielded by the Army National Guard. We were also participating in a number of Guard unit exchanges — the Minnesota Guard with the Norwegian military, the Vermont Guard with the Italian armed forces, and the Oklahoma and Indiana Guard with the British. These exchanges made for great public relations; they established a community-to-community link with our allies and highlighted the strengths of the Guard to our partners. One of the highlights of our increased international presence was that the Michigan ANG became the first ANG unit to drop supplies into the USSR — after the Armenian earthquake in December of 1988.

In 1987, Public Law 100-48, the "New G.I. Bill Continuation Act" went into affect. This was a direct result of the tuition assistance program begun three years earlier and entitled "The Educational Assistance Act of 1984." This legislation — indeed, this crusade — had an interesting history; as well, it had a champion, Congressman "Sonny" G.V. Montgomery. And the both have been crucial to the development of the modern day National Guard.

In 1976, the famous "G.I. Bill," which paid the college bills of veterans, was eliminated for those recruits enlisting after December 31, 1976. Aghast at what he saw as a slap in the face of service members, Congressman Montgomery vowed to resurrect this program, which had been a huge, well-documented engine of social and economic change following World War II.

As with anything on Capitol Hill, gaining and then securing the legislative initiative was a long, tough fight. Placed in the 1984 Department of Defense Authorization Act was a three-year experimental program on educational benefits. Importantly, this program included the Guard and Reserve in the benefits package. The pilot program required participating active duty recruits to complete three years of service with an Honorable Discharge in order to qualify for $300 a month and up to $10,800 in educational benefits. For Guard and Reserve, the recruitment was completion of six months of Basic Training and then an enlistment of six years. The consequent benefits package was $140 a month or up to $5,040 during and after the six-year period of enlistment.

The results were so positive — and overwhelming — that three years later, Congressman Montgomery prevailed in a much bigger way. The 1984 pilot program was enshrined permanently, in Public Law 100-48, and included the benefits package for the selected reserves. Moreover, the legislation changed the original 1984 title to the "Montgomery G.I. Bill Act of 1984." The Army and Air Guard believed that this tuition assistance legislation was "the single most effective inducement to recruit and retain members in the Guard." The overall cost of the Montgomery G.I. bill has been rather modest: $20 million in 1985, $81 million in 1989, $94 million in 1991, and $77 million in 1993. These are not great sums in terms of the enormous boost given the Guard by this legislation.

And the boost has been enormous. Guard leaders have been uniformly effusive about the legislation Montgomery almost singlehandedly pushed into law. And the impact lives on. Recently, Secretary of Defense William Perry, himself a recipient of benefits under the original G.I. Bill, put it simply and powerfully when he said, "The result of the Montgomery G.I. bill is that 2.4 million American servicemen and women have furthered their education and bettered their lives under this bill."

That is the extraordinary legacy of Sonny Montgomery's legislation.

While I knew Congressman Montgomery from my many appearances on the Hill, we had also become close friends over the years through a daily gathering that for want of a better term was known to its members as the "The Breakfast Club."

There's a table in the far northeast corner of the dining room of the Longworth House Cafeteria. For many years, a handful of members, among them Congressmen Montgomery of Mississippi, the late William Natcher of Kentucky, Bob Stump of Arizona, Owen Pickett of Virginia, Mel Hancock of Missouri, Scott McInnis of Colorado, Sonny Callahan of Alabama, Congressman (Air Force veteran and now Senator) Ben Nighthorse Campbell of Colorado, Congressman Richard Schultz of Pennsylvania, Congressman John Tanner of Tennessee, and other friends on Capitol Hill would gather here to eat breakfast. The small-talk would range from what was on the front page of the paper, or even the back page; whose kid was in college, whose kid was fouling up; what the Redskins did, or what the current Administration was or wasn't doing. Divergent views were often aired, but always calmly and with a sense of camaraderie.

It was not exactly a fraternity, not exactly an association, but something in between. Sometimes a senior staffer or friend would appear with a Member but anyone new to the table had to be brought by one of the regulars. The acceptance or rejection of a visitor who appeared frequently, was communicated subtly but firmly.

In the beginning, I came a few times with Congressman Montgomery and Congressman Natcher, a long time Kentucky friend. After a dozen or so visits, I too was accepted into the group. Later, when Chief, I held semi-annual gatherings of the breakfast club at our Quarters One, Ft. McNair home for all my table mates from Longworth.

When Congressman Natcher died in April of 1994, Congressman Montgomery made it known to me that henceforth, I was to sit in the Kentucky chair usually occupied by my late friend. I still consider my breakfast companions some of my closest friends in town. Ironically, one of our Congressional members is freshman Jim Gibbons, of Nevada. Jim retired as a Colonel from the Nevada Air National Guard and is one of the 80,000 Guard men and women that I activated in the Desert War. He distinguished himself as a RF-4 pilot in combat and today is the only member of Congress to have been in combat in both Vietnam and Desert Storm.

By the beginning of 1989, I'd been nearly eight years in grade and with only two years to go until retirement, I had every reason to believe I'd retire as a two-star. Later, when young officers would tell me wistfully about being stalled in grade, I'd tell them about my eight and then nine years stalled at the rank of Major General, a story none of them could match. Nevertheless, not a bad rank at which to be stalled as they would tell me.

It was during this time as Vice-Chief that I participated in one of the most moving events of my military career. On June 5th, 1989, we flew to France to take part in the 45th Anniversary of the Normandy landings — D-Day. The Guard played a prominent role in the landings when the "Blue and Grey" 29th Infantry Division, composed of Guardsmen from Maryland, Virginia, and the District of Columbia stormed ashore at Omaha Beach. The spearhead on that morning in 1944 was the famed 116th Infantry Regiment, the "Stonewall Brigade." Interestingly enough, it is a little known fact that nine National Guard divisions saw action in the European Theater of Operations and that four, the 28th, the 29th, the 30th and the 35th, took part in the hard-fought Normandy campaign.

The trip was led by Secretary of the Army John O. Marsh, Jr., who represented President Bush; General Colin Powell, representing the U.S. Army (he was then head of Forces Command in Atlanta); myself as the National Guard representative; Major General Bruce Jacobs; Major General Charles Kiefner; Major General Joseph Boyersmith; Colonel Doug Olson; Colonel Frank Van Fleet; and, Mr. Tommy Hill, all National Guard members.

Former National Guard Chief, General Francis Greenlief, who had fought and been wounded at Normandy during the war, brought a group of National Guard captains to Normandy. Typical of Fran Greenlief's foresight, he wanted these young men to get a sense of Guard history so that they could pass this heritage along when they became more senior officers.

The entourage visited Vierville-Sur-Mer, where in 1969, NGAUS erected a National Guard monument on the remains of a German pillbox located a few hundred yards away from where the 29th hit the beaches that famous day. We laid wreaths on graves in the huge U.S. cemetery, Colville Sur Mer, overlooking Normandy and later marched through the streets of Ste. Mere Eglise.

The French have always had a fondness for the National Guard, stretching back to the Marquis de LaFayette and more recently, because of the Guard divisions that first arrived in France in 1917 as part of the American Expeditionary Force. On June 8th, the senior French political and military leadership, represented by Mr. Laurent Fabius, President of the French Parliament, hosted a huge dinner in Paris in honor of the National Guard. At that dinner, NGAUS honored Count Rene 'de Chamberun — the last living male descendant of the Marquis De' Lafayette — by presenting him the Legion De' Lafayette Medal.

It was an extremely emotional event as Frenchman from both wars spoke of their gratitude for the American soldiers who came to fight for France. The whole evening was filled with praise for the National Guard, which I found to be fitting tribute to the heritage of the organization which had taken its name from Lafayette, and had returned twice in this century to fight for France. Major General Bruce Jacobs (USA, Ret.), a prolific writer and historian of the Guard, orchestrated this superb event, a truly historic moment in the Guard's long history.

For some intangible reason, 1989 was the year for high-profile disasters. Among the most notable was the July 1989 United DC-10 that crashed landed in an open cornfield near Sioux City Iowa. Within minutes, Iowa Air National Guard personnel from the 185th Tactical Fighter Group were on the scene with fire and rescue and medical personnel; the Iowa Army National Guard stood by and gave first aid. Both components were credited with the miraculous number of lives saved through this rapid response.

There was also the 1989 earthquake in Northern California which took place during the baseball playoffs. Within an hour of the quake hitting, every unit in the state was on alert for possible mobilization. Guard units from Sacramento to San Jose were on duty and providing assistance which civilian agencies were unable to perform. In fact, weeks after the quake, the Guard was still on duty, providing water supplies, shower facilities, tents, food, and clothing.

There was also Hurricane Hugo in the Caribbean and the Carolinas. Guard units from throughout the United States took part in the aftermath, and were the central component of the largest U.S. disaster relief effort to that date in history. The Alabama ARNG 109th Evacuation Hospital was sent to St. Croix and 10 months later, was still operating on the island.

In 1989, the Guard conducted more than 900 mobilization exercises, twice as many as the total conducted in the five previous years. We had also logged 2,060 state call-ups, a staggering 1,811 of those related to narcotics law enforcement.

Perhaps the most frequent Air Guard and Army Guard OCONUS deployments during the last decade had been to Panama. We'd been a virtual fixture at Howard Air Force Base flying the "Volant Oak" C-130 supply operation and the "Coronet Cove" A-7 fighter mission. The "Blazing Trails" road building program had begun in Panama and all of SOUTHCOM drew on Guard resources to help out on any given day of the week. On December 15th, 1989, I visited Major General Marc Cisneros, the U.S. Army assistant to General Maxwell Thurman, the commander of SOUTHCOM. Tensions were high in the region and it was obvious that something would come to a head soon.

All of which is to say that the Guard was poised to play a key role when U.S. military forces invaded Panama on December 20, 1989 to oust the regime of Manuel Noreiega.

From the initial design of the operation, code named "Blue Spoon" but changed at the last moment to "Just Cause" by Secretary Cheney, the Air Guard's electronic countermeasures EC-130 unit, the 190th Special Operations Group (SOG), from Harrisburg, Pennsylvania was included in the Joint Chiefs of Staff and Air Force Staff plan. (The 193rd has certainly proved itself to the actives; it is the most frequently mobilized unit in the Air Guard.)

Before the invasion even began, General H. T. Johnston, head of Transportation Command called the Air Guard to ask for support. As

Air Force Historian Gary Gault has written, "Prior to H-Hour, the 145th Tactical Airlift Group [TAG] NC ANG was tasked by the ANG Operations Center to deliver anti-icing fluid by truck and the 118th Tactical Airlift Wing [TAW] TN ANG and 105th Military Airlift Group NY ANG were tasked to fly anti-icing fluid and equipment to Pope Air Force Base, North Carolina for use on the C-141 troop transports cueing up for the invasion. Medical units from the 109th TAG and the 172nd MAG MS ANG were tasked prior to the Operation and responded at 100 percent strength with volunteer personnel."

The invasion began just after midnight on December 20th, with Army and Marine troops going after key Panamanian facilities. The day ended with most of these targets occupied by U.S. troops. Some resistance continued as a result of "dignity battalions" loyal to Noriega, spread throughout the countryside. But the Panama Canal opened one day after the invasion and fighting gradually diminished between December 22 and January 3, 1990.

Air Guard participation in "Just Cause" ran the gamut — from airlift to fighter, and the aforementioned special operations. Major General Phil Killey activated our ANG Operations Center at Andrews AFB at 0545 on December 20th and after the security classification for the Operation was lifted, the Air Guard Crisis Action Team (CAT) became officially operational. Actually, the CAT team at Andrews had noticed the increased activity in SOUTHCOM units and figured something was up prior to the start of official operations.

Less than 90 minutes after coming on line, the center alerted the Air Lift Control Element teams at five tactical air wings, the 118th from Tennessee, 146th from California, the 137th from Oklahoma, the 133rd from Minnesota, and the 136th from Texas, and directed them to load supplies onto aircraft headed toward Panama. Our Aerial Port troops of the 164th Tactical Airlift Group (TAG) from Tennessee and 165th TAG from Georgia loaded up C-5s; and the 105th Military Airlift Group (MAG) from New York and 172nd MAG from Meridian, Mississippi flew 35 missions, with 128 of those sorties carrying troops and supplies.

The "Volant Oak" aircrews already down there flew 22 missions and completed 181 sorties moving supplies and passengers.

The 166th TAG from Delaware got their share of action as they were directed to haul Army Special Forces troops and cargo to Panama City's General Omar Torrijos Herrera International Airport, to the Rio Hato Airfield, and to Howard AFB.

The "Coronet Cove" units also got in on the action. The 114th TFG from Sioux Falls, South Dakota, and 180th TFG from Swanton, Ohio, flew 34 sorties, flying close air support missions, armed reconnaissance, convoy escort missions, and aircraft intercept and identification missions. The 180th from Ohio flew missions against entrenched Panamanian troops, and were on 15-minute alert, 24-hours-a-day for SOUTHCOM close air support requests. The 190th SOG flew 18 sorties during this time.

There were many other units, involved as well. The 172nd MAG, from Jackson, Mississippi, flew missions from 20 December to 12 January and compiled 89 sorties. The 164th Mobile Aerial Port Squadron from Memphis was involved in supply. The 105th MAG commander had 1,500 unit members called to active duty over Christmas to keep the C-5s in the air. In the end, we flew seven percent of the total airlift missions from 17 December through 14 February. Army Guard units training at that time in Panama were also called into federal service and participated in Just Cause.

"Operation Just Cause" required and received a large amount of volunteerism rather than a mobilization and, along with Grenada and Libya, reaffirmed a consistent pattern of National Guard readiness.

The Air Guard Director, Major General Philip Killey, put it best in a February message to all the ANG units that had participated in "Just Cause": "ANG actions in the Operation, while in a non-mobilized status, clearly demonstrated the patriotism, willingness, and sense of duty which these citizen soldiers contributed to the defense of democracy and freedom in a world scenario in spite of dangerous and adverse conditions. This illustrated the ANG capability and willingness to be an effective part of the Total Force policy of the Department of Defense."

Just a few months later, yet another test would come.

Even as "Just Cause" was winding down, I witnessed a study in contrasts involving another nation in the Southern Hemisphere. And I viewed our participation there as emblematic of the varied Guard experience in that region.

This time the Guard was deploying to Jamaica on a road-building exercise. At the nation's central airport, Guard troops rolled out of Air Guard transports with bulldozers, trucks, and other types of engineering equipment, not howitzers, tanks, HUMVEEs, and machine guns. Coming on the heels of our combat and combat support efforts in Panama, this was a vivid demonstration of the broad range of missions within the Guard's capability.

Over the weeks we constructed a farm-to-market road. As we progressed, thousands of Jamaicans bore witness to the U.S. military as a friendly, helpful force. Indeed, I was told by U.S. Ambassador Holden that there had been some tension in anticipation of our arrival. But the anxiety vanished after a few days when word spread through the communities about the sweat-soaked U.S. soldiers working from dawn to dusk, straining to build a road for Jamaican farmers. As they progressed with the road project, they also rebuilt several Jamaican schools along the route and even remodeled a hospital.

The contrast between Panama and Jamaica, in terms of the Guard experience, remains compelling today.

To my great dismay, it was deployments such as these that prompted an attack on the Guard's autonomy and our constitutional role. It was a legal assault conducted as pure political spite by governors hostile to President Reagan's foreign policy. And it ultimately failed.

CHAPTER NINE

" FUERTOS CAMINOS: THE ROAD TO CENTRAL AMERICA"

For many people inside and outside Washington, the politics of the 1980s was best exemplified by a region — Central America — and the constant controversy over the U.S. involvement there. The engine for this conflict was the 1979 Sandinista takeover of Nicaragua and the communist regime established by President Daniel Ortega.

Unfortunately for the Soviet Union, tiny, penniless Cuba had not been the launch pad for the hemispheric worker's revolution the Soviets had hoped for. Now Moscow believed Nicaragua could serve as the base camp for communist expansion in Central America and they established excellent relations with Ortega. It was a large, populous country and its military forces dwarfed those of neighbors El Salvador, Honduras, Guatemala, and Costa Rica.

President Ronald Reagan and his Administration, on the other hand, were determined to confront Communism in every corner of the globe. They had supported the Afghan muhajadeen, funded a large Polish underground, and installed intermediate range missiles in Europe despite massive anti-nuclear demonstrations.

And in Central America, this policy of confrontation began with the funding of the Contras, an anti-Sandinista guerilla force that harassed the Sandinista government. This forced the Sandinistas to divert resources to border defense and away from the destabilization of neighboring countries through communist insurgencies.

In addition to supporting this anti-communist force, the United States also sought a presence in Central America, a way of showing American resolve in the region. "Volant Oak" and "Coronet Cove" were a start.

However, it was apparent that more of a presence was needed. President Reagan was caught in of a dilemma because alarm bells would sound if a true U.S. presence was accomplished by long-term deployments of professional military units.

At the same time, there was a greater appreciation of the capability and readiness of Guard Reserve units and consequently more frequent request, by gaining Active Component commands for participation of Guard and Reserve Component units in operational missions.

Nowhere was this participation greater than in Central America.

In 1983, the Army Guard planned a road building project for Costa Rica but the Costa Rican government placed many burdensome restrictions on the deployment, including forbidding Guardsmen to carry weapons. So instead, in January of 1984, the Army Guard undertook a road building project in Panama, led by then Colonel Billy Navas of the Puerto Rico National Guard. He was no stranger to the area.

In 1981, he'd commanded the first Guard exercise in Panama - "Minuteman III." These training events provided a great opportunity for Guard and Reserve units to experience a real live deployment mission to a foreign location while also providing needed humanitarian support to less affluent countries. Colonel Navas, a superb soldier, would later rise to become Vice Chief of the National Guard and is currently the Director of the Army National Guard.

This 1984 road building effort became known as "Fuertos Caminos" or the "Blazing Trails" exercise. It was a total Army operation consisting of combined engineer assets from the Army Guard, Army Reserve, and active Army. One exercise each was held in Panama and Honduras, the latter in 1986, with approximately 7,000 Guardsmen taking part. Also in 1986, the Army Guard conducted a communications exercise in conjunction with Fuertos Caminos consisting of nine training deployments involving infantry, artillery, medical, and Special Forces units.

In addition to building roads, participating units conducted a multitude of volunteer, off-duty community relations activities such as improving school buildings and distributing clothes donated by local U.S. communities. Another big boost for the communities along the roads was the medical assistance our Guardsmen and women provided, incidental to the military mission.

Over the decade of the 1980s, the majority of Army Guard training operations in the Central and South American region were road-building exercises undertaken by combat engineers and their supporting units. It was superb training for our soldiers. But more important, those units built hundreds of miles of road. It is universally recognized that these roads became lifelines in the remote areas in which they were built and have improved the quality of life for countless citizens of Panama, Honduras, and Ecuador.

Guard deployments to the region were useful to the Administration in three ways. First, they were less provocative than deployments of active duty units. The Guard's reputation was as a force of part-time citizen-soldiers, not a full-time active duty military. Our nation-building operations, such as the construction of roads, schools, and other infrastructure was very similar to our community and state missions. We knew how to help at the local level. Our primary objective in peacetime has always been to add value to the community and build support among the local populace at home. So it was easy for us to perform the same mission in Central and South America. And for this type of mission, Guardsmen and women are a superior alternative to armed soldiers whose primary purpose has always been combat operations.

Second, the part-time nature of the Guard made its deployment to politically sensitive areas more palatable. Guard exercises in Central America were not seen as an open-ended commitment. We were viewed as temporary visitors rather than an occupying force.

Third, Guard units from Columbus, Ohio building a road in Honduras built support for the deployment....in Columbus, Ohio. The use of the Guard community-based defense force in Central America gave U.S. communities a stake in the success of Reagan Administration policies in the region. Teguilpica wasn't just town on a map, it was where John Smith's military police company performed Annual Training. The support of Hometown U.S.A. for anti-communist undertakings in Central America was directly linked to their sons and daughters who had served there.

We in the Bureau thought the Central American training was a great assignment for the Guard. Overseas deployments were always sought after by Guard units because in addition to boosting morale, the deployments were also good for training, retention and recruiting.

But not everyone approved of the heightened U.S. presence or the use of the Guard. Despite the evidence that Nicaragua was attempting to export communism, undermine governments in the region, and brutally subjugating its Miskito Indians, Reagan's Central American policy became a target on the Hill, particularly vilified by certain Members opposed to that policy. Indeed, several Members of the House and Senate took the opportunity to impede the President's goals through legislative action.

In July of 1985, the then-Director of the Army Guard Major General Herb Temple, requested that the 3rd Brigade of the 40th Infantry Division, California Army National Guard (of which Temple had been a member), deploy to Honduras to serve as an opposition force (opfor) in an exercise with the Honduran Army. California Governor George Duekmejian, a Republican, refused the request.

Ironically, in this case, there was no political axe to grind. The fact was that the California Adjutant General, Major General Willard Shank recommended that Governor Deukmejian veto the deployment. General Shank was concerned that the Brigade would be forced to leave its equipment behind with the Honduran units upon completion of the exercise. This was never a factor in any of our deployments.

General Temple, however, was upset by this turn of events and went next to the Texas National Guard's 49th Armored Division to request that an armored task force be put together for the exercise. Initially there was some hand-wringing by then-Governor Mark White, who finally allowed his Guard unit to deploy. He followed them down there to observe the exercise first hand and after seeing the unit in action, he came back and publicly praised the training and the importance of the exercise.

The mission of the Task Force was to serve as an opposition force against the Honduran Army. The training was conducted in an area in which a Nicaraguan armored and infantry thrust into Honduras might occur in retaliation for Honduras winking at border sanctuaries used by the contras. Indeed, a Nicaraguan feint in 1984 prompted the deployment of active component brigades from the 82nd Airborne Division and the 7th Infantry Division (Light).

In 1986, the Guard deployed the first combined combat arms unit in Guard history, an artillery battery from the 47th Infantry Division. Later deployments included units from the 28th Division from Pennsylvania, and the 38th Division from Indiana and Michigan. All this Guard activity took place under the command of the CINC South, General John Galvin who, fittingly enough, had begun his military career in the Massachusetts Army Guard.

Members of Congress, no matter if they were for or against the Reagan policy in Central America, had ample opportunities to vote, debate, and legislate the various components of U.S. involvement in that region. Governors, however, had no way of inserting themselves into the discussion other than through public messages of support or denunciation. Until 1986.

That year, Governor Joseph Brennan of Maine prohibited the deployment of 48 Maine Army Guardsmen to Honduras. Within weeks, at least seven other governors stated that they would also forbid their Guard troops to train in Central American nations. These included Governors Michael Dukakis of Massachusetts, Madeline Kunin of Vermont, Bruce Babbitt of Arizona, Richard Celeste of Ohio, Richard Lamm of Colorado, Frank Anaya of New Mexico, and Rudy Perpich of Minnesota.

This put Guard personnel in an extremely difficult position. The Guard community in each state and territory has a powerful loyalty to its governor, which is only natural inasmuch as he or she after all, is the commander-in-chief until the unit is federalized for active duty.

But the entire thrust of the Total Force policy was to tie the Guard to the actives so that the Guard could be used in any contingency and in any theater. This fundamental policy shift was the driving force behind the Army and Air Guard participation in major JCS exercises from the 1970s onwards. Indeed, it went quite aways back. The Guard had fought for the Dick Act of 1908 precisely because we wanted the capability to serve overseas, and not be relegated to a quasi-internal law enforcement organization.

As a result of the increased emphasis on the Total Force Policy, SOUTHCOM commanders had been relying on Guard units for more than a decade. As Colonels Reid Beveridge, James Burgess, and George Hargrove have noted in their excellent monograph, "The National Guard, the Montgomery Amendment and its Implications," when

SOUTHCOM Commander in Chief General Paul Gorman was confronted with "communist brush fires in this theater, without the requisite active military backup, he lit on the concept of a constantly unfolding series of military exercises utilizing U.S.-based units that would travel the relatively short distance from the United States to Central America, train as units for a few weeks, then return to home station. He visualized the National Guard...as essential in this not only because of the large numbers of units available but also because of the `citizen-soldier' mentality such unit members would bring to the country in question, all too many of which had historically been ruled by military juntas."

However, as overseas Guard deployments became more frequent, the Governors' objections to Guard deployments increased and the issue began to attract national attention.

Once again, into the breech stepped one of the Guard's greatest friends, Congressman Montgomery.

In 1986, he inserted in the Defense Authorization Act of 1987 a simple amendment stating that no governor could withhold a National Guard unit from deployment on account of "location, purpose, type, or schedule for such deployment." However, he allowed that a state emergency necessitating a call-up by the governor would take precedence over any overseas deployment.

Governor Rudy Perpich of Minnesota called Congressman Montgomery's amendment "an unconstitutional invasion of the governor's control of the peacetime training of the National Guard. The Montgomery Amendment represents a states rights issue of historical importance." And in an eerily prescient fashion, Perpich added that the issue "warrants final resolution by the Supreme Court."

Not only did "many object to the Guard's presence in Central America on some sort of post-Vietnam syndrome grounds," says Beveridge, there was also concern about the possibility of U.S. casualties. Jumping on this bandwagon was Michael Dukakis of Massachusetts, whose Army Guard 65th Public Affairs Detachment was scheduled in 1986 for deployment to Panama and Honduras in 1988.

Those of us in the Bureau had few illusions about what was going on here. It was clear to many of us that the Governors were using their Guard personnel in the most cynical fashion possible — as political hostages in order to attack President Reagan's Central American policy. And in the heated political environment of 1987 and 1988, it was a perfect issue.

During the summer of 1988, West Virginia provided the Task Force headquarters in Honduras. Approximately 6,000 Guardsmen from the 1st Army constructed 11.5 kilometers of new road throughout rugged mountain terrain.

And now, even Hollywood didn't fail to cash in on it.

Even as this road-building operation was being planned, Americans were treated to two cinematic perspectives on Central America.

One was a television news magazine piece entitled the "Road to War" which was sympathetic to the communist cause in Central America. Left out was that in El Salvador, U.S. forces suffered 2 dead and nearly 60 wounded in constructing the road. We paid a price for that road, however mocked by some in America, and the road changed the lives of thousands of citizens for the better.

The more egregious event was a made-for-television movie entitled "Weekend War", a factually inaccurate episode depicting a Guard unit deployed in Central America. The climactic scene was a battle between a National Guard engineer platoon and a band of revolutionaries in which the Guardsmen suffered casualties.

It was an outrageous and inflammatory piece of cinema. And in keeping with its hopelessly skewed political message, it was aired in February of 1988, one night before President Reagan gave a nationally broadcast address outlining additional aid to the contras.

Even though most of the noise was coming from six or seven intransigent governors at this time, several active military leaders began to express their concerns about "re-evaluating" Guard missions. They suggested at the very least that federal recognition be withdrawn from those units Governors had prevented from training in Central America.

It was also obvious at this time that the Army Reserve and the Air Force Reserve were most interested in this outcome. A turning away from Guard units and resources would only serve to enhance the role of the Reserves, historically funded at lower levels than the National Guard.

Indeed, as Beveridge notes, General Mickey Walker, Chief of the National Guard said that he "and other Guard leaders...heard the unpleasant Pentagon rumblings of what otherwise might be called a preemptive strike. This would have been the transfer of units from the Army and Air Guard to the Army and Air Force Reserve, which are under the command of the regular services in peacetime."

As General Walker later told Beveridge in an interview, such a situation would have meant looking "at the Guard to become again strictly a state force and not be carrying the load of defense that it is carrying today. We would probably have seen the modern equipment we have begun to get stopped. We would have seen force structure begin to leave the National Guard. It would have had real ramifications for us."

And as Congressman Montgomery said, "They [the Army and Air Force leaders] were concerned about the reluctant governors. They kind of convinced me — did convince me — that the commanders in the Defense Department, the people who call the shots over there, were concerned that it did affect the force structure of the military. They felt if they couldn't use these Guardsmen where they were needed in Central America, the whole force structure was in trouble..."

The Montgomery Amendment passed the House on August 14,

1986, and was signed into law by President Reagan the next month. Beveridge writes, "Enactment of the Montgomery Amendment had the gratifying effect of quieting almost instantly all the anti-Guard noise at the Pentagon."

Then on January 22, 1987, Governor Perpich of Minnesota filed suit in the U.S. District Court of St. Paul challenging the constitutionality of the Montgomery Amendment. His suit asserted that the amendment violated the Militia Clause of the Constitution. Exactly four months later, Governor Michael Dukakis of Massachusetts, who had joined in the Perpich suit, filed a similar lawsuit in Boston. The Dukakis suit claimed that "The administration is using National Guard training in Central America, with aid to the Contras, as part of an ill-disguised effort to overthrow the Nicaraguan government."

When the suits were filed, Governor Perpich had two units scheduled to deploy to Central America, the 133rd Tactical Airlift Wing, a C-130 unit bound for a routine "Volant Oak" rotation, and the 113th Public Affairs Detachment. Governor Dukakis also had the 13-member 65th Public Affairs Detachment scheduled for Honduras.

Oral arguments in the Perpich case were heard in U.S. District Court on June 15th, 1987.

The Department of the Army and the Department of Justice wanted to argue the case based on the Army Clause of the U.S. Constitution, which states that Congress has the authority to raise and support armies. The Guard community, represented by NGAUS and the Assistant Adjutant General of Louisiana, wanted to argue the Militia Clause. The NGAUS argument was heard only at the district court level in Boston in the Dukakis suit.

Major General Ed Philbin, a New Jersey National Guard General officer and lawyer was the prime author of the National Guard brief. He did a superb job and later would become in June of 1995, Executive Director of the National Guard Association of the United States.

On August 7, 1987, U.S. District Judge Donald Alsop ruled against Governor Perpich.

Governor Perpich appealed his case to the three-judge panel of the Eighth U.S. Circuit Court of Appeals in St. Paul, Minnesota, in February of 1988. In December, the panel sided with Perpich and ruled against Judge Alsop and the Department of Defense.

Then the DOD filed a motion to get the case heard en banc; that is, by the full 10-judge 8th Circuit, a rare occurrence. On June 28th, 1989, that panel reversed the three-judge panel. Perpich then appealed that decision to the Supreme Court where it was heard on March 27, 1990.

The Department of Defense was represented by the Solicitor General, Kenneth Starr. The Assistant Attorney General of Minnesota, Hubert H. Humphrey III, argued for Governor Perpich.

Justice Stevens opinion cut right to the National Guard argument: "The second Militia Clause enhances federal power in three ways. First, it authorizes Congress to provide for `organizing, arming, and disciplining the Militia.' It is Congressional choice that the available pool of citizens has been formed into organized units. Over the years, Congress has exercised this power in various ways, but its current choice of the dual enlistment system is just as permissible as the 1792 choice to have members of the Militia arm themselves."

"Second," Justice Stevens continued, "The clause authorizes Congress to provide for governing such part of the Militia as may be employed in the service of the United States. Certainly this authority encompasses continued training while on active duty. Finally, although appointment of officers and `the authority of training the Militia' is reserved to the states, that limitation is in turn, limited by the words `according to the discipline prescribed by Congress.' If service in the armed forces of a global power requires training in distant lands or distant skies, Congress has the authority to provide it. The subordinate authority to perform the actual training to active duty...in the federal service does not include the right to edit the discipline that Congress may prescribe for Guard members after they are ordered into federal service."

The Supreme Court's decision was delivered on June 11 1990. During the courtroom presentation, one of the justices asked a leading question of the Perpich team, which I paraphrase rather inelegantly, "You want all this equipment and the payroll paid for by the federal government. But you want total control. Why then don't you pay for it yourself?"

The decision was nine to zero in favor of the U.S. Government and the DOD, bringing a decisive end to this needless controversy, brought on by the unfortunate decisions — even cynical politics — of a few Governors.

The inescapable fact is that the Montgmoery Amendment secured the Federal mission of the National Guard, a foundation of our existence.

Years later, I ran into a Supreme Court Justice who had heard the case. We spoke briefly about the ruling and then he laughed and said, "General, it was an interesting case. And I wish they were all that easy."

SECTION III. "THE GUARD COMES OF AGE"

CHAPTER TEN

"CNGB"

In the fall of 1989, General Temple called me into his office, Room 2E394. As usual, he got right to the point. "John, I wanted you to be one of the first to know this. I've decided to retire early next year and go back to California. I think you should really consider becoming a candidate again for Chief."

Give the Chief's selection process one more try? I was dubious. The Chief's position traditionally fell to a green-suiter because of the size of the Army Guard. And, after being bypassed twice, it was hardly likely that a board would recommend me on the third try. The military doesn't operate that way. Plus, I'd already spent 13 years in the Pentagon and doubted that any board would want to appoint me to four more. By any measurement, I'd simply spent too many days and years in the Building.

On the other hand, my longevity had given me experience in every facet of the Bureau and the Pentagon. Only legendary civilians like "Doc" Cooke, Administrative Executive for the Pentagon, had more longevity than me. I knew the Hill and was on good terms with all the key Members. In addition, I had been closely involved with the Army National Guard from the day I assumed the position of Vice-Chief.

During the next week or two, I was non-committal. General Temple, however, was insistent and urged that I at least talk to the higher ups in the Air Force to see what they thought. So I finally arranged a visit with both Secretary of the Air Force Donald Rice and the Air Force Chief of Staff General Larry Welch. I met first with Secretary Rice.

"General Temple is going to retire from the bureau early next year," I told him. "He's going to open up nominations for Chief next month and thinks I should put my package in. But I'm just not sure."

Rice nodded and asked me why. I told him I was tempted, but that

I'd been here before. The Chief of Staff had urged me to run in '82. I did but wasn't selected. Then I was asked to run in '86 and I did and wasn't selected again. Now, I said, I'm being urged to run again.

"Sir, this has almost always been an Army position and that's fine because that's probably the way it should be. But I also know that occasionally a blue-suiter should have a chance." My point here was that if at some point we couldn't get a blue suiter as Chief of the National Guard, then jointness wasn't making much progress in the Pentagon or the National Guard.

"But sir, I don't want to jump in and come out of this process zero for three, particularly if you think we've got a better candidate. I was planning to retire next summer and it would be more than a little embarrassing to go out on that note."

Rice said, "Yes, I understand you. But one for three is a pretty good batting average. I think you're the best candidate we have and you should be nominated and get into the competition." General Welch told me basically the same thing and was very supportive.

With this pat on the back, I decided to enter the race. I asked the governor of Kentucky, Wallace Wilkerson, and the Adjutant General, Mike Davidson to nominate me. They enthusiastically agreed to do so.

To be eligible for Chief, a candidate must have served at least 10 years in the National Guard as a senior officer, he or she must currently be a sitting major general, and he or she cannot currently be an active duty general officer. This pretty much limits the field to the Vice-Chief, the two Directors, the 54 Adjutant Generals, and the National Guard generals assigned to the various forward units and the major commands.

There were other candidates as well. Major General Don Burdick, the then-Director of Army was a strong candidate as was Major General Robert Ensslin, the Adjutant General of Florida, and Major General Carl Wallace of Tennessee.

The selection board was headed by the Air Force Vice-Chief of Staff, General Monroe Hatch, and composed of three Air Force and two Army generals. In the aftermath of Panama and in the midst of <u>Perpich</u>, the board met to decide the next Chief of the National Guard.

Although this may sound a bit anti-climatic, I was in Jamaica when I learned that on my third try, I'd been recommended to be Chief.

Not long after, I was interviewed by Secretary of Defense Richard Cheney, who made it a policy of speaking with senior officers recommended to lead major commands. Secretary Cheney asked me why I wanted the job and what I would do if selected. I responded that after 13 years, I had a good corporate memory of the Bureau; I was well-known on the Hill; and, I had a lot of experience working on force structure and budget issues. I thought these were going to be the biggest issues facing the Guard now that the Soviet Union and communism were fading, figuratively and literally. Secretary Cheney approved my nomination and forwarded it to President Bush, who appointed me Chief pending U.S. Senate confirmation.

On February 3rd, 1990 I was confirmed as a Lieutenant General by the Senate and was sworn in as Chief of the National Guard Bureau the same day.

Receiving that third star was one of the proudest moments of my life. Secretary Cheney, Chairman of the Joint Chiefs of Staff General Colin Powell, and Secretary of the Air Force Donald Rice attended the ceremony. General Monroe Hatch, Vice-Chief of the Air Force, and my wife, Linda, pinned me. General Carl Vuono, the Army Chief of Staff spoke and presented me with my three-star flag.

I was honored that the great chiefs that had preceded me were all in attendance at the ceremony — Francis Greenlief, LaVerne Weber, Mickey Walker, and Herb Temple, every one of them a legend in the Building, every one of them a close friend of mine. The other living former Chief, Winston P. "Wimpy" Wilson, the only other blue suiter to be Chief, lives in Arkansas and was unable to travel. Also in attendance were the Adjutant Generals of the fifty states and my good friends Major General John Pesch, former Director of the ANG in the 1970s, and Jim "Doc" Weaver, a former National Guard air surgeon and legend in medical circles.

When I took over the Bureau, I knew that thanks to the men and women who had come before me, I was taking over the best-trained and best-equipped National Guard in the history of our nation.

And perhaps the key reason for this was because of the superb leadership guiding the Guard during the past four decades. There is no question that one of the strengths of the modern day National Guard is its unprecedented succession of strong leaders, people of diverse backgrounds who held together and advanced the Guard during some very tough times, and some very good times. Each one put his own particular stamp on the Guard; combined, these made the Guard a first-rate, professional military force.

The job of Chief is unique — he or she needs to have a constant view of the big picture and cannot be consumed by the day-to-day details and minutia. And the men who came before me were ideal in fulfilling this role.

My immediate predecessor, Lieutenant General Herb Temple, was a combat infantryman and veteran and a close friend of President Ronald Reagan and his wife, Nancy. Temple was a superb manager, highly respected within the Pentagon, and one of my close friends. Temple presided over the Guard during the Reagan era, when the budgets were large and the Guard was prominent. He was firmly committed to development of leaders — both in the officer and Non-Commissioned Officer Corps. He firmly believed that a reputation for leadership, particularly in the officer corps, would boost the Guard image in the eyes of the Actives. Central to this vision was shifting officer training away from the states and to the active officer schools.

He was also a strong advocate of the Overseas Deployment Training (ODT) program and the Key Personnel Upgrade Program (KPUP). As briefly mentioned earlier, KPUP was a program that took motivated, individual NCOs and enlisted soldiers and airmen, and placed them next to their active duty counterparts. This gave the Guard member an intense exposure to a the full-time environment and the full time way of doing things. Then, when the KPUP soldier returned to his Guard unit, he could pass along his skills to his fellow Guardsman.

Temple believed in getting the Guard out of the world they were in — the local armory, the sometimes tedious weekend drills — and exposing them to another world altogether.

"Improve image," as Temple used to say, "and strength follows." He was right. Indeed, General Frederick Woerner, NATO commander during the Temple regime, said that the Guard, it's manner, its professionalism, its confidence, changed before his very eyes during the 1980s.

Temple also believed that the CNGB, by virtue of the huge number of soldiers and airmen at his command, should be placed on the Joint Chiefs of Staff. This is a compelling idea — and a long overdue reform which has yet to happen.

Preceding Temple was Lieutenant General Mickey Walker. A highly decorated World War II combat infantryman, he knew the Guard in the critical post-war years and had risen from troop leader to platoon leader, and all the way to three stars. He remembered the Guard as it emerged from the Korean War, the reorganization of units in the states, the bitter fights with the so-called Pentagon whiz kids, and the low strength figures.

Walker had been in the Pentagon during the 1970s and thus was acutely aware of the battles over strength. From his own experience, he remembered the dark days when units averaged 50 to 65 percent strength, with 85 percent strength looked upon as incredible. Indeed, it was Walker who fought to get the Army National Guard to the magic number of 400,000 — and got there.

His passion was recruiting. He knew a time when the unit leaders — the 2nd Lieutenants and NCOs — did recruiting. And not only did these folks have to recruit, they were held responsible for clothing, training, and feeding the entire unit, a constant fight to scare up resources from underfunded state officials. Walker believed that the essence and spirit of recruiting came from the top and in hitting the 400,000 mark, he proved it to everyone.

Walker was also a strong advocate of the Capstone program, which matched Guard units with active duty units in the various theaters. As he said, this irretrievably tied the Guard to the active duty organization and structure.

He also had an interesting observation about the relations of the Guard components with their active counterparts. Walker believed that the Air Force was oriented toward equipment and that was why the Active Air Force was quick to embrace the ANG. The Army, on the other hand, was oriented toward people, which produced inevitable problems because while there was a limited amount of equipment, there was a surplus of personnel and a fertile ground for friction.

Walker's predecessor was LaVern Weber, yet one more giant in the pantheon of Guard leaders.

Weber, as mentioned earlier, had a real feel for the post-World War II National Guard and bemoaned the fact that we had lost the art of recruiting. As with Walker, Weber knew that in the old days, it was the unit leaders who did the recruiting, which was the traditional aspect of the Guard before the All Volunteer Force and the professional recruiting corps. And no doubt because of his background in Ida, Oklahoma, Weber considered the rural areas the backbone of the Guard.

As Weber rose through the ranks, the Guard began demanding a higher level of skill-training from its troops. Prior to World War II, the Guard commitment was two hours a week, usually on Monday nights. The switch to weekend assemblies came in the mid and late 1950s.

Prior to 1955, the Guard enlistee received much of his training in his unit. This entailed the fundamentals — field stripping a rifle, drill and ceremony, basic infantry tactics, and walk throughs on the various equipment a unit had. The Reserve Force Act of 1955 mandated that the actives train the new recruits, in periods lasting from eight weeks to four months.

While serving in the Bureau and later as Chief, Weber was tireless in promoting these reforms, making sure that every unit in every state was following the new regime.

Another of Weber's accomplishments was bringing minorities into the Guard without a lot of upheaval and loss of focus. Weber is quick to claim, even today, that the integration of the military was the most important social event of the century, paving the way for other institutions to integrate later.

Finally, Weber was nearly fanatical about readiness requirements of the Guard linked to the actives.

The Chief preceding Weber was Francis Greenlief, another combat veteran and infantryman who fought at Normandy. If there was a theme to Greenlief's tenure, it was first, his belief in securing modern equipment for the Guard and second, his role as the father of Army Guard aviation.

It was Greenlief's view that the Army was "just used up" under President Johnson — that it had no cohesion; that the increasing lack of discipline corresponded with the number of draftees inducted; that drug use by service members was a huge threat; and that as a result of so many draft deferments being granted, the Army was taking in too much of a thuggish element. Greenlief believed that in many instances, the Guard units were actually better than many of the active units because of the volunteer nature of the Guard and its everyday responsibility to the community. Alas, the Guard was still shortchanged on equipment.

(*Above*) *Chi Chi Rodriguez and me at an Air Force Commanders Conference.*

(*Above*) *Introducing Secretary of the Air Force, Donald Rice to speak before the Adjutants General from the States and Territories. He was a big influence and help in my Presidential appointment as Chief.*

(*Above*) *Paying a visit to the National Guard's Heavy Equipment Maintenance Site, Kaiserslautern, Germany.*

(*Above*) *Here I am with civilian leaders in 1990, chiseling away at the Berlin wall.*

(*Bottom Right*) *Near the oil fields in Southern Kuwait with our Guard/Reserve Chiefs - L to R. BGen Jack D'Araujo, Deputy Director, Army National Guard; MGen Jay Closner, Chief Air Force Reserve; myself; Maj Gen Phil Killey, Director, Air National Guard; Maj Gen William Ward, Chief, Army Reserve.*

MG Bill Ward, USAR, and myself in discussion with local Kuwait representive at Kuwait City.

I am here in Mt. Carmel, Pennsylvania, hometown of Linda, as the grand marshall of their welcome home Desert Storm Parade. A yellow Mustang to go with the yellow ribbons.

On stage in Branson, Missouri with retired Air National Guard Master Sergeant, Grand Old Opry star "Boxcar Willie" and Lt. Col. Willie Davenport, Army National Guard, one of my staff and a former Olympic Gold Medal winner. We are honoring "Boxcar" as one of the great American supporters of our troops in the military.

In the Pentagon with Maj. Gen Jack Flynn, Adjutant General, New York; United States Congressman "Ike" Skelton, (D-MO), and Secretary of the Army, Michael Stone. Congressman Skelton is a member of the House National Security Committee and a strong proponent of the National Guard.

At Quarters One with National Guard legend, MGen Ray Matera, a former Adjutant General, Wisconsin Guard and former president, National Guard Association of the U.S.

Here with my close Kentucky friend, U.S. Congressman William Natcher, Chairman, House Appropriations Committee, at one of many breakfasts at Quarters 1, Ft. McNair.

148

(Top) *With NAACP leader Benjamin Hooks after he presented me with their highest award in recognition of the National Guard's progress in equal opportunity.*

(Center) *At the Punch Bowl National Cemetery in Hawaii with MGen Ed Richardson, the Adj Gen of Hawaii. Behind me is longtime friend, BGen William Spruance and his wife Eunice. Two of the greatest Guard supporters in our history. Bill was former Asst Adj Gen for Air in Delaware. We are here to honor all the National Guard members killed in the Pacific Theater during WW II.*

(Bottom Left) *With my two famous cousins, Carl Clewlow, center, Former Asst. Secretary of Defense and a role model and mentor to me; and John Stanley Hoffman, Lawyer, Henderson, KY and former KY State Legislator, County Judge, and Cabinet Secretary in Kentucky.*

(Bottom Right) *Introducing Cong. Newt Gingrich to speak to National Guard Conference. He also was and remains a great Guard supporter.*

I was blessed with a superb staff throughout my career. At the senior level, I thought I had the best to work National Guard issues. Here in early 1992 L to R - BGen Jack D'Araujo, Deputy Director Army National Guard; MGen Phil Killey, Director, Air National Guard; MGen Billy Navas, Vice Chief National Guard Bureau; myself as Chief in my office in the Pentagon (2E394); MGen Fred Rees, Director, Army National Guard; BGen Don Shepperd, Deputy Director, Air National Guard, and BGen Larry Arnold, Asst. Director, Air National Guard.

My Kentucky friend, W/O Hager Hollon, the inspiration behind the National Guard Marksmanship Program kept me fully informed of their great work. Here with Colonel Kenneth Buster, Commander of the National Guard Marksmanship Training Unit, during a visit to the "Wilson Matches" at Little Rock - 1992.

Cong. Montgomery went two places for Christmas - to Camp David to be with President Bush and his family and to Quarters One to celebrate with our family.

Visiting a one-room school in Jamaica where the National Guard was building a farm-to-market road. We also remoldeled several small schools like this one after duty hours. We were in the area near where General Colin Powell's family lived.

Quarters One, Ft. McNair with Senator Ben "Nighthorse" Campbell, Colorado, first Native American in the U.S. Senate and legendary Congressman Bill Natcher, KY, Chairman, House Appropriations Committee. Mr. Natcher holds the voting record in the house, never missing a vote in more than 40 years.

Presenting an award to U.S. Senator James Sasser (D-TN.) He was a great friend and supporter and is now the U.S. Ambassador to China.

Visiting a National Guard deployment training site in Antiqua.

Informal dinner at Quarters 1 with Greg and Julie Casey. Greg is like another son to us and has been a part of our family for almost 20 years. At this time he was chief of staff to Senator Larry Craig, Idaho. He has since been appointed Sergeant at Arms of the U.S. Senate by Majority Leader Senator Trent Lott, Miss. Julie is legistative assistant to Congressman Hal Rogers, R-KY.

Ready for another official function at the "Guard House," Quarters 1 with our trusted and superb aide - Sergeant Major David Velasquez. We were blessed to have the best assistant in the Army to help during the busy four years as Chief.

152

In September, 1992 in Homestead, Florida after Hurricane Andrew. I took a Congressional Delegation down led by Cong. Sonny Montgomery to see the Guard and U.S. Military helping restore the community. The worst devastation I had ever seen.

With Maj Jet Jernigan, South Carolina ANG after we returned from a F-16 training mission. Jet is "America at its Best." His unit won the Air Force's "Gunsmoke" competition as the best and they also performed with distinction in combat during Desert Storm.

Discussions with Colonel Wayne Gosnell and Col. Frank Van Fleet aboard our aircraft enroute to Europe to visit the Baltics and the emerging Eastern Europe Democracies.

In November 1992, as I first arrived in Riga, Lativa on our historic trip to the Baltics.

Laying a wreath at monument in Riga, Latvia, on the Latvian Independence Day in 1992.

In my office with Senator John Warner, R-VA, a powerful member of the Senate Armed Services Committee. We are discussing National Guard issues and of course, the Virginia National Guard.

355th birthday of the National Guard. America's oldest military service. Here with guest of honor, U.S. Senator Pete Domenici, New Mexico; (L to R) Lt. Gen Donald Parker, Director, U.S. Army Staff; U.S. Air Force Asst. Secretary Gary Cooper; Asst. Secretary of Defense for Reserve Affairs, Steve Duncan; and far right Lt. Gen Charles May, Asst. Vice Chief, U.S. Air Force.

In the Pentagon with the legendary "mayor of the Pentagon," Doc Cooke. I always called him "governor" because I always dealt with governors. He is Mr. Pentagon and takes care of all administrative and logistics needs for the world's largest office building.

Presenting the top National Guard award, "The Eagle" to U.S. Congressman Jack Murtha, D-PA, Chairman, House Defense Appropiations Subcommittee. Mr. Murtha is a superb supporter of a strong National Guard and a good friend.

Dedication of the new Army National Guard Readiness Center, Arlington, VA. Major General Fred Rees, Director, ARNG; myself; Doc Cooke, Administrative Chief of the Pentagon; Arlington County Board Chairwoman Helen Bozman; Cong. Sonny Montgomery; Lt Gen (Ret) Herb Temple (former chief); Maj Gen Billy Navas, Vice Chief, National Guard Bureau.

At Quarters 1 with our long-time friend and true supporter of the Guard, Senator Ted Stevens, Alaska, now Chairman of the Senate Appropiations Committee.

My staff at NGB (L to R) Carol Lagasse, Rosemary Walts, Maj. Phil Lennert, Col. Frank Van Fleet, me, Maj. Ken Gonzales, Maj. Gen Bill Navas, Maj. Dave Spahr, MSgt. Frances Burke, and MSgt. Barbara Strylowski.

Here I am just short of "heaven" with our six grandsons. Left to Right Matthew Conaway; Daniel Conaway; Samuel Williams; Joseph Williams; Michael Conaway; and Johnny Conaway. Six angels all with famous biblical names.

In my office in the Pentagon with D.C. National Guard Youth.

January, 1993, behind our quarters at Ft. McNair. President Clinton was president for three days and stands here with me and my mother-in-law, Dorothy Narcavage, The President knew me when he was governor. He said "General, they take pretty good care of the Chief of the National Guard with this house here on the Potomac." I replied "Yes sir, they sure do, but not nearly as good as the quarters they provide you." Linda was the photographer here.

Key in my decision making process was my senior staff - the National Guard Executive Council, 1993, (L to R) sitting Brig Gen. Bill Bilo; Maj. Gen. Phil Killey; Maj. Gen. Fred Rees; myself; Maj. Gen. Jack D'Araujo; Brig. Gen. Don Shepperd; Mr. Tom Link (standing) Brig Gen. Larry Arnold; Col. Cheryl Brown; Col. Ken Rhoades.

Breakfast meeting, Quarters #1 with (sitting L to R) Congressman Robert Stump (R-AZ); Congresswoman Beverly Byron (D-MD); standing, me; Congressman Sonny Montgomery (D-Miss), Secretary Derwinski, Head of U.S. Department of Veterans Affairs.

With the most able Secretary of Defense, William Perry and Congresswoman Jane Byrne, D-VA; and Maj Gen Roberta Mills, Tennessee Air National Guard our first two-star female in the history of the National Guard. To the right is my good friend Lt Gen Minter Alexander, Deputy Asst. Secretary of Defense for Military Personnel Policy

158

With U.S. Senate Majority Leader, Robert Dole. A true friend of the military, the Guard and Reserve.

With President Clinton and Speaker Foley.

"The beat goes on," Forrest City, Arkansas in 1993. Thirty years of living Chiefs of the National Guard. L to R - Lt Gen Vern Weber (1974 - 1982); Maj Gen Fran Greenlief (1971 - 1974); Maj Gen Winston P. Wilson (1963 - 1971); Lt Gen Mickey Walker (1982 - 1986); Lt Gen Herbert R. Temple (1986 - 1990); Lt Gen John B. Conaway (1990 - 1994)

159

In Illinois with Asst. Secretary of Defense for Reserve Affairs, Deborah Lee visiting Guardmen and women during the great Midwest floods.

As Chief, meeting with the father of the Total Force Policy, former Secretary of Defense Melvin Laird.

Linda, as usual, entertaining as the first lady of the National Guard. Here with two of our Pennsylvania friends at Quarters One, General & Mrs. George Joulwan, Commander, Supreme Headquarters Allied Forces Europe.

My retirement in the courtyard of the Pentagon. Here are Gen David Jones, former Chairman, JCS, and the person who brought me to Washington; Secretary of the Air Force, Sheila Widnall, the first female Service Secretary; then Deputy Secretary of Defense, William Perry and my friend Cong. Sonny Montgomery, Miss.

At my retirement ceremony in the Hall of Heroes in the Pentagon with General Merrill (Tony) McPeak, Chief of Staff, U.S. Air Force and Secretary of Defense, Les Aspin.

At my retirement ceremony in the Pentagon Courtyard. Linda and I, our final farewell with our great National Guard troops.

Conaway family reunion - Henderson, Ky - 1995 First row L to R - Grandsons Johnny, Matthew, Danny, Michael, Joey. Second row L to R - Me holding grandson Samuel; Dad and Mother. standing L to R - Linda; Julie and son Bo; Ellen and husband Greg Williams; Cyndi and son Dave; Cathy and son Dan.

To Fran, modern equipment was the key to a motivated, competent force. And as Chief and later as a hugely successful Executive Director of NGAUS, Fran fought determinedly to bring better equipment into the Guard. Force structure meant nothing if the personnel were not equipped.

Greenlief also viewed Vietnam through the prism of Guardsman who'd been called up in World War II. He pointed out, and it was a tenet of Secretary of Defense McNamara's as well, "that once you began using the Guard in Vietnam, you spend it — you can't go back for more." He was also cognizant that with so much energy and manpower directed toward Asia, there was a need for backfill for Europe.

Greenlief carries the title of "Father of Army Guard Aviation." He went to and passed — at not a tender age — flight school after being alarmed about the number of Guard aviation accidents. Typical of Fran's hand's on leadership, he saw a problem and instead of setting up a some kind of commission and writing endless memos about the subject, he drove straight at the matter and solved it.

His biggest regret was that the Army and the Guard were slow to appreciate the need for civil disturbance training. The failure to recognize Watts in 1965 and to prepare for such disaster could have helped the Guard in Detroit, Newark, and at Kent State. Like Weber, Greenlief was also present during the opening of the Guard to black Americans. And he gives credit to General Winston P. "Wimpy" Wilson as the true figure in integration, the man who convinced the state organizations to remove the barriers to blacks.

Even as this historic process got underway, Greenlief knew that there would have to be more blacks in the Guard because simply put, the Guard needed strength. And so during the summer of 1971, he announced that his goal was to double the number of blacks in the Guard, from two to four percent. Ever the can-do troop, Greenlief delivered on his promise.

And of course, one of our greatest legends was our Chief from 1963 to 1971, Major General Winston P. "Wimpy" Wilson from Arkansas. General Wilson was appointed by President John F. Kennedy and really brought the Army and Air National Guard through a tumultuous period in the 1960s and set it on the path to become a strong, stable, integrated force it is today.

He had the Guard working closer with the active force than ever before in history. He was the founder of the Air Force's Gaining Command program, which allowed the Air Guard to work closely with Air Force units. He was relentless in our modernization efforts for both components. He was also the first airmen, or "blue suiter" to be appointed Chief, National Guard Bureau. Wimpy was a man far, far ahead of his time.

Every one of my predecessors deserves the ever-lasting credit of everyone who has ever served in the Guard.

The Army Guard in 1989 was 457,000 strong, the 11th largest army in the world and contained 40 percent of the active Army combat strength and 10 of the Army's 28 divisions. The Air National Guard was the fourth largest Air Force in the world and numbered 110,000 personnel who were at the highest state of readiness ever.

The 1980s had given us better equipment, better training, overseas deployments, and a nation-building component.

I knew that I was inheriting some controversial issues from the 1980s, chief among these the <u>Perpich</u> case. But one thing I didn't foresee was that the Guard, on my watch, was to play a vital role in one of the great U.S. military crusades of the post-World War II era.

General Temple had done an outstanding job in bringing the Guard along in readiness levels, professionalism, training and education. One of my primary goals was to further enhance readiness, which I saw as critical in performing both the federal and the state missions.

Another goal was to move the Guard toward performing what I call "new traditional missions." As Vice-Chief, I had seen first-hand the problems beginning to plague America — narcotics, crime, a devaluing of education, unfocused youth, and the rise of a permanent underclass. The Guard had 4,600 units in 3,200 communities and with this presence, I knew we could do our share at the local level — our traditional role — to make real progress against these seemingly intractable social problems — our new mission.

Third, I also wanted to continue the process of building a force that resembled America. The Guard had come a long way in integrating the force under the strong leadership of Generals Greenlief, Weber, Walker, and Temple and I wanted to make sure I continued that progress.

My overarching vision was that we should look like the communities we represented in terms of race, ethnicity, and gender. Later this aspiration would pay off, as it did during the L.A. riots, when the Guard on the streets of South Central Los Angeles was more than 20 percent black and Hispanic and was led by a Hispanic division commander, Major General Danny Hernandez.

However, my most immediate concern was finding someone to fill my old billet. Having left an empty chair in the Vice-Chief's office, it was imperative we fill that position as soon as possible. By statute, the post had to be filled by a green-suiter. The top competitors were Major General Don Burdick, Director of the Army National Guard; Major General Joe Boyersmith, the Army National Guard Assistant to the Special Operations Command; Major General Ed Baca, the Adjutant General of New Mexico; and Brigadier General Billy Navas, the former Adjutant General of Puerto Rico and the current Deputy Director of the Army National Guard.

Brigadier General Navas was eventually selected and became the highest ranking minority ever to serve in the Bureau until Lieutenant General Ed Baca, the former Adjutant General of New Mexico, took over as Chief when he succeeded me in 1994.

Next on my agenda was formation of the Joint Executive Committee (JEC), consisting of the six Bureau generals, the heads of the Army and Air Readiness Centers, the Senior Executive Service (SES) civilian Tom Link, and his deputies, Colonel Ken Stilley and later Colonel Cheryl Brown. The purpose of the JEC was to set the direction for the Guard during my tenure as Chief. Our first action was the development of a 10-point policy statement sent out to all the units.

In June of 1990, we organized a trip to Europe for the Executive Leadership Council (ELC), an organization composed of African-American executives from Fortune 500 companies. General Temple had started the program when Chief and I thought it was extremely worthwhile. The purpose of the ELC was two-fold: We wanted to give these executives an understanding of the Guard so that as role models for young black Americans, they might spread the word about the Guard. We also wanted to involve their corporations in our program of Employer Support of the Guard and Reserve. Also along on the trip were District of Columbia Guard leaders Major General Cal Franklin and Major General Russell Davis.

Before our departure, we had a reception for the group in the White House Indian Treaty Room which was attended by General Powell and President Bush's Chief of Staff, Sam Skinner. We then flew to Brussels for a reception and briefings at NATO headquarters. From there, we flew to Ramstein Air Force Base in Germany where we met with then-Brigadier General Johnny Wilson, now in charge of ordnance for U.S. Army, Europe. As the trip progressed, I was gently prodded by members of the group to take the whole party on a quick jaunt to Berlin, which at that time was experiencing the peaceful convulsions of unification and the destruction of the Berlin Wall.

I called a few folks I knew in Europe and finally, my good friend and fellow Kentuckian, Lieutenant General Ted Rees, Vice-Commander of the U.S. Air Force, Europe, was kind enough to arrange transportation and clearance for a side trip to Berlin.

We flew in the West's air corridor into Tempelhoff air base in Berlin. A bus met us there and we drove right up to Checkpoint Charlie at the Berlin Wall. Ever efficient, the Air Force provided hammers and chisels and everyone in the group got the opportunity to break off pieces of the graffiti-scarred Wall. We returned to our trip itinerary soon thereafter. The trip was such a tremendous success that we arranged another to Central America in 1991, stopping in Panama, Costa Rica, Honduras, Guatemala, and Belize.

As part of the public outreach efforts, I also made a point of participating in the "Boss Lifts" to our "Business and Industry Days" at the Professional Military Education Centers (PMEC). These events were tied to the graduation ceremonies at the centers, and provided a chance for employers to see their Guard employees receive recognition for completing Guard education courses.

The Air Guard I.G. Brown Professional Military Education Center was in Knoxville and run by Colonel Ed Morrissey and Chief Master Sergeant Paul Lankford. The Army Guard's LaVerne Weber Professional Education Center was located at Camp Robinson, in North Little Rock, Arkansas and was run at that time by Colonel Richard Wilhelm.

Our customary drill was to fly employers to the PMEC the afternoon before graduation. We'd have a big reception that night, during which we'd introduce the employers to everyone. The next morning, the employers would have breakfast in the Mess Hall, attend several briefings, including one by me, receive a tour of the facility, and then attend the graduation. We always tried to have several influential corporate and government executives, such as Governor Dreyfus of Wisconsin, as our special guests.

The entire affair was great for public relations and provided a real morale boost for our National Guard personnel. It was also an opportunity for key decision makers to see the Guard up close and personal. And I can tell you from experience, if your patriotism didn't swell up during these graduation ceremonies with all the bands and flags and marching uniformed troops, it never would.

The Academy at Knoxville has been the focal point of all our young officer and NCO training in the Air Guard and I give the cadre there tremendous credit for our ascendancy to the next level of professionalism. This same level of training is also being conducted at the Lavern Weber Professional Educational Center at Camp Robinson in Arkansas, for the Army Guard.

Drug missions were becoming an unusually heavy part of the Guard workload in FY-90, with the Guard pulling an amazing 5,155 support operations. During peak marijuana eradication season, it was not uncommon to have 2.400 volunteer National Guard personnel on duty on a given day. There were a wide range of duties in these support operations, including aerial and ground reconnaissance and surveillance, cargo inspection at airports, border entry points and seaports, transportation of law enforcement personnel within states, and training in close-quarters tactics.

In 1990 the Guard assisted in operations in which 6.7 million marijuana plants were destroyed; $18.3 million in cash was recovered; 34,000 pounds of cocaine, 487 pounds of heroin, and 27,000 pounds of processed marijuana was confiscated; 466 vehicles were impounded; 614 weapons and 63,000 rounds of ammunition were seized; and more than 1,300 individuals were arrested.

US Customs told us that with Guard assistance, they were able to inspect 14 percent of all containers entering the United States, up from 4 percent prior to Guard support. As a result of this increased activity, we added a new NGB division in 1990, the Counterdrug Division.

We also had other victories. Readiness was at an all time high and we were receiving the funding needed to get the job done. There was, for example, $29 billion in the ARNG equipment inventory, an amazing 75 percent of the wartime requirement.

In FY 1990, the ANG had a phenomenal retention figure, losing only 10 percent of our personnel with under 10 years of service. The tactical reconnaissance element of the Air Guard, always something I kept my eye on, went to the Reconnaissance Air Meet in 1990, a worldwide competition at Bergstrom AFB, and the Nevada Air Guard with their RF-4s took first place.

In July of 1990, with six months under my belt, I was fortunate to spend a weekend with the family at Quarters One. This was a beautiful brick home on the Fort McNair grounds, overlooking the Potomac River, in which Linda and I were to live for nearly four years.

My eldest son David, a Navy F-18 pilot on the USS *Saratoga*, was about to depart on a six-month deployment in the Persian Gulf. He'd flown against the Libyans in 1986 and was looking forward to a quiet cruise. He was with his wife, Cyndi, and their sons, Michael and Johnny. My second son, Daniel, an electrical engineer with A-K Steel in Middletown, Ohio, was there with his wife, Cathy, and their sons Matthew and Danny. My daughter, Ellen, who worked on Capitol Hill, was there with her husband Greg Williams, as were my youngest son, Bo, and his wife, Julie, from Evansville, Indiana.

Everyone was there, tumbling around on the lawns and running through every room of Quarters One. Although I do not talk about it much in these pages, my family has always been the foundation of my life, bringing a sense of worth and meaning to me far beyond the number of stars on my shoulders.

Perhaps the biggest issue during the spring of 1990 was the administration's first real attempt to draw down the force. Everyone knew it was coming. The world landscape had changed. The massive threat posed by the Soviet Union had ebbed and although new kinds of conflicts were bound to arise, the pressure was building to trim the size of the defense establishment.

Kim Wincup, the Assistant Secretary of the Army for Manpower, Personnel and Reserve Affairs, testified on March 5, 1990 that "Whatever shape the reshaped force takes, it must be capable of rapid expansion if required by unanticipated shifts in the international security environment." Prescient words, to be sure.

Even though we knew reductions were inevitable, the force structure plans outlined by the Joint Chiefs, with White House concurrence, were startling. The Army Guard, currently at 457,000 personnel, was to downsize to 321,000 by FY 1995. The Army Reserves would drop from 315,000 to 230,000.

The Air Guard, however, would fare better. It would essentially remain stable at 118,000 because we were tasked with a number of Air Force missions. As well, the Active Air Force was scheduled to come down from 600,000 in 1990 to 435,000 by FY 95.

The Guard Bureau, as with the other components, was essentially told by the Administration, "Here's your number for FY 95. You tell us how you're going to get there."

Such a force reduction policy was unprecedented and seemed imprudent to me. My reasoning was that when you make large reductions in your active force, you're insurance policy and ace in the hole is your Guard and Reserve forces. At the very least, you should leave them alone, if not increase their size. This is especially true if you want to maintain a force with the capability to fight and win two regional contingencies. If you shrink the actives, you need a stable Guard and Reserve for the manpower they provide if you expect to fight regional wars. You also should not reduce the Guard and Reserve until you have reduced the Active force to their planned level. This allows the Guard and Reserve to absorb Active personnel who want to continue serving.

But this was not the strategy of the decision makers in the administration. Their concept was to reduce all the service components down on the same ramp. Unfortunately and inexplicably, they weren't taking into account the dual mission of the Guard or the attitudes of the 54 governors and the 535 members of Congress.

Strength reduction became the intense summer debate of 1990. Until August 3rd.

CHAPTER ELEVEN

"THE GUARD IN DESERT SHIELD AND STORM"

"By the authority vested in me as President by the Constitution and the laws of the United States of America, including sections 121 and 673b of title 10 of the United States Code, I hereby determine that it is necessary to augment the active armed forces of the United States for the effective conduct of operational missions in and around the Arabian Peninsula. Further, under the stated authority, I hereby authorize the Secretary of Defense to order to active duty units of the Selected Reserve."

George Bush, Executive Order 12727, Ordering the Selected Reserve of the Armed Forces to Active Duty
August 22, 1990

October 27th, 1990.

Aboard the National Guard C-22, we flew east toward Riyadh. The plane had traced a route across the eastern Mediterranean, turning south at Turkey, down the coast of Israel, across the Suez then to Jettah, Saudi Arabia, where the pilot had simply turned left to cut over to Riyadh.

As we circled the air strip, I heard the pilot announce us as "Boxer Zero One", the call sign for the Chief of the National Guard Bureau when traveling with the 201st Airlift Squadron out of Andrews Air Force Base. The next morning, we were scheduled to meet with General Norman Schwartzkopf, the theater commander of the largest American combat force assembled anywhere since Vietnam.

At the time, there were several thousand National Guard soldiers and airmen living in tents and holes in the vast expanse of Saudi Arabian desert. How this entire situation had come about was a testament to the key role of the Guard in this sudden and unforeseen contingency known as Operation Desert Shield.

President Bush's August 22nd mobilization order sent the National Guard Bureau into high gear. The Army had the authority to order a maximum of 25,000 Guard and Reserve troops for combat support and combat service support. The number for the Air Guard and Air Reserve personnel was 14,500. The day after President Bush's announcement, I sent the following message to the states:

"From: Chief, National Guard Bureau

Alert Order [#1] for Presidential Call-up of Selected Reserve, date-time-group 241405Z, 69 Army National Guard units federalized in support of Operation DESERT SHIELD."

Ironically, the first Army National Guard unit to be notified of the call to active duty was determined by a coin toss. Two separate unit mobilization orders had come into the Emergency Operations Center of the Alabama Army National Guard from the Department of the Army at 0200 hours on August 27th. Realizing the significance of the occasion, the three officers on duty flipped a coin to determine which unit would be notified first. Thus, the 1241st Adjutant General Company (Postal) Alabama ARNG became the first Army Guard unit to be involuntarily federalized since 1970. The 1207th Quartermaster Detachment (Water Purification) was second.

But even before the official mobilization orders were cut, the Guard had already demonstrated its commitment. Five South Carolina Army Guard volunteers from the 228th Signal Brigade arrived at Central Command Headquarters on August 9th, some of the first U.S. troops to enter the theater.

And, in numbers that would swell into the thousands, individuals volunteered to go on active-duty status. Indeed, the 105th Military Airlift Group from Stewart Air Force Base, New York, began flying C-5 missions on August 6th, within 72 hours of the Iraqi invasion of Kuwait. Nearly 90 percent of the 105th's pilots, flight engineers, and loadmasters volunteered to fly missions to the Persian Gulf. The 190th Air Refueling Group from Topeka, Kansas had deployed six KC-135 aircraft to the theater on August 10th; ANG aeromedical units began moving to the Gulf a day later.

Another unit that came forward, as they always have in the past, was the 117th Tactical Reconnaissance Wing (TRW), an RF-4 unit from Birmingham, Alabama; true to form, they had more than 300 volunteers in the United Arab Emirates by August 30th. The Alabama Air and Army National Guard were the folks who seemingly always had their hands up for missions and we affectionately referred to them as the "Mercenary Volunteers." When speaking around the country, I would frequently observe that I didn't know what was in the water down there, but it seems as soon as you're born in Alabama, you raise your right hand and take the Guard oath. They routinely had between 25,000 to 30,000 soldiers and airmen in the Alabama National Guard, the highest per capita in the nation.

Another example of volunteerism was the venerable 190th Special Operations Group from Middletown, Pennsylvania, which deployed four EC-130s, the Volant Solo aircraft, to the Gulf on August 28th. Like many units, the 190th's deployment began as an all-volunteer operation with a rotation of personnel every 35 to 40 days.

We in the Bureau decided not to mobilize the 190th as long as the volunteer status kept the unit running. We kept that status until late January when changes to the mission called for a partial mobilization.

Even in an all-volunteer status, the 190th was responsible for an incredible level of operation. With an average of 14 flying hours per day for over 60 consecutive days, their crews and, most importantly, their maintenance people were stretched to the limit. It was a testament to the skill and professionalism for the unit to keep working at this tremendous pace. All told, in the first three weeks of Operation Desert Shield, the ANG had 2,800 people from 68 units in 40 states volunteer to serve on active duty. It wasn't until August 24th that the 183rd Military Airlift Squadron of the 172nd Military Airlift Group based at Jackson, Mississippi, the 137th Military Airlift Squadron of the 105th Military Airlift Group, from Stewart Air Force Base, New York, (most of whose personnel had already been participating in Operation Desert Shield for several weeks) and the 136th Aerial Port Squadron, Texas Air National Guard, became the first ANG units to be formally activated as part of the call up.

In conjunction with the heavy volunteerism and the formal unit activations there were a great number of inspiring and heartwarming stories of units being mobilized prior to shipping out. Major General Carl Wallace, Adjutant General of Tennessee, personally said farewell to each unit mobilized and presented the unit commander and First Sergeant with a Tennessee flag. When the 547th Transportation Company from the District of Columbia Guard was mobilized, there was an outpouring of support from the D.C. community — streets lined with flag-waving citizens, yellow ribbons tied to trees, and as always, the emotional scenes with husband and wives saying goodbye to each other and their children. Major General Cal Franklin, D.C.'s Commanding General, was at each event in the District.

The family and community support for the call-up throughout the nation was tremendous, offering solid proof of the popular support for Desert Shield and President Bush's decision to call up the Guard and Reserve.

In his autobiography, General Schwartzkopf recalled that when he got to Riyadh, he knew he'd have to call on the Guard and Reserves for their special capabilities, noting that he needed, "cooks, water purification, stevedores, truck drivers, heavy vehicle mechanics, engineers, and quartermaster companies that did everything from mail to laundry." These were less glamorous units than the jet pilots and tank drivers but they make an organization run. The Air Force, on the other hand, had a critical need for transport and tanker capabilities as well as communications and engineering units.

There was a catch, however, in the mobilization announcement made by Secretary Cheney. It was the kind of glitch which would fester and prove to cause serious problems later. On August 24th, Secretary Cheney published implementing instructions which allowed the Army to call up only combat support and combat service support units. As no less than General Schwartzkopf would later write, "This decision to eschew calling Army Guard combat units, apparently struck at the staff level in the Department of Army in connection with the staff of the Joint Chiefs of Staff (JCS), came one day after General Carl E. Vuono, Chief of Staff of the Army, told senior military association executives, including a representative from NGAUS, that the call up of the 48th Infantry Brigade [a mechanized unit serving as the Round Out Brigade for the 24th Infantry Division] would be announced the next day. It was not to occur for more than three months."

It is important to point out that the Navy, Air Force, and Marines were under no restrictions with regard to calling up their reserve component combat personnel. In fact, ultimately, the U.S. Marine Corps Reserve's 8th Tank Battalion was mobilized, deployed and participated in the attack on Kuwait City in late February of 1991, although they were not as well-equipped nor at the readiness levels of the Army Guard units when they were mobilized.

On August 27th, Headquarters, Department of the Army, federalized 19 ARNG units with 482 soldiers in 14 states. All 19 units met deployability criteria and reported no major problems with recalling and assembling their soldiers. By September 1st, just 10 days after the President's announcement, nearly 5,000 ARNG soldiers had been federalized in 20 units.

On the 7th of September, Secretary of Defense Cheney reported that the U.S. had 100,000 U.S. troops in the Gulf. Two days later, President Bush and President Mikhail Gorbachev met and issued a joint statement demanding that Iraq withdraw from Kuwait. By mid-September, the United Nations Security Council had denounced the invasion, called for withdrawal of all Iraqi troops from Kuwait, demanded that Iraq release the British and Americans held in Kuwait and detained by the Iraqis, imposed trade and financial embargoes on Iraq and Kuwait, and determined that only UN Sanctions Committee could permit, food, medicine, and other humanitarian aid to enter Iraq and occupied Kuwait. One month later, under UN Security Council Resolution of October 24, the Iraqis were held liable for war damages.

During this same time, President Bush was steadily building an international coalition to array against Saddam. On September 14, the United Kingdom announced it would deploy 6,000 troops and 120 tanks to the Gulf. The next day, the French government declared it would deploy 4,000 troops to Saudi Arabia. Not long after, Egypt agreed to send a mechanized infantry unit of 15,000 men.

By September 15th, the United States had 150,000 troops, 420 combat aircraft, and 250 support aircraft in South West Asia. One month later that troop total was nearly 200,000.

In late September, I had the same conversation with Secretary of

Defense Cheney that I'd had with Colin Powell on August 9th, in which I pretty much said, 'We have all the units, including combat formations you need to augment the Active Forces. I recommend a further call-up of the Guard, including combat units, to show Congress and the American people that the Total Force, built with great effort, actually works."

By 30 September, 6,900 ARNG troops had been federalized; just 386 ANG personnel had been activated but an amazing 4,000 were serving as volunteers on active duty. This willingness of the men and women of the National Guard to volunteer exemplifies the finest tradition of the Guard service to this nation. Of course, this did not surprise me. Every day of every year I saw this kind of dedication in response to local and state emergencies.

During September and October, I'd spoken by telephone several times with General Schwartzkopf in Riyadh regarding our National Guard units under his command. He was always upbeat about our men and women, assuring me they were doing their jobs well and that their morale was good. Indeed, I consider him one of the great battlefield commanders since World War II, a man who knew his troops, had an instinctive grasp of the public's mood, and was a superb leader.

General Schwartzkopf was the theater commander and as such, exercised tight control over the military and civilian personnel coming to the theater. He received a great many requests from Members of Congress, DOD civilians, and American and foreign military commanders to visit the troops. General Schwartzkopf knew that he'd become a professional greeter if he allowed everyone with a passport to come see the operation in Saudi.

I was aware of his reluctance to host visitors but I was convinced that it was important for me to see the job the Guard was performing firsthand.

I sent a fax to General Schwartzkopf's office in October and soon thereafter, got his clearance to come over and see our Guard troops. There was one condition attached: my traveling party must be small, just five or six people due to the logistical and transportation problems in Saudi Arabia during the buildup.

On October 26th, myself, Major General Don Burdick, Director of the Army Guard; Major General Bill Ward, Chief of the U.S. Army Reserve; Major General Phil Killey, Director of the Air National Guard; my executive assistant, Lieutenant Colonel Bill Davis, and several other staff, left for the desert.

We took off from Andrews Air Force Base on an autumn evening and flew to Ramstein Air Base, Germany, where we spent the night. The next day we flew to Ishmir, Turkey and that night we flew over the desert into Riyadh. While in the plane, we changed into our desert camouflaged fatigues.

I caught my initial impression of Saudi Arabia peering out of the windows of the C-22: long, thin lines of light stretching out into the desert, superhighways leaving the big cities in every direction like the spokes of a wheel.

After driving into downtown Riyadh from the airport, we went to a hotel where many of the coalition troops were staying. The next morning, we went to Central Command headquarters. The first thing I noticed, which pleased me, was that both active and Guard and reserve officers and enlisted were working together in the Command Headquarters. We were briefed by Marine Brigadier General Johnson on the overall situation.

After filling us in, both he and Brigadier General Buster Glosson asked about the mood in America. These guys hadn't been out of Saudi since arriving here in August and I don't think they really trusted the press reports they received. We said the overall morale of the American people was good and that the public was increasingly engaged in news of the buildup.

Then we met with General Schwartzkopf.

He was sitting at his desk and I could see a bed and his living quarters in the same room also. With us, he was not the mercurial guy of whom we'd hear so much about later. He knew Generals Ward and Burdick from the past. Indeed, General Burdick had been commander of the 48th Brigade when Schwartzkopf was 24th Division commander; General Ward was a 1950 West Point graduate and had known Schwartzkopf for many years.

General Schwartzkopf got right to the point and told us he needed more Guard and Reserve combat service and combat service support units. In about the same breath, he reiterated that the units already in the Gulf were performing admirably.

And then I brought up the two round-out brigades and the fact they hadn't been called up yet.

He said to me, "I hear ya John, I hear ya. That's for the politicians back in Washington to figure out. What I need now is more support units and that's what you guys have a lot of. If we get call-up authority for a longer period of time, I'd love to see the brigades called up and deployed over here." It was obvious he did not want to deal with the guard combat brigade issue. This surprised me because he gained the 48th Brigade as a roundout brigade when he was 24th Infantry Division Commander at Fort Stewart in Georgia. At the same time, it was clear he was very pleased with our Guard units over there. And I knew he had much on his mind besides the round-out Brigades.

He also wanted us to see Major General Gus Pagonis, the Desert Shield logistics czar, who was using a lot of the Guard and Reserve units. He went on to say that he liked the Air Guard tactical control units, the one assigned with the Central Command here in Riyadh and the other with the 24th ID out in the northern Saudi desert. He also said that the best thing we could do would be to go out and see the National Guard troops and help ease their nervousness regarding the 90-day call-up deadline closing in on them with no real movement towards an extension. He said, "Look, John it's pretty damn obvious they're [the

Guard personnel] not going home — we're working right now for an extension and we're gonna get it. They'll have to stay."

Schwartzkopf finished by saying he realized that having the Guard over here generated a lot of public support for the operation and that the support would probably grow as we shipped more units over.

We then met with General Buster Glosson and General Charlie Horner, the air strategists who planned the relentless forty-day campaign against Saddam's military targets. They briefed us on the Air Guard contributions thus far to the operation. We were also pleased to see that the Air Guard and Reserve officers were represented on Horner's Ridyah staff, including Brigadier General Mike Hall, Wing Commander of the New York Air Guard F-16 unit, the famed "Boys from Syracuse."

We left the bunker and traveled out to the new base being built near Ridyah, which was later to host the F-16 units from South Carolina and New York and the C-130 unit from St. Joseph, Missouri, with all the planes operating from one strip.

Next, we went to the United Arab Emirates and saw the air base there with its long runways, huge hangers, and tent cities; the Birmingham guys and gals were ready to stay there forever. The commander was from Shaw Air Force Base in South Carolina and he'd fostered a fantastic active-Guard integration on the base.

Next we flew to Dhahran and visited with the 1st Tactical Fighter Wing from Langley, commanded by Brigadier General McBroom. Finally, we went to see Major General Gus Pagonis and had lunch at his Headquarters. After chow, we went out to the field to see the water drilling and purification unit from North Dakota Army Guard. That's when I finally realized what our folks were up against. Walking around out there in the sun, with the desolate landscape reaching to the horizon in every direction, the remote feeling of the encampment, the fleas, the sand storms — all of this brought home what our National Guard soldiers were going through.

A lot of them, as General Schwartzkopf had said, were perplexed. When I spoke with some of the enlisted troops, the typical comment was, "Hey sir, our orders are up in 10 days. What's gonna happen?" It was obvious that some of them didn't want to hear my answer, which was "The issue is being worked in Washington for a 90-day extension."

In addition, there was also a lot of uncertainty about the mission. The troops wondered, "Are we gonna sit here for six or nine months and charge them or are they going to charge us?" Uncertainty was the order of the day. And frankly, the so-called "big picture" was not really clear to the troops until December when Saddam was given a date to withdraw from Kuwait. From their ground-level view, most of the troops with whom I spoke didn't think he would retreat. So when the January 15th drop-dead date was announced, everyone got a real sense of purpose.

General Pagonis was overjoyed with our troops. He simply was not prepared for the innate talents our troops displayed, particularly our senior NCOs, many of whom had a longstanding knowledge about the equipment and procedures that the younger, less experienced active duty soldiers didn't posses. The Guard personnel were typically the men and women from the trucking firm, the water board, the engineering business, or the county administration office in Hometown USA. To them, the jobs they were performing were the jobs they'd been doing their entire working lives. Furthermore, they had long years of service in their Guard units, training for the mission they were now performing. To a logistics maestro like General Pagonis, they were the kind of wizards that could make a complicated logistics operation hum like a perfectly timed engine.

It was astonishing to see the mass of equipment coming in to his base at Dhahran. My first thought was that there simply couldn't be enough truck drivers to haul this mass of gear all over Saudi Arabia. It was also amazing to see the modern ports with state-of-the-art facilities to handle this influx of cargo. All I could think was, thank goodness the Saudis had the foresight — and the money — to erect this incredible infrastructure. The fact is, we will never go to war again with this kind of back-up logistics base.

Significantly, the port facilities also brought home to me the fact that the long pole in the tent is sealift — the ability to get the units there with their heavy equipment.

On the next leg of the trip, we flew to Jeddah to see the Air Guard KC-135 tanker operation, a vital ingredient in a theater this large. It was a beautiful airport — about like Dulles or Dallas/Fort-Worth if you double them in size and design.

Equally amazing was the smoothness of the operation. What a sight — the Air Guard units were from Tennessee, Pennsylvania, and Kansas and were working interchangeably with Active Duty and Reserve units everywhere you looked. In fact, the senior ranking officer, Colonel Mike Byers, a Guardsman from Kansas, was the Joint Task Force Commander. The great thing about the Air Force is that no one cares what service — active, Guard, or Reserve — is in charge. It is always the senior man or woman. And if they can't hack it, it's the next senior person in line. Colonel Byers did a superb job and remained the commander throughout the entire war. He also worked seamlessly with Saudi Air Force personnel and their maintenance equipment, performing continuous refueling exercises with them. This operation was a superb example of the Total Force in action. Both Generals Burdick and Ward were deeply impressed with this Air Force integration.

That night, as we left Saudi Arabia in the jet, I looked down and saw the distant lights of the U.S.S. Saratoga battle group floating in the Red Sea. I felt a deep sense of pride as well as concern as we flew over the aircraft carrier on which my son, David, served. I knew it was only a matter of time until he would be flying combat missions in the skies over Iraq.

We flew up the Red Sea going north, over Egypt, across the Suez, past Israel, and then to Ishmir where we landed and spent the night. The next morning, we were off to Madrid, Spain, then over to the Azores to refuel, then to St. Johns, Newfoundland. And then finally home to Andrews.

The same week we returned, on November 8th, President Bush ordered 100,000 more troops to Southwest Asia in the event offensive military action was necessary. Five days later, he issued Executive Order #12733 extending the period of active duty for those called up under 10 USC 673b for an additional 90 days.

On November 14th, the Secretary of Defense issued a Memorandum: "The Call of Selected Reserve Units and Personnel to Active Duty." Under this mobilization, the Army was given authority to call up 80,000 personnel and the Air Force 30,000. One of the most significant aspects of the call up was the provision for the 90-day extension for Guard and Reserve personnel.

The 90-day extension was inevitable. Although some of the troops weren't happy, at least they knew where they stood. And in terms of the extension, the gears had been set in motion much earlier.

For some time, it had been evident in Congress that the Section 673(b) time restriction of 90-plus-90 days without congressional approval was antiquated. The 90-day policy actually was a product of the American response to the 1973 Arab-Israeli war. At that time, the Israelis had lost a great deal of equipment in the early days of the conflict and there was big push by the U.S. Air Force to resupply them.

Subsequent to that war, Air Force leaders wanted to beef up their force structure to provide the capacity to respond to surges of this type. Congress balked at increasing force structure but as a compromise, agreed to enact language that would grant call-up authority for an operational mission — one requiring less than three months of call-up time, and thus, one not requiring a Presidential declaration of a national emergency.

As noted in a RAND policy paper after the war:

"Congress authorized the President to call reserve units for operational missions in limited numbers and for limited periods in Title 10 U.S. C, Section 673(b). Prior to this Section 637(b) authority in 1976, the President had to declare a national emergency for mobilization in order to gain access to reserve units. Having a new mechanism enabled substantial military capability, especially support, to be placed in the reserve under Total Force Policy."

The new authority for making reserves available better accommodated international and domestic political needs while the older authorities for partial or full mobilization better accommodated the military and its planning process by making more units and individuals available and for longer periods. The new authority was perceived as useful to military in certain cicumstances but, unless it was only a step to a larger mobilization, meant that the contingency would need to be of short duration and limited in size.

A contingency of the type fought in Desert Storm/Shield was not the most demanding one for which the military planned. The U.S. force structure available to President Bush in the summer of 1990 had been built, trained, and equipped to face the Soviet United in global conflict. Military planning for use of reserves in such a global conflict directly influenced expectations by reserves for mobilization and deployment.

When the Total Force policy was first formulated in 1971, the Selected Reserves end-strength was 28 percent of the active and reserve component end-strength. By the time of the Persian Gulf Conflict, it was 36 percent overall and 55 percent in the Army. The 1980s decade of investment in active and reserve component forces had a pay-off in a very robust, well-trained, and modern military structure. In 1990, there were over 2,00,000 active duty people and 1,100,000 selected reservists. Our conventional forces were sized and equipped to fight with the aim of being able to win quickly and decisively. A priority throughout the 1980s was to maintain high levels of readiness supported by operating tempos at levels sufficient to provide challenging training. The Total Force policy provided President Bush — through a mix of assets including active, Selected Reserve, and Individual Ready Reserve (IRR) — with options for employment of force.

In an attempt to rectify the situation of a maximum 180-day callup, a proposal to double both time periods was pushed by Congressman John Murtha, (D-Pennsylvania), the powerful chairman of the Defense Appropriations Subcommittee and Congressman Montgomery. A narrowly defined clause was drafted and passed that gave the President authority to activate Guard and Reserve units for an initial 180 days (90 days plus the 90 days without Congressional approval) and an additional 180 days without congressional approval for duty in South West Asia. Later, the day after the air war began, as the 180-day window was closing in on our units, President Bush requested a partial mobilization, which legally allowed mobilization of one million Guard and reservists for up to two years.

In a press conference held at the Pentagon in November, Secretary Cheney announced U.S. forces in the Gulf would almost double and that there would be a call-up of the three Army Guard round-out brigades. He also said that he wanted these units to train to active component standards and rotate through the National Training Center [NTC].

The NTC, located at Fort Irwin, California, is the Army's preeminent combat training center. The NTC is a fully instrumented tactical maneuver area that utilizes the latest in laser, computer, and video technology. This sophisticated equipment is capable of tracking units, vehicles, and individuals, displaying virtually everything on computer screens for instant analysis by onlookers. The NTC serves as the Army's major training facility which most nearly simulates actual combat conditions. It's well known throughout the military establishment that units training at the center are pushed to the highest level of performance.

Secretary Cheney's announcement meant the entire 48th Brigade had to report to the NTC, despite the fact that one of the battalions of the 48th had gone through NTC this past July. The 155th Armored Brigade, Mississippi was slotted to round out the 1st Cavalry Division, while the 256th Armored Brigade was programmed to round out the 5th Infantry Division.

But there was a sudden change of plans. Instead of using the Round Outs, however, the 197th Separate Infantry Brigade (Mechanized), an active-component school brigade from Ft. Benning, was used to roundout the 24th; the active component 1st Brigade of the 2nd Armored Division was used to round out the 1st Calvary Division; and the 5th Infantry was not looking for round-out troops yet because they were still in CONUS. To add further to the change of plans, the 155th was now scheduled to round out the 4th Infantry Division at Fort Carson, Colorado, effectively pushing out the 4th Division's legitimate Guard Round Out brigade, the 163rd Armored Brigade from Idaho.

To put it mildly, it was one helluva force contortion. And no one in the Guard was convinced by the Army explanation that the Round Outs needed all this additional training beyond post-mobilization training.

When the 48th and 256th reached their mobilization stations on November 30th (the 48th at Ft. Stewart, Georgia and the 256th at Ft. Polk, Louisiana), the unit commanders were told that the combat readiness rules had been changed. Basically, they were told that the units would have to be retrained, going through a long, drawn-out instruction process commonly referred to as "crawl, walk, run." As General Schwartzkopf later wrote, "Although all [the brigades] were rated `combat ready' by their parent organizations prior to August 2nd, none was deemed combat ready when it reached the mobilization stations."

Later, in April of the following year, some senior Army officials stated that the round-out concept was best performed at the crew, platoon and company level using Guardsmen as fillers. But this simply was unacceptable. Individual soliders being used as fillers had been a concept ended with the Dick Act of 1908. Indeed the use of individual American soldiers as "fillers" had been rejected by Gen. J "Blackjack" Pershing during the WWI deployment of U.S. troops in France. Immediately I met with the Army Deputy Chief of Staff for Operations General Denny Reimer to work this issue.

The controversy surrounding the Round-out brigades was deep and complex. It grew from a tradition of differences between the

National Guard and the active component which has festered for many decades and tainted, somewhat, joint active-Guard/Reserve combat manuever operations in Desert Storm. It was a lesson that would have ramifications for the Total Force Policy and the commissions established by Goldwater-Nichols to consider total force policy.

On the 22nd of October, I received a memo from the Joint Staff assessing our role in Desert Shield. It reported that the Guard and Reserve units were performing well but that the activation of the Reserve components was "not tailored to a no-notice of short-warning operation." The memo went on to say that the Roundout Brigade Concept was not useful given the rapid deployment requirement and the time required to train up and move heavy equipment to the area of battle. The memo codified what had already been done and undone by active Army commanders.

These Round-out Brigades and the poor treatment they received from the active military leadership became a recurring theme for months to come and had created anew the longstanding issues of Active Army intentions for employing combat Guard units.

With the August 7th Presidential Declaration of a National Emergency, the Army immediately alerted its prime contingency force, the XVIII Airborne Corps, consisting of the 82nd Airborne Division, the 101st Airborne Division (Air Assault), the 1st Cavalry, the 24th Infantry Division (Mechanized). I said, 'Whoa there, folks. We have two round-out brigades with those divisions — the 48th with the 24th and the 155th with the 1st Cav. What are you going to do with them?"

The answer was, "We can't use them right now. There's no authority to call out the Guard or Reserve and we're moving out now."

So, as I've explained, we gnashed our teeth while the two divisions got two active brigades as fillers. In fact, this could have and should have been a turning point for the 48th. This brigade was in the same State as the 24th ID, they were well-equipped with M-1 tanks and Bradley Fighting Vehicles, and a large number of Brigade personnel had just returned from an NTC rotation in July. Most important, they'd been working with the 24th for more than a decade. Not to be forgotten either, was that both the 48th and the 155th were headquartered in states with powerful congressional delegations (Georgia and Mississippi), a fact which could not have escaped Pentagon planners.

It was disappointing to many of us in the Guard that General Schwartzkopf, the former 24th ID commander who knew the 48th Brigade, didn't want them over there immediately and that our Forces Command Commander in Atlanta, General Burba, couldn't make it happen.

The bottom line was painfully clear to us in the Guard. There were plenty of active Army units that wanted to get into the fray and there was little real chance the active Army leadership would send Guard troops in the active's place, war plans or no war plans. The fact was and remains, the active Army missed a tremendous opportunity to solidify their total force policy position with the 48th.

Colonel Douglas Hollenbeck was the National Guard Bureau officer attached to an organization known as the Total Force Policy Study Group (TFPSG), established by Congressional decree in February of 1990. Right from the start we knew the process for the TFPSF would be different from that of past panels. Instead of the Department of Defense cadre selecting the Group members, Congress did, and the Members made sure the Guard and Reserve Chiefs and their representatives were part of the group.

This panel was tasked with examining the vast and far-flung U.S. military establishment and then design a force structure appropriate to the challenges of the post-Cold War era. As such, it was presumed the panel members were knowledgeable about the strengths, weaknesses, and the dynamics of the Active and Reserve components.

As Colonel Hollenbeck, the panel's Guard representative, later recounted to me, at the beginning of the group's August 7th meeting, a member said with sincere surprise, "You won't believe this but the cables say that Schwarztkopf is screaming about getting all these service units right now and he says they're only found in the Guard and reserves!" Colonel Hollenbeck told me he looked at the member, who had supposedly spent five months studying these very issues, and asked, "Why are you surprised?" For all of us, it was a telling statement on the attitude and level of understanding about the National Guard and reserve.

Despite a decade-long record of global Guard deployments, which incidentally, included the 48th Brigade's participating with the 24th ID in several "Bright Star" joint exercise in Egypt under CENTCCOM, the active Army still had concerns about the Total Force policy. I believe some senior active officers thought there could be little or no reliance on the Guard and Reserve for a real-world, contingency mission because our troops couldn't be counted on politically, i.e. that civilian leaders would be too frightened or intimidated to move to a call-up.

The irony was that this was the exact opposite of the lesson to be learned from Vietnam. There, the reluctance to mobilize the Guard and Reserve was directly responsible for the reliance on a politically disastrous and socially inequitable draft. A call-up would have explicitly defined the emerging conflict and what America's role in it would have been.

Thus, prior to the call-up, there was a lack of understanding about the importance of the Guard and reserves in battle planning.

However, to their everlasting credit, it was General Schwartzkopf, General Powell, and other military leaders, who led efforts to persuade

President Bush to move towards the call-up. But it probably would not have happened by August 23rd without the additional influence of Chairmen Montgomery and Murtha on President Bush.

The timing of the U.S. military commitment to the Gulf couldn't have been better and the Total Force Policy Study Group (TFPSG) members closely followed the entire scenario as it played out. The senior officer in charge of the Group was a Marine Colonel, a fair man, even though it was the Corps' unofficial policy that no Marine Corps Reserves would get to any conflict until every active unit was committed to the contingency. The official policy stated that Marine Corps Reserve units would not be used until 60 days into the conflict.

The TFPSG studies were driven by a proposition advanced by Assistant Secretary of Defense for Reserve Affairs, Stephen Duncan. This became known as the "rebuttable presumption" and went as follows: Given that there is a disappearing worldwide communist threat coupled with the need for shrinking defense budgets, all the force structure should be put in the Guard and reserve components. The Active Components would have to prove they and they alone were the only ones able to perform the various missions.

When the group's interim draft report was released, I found it favorable to the Guard and Reserve. Anticipating a steep decline in defense spending, the report advocated the transfer of significant force structure from the Actives to the Guard and Reserve.

The two key variables were that first, we had increased warning time for a conflict, given that the once-formidable Soviet Army and Warsaw Pact troops had splintered and begun to fade away.

Second, the report acknowledged that we didn't have enough sealift to get more than a limited number of our equipment-dependent active forces to any theater. The bottom line was that it didn't make sense to have a lot of these big, heavy active divisions trained to a razor's edge at great expense if we couldn't get them to the battlefield for at least three months.

If we couldn't get our active heavy units to the battlefield, then the entire Round Out concept was flawed.

Other group members had their particular models. The one plan that seemed to fit in with Desert Shield was advanced by Frank DeParles. He advocated using the Round Out concept for the creation of a second contingency corps using active divisions that consisted of only two brigades. That contingency corps, for example, would go to Korea in case of increased tensions there.

The fact is, the Round Out brigades had always been in the Middle East war plans, which were predicated on our simultaneously fighting a large, maneuver European land war. Our Guard units had the Capstone mission in the Middle East. But when it became apparent that Europe's mechanized Armageddon would probably never be fought and that the Middle East may well yield the only war in town, then suddenly, the Round Out concept was flawed.

Many in the Army National Guard reasoned that the whole controversy was generated by the survival instinct of the active Army, which
had built its entire force structure — not incorrectly — on fighting a war
on NATO's Central Front. And so when the Warsaw Pact crumbled and
disappeared, the question became one of justifying the Active force
structure. And that came at the expense of the Army Guard. In fairness
to all parties, this was not unlike many other force restructuring and
deployment battles in this century.

The Round Out Brigades did have advocates. Just two days after
the Presidential mobilization, Congressman Sonny Montgomery wrote
a series of letters to both President Bush and Secretary of Defense
Cheney, stating, "As you know, the National Guard and Reserves are
an essential part of the Total Force Policy and with the increased
emphasis we have put on the reserve components in recent years, I am
fully confident that they can answer this challenge. If we believe in the
Total Force Policy, we ought to be mobilizing combat units and not just
be concentrating on support units." Four days later, he wrote again: "I
cannot urge you enough to use this opportunity to prove the validity
of the Total Force policy that we have been working for the past 20
years." Prescient words, to be sure.

Later, in October, Montgomery was joined by two of his Armed
Services Committee colleagues, Congressman Les Apsin and Congresswoman Beverly Byron, in the following remarks on the House floor:

"The men and women in our National Guard and reserve units
work hard to serve their country. The suggestion, unintended or not,
that their work is neither fully appreciated or really needed in time of
hostilities would have a disastrous influence on morale and performance. The failure to make greater use of reserve units in this crisis
raises the broader question of when — and even whether — they would
be used in the future. In Operation Desert Shield, the Department of
Defense has had unique opportunity to test the reserve system,
including combat, combat support and combat service support units
— as part of the Total Force."

"To this point [October 1990], the Pentagon has chosen not to do
so...If the reserve component roundout units are not to be used, or are
deemed unusable when a short-notice war appears possible, then the
viability of the whole roundout concept may be considered suspect.
This would carry profound implications for the organization of the
Armed Forces of the United States in the future."

At the same time, there were all sorts of unofficial reasons floating
around for not sending Guard combat units to the desert. One was a
fear that the 48th would mobilize, deploy, and subsequently experience
high casualties, resulting in a "Task Force Smith" style inquisition.
(Task Force Smith was the hopelessly ill-trained and ill-equipped active
Army unit hastily sent to Korea in the fall of 1950 which was summarily
routed with huge casualties by the North Koreans.)

Many in the Army Guard felt the active Army wanted to send as many active formations as they could to this great unfolding conflict. In the end, it wasn't lack of training or call-up authority, it came down to whose tanks, trucks, and other equipment were going to get on the ships first. And it wasn't the Guards'.

There were other thoughts on the Round-out concept. A few observers noted that the Desert Shield deployment would probably indicate the war stopper is not the capability or availability of the Round Out brigades, but the lack of sufficient sealift to deploy the Army's heavy units to meet the CINC's operations plans.

Second, as General Schwartzkopf pointed out, on August 7th, while the ready brigade from the 82nd Airborne was deployed to Saudi Arabia, "President Bush also signed a Declaration of National Emergency. The significance of this, although perhaps not realized at the time, was the declaration gave the DOD [Department of Defense] the authority it later required to implement a partial mobilization, which permits the call of one million members of the Guard and Reserve for up to two years. This authority was not utilized until January 18th, 1991. Ironically, when the DOD declined to authorize the call-up of combat troops later in August, it cited the limitations of 90 plus 90 days when, under a partial mobilization, it never would have been under any such restriction."

As far as the TFPSG was concerned, the endgame for the Reserve Components had already been played.

Many remember the date, August 2nd, as the day Iraq drove into Kuwait, stunning the world community. The Kuwait army was rolled up and practically destroyed. At the same time, about 13,000 miles away, President Bush was giving a speech that became probably one of the least covered events of his Presidency. He spoke to the Aspen Institute, articulating a course that had been supplied him by DOD Undersecretary Wolfowitz and the active duty military chiefs. Essentially, the TFPSG had been outmaneuvered. Because the President's speech that day codified a policy ensuring the Army Guard and Reserve would suffer as great or greater cuts than the active duty Army. Though separate and distinct, the delay regarding the Round Out brigades had become par for the course.

In September and October, Saddam looked 10-feet tall. The public, the press, and even the military establishment were all grappling with the idea of a drawn out, costly land war, possibly sparked by a sudden Saddam push into Saudi Arabia. Many in the government were cautioning that any conflict could well be another Korea.

However, by mid-November, it was apparent that Saddam had missed his window of opportunity for driving into Saudi Arabia, attacking U.S. forces and inflicting severe casualties. Certainly our air power could have helped stave off a catastrophe befalling our outnumbered troops prior to November. However, the level of casualties — maybe in the thousands of dead and wounded in a few days — would have appalled Americans and created intense public pressure for withdrawal and negotiation.

And although I'm hardly a diplomat, I felt that it was during this time that control over the entire situation subtly shifted from Saddam to us and we began calling the shots. I think he sensed this and thought that he could negotiate a settlement. First, he extended invitations to family members of "guest" hostages to visit them during the holiday period. Then, he offered to release 2,000 male hostages in December. Finally, he proposed to free all German hostages.

On November 22nd, President Bush visited the Gulf to spend Thanksgiving with U.S. forces.

On November 29th, the United Nations Security Council allowed Iraq one final opportunity to comply with all previous resolutions and then authorized "all necessary means" to remove Iraqi forces from Kuwait if Iraq did not meet the deadline to withdraw by January 15, 1991. I believed at that point — incorrectly as it turned out — we probably wouldn't use offensive action. I was convinced we'd pressure them through whatever means necessary to withdraw. And I figured that Saddam had to have grasped the enormity of the forces against him, forces that were growing daily, and that he knew that coalition air power could bring the war to his cities, not only destroying his military infrastructure, but also his entire society.

I was wrong on both counts; the air war was less than seven weeks away.

It was also in November that several Guard combat support brigades were finally federalized. First was the 142nd Field Artillery Brigade from Arkansas, composed of three subordinate field artillery battalions: the 1-112th Field Artillery, the 2-142nd Field Artillery, and the 1-158th Field Artillery. This last group, from Oklahoma, was the only unit in the Guard equipped with the Multiple Launch Rocket System (MLRS), a devastating weapon that scatters a hailstorm of anti-personnel bomblets over acres and acres of ground.

In addition, three Engineer Groups were federalized: the 256th from Georgia, the 104th from South Dakota, and the 176th from Virginia. On December 9th, the 146th Field Artillery Brigade from Tennessee, composed of the 1-623th Field Artillery from Kentucky, the 1-181st Field Artillery from Tennessee, and the 1-201st Field Artillery from West Virginia, was sent to mobilization stations.

On December 1st, the ARNG had deployed 8,582 personnel in Southwest Asia and a total of 36,689 had been federalized from units located in 47 states and territories.

By the 28th of December, just four weeks later, one out of every four personnel — 25 percent — in the desert in Saudi Arabia were Guard or Reserve personnel, a surprisingly high ratio. An equally astonishing figure was that on any given day during Desert Shield, 50 percent of the ANG's C-130s were flying somewhere in the world.

The day after Christmas, two ANG F-16 units were mobilized and quickly deployed to Saudi Arabia. One was the 169th Tactical Fighter Group from Columbia, South Carolina, which had won the 1990 U.S. Air Force Gunsmoke competition as the best fighter unit. The other was the 174th Tactical Fighter Wing from Syracuse, New York — the famed "Boys From Syracuse."

On New Year's day, 11,309 ARNG soldiers were in South West Asia, of a total of 50,597 federalized.

One of the major problems with our call-up was that the Army Guard's mobilization system had not changed since I was mobilized 22 years before during the Pueblo crisis. Almost nothing was automated — it was stubby pencils, carbon paper and push real hard because you're making five copies. Frankly, it was distressing for me to see this and I vowed to help change the entire system. Meanwhile, the Air National Guard was being mobilized and shipped out with all their records and supplies, all of it automated with the Air Force structure.

And there were other minor irritants. I found among some commanders a reluctance to break up units, particularly ARNG units. U.S. Forces Command (FORSCOM), the 2nd Army, the Adjutants General, and sometimes even the Department of the Army were ordered to dismantle larger formations into smaller formations. Early on, I realized that downsizing a division or brigade was the only way that some units were ever going to get to the war.

For example, given the real fear about Saddam using chemical weapons, I thought that the Department of the Army should take a chemical company, or even a battalion, and get them over to the theater. You can never have enough soldiers trained to minimize the horrible effects of combat chemical weapons, right? But it did not happen.

Then, some of the Adjutants General would tell me, 'We want to go as a complete unit.' But the fact was, it wasn't always going to happen that way — the Air Force and Army had vastly different missions and vastly different active-reserve relationships. In fact, the Air Guard put together any size packages in terms of personnel and equipment that the Air Force requested.

I had two Adjutants General, for example, who had divisions spread over several states. 'We want to go' they said 'But don't call us unless you call the entire division.' And while I understood their intense feeling about unit cohesion, I knew that the decision was ultimately out of my control. If General Schwartzkopf wanted a Quartermaster Battalion, that was what he'd get, even if I had to mobilize it separately from the Division structure.

So I'd reply, and it became my standard reply, "What do you mean? Are you going to sit back and wait for World War III? You're not going to get into this war at the division level. The only way you'll get into the fight is if I come after brigades, or even battalions." I didn't even give them the shock of saying companies. The idea of calling up an entire division was remote at this point. And it wasn't as though large unit cohesion was a feature of the Air Guard. We only had a couple of

Air Guard wings going; the rest were calling out squadrons, parts of squadrons, and or smaller units by UTCs — the individual Unit Training Code which identified a particular unit sometimes down to the detachment level.

The insistence on wanting to go in one piece was really a manifestation of a larger issue that the field folks deserve much credit for: <u>Everyone</u> wanted to be in on the action. Except in a few isolated instances — for example, doctors who complained about serving in active duty status after the military had paid their medical school bills — there was an absence of complaints about serving. Everyone wanted to get to the Gulf. And why should that be so surprising? The Guard trains hard for the day the call comes. The theory behind the All Volunteer Force — that they would be motivated for battle, not ambivalent or even reluctant — was inculcated in both the Air and Army Guard. In reality, the vast majority of the state Adjutant Generals would willingly provide whatever mobilization packages the Army or Air Force needed.

One week into 1991, I flew to Ft. Campbell, Kentucky with legendary House Appropriations Chairman William Natcher of Kentucky to visit the soldiers of the 196th Field Artillery Brigade of Tenessee, Kentucky, and West Virginia, awaiting deployment to South West Asia. The brigade strength was at 96 percent and the mission-ready equipment was already enroute to Saudi Arabia. I came away extremely impressed — this group was in high spirits and well-prepared. And needless to say, Chairman Natcher was also impressed with his Kentucky unit.

It was also in the first week of January that Linda and I were invited to dinner at the Chairman's home for an event in honor of a foreign military leader. General Powell was and is a gracious man, as is his wife Alma. That evening, he came up to me at one point and said, "I hear your troops are doing a helluva job out at the National Training Center (he meant the 48th Brigade). We're gonna need them over in the desert and we'll ship 'em out as soon as they finish the training." I replied that it would be a great move by him and the Army to show this total force cohesion since we would have to operate that way in the future with reduced budgets. I also told him that the deployment would help the Army in the long run with Congressional support. Unfortunately, it never happened because of all the delays in calling them up and the short, 100-hour ground war.

There was one positive note that was sometimes lost in the constant hand-wringing over the fate of the 48th and the 155th, and to a lesser extent, the 256th. The training conducted in the states was valuable for one reason. What if another regional contingency had broken out? Even if this potential contingency hadn't resulted in conflict, there would have been a need for maneuver brigades and there would have been two, perhaps three ready to ship out and fight.

On January 8th, President Bush asked Congress to approve a resolution authorizing the use of "All necessary means to drive Iraq out of

Kuwait." Four days, later, Congress narrowly passed the measure in a vote that underscored the political party split on the issue.

Throughout the buildup for war, there was only one bad mark on the scope — an incident in which some Shreveport, Louisiana soldiers from the 256th Field Artillery Battalion training at Ft. Hood, Texas, violated orders and regulations. It was a case of conflicting layers of supervision — one Guard and one active — vexing a large group of men who had just spent many days training in the field. There was confusion as to orders — orders given, rescinded, and then countermanded. The Army had a great deal of people training at Ft. Hood, both for casualty replacement as well as to cycle fresh troops through the desert in anticipation of a long campaign. We heard from several sources that the trainers were not always ecumenical in their treatment of the hometown Guard troops.

Fifty three soldiers took unauthorized leave from Ft. Hood, but were soon apprehended. Of the 53, 15 soldiers violated the 50-mile pass distance from the post and 38 were actually deemed Absent Without Leave (AWOL). Each of the 53 was given an Article 15 by the Deputy Commander of the 256th.

The Adjutant General of Louisiana, Major General Buddy Stroud, handled the entire situation as well as it could be handled. Later, in an memorandum to General Powell, I explained exactly what happened and made no excuses for the Guardsmen, who were guilty of unprofessional and un-military behavior. Although I was disappointed this had to happen in the midst of our singular opportunity in Desert Shield to prove our worth, I also knew the incident was a result of the frustration that can build up in a unit.

Certainly Guard units, given their part-time mindset, are susceptible to this behavior. But as I told countless folks later: The entire incident was so unusual because it was totally isolated. Nothing like it happened before or after. It left a bad taste for a few days and got headlines and then it went away. That's war. You're not going to see the lockstep movement of tens and hundreds of thousands of personnel and not have some problems. The active forces also have their serious personnel issues in war and peacetime. After all, we are a mirror image of our society.

The Air Guard flew combat missions from day one. One reason was because Major General Killey and Brigadier General Don Sheppard worked closely with the active Air Force to get the right active-Guard mix in the theater. General Bob Russ, commander of the Tactical Air Command, and General Tony McPeak, the Air Force Chief of Staff, were both extremely supportive of the Guard.

And it showed. They were firmly in favor of sending combat Air Guard units to the Gulf, and some of our units deployed ahead of the actives. After 46 days of combat, not one ANG plane or pilot was lost.

Even after the war, the ANG flew patrols for Operation Southern Watch, amounting to thousands of sorties. I'm proud to say that our Guard and Reserve force were equal to our active forces and those of our Coalition allies in every respect. This is a tremendous tribute to the active Air Force and their embrace of the Total Force each and every day.

Throughout this period, the United Nations Security Council placed consistent diplomatic pressure on Saddam. To a great degree, the UN was prodded and persuaded by the diplomacy of President Bush and Secretary of State James Baker, whose ideal complements in managing the buildup in the desert were Defense Secretary Cheney, General Powell, and National Security Advisor Brent Scowcroft. During the same time, the rest of us gathered daily in the Pentagon to assess the situation of our forces in the Gulf. I typically attended the 7:00 a.m. Air Force meeting in the Air Force Tank. Then I would rush over to the 7:30 a.m. Army meeting in the Army tank consisting of large briefing screen and theater-style chairs. The Service Secretary as well as the service staffs, attend each meeting as well as the senior Guard and Reserve chiefs and occasionally, the Secretary of Defense and his staff.

On the evening of January 15th, you could observe a most visible sign that something unusual was going on at the Pentagon — dozens and dozens of pizzas were being delivered to the South Parking lot. For anyone who might have noticed, the same flurry of delivered pizza preceded the kick off of Operation Just Cause. The large cheese with pepperoni were flowing, once again.

The air war was about to begin.

I remember the Air Force meeting on the morning of January 17th, just a few hours after the first night of the air war had ended. We had anticipated a 10 percent loss of aircraft — 30 to 50 planes. There was simply no reason to think differently. This was an intricate operation involving hundreds of different types of aircraft from all the services, flying from many different points on the compass, converging on numerous targets, all of it against a solid air defense system — and all of this at night. This was as tough as it gets.

I was stunned — and pleasantly surprised — as were my colleagues, by the initial reports prior to the first meetings of the day. Amazingly, not one aircraft had been lost. In addition to this great news, there were other coups for the Guard. Aircraft from the 174th Tactical Fighter Group from Syracuse and the RF-4C units from Nevada had been in on the first night's raid. And, the best news was that an F-16 from the 169th Tactical Fighter Group, South Carolina, got the first air-to-air kill, knocking down an Iraqi F-1 Mirage east of Baghdad.

Then, the bottom dropped out from under me.

At the morning Air Force staff meeting, we learned that an F-18 from the aircraft carrier U.S.S. Saratoga was unaccounted for, presumed shot down. Our son, David, was an F-18 pilot on that ship.

The rest of the briefing dragged on for an eternity. I was still in shock at the end of the Air Force meeting.

Lieutenant General Jimmy Adams, the Air Force Deputy Chief of Staff for Operations Air Force, knew immediately what was going on. He came up to me and before I got up from my chair, said quietly that he'd find out everything he could for me about the missing F-18.

The Saratoga was already somewhat of a starcrossed ship. A month earlier, 29 members of the ship on shore leave had been drowned when a ferry overturned and sank near Haifa, Israel.

Following the first night strike, the networks began running the story that morning after confirmation of the missing plane by the Pentagon. By 7:30 a.m., the family started calling my office about David. The irony was that we had contingency plans for the states, the Adjutants General, the units, the Governors, and the Air Force and the Army for dealing with emergencies such as this involving the Guard. We had covered everything except for one thing: How to deal with my large family and all of our close friends, whose deluge of calls jammed up the office phone lines all morning.

General Adams got through at a little after nine. He said simply, "John, it's not your son. I can't tell you who it is, but it wasn't David." I said a silent prayer of thanks and immediately phoned David's wife, Cyndi, in Jacksonville, Florida to reassure her. She was overjoyed but then immediately asked who it was because she belonged to a tight group of F-18 pilots' wives at Cecil Field. I told her I didn't know who had gone down. All I could tell her was that it wasn't David. Cyndi told me every wife was panicked and upset. I answered that I would work through all the channels to get word to them as soon as possible. But at this point, there was nothing anyone could do.

Then and now, I always thought having David over there gave me a good insight what it was like for those folks with family members in the Gulf. After each day of the air war, we'd all wait expectantly for the day's news. On General's row at Fort McNair were four of us with sons in combat in Desert Storm. Every night, before going to bed, I would walk out on the porch of Quarters One and take a long look down the homes on the row, wondering how we had all fared that day.

Less than 12 hours after the air war had begun, President Bush, drawing upon Title 10 U.S. Code Section 673, signed Executive Order #12743, authorizing a partial mobilization and ordering units and individual members of the Ready Reserve of Armed Forces to Active Duty. This was an unprecedented move. It meant the mobilization could extend to one million men and women, and that all of these Guard and reserve soldiers and airmen could be mobilized for up to two years.

A momentous political line had been crossed, but it was overshadowed by the television pictures of bombs slamming into buildings in Baghdad.

The mobilization meant we had to cut new orders for everyone. We knew this would be an extremely complex process. For example, how were we going to handle the personnel who had already served over there for several months? Should we give them two years from the date of the partial mobilization decree or should we subtract the time served on active duty status? We finally worked it out that the maximum one-year orders for everyone would include the portion of time our Guard folks had spent on active duty, whether in the theater or not. Thus, if a Guard members was called up on 1 September 1990, he or she would be released by 31 August 1991.

During the next few weeks the air war punished Saddam, decimating the infrastructure of Baghdad, pounding Iraqi troops throughout Iraq and Kuwait, and tearing apart the equipment it had taken Saddam years to acquire. Once again, we thought Saddam would come to terms. The ongoing destruction of his capital city, the blooding of his military forces, the growing uselessness of holding Kuwait — we thought he might want to get out and fight another day. But we were wrong again. And we were unfortunately right about another conclusion: like the fanatical dictators of his lineage in this century, from Hitler to Stalin to Mao, the suffering of his own people meant nothing to Saddam.

On February 4th, Secretary Cheney took time out from his hectic schedule to brief the Adjutants General from all over the country, who were meeting that week in Washington. Secretary Cheney was forthright about our aims — to remove Iraq from Kuwait. At the time, the air war was just 18 days old and the ground war only 20 days off. And, he did state that he wanted to send the 48th and 155th Brigades to Southwest Asia.

On February 21, the ARNG's 142nd Field Artillery Brigade from Arkansas arrived in the theater, along with the 158th Field Artillery Battalion (MLRS) from Oklahoma. Two days later, the 1-158th would have the highest fire rate in the 3rd Army.

Given Saddam's intransigence and stupidity, the ground war was launched on 23 February with our Army Guard elements that were in theater flowing right along with the VII Corps and XVIII Corps.

In just 100 hours, it was over.

The last entry in the Army Guard After Action Report read: "28 February 91 — The President announced a conditional ceasefire effective 2400 hours this date. Conditions include the release of allied POWs within 48 hours and public announcement by Iraq's president on complete acceptance of all UN resolutions and battlefield conditions." And there was the laconic last word, "At 0100 local time the 256th Engineer Group Headquarters (GAARNG) stopped for sleep on MSR Colorado in a minefield."

In April, I visited the Gulf once again. This time I took along Major General Bill Ward, Chief of the Army Reserves; Major General Phil Killey, Director, Air National Guard; Major General Jack Closner, Chief of the Air Force Reserve; Brigadier General Jack D'Araujo, the Deputy Director of the ARNG; my longtime, trusted assistant, the ubiquitous Colonel Frank Van Fleet; and Lieutenant Colonel Tom Berry, my long-range strategic planner.

I felt fortunate to go — various Assistant Secretaries and four-star commanders had not yet gained approval to visit the theater. As soon as General Schwartzkopf cleared the trip, we were off again for the desert.

The trip was hosted by our good friend, Lieutenant General Gus Pagonis, who at this point still had some 20,000 National Guard soldiers working for him.

We flew into Dhahran, then to the bases at Al Karg, KKMC (King Kahlid Military City), and Kuwait City. At each stop, we spoke to the troops both in groups and individually. At KKMC, we met with thousands of troops in a big theater there and were introduced by base commander Brigadier General Brown. KKMC was a desolate place, a huge complex 80 kilometers south of the Saudi-Iraq border. It's military value lay in its proximity to the front, allowing quick resupply to deployed units. Flying across the vast expanses of sand and scrub, I realized first-hand the true importance of aerial tanker support in a theater that large.

The single most asked question, as it has been with soldiers since armies first fought, was: 'When do we get to go home?' It wasn't that the soldiers were being cowards or outwardly hostile about their present situation; rather, it was confusion over the redeployment policy and concern about their families and their future back in the states. As I wrote in my post-trip memorandum to General Sullivan and Chairman Powell, there was a lack of clear understanding as to the redeployment priorities. What the troops observed did not fit their interpretation of the policy of 'first in-first out.'

At each base, we explained the importance of the mission our airmen and soldiers were performing. We pointed out the fact that all returning equipment had to be properly serviced and repaired before being shipped out. We also observed the remaining troops still inside Iraq and in Saudi Arabia had to be supported. There were other factors as well — helping to reconstitute the contingency corps, deactivating unit requirements, and support of the refugees.

Frankly, it's a never-ending challenge for commanders and troops to communicate effectively because of the problem of selective listening on the part of both.

There was no question but that there was an extraordinary amount of work to be done. Many thought it was a phenomenal feat to get all that equipment over there. But it was an even more impressive enterprise to get it all back. Travelling around the desert in a C-130, we saw row after row after row of vehicles — HUMVEES, tanks, armored cars and personnel carriers, trucks, towed artillery, pallets and boxes and drums and canvas bundles — all in desert cammo with an occasional splash of woodland green from units that had arrived late from Europe or the states with not enough time to get repainted. Then there was the mass of captured Iraqi equipment. Most of it was pretty crude stuff and much of it was vintage 1960s and 1970s material from the Soviet Union.

Then came the most memorable part of the trip: I got to fly a St. Joseph, Missouri Air Guard C-130 into Kuwait City from Dhahran.

What a sight! As we went across the desert, we could see the tank tracks and vehicle tracks in the sand, stretching from horizon to horizon. These endless lines stretching out over the desert gave you only an inkling of the vast maneuvers and distances the coalition forces fought over. And the desert traces only provided a glimpse of the scope and tremendous size of the coalition forces. Interspersed among the tracks were the oil well fires, the bright flames leaping up from the desert floor, and then the red and yellow tongues dissolving into tremendous billows of black smoke, blotting out the huge portions of sky.

I landed the reliable ole Herc at Kuwait International. We met with the Alabama Guard medical units there and personnel from an ANG Aerial Port Squadron.

Next, we met with the Kuwait officers who, like General Pagonis, had nothing but praise for the Alabama Guard personnel assigned to the airport to provide medical support. We drove through the damaged downtown and out to one of the oilfields.

We then stopped at the infamous oil pumping station which Saddam had opened so that pure crude oil flowed into the Gulf, threatening the entire Gulf ecosystem. There was huge collection of pipes intersecting in big "T", which was about the size of a small house. The Coalition strike against that facility was like putting a bomb in the left ear of a coyote running through the desert. But they did it.

Everywhere we looked, oil well fires raged. We couldn't get within 50 yards of an oil well because the heat was so intense. It was hard to imagine how our troops managed in that kind of environment. Weighted down with equipment, flak vests, bulky chemical gear, their adrenaline racing with the strain of combat and unexploded mines, the air they breathed was black with smoke, so thick that it blotted out sunlight.

Next, we toured some of the many bunkers and dugouts the Iraqis had carved into the desert west of Kuwait City. As we drove through the city, it was evident that this Iraqi army of occupation had stripped the city of everything remotely useful. In some of the foxholes we found seats taken from cars; sofas, chairs, cabinets, chests, and curtains were strewn about the countless dusty holes cut into the desert floor. There were every kind of electrical appliances you could think of — toasters, lamps, microwave ovens, clocks, radios, and stereos, even though there was no electricity. In one bunker, we found a metallic-blue steel safe, the door shut and the combination lost for all time.

Then we saw the "Highway of Death," an unbelievable jumble of vehicles of all kinds — school buses, passenger cars, pick-up trucks, tanks, jeeps, station wagons, vans, and even motorcycles. Many of the vehicles contained the same type of flotsam we'd seen in the trenches — huge bundles of clothing on hangers, wooden furniture, boxes of household wares — the debris was flung everywhere.

During the next six months, our U.S forces would leave the desert where they had achieved so much. While we were there, they were already beginning to flow back to their bases and their homes. By September, the last National Guard troops would depart the Kuwait theater of operations for America.

Although I'll admit to an institutional bias, I must say that the Air and Army Guard After Action Reports make for good reading. While the Guard performance was outstanding, the phrase "Lessons Learned" pops up frequently, as it should. The dynamics of the call-up for Desert Shield / Storm have set a standard for how this type of action should be done in the future and we don't want to repeat the same mistakes next time.

In Certain Victory: The U.S. Army in the Gulf War, put together by the Office of the Chief of Staff of the Army, it was written that "The performance in Desert Storm of units like the 212st Engineer Company from Dunlop, Tennessee and the 352nd Civil Affairs Command that helped to restore civil government in Kuwait testify to General Abram's commitment made eighteen years before to fully integrate the Active and Reserve Forces."

Said RAND, "Under Total Force Policy, the reserve forces are intended to be available and ready as the initial and primary augmentation of the active forces in any contingency. Judged by these criteria, Total Force Policy, while not without some problems and not without some controversy, was effective in the Persian Gulf Conflict."

For the Air Guard, Operation Desert Storm/Desert Shield was an unqualified success. The individual and unit response was unprecedented in terms of its readiness and mission-prepared status. The actives used both Air National Guard and Air Force Reserve to a great degree in their structure. At any time of day during Desert Storm, for example, the Air Force had 50 percent of the ANG's C-130s and most of our KC-135s in the air.

Another example: Early in the war, the Air Force leadership had a critical shortage of crash fire fighters. Our typical Civil Engineering units have 150 personnel, of which 26 are crash fire fighters. The Air Force didn't need the remaining 124 personnel in the engineering unit so they asked General Killey if he could pull just the 26 fire fighters for active duty. And he did, even though some commanders were concerned. The point is, you are serving a customer and it would be a waste of money and manpower to call up all 150 personnel to get at the needed 26. This type of flexibility underscored the solid ANG-Air Force relationship.

The ANG mobilized 121 units in support of Operation Desert Shield/Storm with, 3,000 personnel volunteering for active duty. Approximately 5,118 were mobilized in theater, 5,315 were mobilized in CONUS, and 692 mobilized elsewhere for a total of 12,270 Air National Guard personnel in direct support of Desert Shield/Storm. The ANG transport fleet flew 1,074 missions, transporting 6,000 personnel and 4,000 tons of cargo. The ANG tanker fleet flew 1,979 missions, dispensing 90 million pounds of fuel to more than 5,000 aircraft. Our fighter wings flew a total of 792 combat sorties during the first 14 days of the air campaign and by the end of the conflict, had flown 3,645 total combat missions and had spent 8,593 hours over enemy territory.

As Air Guard historian Joe Gross has pointed out, this mobilization represented the "first time in ANG's history that the majority of personnel involuntarily recalled for active duty had not been members of combat flying units. Moreover, the majority of mobilized Guardsmen had not been members of any type of flying unit at all. The total number of Air Guardsmen called up from airlift, tanker and fighter units had been 4,494, less than half of those recalled to active duty. Instead, such units as medical and aeromedical evacuation (2,151), security police (1,688), services (546), firefighters (420), mobile aerial ports (387), combat communications (271), and engineers (248), provided the majority of the mobilized ANG force. They reflected not only the Air Force's needs in the Persian Gulf but the dramatic changes in the Air Guard's composition that had occurred in the 1980s."

I've already mentioned the signs of Total Force unity I saw in the desert, and the same teamwork was evident at the staff levels as well. The Air Guard, for instance, was represented on the Air Force Contingency Support Staff (AFCSS), at the major commands, and at the numbered Air Force Headquarters.

The volunteerism in the Air National Guard was phenomenal. More than 2,800 people from 68 Air National Guard units in 40 states voluntarily served on active duty during the first three months of Desert Shield/Storm.

The ANG's Operational Readiness Inspection (ORI) phase list, practiced so long and so hard throughout so many years, proved to be invaluable. The ORI was a critical tool for verifying the unit's C-rating. The Army did not use an ORI system and thus was not as skilled at measuring unit ratings. The Air Force administered ORIs on a regular basis to all Air National Guard units and thus had confidence in their units' readiness reporting. In fact, in 1990, 75 percent of all ANG ORI evaluations were rated either excellent or outstanding.

Finally, re-deployment and demobilization of ANG and ARNG personnel and equipment from all over the Continental United States and outside the Continental United States (OCONUS) — the least glamorous part of a call-up but important for morale and accountability — was handled generally well.

Overall, the ARNG did equally well. Unfortunately, they weren't

allowed to be rated against a common and shared standard. Much ink
has been spilled on the subject of our round-out brigades, which will
no doubt provide a continuing study for think tankers and Guard and
active leaders for years to come. In fact, the 48th Brigade finished its
NTC rotation by participating in the largest battle ever fought at the
NTC. This was on March 1, one day after the ground war ended and
after the unit had spent 56 days in the field. Major General Fred Rees, then
Adjutant General of Oregon ARNG and later Vice-Chief of the National
Guard Bureau, observed that there has probably never been a more ready
National Guard maneuver unit. The 48th also earned accolades from
Colonel Patrick O'Neal, the Opposition Force brigade commander, the
enemy at NTC: "In my opinion, they're as good as some of the finest
brigades and at platoon and company level, better than most. You have
excellent, competent leaders who are aggressive and ready to fight."

But I will admit that all the nice words in the world didn't assuage
our frustrations about the treatment the 48th received. Equally frustrat-
ing was the double standard. The Marine Corps interpreted Secretary
Cheney's orders differently and in my opinion, not only sent less-
equipped, less-trained Reserve units to the desert but also put them in
combat alongside the active Marines. The Commandant of the Corps,
General Al Gray, was very astute in the politics of Washington. By
using his Reserves, he did two things: He demonstrated to Congress
and others in the military establishment that the Corps had faith in its
Reserves, even to the point of putting them in his first assault waves.
Second, he showed that by having to use Reservists for this contingency, the Corps could not afford to take manpower or budget cuts later
on in the draw down. The Marine Corps Reserve manuever units
performed very well and given my reserve component institutionel
bias, I was very proud of them.

Other Guard prodigies were accomplished. The ARNG's 20th
Special Forces Group from Alabama was mobilized on February 20th
while the active duty 3rd and 5th Special Forces Groups were already
deployed in the theater. There was an immediate need for back fill and
the 20th accepted the challenge, finishing their 90-day certification
training in just 45 days. General Carl Stiner, Special Forces Commander,
personally told me they were a superb unit.

All told, a full accounting of the sheer numbers of the ARNG call-up
provides a clearer picture of what the Guard accomplished. The Department of the Army federalized 398 Army National Guard units and 62,411
troops from 48 states, the District of Columbia, and Puerto Rico. A total
of 297 units and 37,848 personnel went to South West Asia; 16 units and
3,378 soldiers went to Europe (including Turkey); and 85 units totalling
21,185 federalized personnel remained in CONUS for support. Ninety-
seven percent of all the ARNG units federalized were deployed in
less than 30 days; eleven medical field hospitals were called and
nine went to the desert. Thirty mobilized units were battalion sized
or larger and sixty Colonel and Lieutenant Colonel commands success-

fully deployed to Southwest Asia. As Army Chief of Staff General Gordon Sullivan pointed out, the ARNG had 1,200 volunteers for active duty even before the August 22nd, 1990 mobilization by President Bush.

For me, the most compelling statistic was that the ARNG had 387 units that met the Army's mobilization criteria for deployment when federalized; fully <u>97 percent of our units were ready when called</u>. This is incredible. And it was due to the readiness check managed by the National Guard Bureau and by the state commands.

As RAND would later assert, "The readiness of the individual reservists was generally high in Operation Desert Shield/Storm."

An amazing 99.9 percent of Army National Guard personnel who were called up reported for active duty. Ninety-four percent were ready for deployment; the remaining 5.9 percent were either waiting for initial duty training, high school students, members attending Officer Candidate School, missing panographic x-rays, or were medical personnel willing to go anyway but prevented from doing so due to critical civilian jobs.

The "Army National Guard After Action Report, Operation Desert Shield, Operation Desert Storm" provides valuable insights on these and other matters. Subtitled "The Army National Guard as a Strategic Force", the publication offers a superb picture of the Army Guard's role in the operation.

The report points out that a decade of active and Guard interface had helped meld the two components. "The Army's implementation of the OSD Total Force Policy and the equipment and manning levels provided by the Army, OSD, and Congress contributed to the high degree of success in the deployment of ARNG commands."

Even though it was sometimes maligned, the Mobilization System was also mentioned. Most commanders stated that the system worked well when used, and that great benefits were realized from the mobilization exercises each unit was required to operate once a year.

In addition, "The extraordinary support given to the ARNG units by their communities greatly enhanced the overall public support for Operation Desert Shield. The federalization of the Selected Reserve should be considered early in a conflict to garner the will of the people in support of national objectives."

But the thing that was most revealing was the National Guard Bureau debriefing sessions, held on May 20th and 21st, which were conducted with the unit commanders returning from the desert. They attributed the Army's success to a list of things — the Total Force Policy, the Capstone program of linking units to places and units, Overseas Deployment Training (ODT), KPUP (Key Personnel Upgrade Program), and the Joint Chief of Staff exercises. (KPUP was a favorite of National Guard leaders and provided Guard personnel the opportunity to train and work alongside their active duty counterparts for short periods of time.)

As the report noted, the commanders "gave high marks to CAPSTONE [and were] especially complimentary of the VII Corps and the integration which had been achieved by CAPSTONE Battle Book preparation, training with VII Corps wartime command both in Europe and CONUS, and JCS exercise such as REFORGER."

Those returning commanders said the Overseas Deployment Training (ODT) program gave their units invaluable experience in coping with the tangible and intangible aspects of working in an overseas theater. The Key Personnel Upgrade Program (KPUP), developed by Major, later Colonel Frank Van Fleet from an idea of then Brigadier General Herb Temple to build confidence and professionalism, sent key personnel to train with active component units in the field, was also commended by both active and Guard commanders. This program had been a favorite of Lieutenant General Temple, who as a former infantryman, knew that KPUP provided enhanced tactical and technical experience to individual Guardsmen, who then could share this knowledge with their fellow troops.

For me, the after action reports and the two-day de-brief session was reassuring, almost like a benediction. These were all the programs and initiatives we'd toiled for during the 1970s and 1980s. They had all worked remarkably well under the pressure of a wartime situation and were a testament to all the sweat and blood we'd put into the Guard during those years.

To sum up, I thought the Guard performance in Desert Shield and Desert Storm was excellent, and the ultimate validation of the Total Force Policy.

But what did the others say?

Congressman Montgomery noted, "I think the White House realizes now that by calling up the Guard and Reserves from over 6,000 communities, the community support was assured as their loved ones marched off to this conflict."

Said Army Chief of Staff General Gordon Sullivan:

"I believe the architects of the Total Force should be proud of the results of their efforts. Lesson number one from these operations is we made it happen. We, the Total Army, deployed more soldiers and equipment farther and faster than ever before in our history. We, the Total Army, in concert with our sister services and allies, defeated the fourth-largest army in the world in a campaign that will down in history as a classic. The Army National Guard played a vital role in the Total Force Victory."

Said General Hansford T. Johnson, Commander of the Military Airlift Command and the U.S. Transportation Command, "I asked the Guard and Reserve to consider putting together a provisional unit. That was in the morning, and that afternoon they came back and said, `Here's two units. The Guard will be led by Charleston, West Virginia and the Reserves by Dobbins AFB in Georgia. Where do you want them to go?' When the history of Desert Shield and Desert Storm is written, America's Reserve and Guard forces will receive a great deal of credit for America's success. Quite simply, we could not have done it without them."

Lieutenant General Charles A. Horner, the allied air leader, said that the Guard and Reserves, "performed very well. I'm absolutely truthful about this, but I cannot tell the difference between active, Guard, and Reserve. And that's they way it's supposed to be."

Secretary of Defense Richard Cheney said, "We could not have done what we did in the Gulf without the tremendous performance of a quarter of a million Guardsmen and reservists...they did everything, and they did it extremely well."

And finally, President Bush, in an historic speech to a joint session of Congress in March in 1991, proclaimed that "the magnificent victory in Operations Desert Shield and Desert Storm belongs...to the regulars, to the reserves, to the National Guard. This victory belongs to the finest fighting force this Nation has ever known in its history."

Three months later, Linda and I were honored to sit in the reviewing stand with President Bush and Congressman Sonny Montgomery at the National Victory parade as we watched American soldiers, sailors, marines, airmen, and Coast Guardsmen march down Constitution Avenue on a beautiful, sunny Washington day.

And later still, in fitting Guard tradition, I would serve as the parade marshall at other celebrations. Not those in New York, Los Angeles or Chicago, but the events in places like Webster Springs, Kentucky and Evansville, Indiana.

And even Mt. Carmel, Pennsylvania, my wife's home town. Fittingly enough, that parade was not on Constitution or 5th Avenue, but on Oak Street. President Bush and Secretary Cheney were not in attendance, but the Sons of Poland, the Elks, the Knights of Columbus, the Shriners, the Veterans of Foreign Wars, and the Pennsylvania National Guard were all there. Mt. Carmel was alive with flags and banners and cheering townsfolk on a bright, breezy day.

After the parade, I stopped by the VFW and the American Legion Halls. Guardsmen and veterans were there, all ages and all walks of life; in wind-breakers and jeans, t-shirts and baseball caps, celebrating the return of their sons and daughters from the desert. And as the oldtimers gathered around me, they told me stories about their wars.

Section IV. "A Guard For The Future"

CHAPTER TWELVE

"AFTER THE STORM"

What is the first thing a triumphant nation does following a hugely successful conflict? Why, decimate its victorious forces, of course.

Just weeks after returning from the desert, I once again plunged into the debates over the draw-down of the active and reserve components. The average Guard member was not aware of the battles that ensue in Washington over force structure, the quarrel over "faces and spaces". But these disputes had begun in 1989 and 1990 and now they quickly became acute. Indeed, the Persian Gulf War occurred during the acrimonious active, Guard, and Reserve discussions on force structure. The irony of the Total Force war interrupting the debate was certainly not lost on the Washington participants.

The services had met in late spring of 1990 with William "Scooter" Libby, an assistant to Undersecretary Paul Wolfowitz. The services and their civilian leaders were desperately seeking a way in which to pre-empt the conclusions and recommendations that the Group seemed certain to reach, which were clearly not favorable to the actives, particu-larly the Army. There were only a few ways to accomplish this. One way was to substitute a force structure policy that had the acquiescence of the highest civilian level, i.e. the White House.

The policy which end-run the discussions of the TFPSG was called "Base Force." Base Force and Reconstruction theory, as described by the Secretary of Defense and the Chairman of the Joint Chiefs of Staff, provides the nation with a capability to meet the operational needs of the National Security objectives. It has also been described as the minimum force essential to our future defense needs. The centerpiece of the theory is a base force with a "contingency" capability and the ability to "expand or reconstitute" the force if or when needed. It differs from previous defense strategy in that it substantially decreases reliance on the citizen-soldier forces, involving them only in the larg-est-scale conflicts.

In Desert Storm, approximately 250,000 citizen-soldiers from all services had to be called to ensure the success of an operation. Under Base Force theory, Guard and reserve involvement in any future opera-tion on the scale of Desert Storm would be far less, particularly in the Army.

Reconstitution theory would result in the country doing away with much of the citizen-soldier forces in peacetime in order to afford a large, non-threat driven active force. If a force larger than the active and remaining citizen-soldier forces is required, new units would be formed with individuals from the Individual Ready Reserves (IRR) and prob-ably, although not well advertised, the draft.

Reconstitution relies on the following arguable assumptions: (1) there will be sufficient personnel in the IRR to reconstitute forces while simultaneously providing for casualty replacements; (2) intelligence will be available up to one or two years prior to conflict to reconstitute a draft, and (3) it will be relatively easy to call up a large number of trained, equipped and ready, all volunteer, citizen-soldier forces in the event of a large-scale crisis, individuals who met and trained once a year.

The final element of Base Force Theory is the "contingency force", or rapid reaction force. The mission of this force is to be available to the National Command Authority for (1) immediate worldwide de-ployment in support of forward deployed US forces; (2) to defend allies; and (3) to show the flag or conduct offensive or counter-attack opera-tions.

The man who articulated 'Base Force' to the nation was President George Bush.

As I stated earlier, the President had announced the Base Force policy on August 2, 1990 in Aspen, Colorado, the date that national and international attention was focused on the Iraqi invasion of Kuwait. Ultimately, this conflict would prove the need for a strong Guard presence in the Total Force.

While the administration was grappling with the Persian Gulf situation, the TFPSG met to discuss its draft report. Mr. Libby said something to the affect that "Well, we can't have a report that conflicts with the President's policy." The statement was so abrupt that people around the room became immediately and visibly concerned. Mr. Libby went on to describe the President's speech of August 2nd, and then, conveniently distributed copies of the President's remarks.

That was pretty much the end of the TFPSG. Given the President's remarks, the group could do little more than revise its report to comple-ment the Base Force policy. Indeed, the degree to which the announce-ment chilled the group was evident in the meetings scheduled before and after the Libby announcement. The group normally met twice a month; afterwards, it met just one more time before issuing a final report which simply faded away into bureaucratic and academic oblivion. The Guard and Reserve were a powerful group on the Hill and throughout America, but we knew the difficulty of working these issues in the Building. The whole discouraging episode demonstrated how infighting, turf battles, and egos can sometimes dictate national defense policy.

And Base Force was articulated by President Bush, who on February 22, 1989, just after he was inaugurated, had stated, "I will continue to adhere to and emphasize the Total Force Policy. Consequently, the National Guard and the other Reserve Forces will continue to be relied upon as full partners of the active duty forces in time of need."

Beyond the pitched battles over manpower, other events were taking place in the Guard. Late in 1991, in response to the increasing international scope and reach of the Guard, the NGB Foreign Liaison section began a new endeavor called the International Training Activities Program (ITAP). ITAP took the experience and lessons learned by the Guard in Central and South American nation building and combined them into a joint Army and Air National Guard Program. The goal was to allow National Guard units to deploy and operate in an isolated overseas environment while providing assistance to the development of Third World countries. By November of 1991, we had a joint engineer and medical team on the ground in Senegal, Africa.

In conjunction with our international initiatives there was an increased interest in the Guard among the international community. In the first three months of 1991, military and civilian delegations from more than 50 nations visited the Bureau and Guard facilities and installations throughout the U.S. In May, I sponsored a Military Attache Orientation Briefing at the Bureau that attracted over 200 members of the Washington corps of military attaches. The next month, I took 27 attaches from 19 nations to National Guard facilities at Camp Roberts and Camp San Luis Obispo, California, the North Black Hills camp in South Dakota, and the Joint Readiness Training Center at Fort Chaffee, Arkansas. Linda and I hosted more than a few functions at Fort McNair Quarters One for defense attaches, for good reason. In any given year, the Guard was operating in over 40 nations, providing engineer, medical, and other support to foster nation building while providing excellent training for our soldiers and airman.

Clearly, the Guard's performance in the Persian Gulf War had kindled the interest of the international military community. The increasing reliance of the world's greatest military power on the use of its citizen-soldiers was attracting the interest of military professionals around the world. No other country in the post-World War II era had projected their reserve forces like the United States had in Desert Storm.

And, surprisingly, so few nations had a trained reserve force. Israel had proven reserves. But other allies, such as Britain and Germany, looked at the National Guard as a model. Indeed, the British have begun to transform their Territorial Army along National Guard lines.

This lack of a "home guard" for want of a better term, was interesting given that all nations have local and regional emergencies that require an immediate and effective response.

Small wonder, as defense budgets continued to decline worldwide, that there was a corresponding rise in regard for the National Guard example as an alternative to large, expensive standing armies.

One element of the Persian Gulf conflict that continued to bother me was the primitive nature of procedures at mobilization stations across the United States. Here we were in the 1990s, an information age saturated with computers and electronics, and we were still fiddling around with pencils, typewriters, and carbon paper. We wanted to take action to change this and in 1991, we began to do just that.

Mobilizing even a single unit requires vast, timely flows of information — medical and dental records, technical documents, family records, military data — and the ability of all of the various agencies, state and federal, to communicate with each other.

The Reserve Components Automation System (RCAS) was first proposed in the 1988 Department of Defense Appropriations bill and its purpose was to computerize mobilization and unit planning for the Army Guard and Army Reserve. General Temple saw the great need for such a system and championed the start of this automation.

By mid-1990, the total Army Guard and Reserve force structure was comprised of approximately 9,800 units. These units were slotted for mobilization from more than 4,700 sites located in 50 states, three United States Territories, and the District of Columbia. We in the Bureau figured that there had to be a way to link these diverse and far flung units to a single, integrated system. We envisioned terminals in every armory and Reserve Center connecting to the fifty-four state and territory Headquarters, Reserve Commands, U.S. Forces Command, and the Bureau. We envisioned the individual soldier carrying around a computer disk instead of a bulky 201 Personnel file.

In September of 1991 the last ANG units left the Gulf, after having flown missions for 15 months. But even as 1991 had served to illuminate the Guard's substantial external role, 1992 would serve to highlight the Guard's internal role, beginning with an eerie symmetry to an event a quarter century past.

On August 11, 1965, a drunk driver's arrest in South Central Los Angeles helped trigger the Watts riots. Seven days later, 34 persons were dead, more than a thousand were injured, and 600 businesses had been destroyed. Long thought of as the beginning of an unprecedented period of protest and civil disturbance, Watts was just one instance, albeit extraordinarily deadly, on a time-line along which disorders gradually reached a level of violence and mayhem thought impossible in a democratic society. The Guard was there throughout all of it.

The most prominet event presaging the social upset yet to come occurred eleven years before Watts with the 1954 U.S. Supreme Court decision which outlawed racially segregated schools. That same year, in the small town of Clinton, Tennessee, a group of whites which eventually grew to more than 1,000 people, gathered around the high school at which the first black student was to enroll. A small unit of 200 Guardsmen under Colonel (later Major General) Warner Giles, with bayonets fixed but sheathed, pushed the crowd back and dispersed it.

A year later, Arkansas Governor Orville Fabus sent 75 Guardsmen to prevent the enrollment of nine black students at Little Rock High. This misuse of the Guard in connection with such a loathsome event so angered the nation that President Eisenhower sent the 101st Airborne Division to Little Rock and simultaneously federalized the entire Arkansas National Guard (a total of 9,873 personnel). When the 101st departed, a force of 450 Guardsmen remained behind to serve as a presence at the school for the rest of the academic year.

Flash points appeared elsewhere in the South. In Mississippi, there were 26 Guard call-ups for civil disturbance duty between 1961 and 1969. The most serious occurred in 1962 at the University of Mississippi in Oxford, where James Meredith — (a brave and historic figure who later was shot and wounded by segregationists) was determined to be the first black student to attend Ole Miss. The Federal Marshals who were sent to assist him on enrollment day were pelted with debris. The situation ultimately became so explosive that the Mississippi Guard was federalized and along with units from the active Army, was ordered to Oxford. It is interesting that the town's own unit — Troop E, 108th Armored Cavalry — moved to the scene immediately and was met by violent protestors. By the time it was all over, 40 Guardsmen had been injured by objects thrown by protesters.

The Alabama Guard was called out twelve times over an eight year span beginning in 1958. At one point in 1961, 16,643 Guardsmen were called into the Federal service to Guard the "Freedom Rider" bus caravan. Four years later, the Alabama Guard provided personal security for Dr. Martin Luther King, Jr. and his colleagues on their historic march from Selma to Montgomery. In 1963, John F. Kennedy was forced to call the entire Alabama Guard into federal service to protect the civil rights of and permit the enrollment of African-Americans at the University of Alabama over the obstructionist tactics of Governor George Wallace.

Then came the Watts riots. More than 13,000 California National Guardsmen were mobilized, at the time the largest state call-up of its kind in Guard history. In 1965, the 40th Division had already assembled at their local armories prior to movement to annual training. When alerted, these units were moved directly into the Watts areas. Evangelist Billy Graham called Watts "a dress rehearsal for what was to come."

In a week's span, from August 11 to August 18th, 34 people had died and 1,000 were injured, including two Guardsman.

The Detroit conflagration in 1967 began just as inexplicably as Watts — this time a police raid on an after-hours drinking establishment. Several days later, 42 people had been killed and property damage was estimated to be in the tens of millions of dollars. Two Guardsmen were killed and 13 were injured from gun shots fired by rioters.

A year later, in 1968, the Democrat Party national convention in Chicago was invaded by nearly 10,000 youthful dissidents who were confronted by Chicago police and 5,600 Illinois Guardsmen. Dozens of people were injured and millions of dollars worth of property destroyed.

The violence and sheer mayhem of this period of unrest pushed the Guard to move to a new and different level of training, planning, and equipment. As retired Colonel W.D. McGlasson wrote, "Newark and Detroit in 1967, with their gunfire and destruction, were the eye-openers. Soon, leaders of both the active Army and the Guard were scrambling to update doctrine for civil disturbance operations, launch 32-hour training programs in all units, distribute protective gear, and initiate new rules of engagement that relegated use of weapons to the `very last resort' category."

The assassination of Dr. Martin Luther King, Jr. in April of 1968 triggered the greatest urban upheaval in our nation's history. Cities across America exploded in numerous disorders — arson, shooting, burglary, looting and murder. Guard units were called into federal service in Chicago, Washington D.C., and Baltimore. Ten days later when the violence had finally subsided, a total of 95,700 Guard personnel had been called out in 22 states.

Obviously, racial disorder was not the only source of social turbulence at that time. There were also an increasing number of protests against the Vietnam War as the conflict became more prominent, more divisive, and more costly. The momentum of these protests began to build in 1967 and as Colonel McGlasson points out, "By 1969, the national spotlight had shifted to campus mob actions, the burning of ROTC buildings, bombings, the vandalism of military facilities, and the ritualistic burning of draft cards and American flags."

The deadly culmination took place at a huge protest at Kent State University in Ohio, where Guardsmen were not prepared for the chaos that awaited them. Having been literally taken out of the field from Annual Training exercises, where they had been for several days and nights, they were pelted with rocks, bricks, and steel construction rods by a frenzied mob of 500 students and non-students participating in the demonstration. Unfamiliar with riot procedures, dazed and frightened, the Guardsmen fired and tragically, four individuals were killed and nine wounded. (One of the students killed and captured forever in photographs with a 14-year-old runaway girl, Mary Ann Vecchio, kneeling over him, was Jeffery Miller, who had just thrown a tear gas canister at the Guardsmen).

It was a sad, lamentable incident. A civil action by the families of the deceased against then Ohio-Governor John Rhodes, the Adjutant General, and the Guardsmen ended with a 9-3 jury verdict in favor of the defendants.

Perhaps Major General James F. Cantwell, the former President of the National Guard Association of the United States, put it best when, responding to relentless criticism of the Guard action, said, "National Guardsmen bear their scars on their souls as well as their bodies from thousands of encounters with lawless, violent elements in our society." No matter, on this one day at Kent State, due to uncertainty and confusion — and the times — the Guard made a tragic mistake.

From January of 1968 to April of 1970, nearly one quarter of a million National Guard personnel were called up for 191 civil disturbances. In the first three weeks of May 1970, over 140,00 Guardsmen were called up in 43 cities and 23 states.

It was a time of utter and complete turmoil in our nation.

It was a very different National Guard twenty years later on April 29th, 1992, when four Los Angeles Police Department officers were acquitted of beating motorist Rodney King.

The not-guilty verdict for the officers involved with King was announced in a Simi Valley, California courtroom at 4:15 p.m. Within several hours, all hell broke loose in South Central Los Angeles.

Sensing something might occur no matter what the court room verdict, the California National Guard's 40th Infantry Division staff had convened earlier that day in Los Alamitos (a Los Angeles suburb) in anticipation of a call-up and to review civil disturbance plans. At 2150 (9:50 p.m.), with the city in utter chaos and the Los Angeles City and County Police Departments totally overwhelmed, California Governor Pete Wilson alerted the 40th for duty, requesting 2,000 troops. The 40th Infantry Division's Engineer Battalion assembled 450 members in just two hours.

As the 40th Division's day logs (unit records) would later state, "This situation is different from Watts in that it is spread out over a much larger area...[it's] somewhat erratic — either a random event or a highly planned and organized operation [which has] caused dispersing of the police over a 15-mile radius...many [youths] have automatic weapons."

Indeed, the 40th's logs provide an outstanding overview, dispassionately written, of the pace and action of the riots:

"The looting appeared...systematic — fires were randomly set. When police and firemen deployed to the fire site, other sites were broken into and looted and then many of those were set afire. [The] concern now is for the first time there appears to be some intelligence indicating that the gangs may be discussing joining together against the Los Angeles Police Department (LAPD). LAPD wants to keep the National Guard around until after this next weekend [May 15th] to see what develops. If the developments are accurate, there could be an all-out war between the LAPD and the gangs. In one looting spree, over 1,000 weapons were taken...some have already been found used in incidents on the street. Although the police fear reprisals against them, there is still much bitterness between the [various] gangs. There is also concern that should the federal investigation of the King incident not produce some action against the policemen involved, then there will be even more violence."

Later, after my visit to the troubled city, I would note that relations among the Task Force participants — active, Guard, various state and federal law enforcement agencies — were very good. The decision of Major General Couvalt (the active component commander) to place 40th Infantry Division commander Major General Hernandez in charge of all military street forces was a smart move, one which facilitated a smooth and uninterrupted operation. (Another interesting sidelight was that the Task Force was enjoying 'host nation' support from the local citizens who wanted to help. There was an outpouring of support of donated food and other items to the soldiers and Marines from many citizens, businesses, and the Salvation Army.)

As of May 4th, the total Army force strength was over 11,000 with approximately 8,800 committed. As the curfew was lifted, the LAPD and the Task Force went to a low visibility profile during the day to allow the appearance that life in South Central Los Angeles was back to normal, which was an uneasy peace in any case. But during the evening, the visibility was heightened.

As I wrote in my report, de-federalization planning, or de-coupling, became a priority of Task Force headquarters after ten days. Major General Couvault planned to withdraw the 7th Infantry Division troops first, followed by the Marine contingent and last, the National Guard. The 40th Division Engineer Battalion planned to deploy for street and neighborhood cleanup support following de-federalization of the other units.

While the day logs provide a compelling overview of what was happening, an equally fascinating description comes from the intelligence summaries from the 40th's G-2 shop. The following is from the period of 2000 (8:00 P.M.) 03 May to 0600 (6:00 A.M.) 04 May 92 and provides a stunning kaleidoscope of the action in a single evening, <u>seven days after the riots</u>:

"031900 — Marines from 1st LAI [Light Armored Infantry] Battalion fired upon from a light blue truck. No injuries reported.

031950 — Car attempted to run over CA-ARNG soldiers at Pico Boulevard and Vermont. CA-ARNG personnel had to dive out of the path of the vehicle. The driver continued ahead 1/2 block. Made a u-turn and came back towards our personnel. Two CA-ARNG fired 14 rounds at car, shooting out the tires, then, as the car continued, hitting the suspects two times in the head. The suspect was taken to the hospital where he died.

032000 — Two CA-ARNG soldiers with 4th Battalion/160th Infantry Regiment in Lenox rescued two girls from an attempted kidnap and sexual assault. The suspect was captured and was a registered sex offender out on parole for kidnapping.

032905 — Sniper fire directed at two CA-ARNG soldiers in vicinity of 90 Freeway and Foxhill Mall. California Highway Patrol closed freeway and are searching for snipers.

032127 — Nation of Islam group held demonstrations at 45th and Western which began at 1648 hours. Approximately 500 demonstrators cheering an Islam leader declaring war on whites. DOJ [Department of Justice] dispatched agents to investigate.

032150 — Automatic weapons fired at CA-ARNG solders in vicinity of 42nd and Central in L.A.

032235 — Anonymous phone call reports gangs going to Nickerson Gardens to jump CA-ARNG soldiers in order to take weapons and uniforms.

032245 — MP [Military Police] reported seeing a white Cadillac with automatic weapons in vicinity of Main and Alizo.

032304 — CA-ARNG soldiers at 26th and Vermont were fired upon. No injuries reported.

032350 — DOJ reported two Compton police officers shot when they responded to a call reporting that a man was on the roof of Compton High School. One officer is in stable condition. The other is unknown at this time.

040453 — About 15 gunshots heard in vicinity of 2200 Redondo Ave.

Conclusions: The large riots and disturbances are over... level of fires, violence and looting has fallen off to well below levels by Los Angeles standards."

During the same period, the report also stated:

"Activity: L.A. County activity is still down. Fire Department reports 828 plus fires, 1,191 rescue calls, and 126 miscellaneous calls. 8,601-plus arrests [including arrests made by L.A. City police], 11 County buildings damaged. City of Los Angeles: 4,665 fires and 8,626 other incidents; 5,647 arrests with 2,412 felonies; 1,300-plus damaged structures and 88 totally destroyed; 190,000 residents still without electricity; 70 percent to be restored by today. Casualties: Deaths — 51. L.A. County — 39 homicides, 13 police/National Guard shootings, seven [due to] traffic. Injuries: 2,383 total, 216 critical; 6 Police, 10 fire fighters. Arrests — 10,470-plus. Current weather: high 84-88 low 54-57; humidity 80 percent, wind South West 10 mph, visibility overcast."

Here's the intelligence summary just 24 hours later, <u>eight days after the riots</u>:

"051000 — CA-ARNG soldier at an accident scene. One suspect went to leave and knocked down a police officer. Two CA-ARNG soldiers locked and loaded their weapons. Then they fired and hit the suspect in the buttocks. The suspect was arrested.

052336 — Three black males pointed weapons at CA-ARNG soldiers in the vicinity of the Crenshaw Mall.

051900 — Members of two gangs may be deploying snipers on rooftops of Shenandoah Street, Garth Street, and Sawyer Street to engage military and police at La Cienaga and 18th Street. The ammunition was purchased in Bakersfield (California) by female friends of the gang.

052240 — Two shots fired at 3rd Brigade CA-ARNG soldiers at Santa Monica and Tarmiane. No injuries.

060020 — At the Vons Market on Rosecrans and Prairie troopers report an individual in a car suspiciously circling a parking lot. A squad car was dispatched.

060020 — At the Boys Market on Hawthorne Boulevard and 118th Street, troops reported the circling of a white car [with occupants] yelling obscenities and threats at CA-ARNG soldiers to kill police officers. Also told our troops that word on the street is that troops were not armed with live ammunition.

060024 — A drive-by shooting was attempted with a .22 cal single shot handgun that was fired once. The suspect was pursued and arrested by Southgate Police.

060028 — Two young men were reported to be observing the Bell National Guard Armory.

060030 — The probation office at 9110 South Central was set on fire. At 052355 it was reported that the probation offices in Compton and Montclair had been set on fire.

060400 — A check point for the 3-185th Infantry at Jefferson and Fraser Boulevards reported five to seven rounds of indiscriminate gun fire. No injuries and no fire returned.

Current weather: Temperature — high 78-80, low 60-63; Humidity 64 percent; Wind, South, 9 knots.

Conclusion: There will be continued below-normal levels of activity. The large riots and disturbances are over. Level of fires, violence and looting has fallen off to well below levels by L.A. standards. The County Equal Opportunity Commission believes that the gangs will continue to target probation offices to destroy records.

Local gangs may increasingly make small attacks against the police and the military. With curfew ended in many locations, the incident may increase tonight. Bloods and Crips (nationwide, organized gangs): Reports indicate that they are still attempting to coordinate joint activities against police and military."

I flew out to Los Angeles on May 4th to see the operation firsthand. In my memorandum to General Powell, I wrote:

"I met with Major General Couvault, the Task Force Commander. He covered the issues surrounding command and control and the undeserved criticisms being stated about the Guard. In his view, regarding the deployment and employment times of the Guard, he stated, `No one could have done it better.'

After the meeting, I flew out to the staging site of the 2nd Brigade, 40th Infantry Division and met with the Army Guard brigade commander, Colonel Metcalf. Following a situation brief by his staff, I was given a tour of the troubled sites, including the location of the shooting incident where the vehicle had tried to run down the CA-ARNG soldiers. That incident is being investigated and I was told by the police that they believed it to be absolutely self-defense."

I also met with Deputy Chief Hood and Commander Banks of the Los Angeles Police Department, who had most favorable comments about the relationship with the Guard and were pleased that they were there. They suggested that the Guard remain through the next week [through 10 May] to ensure a secure drawdown. I attended the 40th Division commanders staff update briefing with Major General Hernandez where I learned that over 11,000 troops were available with 8,800 committed to duty on the street. The strategy was to remain low key during the day at strategic locations in the city to present an atmosphere of calm and then to be highly visible at night.

Because I wanted Guard leaders to learn from these events, I took the Assistant Division Commander of the 40th, Brigadier General William Stewart, to the Adjutants' General conference then underway in Little Rock, Arkansas. There, the Adjutants General could hear first-hand the sequence of events and problems encountered in California, experience which could help them in their planning for handling incidents in their own states.

During my visit and later, I found that the chief concern among the troops was the unwarranted criticisms regarding deployment time. In fact, the CA ARNG, despite some problems (attendant to any mobilization), mobilized, deployed, and employed its first elements of the 40th Infantry Division in sixteen hours time. Even our most vocal opponents considered that to be remarkable given that Guard members came from home or work and assembled at their armories, drew equipment, moved to Los Alamitos to stage and await orders.

The California Guard response was rapid, and timely and reassuring to the residents. Most of the criticism came from Governor Pete Wilson, who many believed had made several critical mistakes.

First, he had not prepared for the obviously explosive situation resulting from whatever verdict the Simi Valley jury reached. For that matter, neither had the Los Angeles Police Department.

Second, Governor Wilson called out the Guard too late — and the riots were in full swing before he realized his error.

Last, he had waited too long as Governor to get to know his Guard, its commanders and strengths. When the critical hour came to use them, they were not used wisely.

I sent Governor Wilson a letter on May 12 and reiterated Couvault's words about the Guard's deployment and pointed out that the Commander of all Army forces, both active duty and Guard, was Major General Dan Hernandez, a Guard commander and a Hispanic. And I said at the end, "I could not have been more proud as I observed these great Americans who had made the transition from their civilian environment to professional soldiers in rapid time, accepted the missions assigned without hesitation, and brought calm to that troubled area. The welcome acceptance by the community of these volunteer National Guard solders reinforced the recognition of these young men and women as `Americans At Their Best.'"

Two years after this major call-up, Governor Wilson would truly understand the worth of his Guard.

Sheriff Sherman Block, Sheriff of L.A. County noted, quite accurately, that by the time Governor Wilson had focused on the personal, political, and public disaster the riots had become and had called for the Marines and Active Army units, additional support was unnecessary because the Guard had helped restore order to the streets "in its usual professional manner."

When I was in Los Angeles, I was able to observe our troops in action with the community. With my own eyes I saw the residents plead with individual Guardsmen, as they stood duty on street corners and elsewhere, <u>not to leave</u>. Indeed, after the initial spasm of violence, crime <u>decreased</u> in those areas, primarily because of the high number of Guard personnel on the streets.

A comprehensive look at the riots highlights some important and simple facts that were overlooked in the rush to assess blame. Within six hours of the notice of mobilization, more than 2,000 Guardsmen had reported to their home station armories. By H-Plus 16, 20 hours ahead of the prescribed Department of Defense "Garden Plot Operation" reaction time for urban disorders, the CA-ARNG spearheaded the domestic military response to the riots. By H-Plus 24, 12 hours ahead of "Garden Plot," the CA-ARNG had 1,000 Guardsmen on the street and 4,000 more in staging areas around Los Angeles. By the time it was all over more than 14,000 California Guard personnel had answered the call.

Most telling was that the crime rate <u>dropped by 70 percent from its 'peacetime ' rate as soon as the Guard arrived on the scene</u>. And not only did we provide security for South Central Los Angeles residents, we provided them with a sense of security. And why not? Our troops were representative of the community itself. These weren't the riot troops such as the ones that had appeared in Watts 27 years past, when less than one percent of the National Guard was composed of minorities. This was a force that pretty much looked like the community it was sent to protect. And this force, despite tough odds, kept an already bad situation from getting worse.

As these and other facts clearly document, the quick explosiveness of the riots in South Central Los Angeles were purely a result of civilian leaders being caught unprepared, not of National Guard tardiness.

From the voluminous accounts of the riots published afterward, two statistics remain vivid in my mind. In a passage from the Army Guard After Action Report (AAR) describing the violence, it was revealed that there were an estimated 102,000 gang members in the Los Angeles basin, with a majority of them possessing automatic weapons.

The other statistic was that in describing the carnage of the riots, the report noted that "One should realize that gangs killed about 771 people during 1991" in Los Angeles. Is it any wonder the residents of South Central Los Angeles begged us to stay? It was the middle of the summer when our last troops left Los Angeles.

Just four months later, the Guard would respond to another disaster, but this one was not man-made.

Initially, Hurricane Andrew was Mother Nature's roll of the dice: it would either hit southern Florida or veer off to the east and expire in the open ocean. Unfortunately, on August 23rd, 1992, it hit the Homestead area south of Miami. Again, superb planning on the part of the Guard Bureau and the Florida Adjutant General resulted in more than 2,000 Guard personnel pre-positioned in the southern region of the state. The storm hit Sunday evening and the Guard was on the street Monday morning. The next day, I visited the area.

I flew over the region in a UH-1 Huey helicopter to get a first hand look at the destruction at Homestead Air Force Base and the surrounding Homestead community. Both were torn to bits. I was struck by the narrow path of destruction: the hurricane had the tightest path of a Category IV hurricane I'd ever observed. The really bad damage was in a path 10 to 20 miles wide. However, associated destruction probably expanded the path to 20 to 30 miles wide. It looked like more like a cross between a tornado and a hurricane, a "hurri-nado," if you will. Even at that early date, we predicted the Florida National Guard would be heavily involved for a minimum of 60 days.

I spoke with the Florida TAG, Major General Ron Harrison, who was on site at the FL-ARNG staging area. He had mobilized 2,400 Guardsmen and women from throughout the state and would eventually call for a mobilization of 6,354 troops. I talked with a number of Guard infantrymen who had pulled guard duty the previous evening and had apprehended many looters. I also observed that one mall, between Homestead and Miami, had seen extensive looting prior to the arrival of the Guardsmen.

Overall, the morale was good. Indeed, it was the best National Guard community support action I've ever seen in terms of pride and esprit de corps. They knew the importance of the mission to prevent widespread disorder. In fact, several soldiers who were called up from the Homestead area had lost their homes and yet they still reported to their mobilization stations.

The local law enforcement officers on site commented that the FL-ANRG expertise, planning, and prompt response in the wake of the hurricane prevented widespread chaos and violence. In the process, Florida Guard soldiers and airmen operated the areas's only water purification equipment, constructed tent cities, pulled patrol duty, and also cleared obstructed highways and roads throughout the area.

There was a tremendous need for clean-up support, which eventually led Major General Harrison to mobilize an additional 2,000 ARNG and ANG personnel for this purpose. The Guard also worked closely with the American Red Cross. Before I left to view the storm's devastation, I spoke with Elizabeth Dole, the head of the American Red Cross, and offered the Guard's continued assistance in helping her agency.

The citizens of the Homestead community began flowing back on Tuesday and Wednesday to the neighborhoods they had abandoned. There was no food, no electrical power, no water, but the Guard had already begun handing out Meals Ready to Eat — the famous "MRE" — by the thousands.

The next day, the overwhelming chaos caused by families returning to their homes destroyed by Andrew prompted Governor Lawton Chiles to ask the President to call for active duty troops, ironically, to provide combat service support — the specialty of the Guard — for the South Florida residents and the Florida National Guard. And so, approximately 20,000 active duty troops from North Carolina and New York began to set up tent cities. This support was needed wholly in terms of manpower to house and feed the thousands of homeless for the next two months.

There was also a major push at this time by the Pentagon to federalize the Florida Guard, a move I strenuously resisted. I pointed out that when Guard personnel are federalized, they come under the 'posse comatitus' law which means that Guard personnel fall under the same laws as active duty military personnel. In other words, we can no longer assist in law enforcement activities unless martial law is declared. Such a move would nullify the Guard's unique standing under state mobilization.

My stance against federalization was in keeping with my reputation in the Pentagon as the "States Rights" general. If we were to be used as active duty troops, who could the state and local law enforcement authorities turn to for assistance with the very critical patrolling and security missions? If the whole point of the Guard was to provide a community presence, why suddenly transform us into active duty troops and end our security mission?

Fortunately, I was successful in making the case to the Administration against federalization. The active component soldiers remained in a support role with tent city construction and the servicing of displaced citizens while we continued the anti-looting patrols. The active duty forces stayed for 60 days while Guard units remained on state active duty an additional 60 days until late December.

Here, as in Los Angeles, there was a problem with "de-coupling" i.e. leaving the operation following the successful stability of the area. Residents simply didn't want us to leave; they trusted in the Guard and the sense of calm and order we brought to an otherwise unsettling situation.

Hurricane Andrew also hit Louisiana, though not as severely as Florida. Nevertheless, as in Florida, outstanding planning on the part of Governor Edwards and the state Adjutant General, Major General Buddy Stroud, helped mitigate the situation. They took quick and decisive actions prior to the arrival of the storm, deploying more than

1,100 LA-ARNG and LA-ANG personnel to staging areas in southern Louisiana, well in advance of the storm's arrival.

I soon left Florida for Louisiana and took a helicopter tour of Houma, Morgan City, Patterson, Jeanerette, and the Atchafalaya Basin of South Louisiana. I quickly concluded the damage was more dispersed than in South Miami. The law enforcement folks, as in Florida, expressed high praise for the National Guard assistance. The extensive advance planning was a critical element in the ability to maintain law and order in the aftermath of the storm.

Several days later, Hurricane Iniki hit Hawaii. Given our advance warning of these storm systems, we arranged an inter-state assistance package and worked closely with the Hawaiian Adjutant General, Major General Ed Richardson. As Iniki passed over Oahu, we had six C-130s from the ANG unit in Channel Islands, California, fly into Hickam Air Force base and then to a base in Kauai. These aircraft are ideally suited for the various conventional and sometimes unconventional missions that arise when disaster strikes. For example, we used the C-130s to transport dialysis patients from the islands to Oahu for treatment because their usual facilities had been wiped out. By the end of September, we'd moved 8,000 passengers, and nearly 3,000 tons of cargo. Major General Richardson and the Hawaii National Guard did a superb job in assisting the citizens of Kauai.

In just two years time, we had fought in Desert Storm, been mobilized for extensive riot duty, and had completed service in addressing one of the most costly natural disasters to hit the United States in this century.

But 1992 wasn't only a year of disasters. It was a period of time in which the Guard continued it's external, international orientation. We ran humanitarian assistance operations in Latin America, the Caribbean, Africa and the Pacific. We conducted infantry, medical, and engineer training in Panama, Honduras, Costa Rica, Saint Kitts, Bolivia, and Belize.

We also continued our "Fuertos Caminos" road building exercises in Panama and in Honduras. Indeed, Task Force 105, led by North Carolina ARNG soldiers, deployed over 4,000 soldiers from 18 states in to Honduras to complete the final 8.2 kilometers of the Yoro Valley Road. Task Force Badger, led by the Wisconsin ARNG, deployed over 2,000 ARNG troops from six states to Panama to pave over 100 kilometers of farm-to-market roads and repair and construct schools in six Panamanian provinces. And over 1,100 infantry and 360 field artillerymen deployed to Honduras to conduct squad and platoon level training with the Honduran Army.

We assisted with Joint Chief of Staff operations, including Provide Promise in Sarajevo. The 167th Airlift Group from Martinsburg, West Virginia was chosen to fly their C-130 Hercules planes 38 times into the contested skies and airport at Sarajevo. Air Guard units also participated in "Operation Provide Relief" in Somalia, ultimately a star-crossed venture. Four ANG units — the 123rd Airlift Wing out of

Standiford Field, Kentucky, my old fighter unit now converted to transport; the 133rd Airlift Wing, from Minnesota; the 135th Airlift Group, Maryland; and, the 146th Airlift Wing, California, and three others from Ohio, Maryland, and Tennessee — responded with 650 sorties to Somalia, delivering 4,000 tons of food and medical supplies. A medical detachment complete with technicians and flight nurses from the Mississippi ANG came to Mogadishu and worked on wounded Americans and United Nations troops.

And, in a ceremony filled with many memories, the 2,000th C-130 built was assigned to my old wing at Standiford Field in May of 1992.

At the end of Fiscal Year 1992, the Air National Guard had 1,500 combat and transport aircraft in its inventory and 118,923 personnel, making it the fourth largest air force in the world. Amazingly, the ANG was only smaller than the active U.S. Air Force, the Navy and Marine Corps air fleet and China's Air Force of the People's Liberation Army.

There was other good news. The Guard was getting smarter. In 1980, 66 percent of all new recruits had a high school diploma, with 73 percent scoring in the I to III range of the Armed Forces Qualification Test (AFQT). A decade, later, high school graduates made up 93 percent of our recruits and 93 percent scored in the top three categories of the AFQT.

During FY 1992, the ARNG implemented a program, designated Project Standard Bearer, to ensure our high priority Contingency Force Pool and Round Out units were fully capable of answering the call on day one of the crisis. Actions were also underway to ensure that all ARNG Contingency Force Pool Roundup and Roundout units were fully manned, totally equipped, and trained and validated to standard. The 38 highest priority contingency force pool units, designated operational units, are packaged to be available within seven days of an alert lasting up to 45 days.

The ARNG in 1992 also began the implementation of an operational readiness program called "Bold Shift." Under this program, the Department of the Army identified 102 high-priority ARNG units from 50 states to participate in the pilot program. One element of Bold Shift, modeled after the extremely valuable Air National Guard Operational Readiness Inspection (ORI), was that states established standardized, Army-wide deployment validation criteria. It was to be a "Total Army", or "One Army" approach, with CONUS evaluation teams composed of one-third Active duty, one-third Army National Guard, and one-third U.S. Army Reserve.

The year 1992 also marked the sixteenth year of our ODT (Overseas Deployment Training) program. This gave the ARNG units training in their wartime missions, provided a forward presence, and contributed to the strategic objectives of regional CINCs. It strengthened CAPSTONE relations and helped get us involved more closely with Joint Chiefs of Staff operations. During these past six years, we had between 19,000 and 34,000 soldiers annually participate in ODT.

We also were tasked by the Army Chief of Staff with the Humanitarian Support Unit Program (HSUP) to supply short-notice humanitarian missions. The HSUP was developed to provide volunteer ARNG units to support worldwide humanitarian missions on a 72-hour notice for up to a 45-day rotation. Of the 89 units nominated by 27 states, 19 were (and continue to be) identified as 72-hour deployable for up to a 12-month period.

Another big move was the start-up of the Operational Unit Program for states to organize high-priority units for service in volunteer status to support contingency missions. This began in 1992 as a way to organize the 38 earliest deploying ARNG units in the Guard to be available for active federal service on a volunteer basis within seven days of a mobilization to support a future Presidential deployment for contingency purposes. Most importantly, this was not contingent on Title 10 673b Presidential selected reserve call-up authority.

There were also ANG Civil Engineer "Prime Beef" and "Red Horse" operations with deployments involving some 8600 personnel to 15 nations in 1992. And 18 teams participated in Base Recovery After Attack Training at Eglin Air Force Base in Florida. This realistic training allowed personnel to learn wartime base support operations and to make rapid runway repairs.

An ideal example of the Guard's continuing technological and professional sophistication is the 629th Military Intelligence Battalion (CEWI), of the Maryland Army National Guard. Led by Lieutenant Colonel Ed Leacock, who has been with the 629th for nearly a decade (which demonstrates the continuity that makes the Guard so effective), the 629th is the only fully manned Combat Electronic Warfare Intelligence Battalion in the Army Guard, providing combat intelligence support to the commander of the 29th Infantry Division (Light), based in Maryland and Virginia.

The battalion received federal recognition on October 3, 1988, and has established a reputation as a premier CEWI unit in the Reserve Components, supporting the ongoing, real world needs of the wider intelligence community.

The unit is exceptional, even by active standards, in several ways. Nearly 65 percent of the battalion personnel have a college degree and nearly 35 percent have master degrees or doctorates. A total of 24 languages from around the world, are spoken by the battalion's linguists, who specialize in the interrogation of enemy prisoners and the interception of enemy voice transmissions.

Many members of the unit responded to the call in Operation Desert Shield, proving timely and much-needed support to the 82nd Airborne Division and the XVIII Airborne Corps in CONUS. Members of the unit also support the Guard counter-narcotics effort and have been in involved in a wide variety of training and joint exercises such as "Ulchi Focus Lens," "Atlantic Trail," and "Reforger."

In addition, the unit is fully equipped and is headquartered in a state-of-the-art armory in Laurel, MD. This facility also houses the first of the National Guard's new Distance Learning Network centers, featuring the latest in local area network computer technology, which can deliver video conferencing to sites around the country.

The above is just a glimpse of the huge engine that the National Guard has become in the last 15 years. Moreover it's important to keep in mind that all of these operations, deployments, and programs were concrete proof and validation of the Total Force policy.

Throughout all of the Guard's nitty-gritty, day-to-day work internally and overseas, the over-arching battles regarding force structure persisted. In the spring of 1992, the Administration again announced its plans to trim the Guard and Reserve on the same ramp, i.e. along the same percentages, as the actives. At the time, I thought this was as dramatic as the 1968 Guard reorganization which cut the ARNG from 18 to 10 combat divisions.

Once again, I protested loudly and clearly. To anyone who had seen the social and political evolution of the last decade, it was crystal clear: We needed a bigger, not a smaller, National Guard. If we had to bring down our active force, I argued, at the same time our population was increasing, we shouldn't move the Guard in the opposite direction. Indeed, I pointed out that our per-capita Guard strength hadn't been this low since 1918. And from a warfighting perspective, I argued that if the Persian Gulf conflict proved anything, it was that a large, trained, motivated Guard was critical to any sustained war effort.

As John Vessey, retired Chairman of the Joint Chiefs of Staff (and a former Guardsmen) said in May of 1991 before the Senate Armed Services Committee on the subject of the cost to train the active troops and the importance of our reserve troops: "We should be asking ourselves about the possible uses of these people (actives) to increase the capabilities of those reserve components which will necessarily become more important to us. I've lived through a number of force reductions and the best ordered of them was chaotic!"

I then tried diplomacy when reason failed. I asked many senior military and civilian leaders: Why are we talking about this massive troop cut in May and June of 1992? Why can't it be played out after the election? Unfortunately, it became clear to me that the Pentagon was primarily interested in the external U.S. military presence, certainly not the internal. Secretary Cheney, National Security Adviser Scowcroft, and other Administration officials were all looking outside our borders, not inside. How ironic. Because the Guard's performance in Desert Shield had been every bit as impressive as its prominence in an unprecedented string of domestic disasters. And I remain convinced that it was in large part the Guard and Reserve call-up that galvanized the community support for the Persian Gulf War.

The Bush Administration plunged on with their efforts. In April

1992, top Pentagon officials made the mistake of announcing that the planned reduction of approximately one-third of the Army Guard and reserve would equate with closure of one-third of the nation's armories.

The news was absolutely devastating. They had made a conscious decision to disrupt the National Guard community. I pleaded with the Administration, emphasizing that the federal government shares in the building of armories, <u>the states provide the land, part of the dollars, and are responsible for all maintenance and day-to-day upkeep for the life of that armory.</u>

Furthermore, in many small communities across the country, the armory is the local community center, a focal point for local events.

I asked them for enough time to restructure the forces so at least one unit remained in most, if not all, of the armories. Finally, I pointed out that Congress was never going to sign off on a measure of this magnitude.

Although I take little solace in this, in retrospect we were eventually proven right. The ARNG strength figure was restored by Congress at the 420,000 figure, not the 366,000 the Administration requested for Fiscal Year 1993 and not anywhere near the 321,000 the Administration had planned for Fiscal Year 1995.

The tension surrounding force structure and the Guard's increasingly important Total Force role was still evident as the annual NGAUS convention got underway in Salt Lake City in September. In my remarks to the 6,500 attendees, I spoke of a Guard in transition — our increased visibility in both internal and external missions. I also recognized in my speech the first appointment of a female General Officer in the National Guard, Brigadier General Roberta Mills of the Tennessee National Guard. General Mills later rose to the rank of Major General, the first female two-star in the National Guard.

I concluded my remarks by noting that America's community-based national defense force had become the benchmark for the world.

Given this Presidential election year, President Bush and Governor Bill Clinton were invited to address the conventioneers. President Bush accepted immediately, no doubt confident he would receive a sympathetic reaction from a room full of veterans, despite his plans to draw down the Guard.

The second day of the convention, and a day before President Bush's speech, the Association suddenly got word that Governor Clinton would attend as well. Indeed, Clinton's decision to attend was remarkable: Hours before the Clinton campaign called the Association to schedule the Democrat candidate for the next day, Congressman Dave McCurdy (D-OK) spoke to the convention on Clinton's behalf.

The Association hastily rearranged the event schedule and placed the candidates back-to-back in the program.

President Bush spoke first, congratulating the Guard for its performance in the desert, and was quick to mention that his good friend, Sonny Montgomery, always kept him straight on Guard issues. He was applauded, but the sense of restraint by the attendees was noticeable.

Governor Clinton came into the hall less than 45 minutes later. Accompanying him were Chairman of the House Armed Services Committee, Congressman Les Aspin and Congressman Dave McCurdy, both seemingly vying to become Secretary of Defense if the Democrats won the White House.

As Governor Clinton walked across the stage toward the podium, I was seated in a chair to his left. As he walked to the podium, he stopped to say hello to me. We'd known each other from numerous Governor's conferences in the past and we chatted for 30 or 40 seconds. Then he proceeded to the podium and began speaking.

Everything in Washington seems to be heavy with meaning and to the many folks who watched or heard about this later, this brief encounter took on legendary proportions.

Governor Clinton began with a few remarks emphasizing the "change" theme upon which his White House run was based. But I noticed that after about five minutes, he folded up the speech on the lectern and began speaking off the cuff. Part of his following remarks continued the campaign themes, and part addressed the Guard and the need to maintain a strong, community-based defense force. He alluded to his experience as a Governor and the high esteem in which he held his Arkansas Guard after seeing them respond to emergencies in his state throughout the 1980s.

Governor Clinton finished with greater applause than that given President Bush. He shook hands with everyone on the dais and then, unlike President Bush, he plunged into the crowd for 10 minutes shaking hands and making small talk.

Immediately after the speech, a reporter collared me and asked the inevitable question arising from the circumstances surrounding Governor Clinton and his military record: "Why did six thousand patriots give a standing ovation to a draft dodger?" I gave an answer befitting my reputation as the "State's rights General". I said we respect and serve both our federal commander in chief and our state and territorial commanders in chief. First and last, we serve civilian leadership and we have respect for whomever is President as well as Governor because they are the commanders-in-chief of the militia in Federal service and their state National Guard. I emphasized that <u>any governor would have received this kind of reception</u>. You might as well get out of the Guard if you didn't respect the governor of the state in which you served. After all, he or she had the power — and often had to exercise it — to put you in harm's way.

The convention appearances by Bush and Clinton received a lot of national attention due to the dual candidate billing and the questions surrounding each candidate's military record.

By the time I returned from Salt Lake, there were only seven weeks left until the election and it seemed there was a feeling of paranoia in the Building.

During the next few days, at least half a dozen high-level Bush appointees stopped me at various times during the day. "I saw you on television talking to Clinton at the convention," they invariably asked, "What'd he'd say?"

Now the person asking the question knew that nothing more than small talk goes on in situations like that. But it seemed everyone was hoping for some bit of undisclosed information, some tip about what Clinton had in mind for DOD. "It was just small talk," I'd tell folks, "Just a few things about the Arkansas Guard and how I was doing."

Despite disclaimers from me and other Guard leaders, a lot was read into the Clinton appearance at the NGAUS convention. There was worry that the Guard was going to go with Clinton — not so much the officers as the enlisted folks and NCOs — and more importantly, their families — at the grass roots level, those folks upset at the turmoil of the armories and the planned Bush Administration drawdown. Plus, as I would later tell folks, Clinton was a governor who had worked almost daily with his National Guard.

On November 3rd, Bill Clinton received 43 percent of the vote, George Bush, 38 percent, and independent candidate Ross Perot, 19 percent. A 12-year era of Administrations considered friendly to the defense establishment had ended.

Governor Clinton had campaigned with an expressed determination to focus on domestic policy, which many people felt had been overlooked by the outward-looking Bush Administration. And the plain fact was that a focus inward did not hold a lot of promise for the folks at the Pentagon. Plus he was a Governor and had a keen sense of the Guard.

Maybe I was to close to the subject. But maybe not. Two years later, when I was retired and on a plane from Nashville to Washington, I ran into a top political consultant to candidate Clinton, who told me, that the Clinton campaign had considered the Guard vote more important than the rest of the DOD establishment combined.

The day after the election, I attended my usual round of meetings at the Building and noticed the discouraged demeanor of the senior Bush appointees. And I will never forget one compelling comment, a thought which I knew was going through the minds of a lot of other folks. He said to me almost bitterly, "It looks like you folks in the Guard got what you wanted."

I'm not sure we in the Guard really wanted this. But it was clear that America's community-based defense force, particularly those folks living far outside the Beltway, voted for what they believed would help them and their hometown.

CHAPTER THIRTEEN

"A NEW CALL"

Five weeks after the election, even as the folks in the Building began to comprehend Governor Clinton's victory and the effect it would have on DOD, I left on a trip that would have been unthinkable even two years before: a journey to the Baltic nations to brief their civilian and military leaders on America's National Guard.

The visit had been arranged in August by the Administration and was part of the U.S. European Command Military-to-Military Contact Program. Like other official United States diplomatic missions being conducted throughout Moscow's former client states in Central and Eastern Europe, the attempt was to make military and political inroads — permanent inroads — into the former Eastern Bloc. The new Russian government was adjusting internally and U.S. officials were interested in establishing a favorable presence in the ring of nations around the former Soviet Union. This was, in effect, the outline of a new NATO front line and the U.S. effort served a dual purpose: It was to forestall a Russian return — by seduction or overt force — to these once captive nations, and, an attempt to help these nations develop democractic governments along Western lines. The non-profit Baltic Foundation of the United States was one of the prime movers behind these increased ties with the West.

The Guard was ideal in this situation. In the Baltic states, there was an acute interest in building an effective "Home Guard" for basic border security, for response to internal disasters, and for back-up of the regular defense forces.

There was a great sensitivity to the political moves of Estonia, Latvia, and Lithuania because although these nations won independence from the USSR in 1991, large contingents of Russian soldiers still remained in each country. One reason was that the Russians, officer and enlisted alike, simply did not have anywhere else to go. There was little for them in Russia, no bases like Fort Bragg, or Fort Benning, Riley, Hood, Stewart, Campbell and others which had the infrastructure to absorb large amounts of soldiers and their families.

Moreover, there were a lot of Russian civilians in these nations, camp followers dating back to the June 1940 occupation. Ever since that time, the Russians had forcibly seized the choicest homes and buildings in these nations. As a consequence, there was acrimony between the Baltic people and everything Russian. No wonder all of this combined for a tense and uncertain situation.

And here came the National Guard.

The administration, primarily General John Shalikashvili, who was then commander of U.S. Forces Europe (USAEUR), Chairman Powell, and Secretary Cheney believed that a delegation of active duty soldiers to those nations, led by an active, warfighting CINC, would send the wrong signal to the Russians, it was typical of the extraordinary political and military acumen of these three men. They knew that the National Guard-led delegation would appear to the Russians as non-threatning and helpful to the emerging democracies and their defense forces.

There were 30 members in my delegation, which included experts in civil defense, several doctors from George Washington University, a few colonels from the Bureau, and state officials from Missouri and Pennsylvania skilled in assessing and providing disaster information and assistance. Our plane, a C-22, also carried medical supplies, humanitarian items, and believe it or not, one brand new tuba requested by the Latvian government. We were briefed at Mildenhall AFB in England in early November and then flew first to Riga, Latvia. Before the plane had even come to a stop, we were immediately presented with evidence symbolic of the giant collapse that had taken place in the Soviet empire. Along one side of the runway on which we taxied were dozens and dozens of Aeroflot airliners. To me, an airman, it was obvious that none were operational — snow and debris was pushed against the wheels, paint peeled off the fuselages, windows were broken, wires hung down from the nose sections, engines were missing, and some wings had broken off and rested on the ground in huge misshapen metal heaps.

Along the other side of the runway were parked rows and rows of Soviet military aircraft — jets, transports, prop aircraft, and helicopters. Most were in the same condition as the airliners.

Even though the visit was supposed to be low key, the Latvian press was there to meet us at the airfield, where we held a brief press conference. An interesting sidelight was the wonder with which some Latvians looked at the African-American crew members on the plane. This nation had been isolated for so long that some people had never seen a dark-skinned individual in person.

We then went to meet the President of Latvia and then went to tour an ex-Soviet military base now occupied by the Latvians. This provided a fascinating look at the military organization and competence of our former enemy.

What I found most striking was that even though our visit had been planned for months, and even though some work had obviously been done on the facilities, *everything looked like it had been abandoned years ago*. And this was an active duty base!

For example, the barracks were wood with cement foundations. But the wood walls were splintered and rotting; the cement foundation was cracked and chipped everywhere. There was no shrubbery or trees, just debris everywhere, both inside and out; used lumber, cement, rocks, oil drums, broken crates, and rusting pieces of machinery. Inside, the barracks smelled like urine and wet rot, and the cots and beat-up footlockers were extremely close together. In the space in which we might put 20 soldiers, the Russian crammed 80.

Several hundred troops were supposed to use the latrine and shower facilities that we would build for approximately 40 U.S. soldiers. And again, these facilities were filthy. We were told that there were hygiene problems with many of the new recruits. No wonder — this entire unsanitary tableau was an invitation for disease.

Riga was similar in terms of its decaying, unwashed look. The entire city, its streets and shops and buildings, were equivalent to a city in the United States, circa 1940. Which made sense because the country had developed up to 1940 and had been frozen in time, thanks to their occupying Russian brothers. It wasn't that the Latvians were a backwards or underdeveloped people; it's just that much of the music had all but stopped for about 50 years and was just starting up again. I was later to see the effects of this seeming nationwide stupor in Lithuania and Estonia.

From a military standpoint, I ascertained that there was already friction between the new independent Latvian Army and the fledgling Home Guard. As I told several members of the delegation, it was a situation with which I was not unfamiliar. In discussions with Latvian political and civic leaders, I learned that the Latvians had a bit more trust in the Home Guard because it's center of gravity was the Latvian cities and towns. And, the Home Guard in Latvia has a lot of clout in the country's legislature because the commander of the Guard is by law a legislator. The Latvian Army regulars are judged to be too close to the despised Russian Army.

We attended a solemn Independence Day ceremony and laid a wreath at the Freedom Monument in Riga. It was moving rite — and it was not hard to appreciate the deep hatred of the Russian military occupation and how it had contorted the history of this nation. And not to be forgotten, a military band played at the event, complete with the brand new tuba compliments of the U.S. Army Reserve.

Later that same afternoon, I planned to attend a church concert featuring the second-largest organ in Europe, installed in a church built in 1201 AD. However, we were on a such a tight schedule that I had no time to change into my civilian clothes and went to the concert in my uniform. As we arrived we saw a huge, graceful building built of cut stone and wood. We came in from the back of the church and suddenly walked in upon nearly 1,000 people listening to the massive organ. Everyone had heavy coats on and breaths clouded from the pews as there was no heat in the chamber and the temperature was in the 40s. Our American entourage was escorted down the main aisle of the church to a group of seats and as we walked, I became physically aware of about 1,000 pairs of eyes following me. We took our seats as the music filled the huge hall.

It was apparent to me, after a few minutes, that a lot of folks were glancing over at me from time to time, from all around the sanctuary. After the concert ended and we got up to leave, a horde of people came over to our group and spoke with our interpreter. Whatever the interpreter said was being quickly repeated through an ever-growing crowed, with people quickly turning to others and speaking rapidly in Latvian. Soon the several dozen people had become at least 300 hundred and our group was surrounded.

Then people began crowding in around me tightly and shaking my hand. I became a little confused and looked over at the interpreter for an explanation to all this. He said that he'd told them I was an American officer and that I was delivering humanitarian relief and meeting with the Latvian military and the Home Guard. But even more compelling was that this was the first person in military uniform to be seen in this church for 50 years.

The same basic scenario — base tours, discussions with top civilian and military leaders, the delivery of supplies — played out in Estonia and Lithuania. Always, there was in the background, hovering presence of the Russian military; the rows of unusable, cannibalized aircraft at the airports, the shabby military facilities, the cities and villages in their 1940s time warp. What I found oddly ironic was that at a time when these nations were struggling to simply survive economically, with their lowest priority being defense spending, there was a great interest by all these military leaders in acquiring U.S. military equipment. Virtually every military official I spoke with asked about the possibility of receiving HUMVEEs, new trucks, communications equipment, artillery, our main battle tanks, Bradley Fighting Vehicles, and support aircraft. And, they all wanted to join NATO, a sign of the changing times.

As I later told Chairman Powell, Army Chief of Staff General Gordon Sullivan and Air Force Chief of Staff General Tony McPeak, the visit received maximum press coverage in all three nations, coverage which was undoubtably beamed to the East. More importantly, the trip made valuable contacts with the Presidents and key officials of all three countries and established the United States' first senior military contacts with the Baltic nations. Not long after we departed, U.S. Senators Sam Nunn and Richard Lugar followed us into the region. Again and again, they received laudatory words about the Guard visit; when the two returned to the United States, they made a point of telling their colleagues about our good work over there.

After my trip, representatives from the three Baltic nations came to the United States as guests of the Baltic Foundation. The Guard established state-to-country partnerships on the basis of the high rate of Baltic populations found in various states. Hence, we paired Estonia with Maryland, Lithuania with Pennsylvania, and Latvia with Michigan. Later, drawing upon these examples, we paired Illinois with Poland, California with the

Ukraine, and Arizona with Khazakstan. There are now many more partnerships. My very able successor, Lieutenant General Ed Baca, is solidly behind the program and it has continued to grow under his leadership.

The most pleasing closure to the trip was when Chairman Powell told me that during this important time in U.S.-Baltic relations, the National Guard visit had been invaluable in introducing these nations to the U.S. military.

It's through these types of partnerships that the United States can serve as a role model on how a democracy and its military can get along. And this also provides a way for Americans to become involved in what is a historic transformation in Europe, one which may well take a generation of contacts to solidify.

Two weeks later, I was back on the road — this time to Panama, El Salvador, and Guatemala. The purpose of the trip was to visit General George A. Joulwan, CINC of Southern Command, who was keen on showing me the key role the Guard and Reserve played in his theater. He hoped our presence would remain there even as budgets began going down.

General Joulwan was adamant about two things: the importance of Latin America to the U.S. and the importance of the Guard in the conduct of almost any military operation undertaken by the actives in the region. I assured him that it was our priority theater because of the cost-benefit ratio of training close to home and because our activities there contributed directly to U.S. national objectives.

General Joulwan was particularly concerned that we continue support of "Phoenix Oak" and "Coronet Nighthawk," the C-130 and F-16 rotations. He told me that El Salvador was a linchpin to the region and that it might behoove the National Guard to look into linking the Guards of certain states with Latin American nations for various future planning exercises.

In El Salvador, we were briefed on the ongoing peace process in the country and the ways in which the U.S. military was supporting these efforts through engineer and medical team exercises.

Guatemala was also a trouble spot, with human rights concerns a result of the nation's 30-year-old rebel insurgency. Embassy officials made the point that the National Guard and Reserve constituted the sole U.S. military contact with the Guatemala military and for that reason we were a key component in the U.S. country plan. I also visited with some Guatemala military leaders, including General de. Division Perussina, Chief of Staff, Armed Forces of Guatemala.

My basic conclusion from the trip was that the U.S. Southern Command was at the forefront of U.S. policy implementation in Latin America. In particular, the efforts of CINCSOUTH in the counter-drug arena directly affected the efforts with which these nations are able to deal with the war on drugs.

Frankly, this visit and the good relations with General Joulwan, who remains one of my best friends in Washington, were a kind of second wind for the Guard in South America, given the outcome of our previous involvement there.

1993 brought another piece of good news.

In 1991, the Army Guard had begun a program called "Standard Bearer", which was a way of ensuring that our high-priority contingency pool and roundout units were fully capable of answering a call immediately. Under Standard Bearer, which was directed by Colonel Mike Squier, the ARNG contingency force units are fully manned, fully equipped, fully trained and are validated by the Active Army. Our 38 highest priority designated operational units are packaged to be available within seven days of an alert for up to a 45-day rotation. By 1993, the residual effects of Standard Bearer had increased the readiness of Army Guard units, with 92 percent meeting minimum deployment criteria. Only 72 percent of the Active Army units could meet this mark.

By the time I had returned from the trip to South America, Washington was abuzz about the assembling of the Clinton administration, particularly who would head the Department of Defense. It looked as though Les Aspin, a former Army desk officer in the Pentagon had the inside track for Secretary; he'd waged a not-so-quiet battle with Congressman Dave McCurdy, a former Air Force Reservist, for the post. Aspin was better known; for years, his Congressional office had churned out "White Papers" on virtually every defense matter. He'd also survived some rough political battles in securing and then maintaining his chairmanship of the Armed Services Committee during the Reagan build-up and efforts in Nicaragua. Aspin's visibility and reputation as a hawk were deciding factors and he officially became Secretary of Defense in January 1993. As it turned out, he was to hold that position for less than a year.

At the time of the inauguration, we were operating under President Bush's Fiscal Year (FY) 1993 budget, which projected the Army Guard dropping to 430,000 in FY 1993, 360,000 in FY 1994, and then to 321,000 in FY 1995, an incredibly steep drawdown of forces. And yet, there was no possible way the Guard — or the actives for that matter — could take such a massive and immediate reduction in personnel. There was no administrative means of mustering out this many personnel in this time frame; there was no administrative or legal technique by which to close down units this fast. Remember, the states owned and operated the armories. Far apart from the administrative morass was that the unprecedented cut would be a public relations fiasco. Two months later, however, the Bush Administration was preparing to shut down.

In addition to the continual battles on the force-wide drawdown, there were other rocky fights for the DOD at the onset of the Clinton Administration. There was the President's executive order on gays in the military, a tough, inexplicable move not handled satisfactorily by almost anyone's measure.

Where, some of my close colleagues and I continually wondered, was the animating national ambition to suddenly tackle the gays-in-the

military issue?   There were the new guidelines on women in combat.
There was the use of Regular Army troops and equipment at the Waco
standoff with the Branch Davidians, in which 83 Americans lost their
lives.   There were several well- publicized instances of Administration
personnel snubbing the military, including an incident involving General
Barry McCaffrey, one of the true heros of the Gulf War.   And of course,
coloring the entire picture was the Clinton's own inconsistencies on his
draft record, which to this day affects his relationship with many uniformed men and women of all ranks.

The one abiding fact was that the force structure battles, like a bad
movie, continued on and on and on.

Inheriting the Bush downsizing plan, Secretary Aspin in February of
1993 issued a "Guidance" on Guard and Reserve Force structure, propos-
ing strength levels "consistent with what Congress has done in the past
with the Guard."

This single phrase was crucial to the Guard evading the proposed
cuts. The Army National Guard force structure ramp thus became the
following: 1994 — 400,000; 1995 — 400,000; 1996 — 386,000; 1997 —
375,000; and, 1999 — 367,000. What a difference from the 321,000 in 1994
proposed by the Bush Administration! Secretary Aspin's new Assistant
Secretary of Defense for Reserve Affairs, Deborah Lee, was a good friend
and very knowledgeable on Guard and Reserve issues. She also was very
supportive of the new ARNG strength numbers.

In an comprehensive effort to reduce the acrimony and inside-the-
building bickering between the three Army components, all the interested
parties agreed to participate in an "off-site agreement."

The term describes literally what it means — meetings held at a site
away from the Pentagon. General Dennis Reimer, the Army Vice-Chief
of Staff, was the Chairman of the group, which included Major General
Roger Sandler, Chief of the U.S. Army Reserve; Major General Fred Rees,
Vice-Chief of the National Guard Bureau; Major General Jack D'Araujo;
Director of the Army National Guard, and myself. Also included because
of their political clout and institutional perspective were four influential
associations — the Association of the U.S. Army (AUSA); National Guard
Association of the United States (NGAUS), Reserve Officers Association
(ROA), and the Adjutants General Association of the United States (AGAUS).
The overall purpose of the group was to stifle the internal and external
feuding and bring coherence, and hopefully closure, to what should be
done about the Total Army in the post-Cold War era.

In the midst of this much-needed debate, we were once again inter-
rupted.

Here came the infamous Midwest floods.

I travelled to Quincy, Illinois on July 13, 1993, to visit with National
Guard leaders and troops assisting with the flood disaster. My first
meeting was with the Adjutant General, Major General Donald Lynn, who
was in charge of the Illinois National Guard troops employed in disaster
operations along the Mississippi. When I got there, over 3,300 Guard

members had been activated. The NGB tasked the Michigan National Guard to provide two laundry and bath units, about 1,250 personnel, to Illinois to provide support to the base camps. As unusual as this may sound, these units were critical to the well-being of the civilian population.

We flew south to Hannibal, Missouri and then to the Illinois base camp at New Canton, Illinois, observing the security mission, the moving of families to higher ground, and the various searches for weak spots in the levees. We saw areas where the levee could not withstand the rising river pressure and simply broke, creating huge lakes across flat cropland. One levee just north of Quincy collapsed and the surging waters flooded over 14,000 acres of prime farm land.

The floods were undoubtably the worst disaster and one of the biggest emergencies I'd ever been involved with. This was not like Andrew which was an hour of real devastation followed by massive clean-up. The flood water kept surging and there was no way to begin any post-disaster mission clean-up until the waters had receded.

A few days later, I flew with Congressman Tom Ewing, Assistant Secretary Deborah Lee, Assistant Secretary of Defense for Reserve Affairs, and Major General D'Araujo, now Director of the Army Guard, to observe the Guard work in Iowa and Illinois. We visited several areas and then toured Des Moines and observed the work of the 1206th Quartermaster Detachment from Alabama, whose soldiers were operating Reverse Osmosis Water Purification Units (ROWPUs) in support of a local hospital. In the city of Des Moines there were over 2,300 Iowa, Texas, Alabama, Arkansas, North Dakota, and Ohio National Guard soldiers and airmen providing flood relief to the city and surrounding areas, and helping to provide potable water for the city's nearly 200,000 residents.

During our helicopter tour south along the Mississippi, we could see many of the 4,600 Guard solders providing assistance. We flew over thousands of acres of what appeared to be deserted farms and small towns — and all the activity was on the levee, bustling swarms of people looking rather small against the huge waters of the Mississippi. This was basic, manpower intensive work — filling and stacking sandbags — and it was heartwarming to see these dirty, muddy Guardsmen working determinedly to assist the helpless citizens of these river towns. I even saw signs during the visit reading "God Bless the National Guard," and "Thank God for the Guard."

General D'Araujo was particularly good during this crisis. He worked closely with the Governors and Adjutant Generals of Arkansas, Alabama, North Dakota, Texas, Ohio, and West Virginia to deploy 28 of these water purification units. The New York Air Guard pitched in with the C-5s of the 105th Military Airlift Group to airlift the ROWPUs and personnel from Alabama to Des Moines in record time. It took only 24 hours from the time I called New York for aircraft to the moment they provided potable water to the citizens of Des Moines. It was a typical Guard reaction to an emergency.

During this time, I was in daily contact with the very capable chief of the Federal Emergency Management Agency, James Lee Witt, whose people were doing a great job. Both General Bud Lawson, Adjutant General of Iowa, and General Lynn were performing expertly and once more, the national and local media showed the Guard responding rapidly and effectively to ameliorate another crisis.

Later, I traveled with Ms. Lee and Major General D'Araujo to St. Joseph, Missouri and Kansas City, Kansas to observe more flood damage and visit with Guard personnel, along with the Adjutant General of Missouri, Major General Raymond Pendergrass.

Even before the floods had receded, I made the decision to leave my post as Chief at the end of the year. Yes, I was eligible for reappointment for a second four-year term. But I felt it was time for a new generation of Guard leaders to take over. Throughout my almost 17 years in the Building, I'd worked hard to recruit and retain officers to compete for Deputy Director and Director positions, as well as other top posts within the Bureau. The result was bringing in Generals Rees, Killey, D'Araujo, Navas, Sheppard, and Weaver, and a lot of other folks for other crucial, senior jobs.

Early on, I'd made a conscious decision to go after people who were prior active-duty and Vietnam combat veterans, and had experience with state-federal call-ups. I knew that the active folks respected this kind of experience. The result was that I considered the 1993 National Guard Bureau leadership the greatest collection of generals the Bureau had put together in recent history.

There was no reason for me to stay on any longer — it was time for new leadership to take the reins.

And so in the spring of 1993, I went to the Army and Air Force service secretaries and to the service Chiefs of Staff and told them I planned to retire at the end of the year and that I thought we should start the selection process as soon as possible. Everybody in town knew that the new Administration had been slow in personnel matters and I figured that we should get out ahead of the whole process.

The drill for selecting a new chief was straightforward: There would be an announcement of the opening for Chief, NGB and a 30-day nomination period for the Governors. By the close of the process in April, five qualified candidates had come in: Major General Jim Barney, Division Commander in Indiana, Major General Phil Killey, the former Adjutant General of South Dakota and current Director for Air; Major General Bill Navas, former Vice-Chief and later military assistant to the Chairman of the Reserve Forces Policy Board; Major General Fred Rees, Vice-Chief of the National Guard Bureau; and Major General Ed Baca, the Adjutant General of New Mexico — a total of three from the building and two from the field. Background checks were conducted on the candidates in April and May and in June, the five-member selection board met. Chaired by an active Army four-star, it contained an active Army three-star, a two-star Army Guard Adjutant General, an active Air Force three-star, and a two-star Air Guard Adjutant General.

After consideration of the candidates, the board would recommend one candidate. The recommendation would go to the Air Force and Army Chiefs of Staff, to the Service Secretary, the Joint Chiefs of Staff, to the Assistant Secretaries in Office of the Secretary of Defense, and then to the Secretary of Defense. All the while, the DOD General Counsel would examine the background of the nominee. Then the nomination went to Secretary Aspin. He, in fact, received the board recommendation in August of 1993. He approved the board's nomination and sent the recommendation to the White House for final approval.

The annual NGAUS convention was being held in Biloxi, Mississippi that October and we wanted a Chief's announcement by then inasmuch as I was retiring from the Bureau on December 1, 1993. A nominee presented at the convention would have been a spectacular announcement for the new Administration in front of more than 5,000 Guardsmen and women.

Even before the NGAUS conference, both Democrat and Republican Governors had been calling the White House, anxious to get a Chief in place and working with the states. I had personally told Secretary Aspin and his staff that we had to move on this.

In late October, I went before the U.S. Senate to be confirmed for retirement on December 1.

The retirement procedure for three-star and four-star generals is rather unusual. These two ranks are considered by the military to be only temporary billets. When you are confirmed by the Senate for Lieutenant General or full General, you must return to the Senate to be confirmed at that grade for retirement.

It was at this point in the year, with no successor chosen by the White House, that I was told by some Senators that they would have postponed confirming my retirement — my official term as Chief expired in January, 1994 — if they'd known that the Administration would be this slow with this expected appointment.

By November 1, 1993, there was still no Chief, fully three months after the official DOD recommendation had been made. Most disturbing was that I had intentionally begun this process early so that my successor entered the budget process at the beginning of a Congressional budget cycle, rather than the middle or the end. This timing would also allow the new Chief to get up to speed during the December and January legislative lull. Instead, the White House delayed the whole process.

When Major General Ed Baca was formally selected as Chief, more than nine months had passed since the board had made its recommendations.

Even with the frustration and delay over the Chief's selection, I was ready to hang up my uniform. But I wanted to do it gracefully. Despite my longevity and a huge Guard network of friends, I didn't want to make too big of a scene. It had been the practice in the past for all the state delegations to come to Washington for a huge retirement party. The planes would roll in from all over, jamming Andrews Air Force Base, filled with Guardsmen of every rank.

I wanted to change this practice. So I tried to visit as many groups in as many units as I could to personally thank them for all the support they'd given me over so many years. I went to the Enlisted National Guard Association of the United States (EANGUS) convention in Columbus, Ohio in August. I attended the Air Force Association conference in New York where I received the Max Kriedler Award. I was the first Air Guard General to receive this award, which in the past had gone to men such as Tony McPeak, the Air Force Chief of Staff, General Colin Powell, and to Bob Hope.

There were big receptions at the Andrews Air Force Base Readiness Center, where I'd been the ground breaker and the ribbon cutter as Director of the Air National Guard, a nice juxtaposition. I also travelled to the Guard Academies. The I.G. Brown Air National Guard Professional Military Education Center in Knoxville honored me with a ceremony and dinner and named their library after me. At Camp Robinson, Arkansas, the home of the Army National Guard LaVern Weber Professional Education Center, they honored me by naming the main auditorium after me.

It was also a fitting climax to be honored by the new Army National Guard Readiness Center in Arlington, Virginia which I had dedicated in a groundbreaking ceremony as Vice-Chief and later opened as Chief.

In Washington, a retirement ceremony committee was put together, with Colonel Bryan in charge. It was decided to have the event at the Crystal Gateway Marriot, which has a banquet room capable of seating more than 800 people.

The retirement ceremony itself was scheduled for the Pentagon's Center Courtyard. The Army Fife and Drum Corps, an Honor Guard, the Air Force Ceremonial Band, and several dozen Army Guard soldiers and Air National Guard airmen in desert BDUs from the Maryland and Washington, D.C. Army Guards were in attendance. There was the passage of the state flags as myself, Secretary of Defense Aspin, and General McPeak, and other senior military leaders stood on stage. Also in attendance were then Deputy Secretary of Defense William Perry, Secretary of the Air Force Sheila Widnall, Congressman Sonny Montgomery, Senator Ted Stevens, Senator Wendell Ford, Congressman Jim Moran, and many others.

I received the Department of Defense Distinguished Service Medal, the highest award the Department presents in peacetime, the Army Distinguished Service Medal, and my second Air Force Distinguished Service Medal. I also ended up receiving 40 different state Distinguished Service medals.

The Pentagon reception was held at the Hall of Heroes. Later that evening, there was the final retirement ceremony, attended by Secretary Aspin; Senator Ted Stevens; General Bennie Peay, the Army Vice-Chief of Staff; the Air Force Vice-Chief of Staff, General Monroe Hatch; Assistant Secretary of Defense Debbie Lee, and many others.

My favorite event of the evening was a patriotic video put together for me by my friends, Lee Greenwood, Chi Chi Rodriguez, and Boxcar Willie, certainly an All-American way to end the evening. They are all public-spirited Americans and great role models, and I have worked with them throughout my career at many military functions. It was a night I'll simply never forget. *

1 December 1993.

I got up this morning and for the first time in nearly 30 years, put on civilian clothes. Tonight, I had dinner at General McPeak's home in the company of some true military legends — former Air Force Chiefs Charlie Gabriel, Larry Welch, and David Jones (also Chairman of the Joint Chiefs of Staff); Vice Chief of the Air Force General Mike Cairns, Secretary Aspin and his assistant, Larry Smith. We talked about — what else! — force structure. Aspin had been having these informal meetings with senior leaders on a weekly basis in order to strengthen his ties to service. He'd had a rough year. The issues of gays, women in combat roles, the bottom-up review, Somalia, and several others had taken their toll on him. And a year in the Pentagon hadn't changed his personal style. He was still a rumpled dresser, he was perennially late to meetings and events, and he had reputation for being indecisive. None of these things endeared him to an institution, the military, whose ethos was crisp method and discipline.

In spite of his expert knowledge of the military and his desire to listen, as these dinners demonstrated, just one week later, Aspin was asked by President Clinton to resign. I will always consider him a loyal American who did much to advance the readiness of our military.

My real epiphany came the day before on November 30, my last day in uniform. I attended the Air National Guard Senior Commander's conference as the guest of honor. And as I stood at the podium looking out at the hundreds of blue uniforms — I felt as though I shared something with everyone in the room. At one time, I'd been privileged to be one of them — a senior officer in charge of a hot, dusty airbase, dealing with Airmen Second Class and searching for engine parts and filling out DOD forms in triplicate — the place in the Guard where in that inelegant phrase, the rubber meets the road.

Most of all, the evening was an eerie symmetry to my first days as Deputy Director, filling in as a rookie sub for Major General John Guice at a Senior Comander's conference seventeen short years ago.

---

* Indeed, one of my closest friends is Chi Chi, who has two loves — the military and America's youth. I consider him one of the greatest and most compassionate Americans I have ever known.

CHAPTER FOURTEEN

"STAND DOWN"

"So far has the Army Guard come from those early postwar years of two-hour drills, repetitive cycles of recruit training, ramshackle armories, crude base facilities, substandard equipment, and nickel-and-dime funding, that it is now difficult to even draw a comparison between then and now."
    W.D. McGlasson, U.S. Army Historian
    November, 1988

Succinct and straightforward, the above statement is compelling in its description of the journey of the modern National Guard.

Today, in the mid-1990s and on the threshold of its fifth century, America's National Guard has emerged as a strategic deterrent essential to the short-term and long-term projection of American force. No other nation in the world has projected power with reserve forces like the United States did in Desert Storm. At the same time, the Guard continues to serve the diverse needs of virtually every community in the nation.

In 1997, the guard remains a key componant of the U.S. military establishment. Military analyst Philip Gold of the Discovery Institute writes that President Clinton's Department of Defense Bottom Up review, (required every three years under the Goldwater-Nichols reform legislation) anticipates and plans force structure for two simultaneous wars. As Gold points out, this scenario is simply not possible without a massive callup of Guard troops. Indeed, he notes that there were mobilizations of Guard units in even the smaller contingencies such as Somalia, Haiti, and Bosnia.

Another important point emphasized by Gold is that while Guard units are sometime criticized for their part-time nature, they retain a substantial share of combat veterans. This was true in the late 1970s and early 1980s with Vietnam-era personnel leaving active duty. Moreover, a new wave of combat veterans joined the Guard following the Persian Gulf war and the consequent downsizing of the defense strucure.

Back in April of 1990, having served as Chief for only three months,

I laid out a blueprint of what the Guard must achieve in order to serve as part of the nation's strategic deterrent force. In testimony before the Senate Armed Services Subcommittee on Manpower and Personnel in April of 1990, before the Gulf conflict, I said, "For deterrence to be credible, the Army and Air National Guard must demonstrate our capability in highly visible locations in concert with Total Force operations. National Guard soldiers and airmen must be fit to fight, indoctrinated in joint-military operations, trained in peacetime to use the equipment provided, and taught to sustain themselves in hostile environments. National Guard equipment must be state-of-the-art, compatible with its active component counterparts, and technologically superior to that of our adversaries. Training must be realistic, and conducted in those places where the U.S. military could be one day called to fight. On the battlefield of the future, Guardsmen will be called to serve alongside their regular Army and Air Force counterparts — and they will be no less vulnerable to the capabilities of the enemy. Therefore, Guardsmen must be trained in peacetime for the rigors of war. In view of this, the value of Army and Air Guard participation in varied locations both at home and overseas contributes significantly to our ability to achieve wartime objectives."

Moreover, I added that only 2.4 percent of full-time flag officers were Guard generals and they oversaw a force of 510,000. Overall, I felt my remarks to the panel were a definitive statement of policy, exceedingly important to articulate as the decade of the 1990s moved underway.

Only four months later these observations would be seen in a brand new light. There is no question that the National Guard's mobilization for Desert Shield/Storm was the culmination of my career in uniform and more important, the affirmation of the Guard's central role in the American military establishment. It was in this conflict that the Guard proved itself to be a full-fledged member of the Total Force.

As the Guard has transformed itself to become a vital component in a potential American face-off against an external threat, we've also examined ourselves in light of changing internal problems. Not only is there a seemingly higher rate of catastrophic natural and man-made disasters requiring thousand-plus personnel callups, there is a significant increase in violent crime and other social pathologies in our inner cities, particularly among our youth. It's something that we, as the nation's community-based defense force, can't ignore.

I recall with a mixture of dismay and disbelief a Congressional Quarterly compilation of the top difficulties in the public schools as identified by teachers over the span of half a century. In 1940, the top problems in our schools were "talking out of turn, chewing gum, making noise, running in halls, cutting in line, dress code infraction, and littering." In 1990, it was "drug abuse, alcohol abuse, pregnancy, suicide, rape, robbery, and assault."

It staggers the mind to consider the implications of such an environment for our children — and our nation's future.

Does the Guard have a role in trying to correct this?

Unquestionably, yes.

In speeches to audiences while I was Chief, I never failed to point out an interesting parallel, a comparison between the World War II generation and successive cohorts of American men and women. In the decade of the 1940s, nearly 14 million men and women — out of a population of 135 million — received military training, which provided these individuals with a foundation of, self-discipline, initiative, patriotism, and fraternity. Some went through the ultimate test — the crucible of combat.

In succeeding decades, fewer and fewer individuals received such training. And indeed, during the 1960s when the need for military manpower was its strongest since the Korean War, the existence of officially sanctioned exemptions from military service — most notably for college — created a contortion of that bond between citizen and state. The outcome was a military consisting predominantly of men from lower income groups and minority groups. Brave and many times unrecognized, these men bore the brunt of the Vietnam War.

In the decade of the 1990s, there will only be about 2.8 to 3 million men and women receiving that any kind of training, even as the draft-age cohort continues to grow and our population is double that of 1940. It's probably safe to say that (1) the structure and discipline of military training instills values that enforce positive social behavior; and, (2) that positive social behavior is certainly missing in the environment of our urban areas and inner cities.

Even as the Cold War began to wind down, many of us in the Building and elsewhere were cognizant of this nagging problem and its effect on our young people. It's also something the Guard felt more keenly than other components given our community foundation.

Thus, we began to look at ways we could help. We began to focus our efforts on using our large personnel base and broad physical presence, particularly in urban areas, to help youths. At our urging, in the Fiscal Year 1993 Defense Authorization and Appropriations Acts, Congress funded the National Guard Bureau to enter into agreements with the Governors for the purpose of conducting programs targeted at youth. My very able public affairs chief, Dan Donahoe, was assigned the additional responsibilities of overseeing these youth programs.

The goals of the program were to provide young people with the values, self-esteem, skills, education, and self-discipline to succeed as students and adults. We put together four basic programs, all meant to be preventive rather than remedial.

Probably the most visible of our programs is the Civilian Youth Opportunities Program, the aptly named "ChalleNGe." This is a five-month residential program, with a one-year post residential mentoring component for students 16 to 18 years of age who are drug free, have never been convicted of a felony crime, are unemployed, and are high school drop outs. The core components of the program are the attainment of a GED or high school diploma, training in basic vocational skills, instruction in leadership, health and hygiene, and physical fitness.   More than a dozen states currently conduct the ChalleNGe program.

There is a military-style structure to the five-month camp, complete with drill sergeants, barracks, unit formations, and uniforms. Admittedly, this is a tough balance to maintain: strict regimen mixed with a bit of understanding. Every day of the five months must place a heavy demand on these kids or they will have absorbed nothing of the program.   On the other hand, the training cannot be too hard or punishing because it will scare away its intended beneficiaries. Youths have the opportunity to literally walk out of the gates of these state-run facilities at any time. And indeed, they sometimes do.

Another program is the Youth Conservation Corps (YCC), a six-week residential version of the ChalleNGe program without the emphasis on attaining a GED or diploma. This is conducted at National Guard bases and like the much-heralded Civilian Conservation Corp programs from the 1930s, emphasizes outdoor work. Another program, the Urban Youth Corps is a six-week, non-residential version of the YCC conducted at inner-city armories. The fourth major Guard endeavor is Starbase, a program for youth in Kindergarten through 12th grade which exposes inner-city school students and their teachers to real world applications of math and science through experiments in aviation and space-related fields. The program also addresses drug-use prevention, health and self-esteem.

I'm aware that some people question if there is a Guard role in such social endeavors. Others, including many in state government and in the National Guard Bureau, believe that the unique Guard structure and presence is ideal for these programs. We have a longstanding base in the community and the ability to operate a quasi-military program.

And it's not just Guard leaders who feel that the Guard has something to offer in this arena. In May of 1992, I was contacted by Congressman Newt Gingrich, then serving as Minority Whip in the U.S. House of Representatives. He requested a meeting with me to discuss "Adding Value to America" ideas and with him was Congressman Steve Gunderson (R-WI), deputy minority whip, and several staff members. We reviewed a variety of youth and inner city oriented programs, the Civilian Conservation Corps, what the National Guard currently does in State status supporting youth programs, and the particular National Guard units which could perform missions in the inner city.

During this time, I also met with the Chairman of the Senate Armed Services Committee, Sam Nunn, and Chairman of the House Veterans Affairs Committee, Sonny Montgomery. We had many discussions on the problems faced by youth in America and talked about what the Guard, as America's community based-defense force, could do to help.

In addition to assisting inner city youth get a toehold on life, we looked at another aspect of inner cities in which the use of Guard personnel was contemplated: law enforcement.

Although this is a bold idea, it is not far fetched. First, you begin with the premise that the use of the National Guard by the states today represents an extension of Guard activities that would not even be contemplated 15 years ago. Additional missions for the Guard are not out of the realm of possibility.

Next, you consider the nearly unassailable fact that municipal police departments across the nation are overwhelmed today by crime.

To many local officials, the spoken or unspoken word is that to fight the ever-increasing crime menace, all of the Guard manpower, equipment, and expertise in their communities is an unused resource.

Sometimes, this desire to use the Guard has sometimes won Congressional approval: Both in 1981 and 1988, Congress passed legislation permitting use of the Guard in domestic drug control efforts.

As mentioned earlier, in 1977 in Hawaii, the Guard gave helicopter support in efforts to detect and seize marijuana fields. Just 13 years later, drug programs were ongoing in every state and territory (and they continue to be to this day). Such an expansion of the Guard role was astonishing, and yet, it was necessary and desired.

In my remarks to audiences across the country, I would continually emphasize that Congress provides federal funds for state governors to use National Guard in a counterdrug role and that on any given day, approximately 4,000 Guard members are involved. In 1994, for example, Congress allocated $164 million for 6,000 Guard personnel to assist 2,000 local, state, and federal agencies. Currently, there are 16 different counterdrug missions of the National Guard, including reconnaissance, radar support, vehicle inspection, drug detection, eradication, drug-lab testing, film processing, and weapons support.

Hence, the inescapable question becomes, if the Guard is used in this capacity, why not use us in other urban law enforcement endeavours?

In the District of Columbia, for example, the National Guard is in helicopters, performing aerial survey, photo reconnaissance, aiming bright searchlights on known crime areas, and performing data entry, communications, and other administrative tasks. On virtually any given day of the year, the D.C. Guard has 22 personnel serving on active duty in support of the D.C. police. And it's probably not enough. Also, the Puerto Rico National Guard is being deployed daily to help with law enforcement and presence in San Juan.

To use the Guard in a law enforcement role, National Guard members would have to undergo rigorous criminal law enforcement training and be schooled in search and seizure and arrests. Of course, there are limitations on use of the Guard in domestic law enforcement — first, the constraints on the time away from civilian jobs, and second, the aversion to use the military until the needs become urgent and acute. Moreover, there are certainly relevant concerns about civil liberties.

One alternative to random and sporadic callups of the Guard might be specific legislation. For example, in the 1993 crime bill, Section 90107, there was made allowance for designation by a state or local official of a "major violent crime or drug emergency area" to be determined by the President. The President's determination would be based on the immediate need to save lives, protect property, and provide public safety. And such a determination could clear the way for state mobilization of the Guard to respond to the emergency.

Discussion of a greater Guard role in domestic law enforcememt raises concerns. I recognize that.

And last, as I've said before when asked about the National Guard role in domestic affairs, I'll never forget the pleas of South Central Los Angeles residents, who, when our deployment was up in May of 1992, begged our soldiers to stay.

In August of 1993, I met with Attorney General Janet Reno to discuss possible National Guard support of the U.S. Border Patrol along the U.S.-Mexico border. Legislation had been offered by Senator Barbara Boxer, from California, which would require Guard personnel to provide manpower to the Border Patrol in an effort to reduce illegal alien activities along the border. Senator Boxer's legislation would have required approximately 500 Guard personnel on active duty annually with a price tag of $15 million. Congressman Duncan Hunter, Chairman of the House Subcommittee for Procurement of the National Security Committee, has been a strong proponent of increased use of the Guard on our borders.

While we in the Bureau were flattered to be considered for this role, I personally believed the long-term manpower needs contemplated by the legislation would have a devastating impact on the Guard's ability to maintain readiness for wartime mission requirements. However, I believed that other alternatives should be considered that would allow us to provide support and yet have less impact on our primary mission readiness. Attorney General Reno concurred with my assessment of the situation and agreed that we might be able to provide some support if the authority was given and we received sufficient funding.

Overall, this focus on non-traditional roles, whether it be crime fighting, assisting youth, or even patrolling the border was good for the visibility of the Guard. And it reinforced the idea that often it is internal forces which seem to present the most intractable problems to a nation's peace of mind.

It's almost universally recognized that the Guard has come of age in modern times. I and so many of my colleagues remember the days Colonel McGlasson describes, when it was a thin operation, under fire from the active components, caricatured by civilians and political leaders, and even unwanted by some of the communities in which we were based.

Testifying before the Senate Armed Services Subcommittee on Manpower and Personnel in April of 1990, I asserted,

"The contemporary National Guard is quite unlike the Guard at any time in its 353-year history. The Total Force policy of the seventies came to fruition in the eighties as National Guard members demonstrated that when given responsibility, backed by resources and training, the Guard could meet active Army and Air Force standards. Stressing the three pillars of military professionalism - modernization, education, and training - Guard units today enjoy the highest readiness ratings in peacetime history."

"The eighties was a time to lay the foundation for the Guard's long-term effectiveness as a valuable member of the Total Force. The 1990s will be the time to build upon this demonstrated record of achievement."

The past twenty five years have gone very fast for me. I have seen the National Guard grow into a modern, well-trained and motivated military force, closer to the active components than any previous time in history.

Our forefathers, when debating the role of the militia for the future of the newly created Nation, believed very strongly in the responsibility of the citizen to serve and defend his homeland.

This is not to say that a professional force is not needed; indeed, quite the contrary. George Washington saw the need for a rapidly deployable army — by the standard's of his time — and the same is true today. Events effecting our national interests happen with lightening speed and it is crucial we have a highly trained, easily deployed and ready force to meet these frequent tests.

It's worth remembering that the Guard was more than 140 years old when President Washington considered building a professional army for the nation. The Guard remains one of Americas oldest institutions. And along the way has come one of the nation's oldest refrains, heard when immediate help is needed, when there is a need for unique talents, when lives and property are at risk in hometown U.S.A. or halfway around the world:

"Call out the Guard!"

EPILOGUE

1 November 1994

I'm driving through southwest Washington after a meeting on Capitol Hill. I'm headed to the retirement ceremony of Colonel Joe Gross at Andrews AFB. Gross is a Guardsman and an excellent historian whose book, *Prelude To The Total Force*, remains the classic work on the Air National Guard. It's a cold, overcast day and I've got some time to kill before the event. Suddenly I get the urge to drive by our old home, Quarters One at Fort McNair. It's been almost a year since we left that wonderful house, giving a final salute to my military career.

I entered through the huge brick entrance gates, saluted by the crisp, professional Army E-4 standing guard, and drove slowly along the wet streets of the base, quiet at this time of day. I rounded the bend that gives a panoramic view of the parade ground and "Generals' Row," 15 brick houses, each one occupied by a general. Each one is set alongside the Potomac River, which today is barely rippling under those long grey skies.

There, in front of our one-time home, Quarter's One, is a huge orange-and-white Van Lines moving truck, doors open and furniture sitting everywhere. Earlier in the year, Lieutenant General Edward Baca had been appointed Chief and today he was moving in.

It was an overwhelming moment for me; I understood then that the last chapter of my three decades of life in the Guard had closed.

The Guard continues to be a valuable partner in the Total Force with each passing year. It seems that everywhere you look, we're in the picture. It was an Air National Guard K-135 Stratotanker that fueled up Air Force Captain Scott O'Grady 10 minutes before he was shot down over Bosnia. And it was planes from the New York 107th Air Rescue Group and the New Hampshire 157th Air Refueling Group that supported the rescue operation, which plucked O'Grady from the ground.

Indeed, in September of 1996, the first units that had been mobilized for Bosnia. Were coming home from Operation "Joint Endeavor" and included the 715th Public Affairs Detachment from Washington DC; the 102nd History Detachment from Kansas; the 29th Public Affairs Detachment from Maryland; the 210th Military Police Detachment and the 1776th Military Police Company from Michigan; the 130th History Detachment from North Carolina; the 114th Public Affairs Detachment from New Hampshire; Detachment 4 from STARC, Pennsylvania; the 57th Transportation Company from South Dakota; the 30th, 1128th, 1129th and 1130th Finance Detachments from Tennessee.

And the Guard's role in the peacekeeping process in that area of the world is hardly over. Army Guard units were still being mobilized for up to 270 days in August 1996 to replace those that came home. In fact, 25 Guard units totaling 1,060 personnel from Massachusetts to Hawaii were to be part of the second "Joint Endeavor" rotation.

This precedent for the Clinton administration had been set two years previously on 12 September 1994. That was when President Clinton announced that Guardsmen would be mobilized for the planned invasion of Haiti. This was an unmistakable warning shot to Haitian military and political leaders that the situation had become deadly serious. The Guard deployment in Bosnia was a continuation of that model.

In another theater, a battalion of Guardsmen from the 29th Infantry Division keeps watch over the Sinai Peninsula, peacekeepers in a land of conflict since Biblical times. Guardsmen are in every theater in which this nation deploys active duty troops. The fact is, the Total Force has become so ingrained in the nation's military establishment that Guard deployments are simply a routine event.

Hurricanes Fran and Eduard hit our coasts with unprecedented ferocity during the summer of 1996 and the number of Guard personnel mobilized went into the thousands. There was a heavy Guard presence at the 1996 Atlanta Olympic Games. And of course, it is commonplace to find the Guard is training at bases throughout the nation, even as call-ups remain at an average rate of two a day.

But there have also been changes in the Guard community. My good friend, Congressman Sonny Montgomery, "Mr. Guard" in Congress, has retired and I know the Guard community waits for a Member or Members to step up to fill his shoes.

There is the new recruitment and retention campaign for the Guard, built around the slogan "You Can." It calls to mind the many campaigns of the past, each with their particular phrase intended to summon forth legions of recruits.

And the struggles over strength continue.

Following retirement, I was yet again involved in the ongoing (and seemingly eternal) effort to get a handle on defense restructuring. The vehicle was the Roles and Mission Commission established by then Secretary of Defense Les Aspin. I was a non-paid consultant to the Commission and after attending several meetings, I found that I was reliving the same force structure battles of the past.

Indeed, I had many conversations with Dr. John White, Chairman of the Commission and now Deputy Secretary of Defense, and I emphasized to him time and again that the Guard is a unique asset, and that no government entity (local, state, or federal) can do the job as quickly or efficiently.

One recent proposal has been to transfer some of the combat punch of the Army Guard (approximately 12 of 42 ARNG combat brigades) into the combat support and combat service support role. This redesign is contemplated so as to minimize the number of Guard positions lost as the active Army and the Guard manpower levels decline.

I continue to spend a lot of time on the Hill and I go to breakfast several times a week with many of the same old faces, including my successor as Chief, Lieutenant General Ed Baca. Members will often come over to the table to say hello and ask about the units in their districts.

Most of all, I try to remain visible around town, and perhaps to the point of gentle aggravation, remain an advocate for the Guard.

I do this for two reasons. First, even though I hung up the uniform, I simply cannot turn away from an institution which so profoundly shaped my life.

Second, and more important, I believe with every fiber of my being in the Guard and its service to this nation.

There is not a day that goes by that I don't reflect on what an honor it was to be associated with such a respected military tradition.

I believe every American should be comforted by the fact that there are neighbors and strangers who will drop everything they are doing and will rush somewhere to help their fellow citizens, for as long as it takes, for whatever it takes.

This is what public service is all about, and this idea of service is inculcated in the newest recruit, the gruffest NCO, the greenest officer and the most veteran Adjutant General.

Sometimes, late at night, I'll turn on the radio and hear about the progress of a storm or other calamity befalling a town, or an entire state, and I'll think that somewhere, at an armory or air base, orders are being issued and plans laid out. In Hometown USA, phones are being answered, uniforms are being yanked out of closets, boots are being laced up, and good-byes are being said to loved ones.

The call has gone out, and just as it has responded during the past 360 years, the Guard is on the way, responding to another community calamity to help restore domestic tranquility.

ACKNOWLEDGMENTS

Rather than the work of two individuals, this book bears the imprint of many men and women. Indeed, it's impossible to write about the National Guard and not become involved with the huge Guard family, both in Washington and around the nation.

First, we are hugely indebted to the heart and soul of the Guard residing at One Massachusetts Avenue Northwest, the venerable National Guard Association of the United States. We spent many months here, meeting with dozens and dozens of individuals, conducting hundreds of hours of interviews, and reviewing thousands of different sources, including books, personal histories, academic works, state and federal government documents, and NGAUS papers. Of particular note were the many days and weeks happily spent in the Edward Martin Library, a huge and unique historical collection of publications on the National Guard. The library is a gold mine for the histories of the Guard in the individuals states. As well, it contains the definitive collection of historical documents relating to the Guard at the federal level. We want to thank the ever-gracious librarian, Maj. Tom Weaver, for his patience in helping us discover and retrieve sources of all kinds.

NGAUS wasn't only the library, it was all the people who helped us, whether it be with insight about the Guard, tracking down a key document, or simply supplying us with a cup of coffee.

Thanks should first go to Major General Robert Ensslin, NGAUS Executive Director for allowing us to work in the NGAUS offices, and to Major General Edward Philbin, the current Executive Director. We also want to recognize the cast of NGAUS colonels who provided assistance (all of whom, by the way, have seen first-hand the dramatic transformation of the Guard): Colonels Chuck Schreiber, Dick Hostetler, Pete Denman, Paul Haynes and Ed Morai.

Helpful at every turn were the two wonderful ladies we called the "gatekeepers," Betty Hall and Sandy San Luis. Also deserving thanks were Kathy Dawson, Pam Johns, Pam Kane, Vic Dubina, Bonnie Carter, Pam Johnson, Tammy Milam, Rodney Oden, Cathy Privat, Mary Sullivan, Mary Willis and Cheryl Young. A special thanks to the wonderful Bernadette Phelps, who tracked down all sorts of obscure congressional testimony. These individuals provided a supporting cast that every writer would be fortunate to have.

Second, our profound thanks to the former National Guard Chiefs: Generals Vern Weber, Francis Greenlief, Herbert Temple, Mickey Walker and Wimpy Wilson, all of whom sat through hours and hours of interviews in the preparation of this book. Their insights and institutional memory form the backbone of the story of the modern day Guard and their contributions inculcate virtually every page of the book.

There are several others who deserve special attention. One is Colonel (now Brigadier General) Reid Beveridge, a recognized expert on the Guard's involvement in Central America, for reviewing portions of the text.

Also, our gratitude to Major General Bruce Jacobs (USA ret.), whose many pieces in *National Guard Magazine* and elsewhere seeped into our understanding of the modern Guard. Bruce Jacobs is a first-rate historian and has seen and written about it all during the past five decades.

Moving over to the Pentagon, there are several individuals who deserve credit for helping to shape this book. A person of immense help was Colonel Douglas Hollenbeck, who helped guide us through the force structure sagas. Then there are the very capable folks at the National Guard Bureau Historical Services. It's chief, Lieutenant Colonel Len Kondratiuk, is a superb historian and has an extremely wide knowledge of both Guard and active affairs. We've already spoken of Charles Gross, who is the premier Air Guard historian in the land. Gary Gault, also a historian with Historical Services, is also a recognized expert on the modern Air Guard and its operations. Also helpful in that shop were Senior Master Sergeant and Senior Enlisted Historian Windell R. Mimms Jr. and Lieutenant Colonel James Lightfoot. The Guard's Chief of Public Affairs, Daniel Donohue, is to be commended; his shop can always be counted on to put out useful, comprehensive information on the Guard, including the award-winning monthly newspaper, *The On Guard*.

Several individuals reviewed the manuscript, providing constructive criticism and just plain good advice. These included Lieutenant Colonel Mike Hill (ret.) and Colonel Frank van Fleet (ret.). Then there were the inestimable insights of my old friend, Brigadier General Stu Stewart, who provided us with some colorful accounting of the Guard's early years.

We had hundreds of discussions with Guardsmen, current and former. Some of the most valuable discussions were with members of the Maryland Army National Guard. Some of the people who provided shrewd observations were Sergeants Larry Gray, Gerald Thompson, Edgar Pruitt, Regan Plumb, Antonio Jones, Greg Holobaugh, Jeff Ezell, Linda Buchanan, Paul Pierson, Dennis O'Bryan, Steve Keefauver, and Terry Dodd. Others included Lieutenant Colonel Edward Leacock, Major Ed Schieman, Captain Kerry McIntyre, Captain Richard Amott, Captain Charles Deleon, WO3 Dennis Henley, WO3 Roosevelt Holliman.

Finally, providing key support throughout were our family members, including our wives, Linda and Beatrice, and our children: Ellen, David, Dan, Bolyn and Devlin and Braden.

A book of this breadth necessarily has many contributors and we were fortunate to have the support of all of these men and women during our collaboration.

LTG John Conaway
Jeff Nelligan
July 1997

A NOTE ON SOURCES

Rather than structure a formal bibliography, we thought the reader might find more useful an informal list of some of the more important sources used in compiling this book.

Essentially, the sources are broken down into the following types: articles from periodicals, monographs and academic studies, published books, the personal notes and papers of John Conaway, documents from various federal government agencies, and, testimony before Congress.

There were several sources that proved indispensable, offering a detailed look at the Guard and its development. One was the Annual Chief's Report, which is produced by the National Guard Bureau under the chief's name, and documents that the Guard has done during the previous fiscal year. The interested reader can obtain a good, year-by-year understanding of the Guard through these reports. Our research began with Chief's reports from the early 1960s.

Another useful source was *National Guard Magazine*, whose articles never failed to focus on timely issues of interest to Guard men and women.

Congressional testimony is always valuable in finding out where the principals are, officially, on a certain issue. Though there are hundreds of individuals who've addressed Guard issues before Congress, we have listed below the testimony we found particularly useful.

In addition to the sources listed above, the monthly magazine published by the National Guard Bureau, *The On Guard*, is always a good read and moreover, full of solid insights on the Guard.

Following this is a list of sources and publications that are easily obtainable for the reader who wishes to pursue the subject further.

MISCELLANEOUS SOURCES

The History of the National Guard Bureau, by Julius Rothstein, Historical Services Office of Public Affairs, National Guard Bureau.

The Chiefs of the National Guard Bureau, by Julius Rothstein, Historical Services Office of Public Affairs, National Guard Bureau.

The Abrams Doctrine: Then, Now and In The Future, a National Guard Association of the United States Symposium, July 1993, report and transcript.

The Air National Guard in Desert Shield/Desert Storm: Lessons Learned, January 1992, National Guard Bureau.

Army National Guard After Action Report, Operation Desert Shield,

Operation Desert Storm, 2 August 1990-28 February 1991: The Army National Guard as a Strategic Force, June 1991, National Guard Bureau.

Interim Report of the Total Force Policy Study Group, 15 August 1990, Department of Defense

The Air Guard: A Short History by Joe Gross, 1994, National Guard Bureau.

The Air National Guard in Operations Restore Hope and Provide Relief by Gary A. Gault, National Guard Bureau, Historical Services, February 1994.

The First One Hundred Years, National Guard Association of the United States, June 1978.

A Brief History of the Militia and the National Guard, by Renee Hylton and Robert K. Wright Jr.; Ph.D.; Departments of the Army and Air Force, Historical Services Office of Public Affairs, National Guard Bureau, August 1993.

Task Force Ordered to Tone Down Pro-Reserve Study, Rick Maze, *Air Force Times,* 17 June 1991.

Roles Panel Doesn't Roil Anybody, David C. Morrison, *National Journal,* 10 June 1995.

Mobilization for the Vietnam War: A Political and Military Catastrophe, by John D. Stuckey and Joseph H. Pistorius, *Parameters, Journal of the US Army War College,* September 1984.

Selective Service Without a Draft, by James B. Jacobs, and Dennis McNamara, *Armed Forces and Society,* Spring 1984, Vol. 10 No. 3.

Strategic Plan 2000 AD: The Long Range Plan of the Combined National Guard Association of the United States, NGAUS, December 1990.

Goldwater-Nichols Department of Defense Reorganization Act of 1986, Public Law 99-433.

Historical Perspective of a Current Problem, Why and How Governors Control National Guard Training, Major John T. Muegge, US Army Command and General Staff College, Fort Leavenworth, KS, 1987.

The National Guard, the Montgomery Amendment, and Its Implications: A History of the National Guard Experience in Central America, the Controversy Over State Control in Peacetime, the Enactment of the Montgomery

Amendment, and an Afterward by Colonel Reid K. Beveridge, DEARNG; Colonel James M. Burgess, ILARNG, and Colonel George L. Hargrove, US Army War College Research Associates, Fletcher School of Law and Diplomacy, 1 May 1990.

The Annual Report of the Reserve Forces Policy Board, Office of the Secretary of Defense, March 1996.

Report to the Secretary of the Army: Army Force Structure Lessons to Apply in Structuring Tomorrow's Army, GAO Report, NSIAD-91-3 November 1990.

BOOKS

Thunderbolt, From the Battle of the Bulge to Vietnam and Beyond: General Creighton Abrams and the Army of His Times, by Lewis Sorley Simon and Schuster, 1992.

Kent State: What Happened and Why, by James A. Michener, Fawcett Crest, 1971.

Citizen Soldiers: An Illustrated History of the Army National Guard, by Renee Hylton, NGB, Historical Services Division, Office of Public Affairs, Washington DC, 1994.

The United States Air National Guard, by Rene J. Francillon, Aerospace Publishing London, Airtime Publishing USA, June 1993.

Prelude to the Total Force, The Air National Guard: 1943-1969, by Charles Joseph Ross, Office of Air Force History, United States Air Force, 1984.

NATIONAL GUARD MAGAZINE

From Watts to Kent State: The Guard's Time of Testing by Colonel W.D. McGlasson (ret.) *National Guard*, May 1991.

A Foggy Future for a Ready Army and Air National Guard, by Major General Robert F. Ensslin Jr. (ret.), executive director, NGAUS, *National Guard*, October 1991.

Too Many Regulars in the Base Force Strategy, Colonel Ralph E. Kahlan, *National Guard*, August 1991.

State Callups: The National Guard in Action, *National Guard*, April 1988.

Largest Army Guard Reorganization Since 1968, *National Guard*, April 1988.

National Guard Training: Then and Now, by Colonel W.D. McGlasson (ret.), *National Guard,* November 1988.

The Active Guard/Reserve Program: In Search of an Identity, Colonel Joseph Galioto, *National Guard,* January 1988.

The Best Kept Secret in Central America, by Tech Sergeant John Tyson, *National Guard,* May 1988.

CAPTSONE: War Plans Key Factor in Mobilization, National Guard, January 1989.
Pushing the Limits of Posse Comitatus, by Major Aleksandra M. Roche, *National Guard,* August 1989.

Fuertes Caminos, The MP Mission is a 24-Hour Operation, by 1st Lieutenant Pamela Kane, *National Guard,* May 1988.

Desert Guard I: The Louisiana Brigade is First to Command NTC Unit Rotation, by Brigadier General (P) Frank Denton, *National Guard,* February 1988.

The Future of the National Guard and Reserve by Lieutenant Colonel Reid Beveridge, *National Guard,* July 1990.

The Hows and Whys of Mobilization for the Unit Commander, by SGM R.W. McDonald, *National Guard,* January 1989.

The National Guard in Armenia, by Major Leonid Kondratiuk, *National Guard,* February 1989.

Drug War - Rules of Engagement, Expansion Concern Guard, Captain Jean Marie Beall, *National Guard,* October 1988.

Major General Milton A. Reckord's National Guard Legacy Lives on by John K. Mahon, *National Guard,* October 1991.

Just Cause Provides Lessons Learned in Combat Operations, National Guard, August 1991.

The Air Force ORI: The Inspection That Proves Combat Readiness by LTC Reid Beveridge, *National Guard,* April 1991.

Berlin '61 Mobilization: Getting Inside Khrushchev's Head by LTC Reid Beveridge, *National Guard,* January 1991.

50th Anniversary: National Guard Mobilized for WWII, Colonel W.D. McGlasson (ret.), *National Guard,* September 1990.

Operation Just Cause: This is What We Train For by LTC Frank Adinolli, Capt. Ken MacNevin, Lt. Randell Parlett, and SSG Jerry Deyo, *National Guard*, March 1990.

The Devastation of a Hurricane, Capt. Ken MacNevin, Sergeant Bob Garrett, Pfc. Dawn Shelton, Pfc. Edna Rivera, *National Guard*, February 1990.

Soviet Perception of the Army National Guard: A Force To Be Counted, Captain Paul Vivian, North Carolina AARNG, *National Guard*, January 1990.

The Middle East Mobilization Major General Charles Kiefner, President of NGAUS, *National Guard*, September 1990.

Desert Shield: Retraining is Not Needed by Lieutenant General Herbert R. Temple Jr. (ret.), *National Guard*, February 1991.

When the Guard is Called, The Nation Follows, by Captain Jean Marie Beall, *National Guard*, January 1991.
Total Force Policy Examined in Wake of Desert Storm, Major General T. Easton Marchant, National Guard, August 1991.

Latin America: US Southern Command Offers Realistic Training, March 1990 by Sergeant Gwen R. Rhodes and SPC Steve S. Collins, National Guard, March 1990.

Speakers Praise Guard's Desert Shield Service, Editors, *National Guard*, December 1990.

*Guard Education Center*s Colonel W.D. McGlasson (ret.), *National Guard*, June 1991.

The Guard's 20th Special Forces Breaks Mob-Training Records, Capt. Jean Marie Beall, *National Guard*, August 1991.

The 48th Brigade, A Chronology from Invasion to Demobilization, by Gen. H. Norman Schwarztkopf Jr., *National Guard*, May 1991.

A Tribute to Black Guardsmen, Lt. Pam Kane, *National Guard*, February 1989.

How The Dick Acts Happened, by MG Bruce Jacobs (ret.), *National Guard*, September 1988.

In addition, there are two extremely valuable issues of *National Guard* magazine:

National Guard - 10th Yearbook Edition, January 1994.

National Guard - 350 years and Going Strong, December 1986.

CONGRESSIONAL TESTIMONY

Opening statement of Gen. John W. Vessey to the Senate Armed Services Committee, 2 Feb 1990.

Statement of Stephen Duncan, Assistant Secretary of Defense for Reserve Affairs, Joint Hearing before the Defense Policy Panel and the Subcommittee on Military Personnel and Compensation, House Armed Services Committee on *Recruiting and Retention Within the Reserve Components*, 1 May 1991.

Statement of I. Lewis Libby, Principal Deputy Undersecretary of Defense (Strategy and Resources) on *The New Defense Strategy*, House Armed Services Committee Defense Policy Panel, 12 March 1991.

Statement by Kim Wincup, Assistant Secretary of the Army for Manpower and Reserve Affairs, before Subcommittee on Manpower and Personnel, Committee on Armed Services, US Senate, 5 March 1990.

Testimony of Christopher Jehn, Assistant Secretary for Defense for Force Management and Personnel, Military Personnel and Compensation Subcommittee of the House Armed Services Committee, 7 March 1991.

Statement of Stephen Duncan, Assistant Secretary of Defense, Senate Appropriations Subcommittee, 19 March 1992.

Statement by Major General John R. D'Araujo Jr., Director, Army National Guard, Subcommittee on Crime and Criminal Justice, Committee on the Judiciary, 5 October 1994.

Statement of Mark M. Richard, Deputy Assistant Attorney General Criminal Division, Concerning Use of the National Guard in Domestic Law Enforcement, Subcommittee on Crime and Criminal Justice, Committee on the Judiciary, 5 October 1994.

Statement of Honorable Pedro Rossello, governor of Puerto Rico, Mr. Harold Johnson, Chief of Police, Sumpter Police Department, Sumpter, SC, Subcommittee on Crime and Criminal Justice, Committee on the Judiciary, 5 October 1994.

APPENDIX

Chiefs of the National Guard Bureau (Rothstein)

History of the National Guard Bureau (Rothstein)

Roles and Missions of the National Guard

Abrams Doctrine: Then, Now and in the Future
(NGAUS publication)

Total Force Policy Memorandums

President Bush's Reservist's Day Proclamation

National Guard 10 Commandants for the 1990s

The Chiefs of the National Guard
by Julius Rothstein Historical Services
Office of Public Affairs National Guard Bureau

Colonel Erasmus M. Weaver, Jr.,   1908-1911

Graduate of the United States Military Academy, class of 1875. Professor of Military Science at The Citadel, the South Carolina Military Academy, Charleston, South Carolina, 1883-1885. Remained a lieutenant for 23 years before being promoted to captain. Instructor, Department of Chemistry, United States Military Academy, 1888-1891. General Weaver was the first Chief of the Division of Militia Affairs, 1908-1911. After duty with the Division of Militia Affairs, he served as Chief of Coast Artillery, 1911-1916. Noted as one of the fathers of the modern artillery.

Brigadier General Robert K. Evans,   1911-1912

Graduate of the United States Military Academy class of 1875. After being commissioned a second lieutenant he served as part of the guard at Alcatraz Island, 1877. Following duty at different posts in the west, General Evans served at Ft. Leavenworth, Kansas, 1891-92.

His various campaigns include the Indian Wars; the Spanish-American War, seeing action at: El Caney, San Juan, Santiago, 1898; and the Philippine Insurrection, 1899-1900, where he received the Silver Star Medal with one oak leaf cluster. Served as the Commander, Philippines Department, 1917-18.

Major General Albert L. Mills,   1912-1916

Graduate of the United States Military Academy, class of 1879. Served on the Indian Frontier from 1879-1885. Professor of Military Science and Tactics at The Citadel, the South Carolina Military Academy, Charleston, South Carolina, 1886-87. Twice commended for actions in the Spanish-American War, participating in the Santiago, Las Guasimas, and San Juan campaigns. Received the Medal of Honor for distinguished gallantry near Santiago, Cuba, July 1, 1898. During this action, familiarly known as "the charge up San Juan Hill," General Mills (then a captain) was leading a detachment up Kettle Hill when he was shot through the head; although temporarily blinded, he continued to command his men. He was absent from duty until August 1898 while recovering from the effects of his wounds. After returning to duty, General Mills was appointed Superintendent, United States Military Academy, a position he held until August 31, 1906. During his long term at West Point he initiated numerous changes including the practical suppression of hazing, and the expansion of the Military Academy. After serving as Chief, Division of Militia Affairs from 1912-1916, he requested a transfer to the Hawaiian Department. In his request he stated, "In view of the prospective legislation (National Defense Act, 1916) which will probably require a complete reorganization of the National Guard, I feel that I must leave the Division of Militia Affairs in the hands of some one thoroughly conversant with the needs and conditions of the National Guard." General Mills died while serving as Chief of the Militia Bureau, of September 18, 1916.

Major General William A. Mann,   1916-1917

Graduate of the United States Military Academy, class of 1875. As a lieutenant in the 17th Infantry, participated in the Pine Ridge Indian campaign of 1890-91. He accompanied his regiment to Cuba during the Spanish-American War and took part in the battle of El Caney and in the siege of Santiago; he was awarded the Silver Star for gallantry in action. After fighting in the Philippine Insurrection, he was promoted to major in 1904 and returned to the U.S. for duty at the War College. General Mann's term as Chief of the Militia Bureau only lasted one year. Left the Bureau in November 1917 to command the 42d (Rainbow) Division, composed of National Guard elements from 27 states.

Major General Jessie McI. Carter,   1917-1921

Graduate of the United States Military Academy, class of 1886. Last Regular Army Officer to hold the position of Chief, Militia Bureau. A great supporter of the National Guard, but saw much room for needed reforms. Believed that "one of the greatest obstacles to efficiency in the

National Guard is the failure of states to appoint or elect properly qualified military men as Adjutant Generals of the States". General Carter wanted the National Guard to remain under state control, but wanted Regular Army officers appointed as State Adjutant Generals. Left the Bureau temporarily to command the 11th Division during the First World War. He was mustered out of service with his regiment on May 6, 1919. Promoted to brigadier general in anticipation of the reorganization of the 28th Division. Under the 1920 Amendment to the National Defense Act, General Rickards became the first National Guard officer appointed Chief, Militia Bureau. His term as Chief lasted from 1921 to 1925, completing a career in the National Guard which spanned six decades.

Major General Creed C. Hammond,   1925-1929

Enlisted in the Oregon National Guard in April 1892; discharged to enlist in the Regular Army in 1895. Discharged in 1897 and enlisted in the 1st Infantry, Nebraska National Guard. Called into federal service May 1898-August 1899; discharged as a first sergeant. General Hammond saw action in both the Spanish-American War and Philippine Insurrection. His campaigns include Manila (Spanish-American War); Manila, Malolos and San Isidro (Philippine Insurrection). Commissioned a second lieutenant in the Oregon National Guard on March 19, 1901. General Hammond advanced through commissioned grades, becoming a colonel, Coast Artillery, in 1911. Ordered into federal service as colonel, Coast Artillery, July 25, 1917-April 19, 1919. Came to the Militia Bureau as an Assistant to the Chief, Militia Bureau in 1922. Appointed Major General and Chief, Militia Bureau on June 25, 1925.

Major General William G. Everson,   1929-1931

Enlisted in the Indiana National Guard on April 22, 1898 and was immediately ordered into federal service with the 158th Indiana Volunteer Infantry Regiment until November 4, 1898. Served as regimental sergeant major, 2d Indiana Infantry, 1900-1903. Commissioned a second lieutenant in the Indiana National Guard on May 19, 1905. Ordered into federal service with the 152d Infantry as a major on August 17, 1917; during the First World War, served in Italy with the 332d Infantry, 83d Division. Discharged from federal service on April 29, 1919 as a lieutenant colonel. Promoted to Brigadier General and Commander, 76th Bde, 38th Division, November 1922.

Major General George E. Leach,   1931-1935

Commissioned a second lieutenant, Field Artillery on April 15, 1905 in the Minnesota National Guard. Saw duty on the Mexican border as a major and later, colonel, Field Artillery, June 1916-February 1917. Commanded 151st Field Artillery, 42nd Division, August 5, 1917-July 14, 1918. Saw action at in Champagne-Marne, Aisne-Marne, St. Mihiel, and Meuse-Argonne. For his service in the First World War, General Leach received the Distinguished Service Cross, Distinguished Service Medal, and Purple Heart in addition to other awards and decorations. Reappointed Commander, 151st Field Artillery November, 1921. After duty as CNGB, returned to command the 59th Field Artillery Brigade, 34th Division until 1940.

Major General Albert H. Blanding,   1936-1940

Began his military career by enlisting in the Gainesville Guards of the Florida State Troops, 1895. In 1899 he was commissioned a captain in the National Guard of Florida. As a colonel, he commanded the Florida troops during Mexican Border service in 1916. With the onset of the First World War, General Blanding was one of only eight National Guard officers promoted by Woodrow Wilson to the rank of brigadier general. As commander of the 53d Brigade, 27th Division, he participated in the Somme and Celle River campaigns. For his action during the Somme campaign he was awarded the Distinguished Service Medal for leading an attack on the Hindenberg Line. He was separated from military service after the war and in 1924 learned through a newspaper article that he was appointed a major general and Commander of the 31st Division. In 1936 President Franklin D. Roosevelt appointed him as Chief, National Guard Bureau. He headed the Bureau during an extremely turbulent time, with the country in the throes of economic depression and pacific sentiment on the rise. During his term he convinced the President to call for a buildup of National Guard strength and equipment. When General Blanding took office, the Guard had no effective antitank weapons and averaged only two tanks per division. Although the Guard was by no means at any level of satisfactory readiness in 1940, General Blanding had initiated the formation of a readily-deployable reserve force.

Major General John F. Williams,   1940-1946

Enlisted in the Missouri National Guard as a private on March 18, 1903 and was honorably discharged on September 1, 1904. General Williams was appointed a first lieutenant, Infantry, Missouri National Guard on April 2, 1917. Ordered into federal service during the First World War as Adjutant, 128th Machine Gun Battalion, 35th Division, August 1917-September 1919. Promoted to major, Coast Artillery on June 8, 1921. Appointed colonel and commander, 128th Field Artillery on April 21, 1923. Promoted to major general and Chief, National Guard Bureau in 1940. He served as Chief for the duration of the Second World War and immediately after the war during the initial reorganization of the National Guard.

Major General Butler B. Miltonberger,   1946-1947

Enlisted in the Nebraska National Guard in 1916 and was called to duty for Mexican Border service. During the First World War he saw action with the 4th Division in the Argonne and returned to the United States as a first sergeant. On May 12, 1923 he was appointed as first lieutenant in the Nebraska National Guard. In 1940 he commanded the 134th Infantry, 35th Infantry Division. During the Second World War General Miltonberger saw action in St. Lo, Vire, Mortain, Montargis, Morhange, Sarreguemines, Bastogne, Alsace, Venlo and the Elbe River. During his duty in the European Theater he received the Legion of Merit, the Silver Star Medal, the Bronze Star Medal with three oak leaf clusters, and the French Legion of Honor, in addition to other awards and decorations. In 1945, as a Brigadier General, he was made Assistant Division Commander of the 35th. he became Chief, National Guard Bureau in 1946. His first mission as Chief was to reestablish the National Guard as a trained, equipped, and deployable force. He instituted a national information and advertisement campaign to encourage recruitment, the first such program in the history of the National Guard Bureau. By August 1, 1947, when he was forced to retire because of physical disability, there were more than 100,000 enlisted and commissioned soldiers in the National Guard. Additionally, more than 40% of the units planned had been Federally recognized, another 20% were organized. In 1950 he headed the "Miltonberger Board," a team of present and former National Guard officers reviewing the Guard Bureau's organizational structure and internal operating procedures. Instead of recommending the creation of a separate National Guard Bureau for the Air Guard, the Board suggested the implementation of procedures which would ease tensions between the two services.

Major Kenneth F. Cramer,   1947-1950

General Cramer began his military career in 1917 when he attended Officer's Training Camp and was subsequently commissioned a second lieutenant on August 15, 1917. During the First World War he saw action in St. Mihiel and the Meuse-Argonne, where he was wounded in action and taken as a prisoner of war. After the war, he joined the Officers' Reserve Corps; appointed Captain, Connecticut National Guard in 1931. Entered Federal service with the 43d Infantry Division as a colone; transferred to the 24th Infantry Division and promoted to Brigadier General and Assistant Division Commander in 1942. During the war General

Cramer received the Silver Star Medal with three oak leaf clusters, the Bronze Star Medal and the Air Medal, and was made division commander in 1945. Following the war he commanded the 43d Infantry Division, 1946-1947. His term as Chief, National Guard Bureau was marked by controversy with the Director, Air National Guard; following an investigation by the Inspectors General of the Army and the Air Force, General Cramer asked to be relieved so that he could command the 43d Division as it was called into Federal service in 1950 for the Korean War.

Major General Raymond H. Fleming,   1950-1953

Enlisted in the Louisiana National Guard and served as a sergeant on the Mexican Border in 1916. Commissioned a second lieutenant in the 141st Field Artillery in 1917. In July 1928 General Fleming was appointed the Adjutant General of Louisiana and served in this position for 20 consecutive years. While serving as Adjutant General, he also commanded the 55th Cavalry Brigade, 23d Cavalry Division. In 1940 he was ordered into Federal service as the state director of the Selective Service System of Louisiana. General Fleming came to the Guard Bureau in 1948 and was the first person to hold the office of Chief, Army Division, National Guard Bureau. He held the office of Chief, National Guard Bureau from 1950-1953. After his term he returned to Louisiana and once again served as the Adjutant General, a position he held for a total of 24 years.

Major General Edgar C. Erickson,   1953-1959

Enlisted in the Massachusetts National Guard in April 1914 and served on the Mexican Border in 1916. Commissioned a second lieutenant in 1917 and served with the 26th Division in France, 1917-18. Served as the Adjutant General of Massachusetts, 1939-1942. Called into Federal service from 1940-1942 as the State Director, Selective Service, Massachusetts. Accepted a demotion to the rank of Colonel in 1942 to go on active service in the infantry. General Erickson was later assigned as liaison officer with the Chinese Nationalist Army for the remainder of the Second World War.

Major General Donald W. McGowan,   1959-1963

Enlisted in the New Jersey National Guard and served on the Mexican Border in 1916 at the age of 16. General McGowan was promoted successively in noncommissioned grades before going to Europe with the 29th Division as battalion sergeant major in 1918. Saw action in the Meuse-Argonne and Alsace campaigns. Discharged in 1918 to attend the United States Military Academy. Resigned from West Point in 1919 and rejoined the New Jersey National Guard. Commissioned a lieutenant colonel while serving as the Assistant Adjutant General of New Jersey, 1936-1941. In 1941 he was called into federal service as Commander, 102d Cavalry Regiment. Participated in the D-Day assault on Omaha Beach. Later detailed as Provost Marshal, Normandy Base Section, 1944; his responsibilities were expanded to include Britanny, the Lower Seine, Belgium and Holland. Commanded 50th Armored Division, 1948-1955. Served as Chief, National Guard Bureau, 1959-1963. The National Guard experienced numerous challenges and reforms during his term as CNGB. The mobilization of 65,438 National Guard troops during the Berlin Crisis of 1961 was hailed as "the most successful mobilization in history." His administration initiated better and more numerous drill and training periods. Also, Officer Candidate Schools increased from 5 to 51. The Guard, during his term, converted from anti-aircraft guns to NIKE-AJAX and HERCULES missiles. Furthermore, the Guard underwent two major reorganizations: The 1959 reorganization under the ROAD (Reorganization Objectives, Army Divisions). Additionally, the first Special Forces units were organized in the Army National Guard during his tenure.

Major General Winston P. Wilson,   1963-1971

Enlisted as a mechanic with the 154th Observation Squadron, Arkansas National Guard in 1929. Commissioned a second lieutenant in 1940. Went on active duty with the 154th in September 1940, and during WWII served both in Washington, DC and in the Pacific Theatre, ending the war as Assistant Photo Officer, Far East Air Forces. In 1950 came to duty with the National Guard Bureau and became Chief, Air Division, NGB in 1953.

General Wilson believed Air Guard units should be measured and trained under the same criteria as Active Air Force units. He integrated the ANG into the operations of the USAF; the Runway Alert Program, which in 1954 gave the ANG the real-world air defense mission, initiated the Total Force concept for Reserve Components. Wilson also converted the ANG from weekly drills to weekend Unit Training Assemblies, a pattern later adopted by all Reserve Components. At General Wilson's urging the ANG was given its first multi-engine jet transports, and began deploying worldwide.

In 1963 Governors from 51 of the 52 States and Territories nominated General Wilson for Chief, National Guard Bureau. The first Air Guardsman appointed to the position of Chief, he emphasized better mobility and increased readiness, and saw the Guard through its mobilization for the Vietnam War.

General Wilson remained in the Bureau until his retirement in 1971.

Major General Francis S. Greenlief,   1971-1974

General Greenlief began his military career by enlisting in the Nebraska National Guard in July 1940. He was ordered to active duty in December 1940 with the 134th Infantry Regiment as a corporal. When he entered Infantry Officer Candidate School in May 1942, he was acting company First Sergeant. General Greenlief was commissioned a second lieutenant in August 1942. He went to Europe with the 134th, and saw action in Normandy, Northern France, Rhineland, and the Ardennes. Received the Silver Star Medal, the Bronze Star Medal and the Purple Heart w/3 OLCs, in addition to the other awards and decorations. General Greenlief was ordered to duty in the National Guard Bureau in 1960 as Executive Officer, Army Division, NGB. As a brigadier general, he was designated Assistant Chief, Army, NGB in November 1962. The following year, General Greenlief was named Deputy Chief, NGB. He was appointed as Director, Army National Guard in 1970. Became Chief, National Guard Bureau in 1971.

Lieutenant General La Vern E. Weber,   1974-1982

Began his military career by enlisting in the United States Marine Corps Reserve in 1942. Commissioned a second lieutenant, USMCR, upon graduation from Officer Candidate School in 1945, and ordered to active duty until May 1946. General Weber left the United States Marine Corps Reserve in 1948 when he accepted an appointment as a second lieutenant in the Oklahoma Army National Guard. Served in Korea with the 180th Infantry, 45th Infantry Division and was promoted to major in May 1952. Was promoted to major in May 1952. Was promoted to major general concurrent with an appointment as Adjutant General of Oklahoma in 1965. Served as Director, Army National Guard, NGB 1971-1974. Appointed Chief, National Guard Bureau in 1974 and was appointed for a second term in 1978. In 1979 General Weber was promoted to lieutenant general, the first Chief to hold this rank. He received this promotion as result of a concurrent elevation of the Chief, National Guard Bureau from a major general to a lieutenant general.

Lieutenant General Emmett H. Walker Jr.,   1982-1986

Enlisted in the United States Army in December 1942, attended Officer Candidate School at Fort Benning, GA and was commissioned a second lieutenant, infantry, on May 23, 1944. General Walker served with the 95th Infantry Division during the Second World War and was awarded the Silver Star Medal and Bronze Star Medal with "V" Device. He separated from active service in 1946 and joined the Mississippi Army National Guard as a first lieutenant in May 1949. General Walker was ordered into active duty during the Korean War as a captain with the 31st Infantry Division, and was assigned to the Far East Command Headquarters, Japan, January 1951-September 1952. After the war he returned to the Mississippi National Guard where he performed various duties including commanding the 4th Howitzer Battalion, 114th Field Artillery, and the 631st Artillery Group. He also served as Assistant Adjutant General of Mississippi, 1972-1976. In 1976 General Walker was ordered to active duty as a brigadier general and Assistant to the Director, Army National Guard. He also served as Deputy Director and Director of the Army National Guard. General Walker was promoted to lieutenant general and was appointed Chief, National Guard Bureau on August 16, 1982.

Lieutenant General Herbert R. Temple Jr.,   1986-1990

Enlisted in the California Army National Guard on June 2, 1947 and served with the 160th Infantry Regiment, 40th Infantry Division. Ordered to active duty on September 1950; served as a Non-Commissioned Officer with the 24th Infantry Division in Korea and received a Korean Service Medal with one bronze service star, in addition to other awards and decorations. Upon being discharged in 1952, General Temple rejoined the California National Guard, and was commissioned a second lieutenant in October 1952. General Temple rose successively through commissioned ranks in the 40th Division to the position of Battalion Commander. Served as Commandant, California Military Academy. Was the Military Assistant to the Governor of California, 1968-1971. Served as Deputy Commander, 49th Infantry Brigade, 1971-74, and commanded the 3d Brigade, 40th Infantry Division, 1974. General Temple came to the Guard Bureau in 1975 and remained until his retirement as Chief, National Guard Bureau, in 1990. During his involvement with the Bureau General Temple held the positions of Chief, Office of Mobilization Readiness; Chief, Office of Policy and Congressional Liaison; Deputy Director, Army National Guard; Director, Army National Guard; and Chief, National Guard Bureau.

Lieutenant General John B. Conaway,   1990-1994

General Conaway began his military career in the Reserve Officer Training Corps program at the University of Evansville. He was commissioned a second lieutenant in the United States Air Force in June 1956. In 1960 General Conaway joined the West Virginia Air National Guard, later transferring to the Kentucky Air National Guard. He was ordered to active duty in January 1968 and served in Alaska, Panama, Japan and Korea. He returned to the Kentucky Air National Guard in 1969. In 1972, General Conaway was appointed Air Commander, Kentucky Air National Guard. In 1974, he was appointed Vice Commander, 123d Tactical Reconnaissance Wing, composed of units of Kentucky, Arkansas, Nevada, and Idaho. In 1977, General Conaway was recalled to active duty as Deputy Director, Air National Guard. In 1981, he was appointed Director, Air National Guard, NGB. He held this position until 1988, when he was appointed to the newly-created position of Vice Chief, National Guard Bureau. In February 1990 General Conaway was promoted to lieutenant general and assumed the office of Chief, National Guard Bureau.

Lieutenant General Edward D. Baca,   1994 -

General Baca began his military career in 1956 with enlistment in Battery C, 726th Anti-aircraft Artillery Battalion, New Mexico Army National Guard. He served as an Anti-aircraft gunner and supply sergeant and graduated from Officer Candidate School in 1962. He volunteered for active duty during the Vietnam conflict, went overseas to Southeast Asia, and upon release from active duty in 1966, returned to the New Mexico National Guard. In 1977, he became the State Military Personnel Officer, then the State Command Administrative Officer in 1979, and was appointed adjutant general of the New Mexico National Guard in 1983. He served in that capacity until his promotion to lieutenant general and assignment as Chief, National Guard Bureau on October 1, 1994. His military education includes the Ordnance Basic Course, the Ordnance Officer Advanced Course, and the Command and General Staff Officer Course. His awards include the Army Distinguished Service Medal, the Legion of Merit, the Meritorious Service Media, the Army Commendation Medal, the National Defense Service Medal with one Bronze Service Star, the Vietnam Service Medal and the Republic of Vietnam Cross of Gallantry with Palm Unit Citation.

The History of the National Guard Bureau
By Julius Rothstein
Historical Services Office of Public Affairs
National Guard Bureau

The National Guard Bureau is the federal instrument responsible for the administration of the National Guard. Established by Congress as a Joint Bureau, of the Departments of the Army and the Air Force, it holds a unique status as both a staff and operation agency. Throughout its more than 80-year old history, the National Guard Bureau has repeatedly proven that the National Guard can effectively perform its duties, with its own personnel, at a high level of professionalism.

The National Guard Bureau dates back to he turn of the century. After the Spanish-American war of 1898 which demonstrated weaknesses in the militia, as well as in the entire United States military. Secretary of War Elihu Root initiated a program of reform and reorganization in the military establishment. The impetus for reform led to the Militia Act of 1903, better known as the Dick Act.

The Beginnings of Federalization

United States Senator Charles Dick, a Major General in the Ohio National Guard, sponsored the 1903 act, which gave Federal status to the militia. Under this legislation the organized militia of the States was required to conform to Regular Army organization within five years. The act also required National Guard units to attend 24 drills and five days annual training a year, and, for the first time, provided for pay for annual training. In return for the increased Federal funding which the act made available, militia units were subject to inspection by Regular Army officers, and had to meet certain standards.

The increase in Federal funding was an important development. In 1808 Congress had allocated $200,000 a year to arm the militia; by 1887, the figure had risen to only $400,000. But in 1906, three years after the passage of the Dick Act, $2,000,000 was allocated to arm the militia; between 1903 and 1916, the Federal government spent $53,000,000 on the Guard, more than the total of the previous hundred years.

With the increase in Federal funding came an increase in paperwork and bureaucracy. Before the passage of the Dick Act, militia affairs had been handled by the various bureaus of the War Department, as the subject dictated. But the 1903 act authorized, for the first time, the creation of a separate section responsible for the National Guard affairs. Located in the Miscellaneous Division of the Adjutant General's office, this small section, headed by Major James Parker, Cavalry, with four clerks, was the predecessor of today's National Guard Bureau.

This section remained under the supervision of the Adjutant General's Office until War Department Orders on February 12, 1908 created the

Division of Militia Affairs in the Office of the Secretary of War. The act also provided for "necessary clerical and official expense of the Division of Militia Affairs". Lieutenant Colonel Erasmus M. Weaver, Coast Artillery Corps, assumed duties as the division's first Chief. An increasing volume of business meant more personnel, and the four clerks had by this time increased to 15.

The Division remained a part of the Office of the Secretary of War until July 25, 1910 when the Chief was directed to report directly to the Army Chief of Staff. The Division continued to perform under the direct jurisdiction of the Chief of Staff until passage of the National Defense Act of June 3, 1916. Then the Division of Militia Affairs became the Militia Bureau of the War Department, under the direct supervision of the Secretary of War.

The Division Becomes a Bureau

The National Defense Act of 1916 is, with the exception of the United States Constitution, the most important piece of legislation in the history of the National Guard. It transformed the militia from individual state forces into a Reserve Component of the U.S. Army - and made the term "National Guard" mandatory. The act stated that all units would have to be federally recognized, and that the qualifications for officers would be set by the War Department. It increased the number of annual training days to 15, increased the number of yearly drills to 48, and authorized pay for drills.

The 1916 act transformed the Division of Militia Affairs into a separate Militia Bureau, increasing its autonomy and authority. Eight new civilian positions were authorized, something which the various Chiefs had been requesting for years; the number of military assigned to the Bureau had grown to 13. The National Defense Act also gave Presidential authority to assign two National Guard officers to duty with the Militia Bureau. The inclusion of National Guard officers in the Militia Bureau was an important step towards creating a centralized planning organization for the National Guard headed by its own officers. The first National Guard officer assigned to the Bureau was Major Louis C. Wilson of Texas in 1916.

On September 11, 1917 War Department General Order 119 stated that the jurisdiction of the Militia Bureau includes "coordination through the office of the Chief of Staff, of the organization, equipment, and instructions of the National Guard under department commanders in a manner similar to the coordination by the Chief of Staff of the organization, equipment, and training of the Regular Army under department commanders." Thus the National Guard Bureau was charged with the responsibility of maintaining high standards in the National Guard.

Prior to 1910 the Chief of the Militia Bureau was a Regular Army officer. This situation changed on June 4, 1920 when Congress passed an amendment to the National Defense Act of 1916. One of the the amendment's conditions stated that effective January 1, 1921, the Chief of the National Guard Bureau would be selected from lists of present or former National Guard officers.

The act reads:

The Chief National Guard Bureau shall be appointed by the President, by and with the advice and consent of the Senate, by selection from the lists of officers of the National Guard of the United States recommended as suitable for such appointment by their respective Governors, and who have had ten or more years commissioned service in the National Guard ...The Chief of the National Guard Bureau shall hold office for four years unless sooner removed for cause, and shall not be eligible to succeed himself (NOTE: it was later amended that the Chief could succeed himself)...Upon accepting his office, the CNGB shall be appointed a Major General in the National Guard of the United States, and commissioned in the Army of the United States, and while serving shall have the rank, pay, and allowances of a Major General.

The first appointee under these provisions was Major General C. Rickards of Pennsylvania. The amendment also provided for the creation of a General Staff committee of National Guard officers which could recommend policies affecting the Guard.

The Bureau was known as the Militia Bureau until it was redesignated as the National Guard Bureau by an amendment to Section 81 of the National Defense Act on June 15, 1933. Furthermore, this amendment worked towards settling the issue of the National Guard as a reserve component. It stated that there would be two National Guards: the National Guard of the several States, and the National Guard of the United States. The former would be the individual State militias, employed in local emergencies and national defense. The latter would be a deployable reserve component of the Army.

The National Guard Bureau During World War II

The National Guard began mobilization on September 16, 1940 and a total of 18 National Guard Divisions (plus one more assembled from National Guard units), as well as 29 National Guard Army Air Forces observation squadrons saw action in both the Pacific and European Theatres. The National Guard Bureau also experienced changes during the war years.

The first of these changes occurred on March 2, 1942 under War Department Circular number 59. This order reorganized the War Department and Army under the authority of the first War Powers Act. It specifically affected the Bureau by designating it as a part of the Adjutant General's Office. On April 27 of the same year, General Orders No. 9, Headquarters, Service and Supply, established the National Guard Bureau as an "independent administrative service of the Services of Supply," under the jurisdiction of the Chief of Administrative Services.

The third major order affecting the National Guard Bureau was Army Service Forces (ASF) circular No. 118 which came on November 11, 1943. It stipulated that the Chief of the National Guard Bureau was directed to report to the Commanding General, Army Service Forces. Finally on May 17, 1945, General Order No. 39 stated that the National Guard Bureau was removed from the jurisdiction of the Commanding General Army Service Forces, and established it as a war Department Special Staff activity.

With the entire National Guard on Federal service, the mission and functions of the Bureau were reduced. A large part of the Bureau's wartime work consisted of managing the State Guards which in wartime took over a great deal of the Guard's state mission, and keeping up the personnel records of Federally recognized National Guard officers on active duty.

The numbers of military office's assigned to the Bureau declined sharply, and the number of the Bureau's civilian personnel went from 140 in 1940 to 49 in 1945. There were practically no promotions awarded to National Guard Bureau civilians, which did not compare favorably with other War Department agencies. This made retaining those few key civilians employees needed in maintaining good relations with the States and working towards planning the post-war reorganization of the National Guard extremely difficult.

Post-War National Guard Bureau

During the war years, annual leave was restricted for all War Department civilian employees. National Guard Bureau civilian personnel certainly could have been spared, since their work-load had been greatly reduced. When the freeze on annual leave was limited in 1945 civilian employees were compelled to use their leave or lose it. At the war's end the National Guard Bureau desperately needed its full military and civilian staff, for the task of reorganizing the National Guard in the states. However, the number of personnel was not expanded quickly enough to facilitate such activity. The frantic post-war reorganization of the National Guard was coordinated by an under-staffed Guard Bureau.

In addition to the reorganization of the National Guard, the Bureau also had to deal with internal organizations. The most important of these was the creation of the Air Force and consequently, the Air National Guard. Under the National Security Act of July 16, 1947, Congress approved the creation of a separate division within the National Guard Bureau for the Air National Guard, thus transferring the functions, powers, and duties from the Department of the Army and the Secretary of the Army to the Department of the Air Force and the Secretary of the Air Force.

After World War II the National Guard Bureau and the Army Air Forces jointly prepared a plan for the Air National Guard. Among the foreseeable problems were supplies of aircraft, type and distribution of units, training, recruitment of trained personnel, and strength in relation to the Air Force and Air Force Reserve. In 1946 a plan calling for the creation of 12 wings, 27 groups and 84 fighter and light bombardment squadrons was authorized and tendered to the States. June 30, 1946 saw the federal recognition of the first postwar Air Guard unit, the 120th Fighter Squadron, based at Buckley Field, Denver, Colorado.

Although the projected date of July 1, 1947 for organizing all Air Guard units could not be met due to drastic cuts in federal funding (the Air Guard only received $154 million instead of the requested $536 million during FY 1947-1949), by May 1949 514 units had been organized and federally recognized. In 1949 the Army and Air Force Authorization Act (Public Law 604, 81st Congress) formally established a legal existence which provided that the Air Force of the United States shall consist of, among other components, the Air National Guard of the U.S., composed of federally recognized units and personnel of the several States. This Act established an independent relationship for the Air Guard, separate from the Air Force. It ensured that the Air Guard would remain state controlled.

To facilitate the dual function of the National Guard Bureau, the Departments of the Army and Air Force, along with the NGB, reorganized the latter agency on October 1, 1948. This reorganization established the NGB as a Bureau of the Department of the Army and an agency of the Department of the Air Force. The reorganization of the NGB included the creation of the Legal Adviser, the Information Office, the Administrative Office, and the Planning Office. It also established the Chief, National Guard Bureau (CNGB) as the head of the two components divisions, the Army Division and the Air Division. It provided for a Major General of the appropriate service, commissioned in the National Guard, to be appointed as Chief of each of the respective Divisions. The Army and Air Force Authorization Act also stipulated that the National Guard Bureau would perform similar functions and duties for the Department of the Air Force as it performed for the Department of the Army and would be formal channel of communication between the Department of the Air Force and the several States on matters pertaining to the ANG.

An Army vs. Air Feud

The Air Guard viewed this mandate as an attempt to restrict Air Guard authority through the Army-dominated NGB. Further, the active Air Force and the Bureau disagreed on the scope and function of each others' duties in relation to the Air National Guard. On the one hand, the Air Force felt that the Bureau should act only as a channel of communications between the Air Force Chief of Staff and the State military authorities. The Guard Bureau, on the other hand, interpreted its mission in broader and more active policy making terms, rejecting the purely administrative role envisioned by active Air Force. The Air Force was angered because it felt the Air Guard was a component of the Air Force and wanted directed control.

By late 1949, the stage had been set for an open confrontation. Maj. Gen. Kenneth F. Cramer, Chief of the National Guard Bureau and an Army Guardsman, relieved the head of the bureau's Air Division, Maj. Gen. George Finch - without consulting the Department of the Air Force. It is reported that a personality conflict existed between the two intensely ambitious men, but the underlying factor in Finch's dismissal was rift between the Air Force and the National Guard Bureau concerning the control of the ANG. The Air Force believed that Cramer was not sufficiently informed about the Air National Guard and had no right to be supreme authority regarding policies of the Air Force established for its state-controlled reserve component.

The situation led to a joint investigation by the Inspection General of the Army and Air Force. Sweeping reforms and changes in the Guard Bureaus were recommended by this inquiry team. In separate reports both General Finch and General Cramer were recommended to be relieved from their duties in the NGB. The team also recommended that the Chief, NGB should be directed to comply fully with provisions of any Air Force directive relating to staff procedures on matters pertaining to the Air Guard.

The Inspector General advised the Secretaries of the Army and Air Force to appoint a joint board of officers who would recommend changes in the Bureau's organizational structure and internal operating procedures. The Secretaries appointed a board commonly known as the "Miltonberger Board," named because it was headed by former Chief of the Bureau Maj. Gen. Butler Miltonberger. On March 31, 1950 the Miltonberger Board reported its findings and recommendations to the Secretary of the Army. The report argued against the creation of separate National Guard Bureaus for the Army and Air Force as being unnecessary, but "...the Bureau's structure and operating procedures must conform to the joint operating policies of both services."

The Miltonberger Board reported that the organizational structure and operating procedure of the NGB were inconsistent with staff principles. In the spring of 1950, changes were implemented to reform the Bureau's organization and operating procedure. In effect, these changes gave more authority to the directors of the Army and Air National Guards, and reduced that of the Chief of the Bureau itself (especially in relation to the Air Guard - although this would be changed when an Air Guardsman became chief of the Bureau). Also, in May 1950, under Special Regulation 10-230-1 the new position of Deputy Chief of the National Guard Bureau was created. The regulation authorized a Major General in the Air National Guard for the position of Deputy Chief. Earl T. Ricks was the first to hold this office.

The two men responsible for the great upheaval in the Bureau's structure eventually left. General Cramer was relieved at his own request to assume duties as commander of the 43d Infantry Division upon its induction into Federal Service on September 8, 1950. General Finch was reassigned to the United States Air Force on September 25, 1950.

On August 6, 1958 Congress passed a bill for the reorganization of the Department of Defense. Among this Act's resolutions was an order to make the NGB a Joint Bureau of the Departments of the Army and the Air Force. It stated that the CNGB headed the Joint Bureau and acted as adviser to the Army Chief of Staff and the Air Force Chief of Staff on National Guard matters. This Act was implemented by AR 130-5/AFR 45-2, 10 July 1959. Under these provisions the Army Division was redesignated "Office of the Assistant Chief, NGB, for Army National Guard", and the Air Division was redesignated "Office of the Assistant Chief, NGB, for Air National Guard."

These offices were redesignated again in 1970 by a changed to AR 130-5/AFR 45-2 which changed the titles of the Assistant Chiefs, NGB, for Army and Air National Guard, to "Director, Army National Guard" and "Director, Air National Guard." These positions remained Major General positions. Additionally, these changes authorized the creation of a Deputy Director for the Army and Air National Guard, each in the grade of a Brigadier General.

In 1979 the Chief of the National Guard Bureau, La Vern E. Weber, received a third star as a result of a concurrent elevation of the CNGB position from Major General to Lieutenant General. Three other Chiefs have since held this rank and office. They are LTG Emmett H. Walker, Jr., LTG Herbert R. Temple, Jr. and LTG John B. Conaway. In 1988, the position of Vice Chief, NGB was created. John B. Conaway, at that time a Major General, was nominated and appointed to fill the position. He had previously served as Director of the Air National Guard since 1981. In February 1990, General Conaway assumed the position of Chief, National Guard Bureau and was promoted to the rank of Lieutenant General. He is only the second Air National Guardsman to hold this highest position in the National Guard Bureau.

From its small beginnings as an office in the Adjutant General's Office, the National Guard Bureau has grown into a major staff and operating agency in the Department of Defense. Its personnel has also substantially increased form one officer and four clerks to a present total of more than 400 officers, enlisted personnel, and civilians.

Today, the mission of the National Guard Bureau is to participate with the Army and Air Force staffs in programs pertaining to the National Guard. The NGB is responsible for administering programs for the development and maintenance of Army and Air National Guard units in the several States, the Commonwealth of Puerto Rico, the District of Columbia, the Virgin Islands and Guam. Finally, the National Guard Bureau is a channel of communications between the states and the Department of the Army and the Air Force.

For more than 80 years the National Guard Bureau has experienced many changes and important historical events, most notably four wars, the post World War II reorganization of the National Guard, and the creation of a separate Air Force. The successful trends set by those who worked for the Bureau in the past will undoubtedly be continued by those presently working in the Bureau to ensure that the National Guard remains a vital component to the Armed Forces of the Unites States.

Roles and Missions of the National Guard
The National Guard Association Of The United States
The Adjutants General Association Of The United States
November 1992

The post-Cold War threat and the current military environment, combined with the domestic economic posture, dictate a fundamental change in the size and force mix of the US military.

The radical changes in the traditional external military threats have precipitated an analysis and reevaluation of US defense needs. Nonetheless there is an undisputed need for a strong, capable and ready national defense.

Central to the decisions affecting component force structure and missions assignment are:

- The domestic and international needs of the nation;
- The congressionally desired size of the standing military;
- The willingness to underwrite the costs of the resultant roles, missions and force mix;
- The ability to move forces to a potential battlefield; and
- The extent to which Congress is constitutionally required to participate in the process leading up to and declaring war.

An historic point, in fact, is that the United States has for most of its history—except during the Cold War—relied upon the community based militia for its defense. The level and mix of forces during the Cold War period were unique in the history of the country.

The end of the Cold War presents the nation with a range of opportunities; return to its pre-Cold War posture; or continue its reliance on a large, Cold War type, active duty force; or embrace the community-based militia defense force thesis, modifying it as necessary to meet contemporary needs.

Secretary Dick Cheney and General Colin Powell, chairman of the Joint Chiefs of Staff, have said that it is appropriate to restructure the entire military. That proposed restructuring includes removing the Reagan build-up growth from the Army National Guard and US Army Reserve. In fact, their proposal removes a substantially larger amount of such force structure from the Army National Guard.

The Guard community recognizes that Army reserve component force structure will probably be reduced to the pre-Reagan buildup

levels. In the Guard, that will be accomplished by the end of FY 1993—
the growth that occurred in the Guard in the 1980s will have been cut.
In fact, National Guard force structure will be reduced to pre-World
War II levels.

An examination of Army force structure and size throughout the
history of this nation is informative. Historically, the National Guard,
America's community-based national defense force[1] has been approximately .19% to .23% of the US population in peacetime. And, prior to
World War II and the onset of the Cold War, the National Guard ranged
from 50% to 100% larger than the standing Army.[2] The National Guard
was the only unit-organized citizen-soldier force prior to 1947.[3]

The number of personnel on active duty and the size of the active
duty forces also grew in response to the Cold War, as a direct result of
the requirements for forward deployed forces—Europe, Japan, Korea,
etc.— and in time of combat—Korea, Vietnam, Iraq, etc.

Decisions on the future roles and missions of the National Guard
will, of necessity, be framed in the broader issues of international
security, economics, domestic needs and the principles of the American
democracy.

The roles and missions of the National Guard, the nation's militia
and primary federal reserve, are founded upon constitutional intent
and the Guard's unique dual status. Fulfilling both federal and state
mandates makes the Guard unique among the US military and presents
special challenges in perpetuating current and designing additional
constitutionally relevant roles and missions for the future.

The Constitution prescribes a national defense capability that is
composed of the smallest necessary standing active forces reinforced by
a strong, capable and trained militia. Subsequent statutory and case law
have enjoined the National Guard as the primary federal military
reserve in the first line of national defense[4] and made it readily available
for swift mobilization at the call of the President.

The history of US warfare provides clear and consistent evidence
that the Framers' vision remains valid. Vietnam proved that the Army
could not win a war the Nation did not want to fight.[5] Conversely,
Desert Storm proved that exercising the constitutional process permits
the Army to win a war the Nation wants to fight.[6]

Historically, the militia of community-based soldiers has provided
the vehicle for congressional and public involvement in the process. The
purpose of the Total Force Policy, aside from the undeniable 50 to 75
percent fiscal savings, was to subject war-making to the political litmus
test.[7] Calling forth the citizen-soldiers provided the elected civilian leadership with an immediate sense of the nation—the national will.[8]

The federal military mission of the National Guard is to provide to
the National Command Authority trained and ready combat and support forces available for call by the President. Concurrently, the National Guard is charged to provide the Governors of the Several States
and Territories trained and ready units with organic chains of com-

mand, control and communications available for call and employment in times of emergency.

The dual roles and missions of the Guard for the 21st century must include forces sufficient to meet constitutional mandates. The federal mission, as it has been for more than 200 years, is to provide forces in the first line of defense. In peacetime, the mission of the Guard is to maintain combat ready forces and conduct federal peacetime engagement operations as dictated by the President and Congress. The Guard's peacetime role encompasses three other activities: the traditional state mission of emergency and disaster response; the war on drugs as part of the Governor's initiatives in support of the national objectives; and, the domestic mission—contributing to the moral and social fabric of the nation through a wide range of federally and state funded and authorized programs.

Traditional combat and support forces that comprise the immediately ready reserve are assigned to the National Guard as an integral part of the nation's first line of defense. Additionally, the Guard is properly the constitutional and statutory institution to which all reconstitution and deep reserve force structure and personnel are assigned. Assigning to and resourcing such structure in the National Guard would also make these forces available to the several states in time of domestic need.

The roles and missions of the National Guard for the 21st century must include:

• Perpetuating its role as the primary federal military reserve;

• Maintaining its role as a major combat force in the first line of national defense;

• Continuing its role as the domestic contingency force, including state domestic disaster preparedness and emergency response—the first line of response to domestic disaster and emergency; and

•Maintaining its role as the primary military force engaged in domestic missions that contribute to the moral and social fabric of nation.

In order to accomplish the dual roles and missions outlined, the Army National Guard must be sustained at is pre-Reagan, pre-Cold-War force structure authorization level of 420,000. Legislation establishing a floor of force structure authorization and funded end-strength of 420,000 is required.

To effectively prosecute its roles and missions, it is essential that major combat and support formations, with organic chains of command, control and communications, be the primary units of the Army National Guard. This requires units that have dual mission capability, ranging from military police, engineers, medical and aviation to infantry, special forces, armor, and artillery.

To accrue maximum potential costs avoidance and return on the taxpayers' investment in the national defense, units and missions should be assigned to the National Guard. Exceptions are warranted where it can be shown that, because of forward deployment, immediate response or unique mission requirements, they must be placed in the active forces. This approach is in the domestic and international best interest of the nation, it is fiscally sound, and it is militarily prudent.

[1.] The Army National Guard is composed of approximately 4,200 units located in more than 3200 communities and all 435 Congressional Districts.

[2] Jim Dan Hill, *The Minuteman in Peace and War.* (Harrisburg, Pennsylvania, Stackpole Books, 1964) ch. 18.

[3] "Approved War Department Policies Relating to Post War National Guard and Organized Reserve Corps" (ORC), War Department General Staff Washington, D.C., October 13, 1945, and December 13, 1946; and, Brigadier General Herbert H. Vreeland, Presentation on behalf of the Senior Army Reserve Commanders Association to the Army General Staff Committee on the Guard and Reserve, May 9, 1949. With the exception of the medical reserve corps established in 108, all Army Reserve units were created as a direct result of an in response to the Cold War. The Cold War mission of the ORC was to provide "formations" (units) that could not be recruited, organized and manned by the Regular Army or the National Guard. The ORC, predecessor to the modern day Army Reserve, was established to "capture" officers departing active duty following World War I, thereby providing a manpower pool — although assigned to virtually nonexistent, paper-only divisions.

[4] 32 USC 102

[5] John R. Handleman, Howard Shapiro and John A. Vasquez, *Introductory Case Studies For International Relations: Vietnam/The Middle East/ The Environmental Crisis, (Chicago: Rand McNally and Co., 1974) p. 24.*

[6] Paul H. Vivian, "Finding the Best Defense for The United States, *Washington Times,* November 18, 1991, p. E2.

[7] The Defense Budget; The National Guard and National Defense, Congressional Record, Washington, D.C., S-4801, April 23, 1990.

[8] Michael Howard, *The Forgotten Dimensions of Strategy,* Foreign Affairs, Summer 1979

The Abrams Doctrine: Then, Now and In The Future
A National Guard Association of the United States Symposium
National Guard Memorial
Washington, D.C. • July 16, 1993

In 1993 the National Guard Association of the United States sponsored a symposium called "The Abrams Doctrine: Then, Now and in the Future." The purpose of the symposium was to discuss the process and pressures General Creighton Abrams, Chief of Staff of the United States Army in the post-Vietnam era, faced in restructuring of the Army, and the validation of his guidelines in today's context.

The post Cold War period, like that of any other immediate post-war period involving Americans, has seen pressures develop to "bring the boys home" and to downsize the military. The Cold War, and World War II before it, saw the largest standing military force in our national history. The Cold War force, unique in the sense that the period could really be called a time of peace and stability, was created because our nation faced a threat like the world has never seen.

The ups and downs during this period were fluctuations caused by the ability to pay for such a large standing force and the political determinations of how immediate that threat was. The Vietnam era was a fissure that tested political will and was the beginning of a period of national, political and economic reconsideration. Dealing with political and economic pressures, national leaders had to create a new military while simultaneously still face the Soviet Empire.

The situation with which General Creighton Abrams had to deal as the Vietnam war ended and what we face today, we feel strongly parallel and have lessons for tomorrow. The nation has budgetary challenges; the public wants to downsize the military. A dramatic difference is that the single monolithic threat has disappeared, replaced by multi-faceted uncertainty.

It is our supposition that Creighton Abrams set out to institutionalize and integrate the relationship between the active forces and the Guard and Reserve for three reasons. Number One, to make integration of the Active Forces and the Guard and Reserve structure so tight that no major commitment of American forces could be accomplished without a reliance on the Guard and Reserve. Number Two, to ensure that integration of the Active Forces, Guard and Reserve was so close that a future mobilization, to even be contemplated, would require public support to commit our nation's forces. And Number Three, to assure that maximum use is made of Guard and Reserve cost-efficiencies.

This report is an edited transcript of those proceedings. A distinguished group of panelists met in the Walsh-Reckord Hall of

States in the National Guard Memorial building on July 16, 1993 and discussed the creation of what has become known as the Abrams Doctrine, reconsidered its implementation and conjectured upon its continued validity.

The following is a summary of the conclusions reached by the respective panels.

An Historical Perspective of the Abrams Doctrine

Moderator: MG Bruce Jacobs (ret.),
Chief Historian, Historical Society of the
Militia and National Guard

Panelists: GEN John W. Vessey, Jr. (ret.)
former Chairman, Joint Chiefs of Staff
Dr. Lewis Sorley
Historian and author
LTG Herbert R. Temple, Jr. (ret.)
former Chief, National Guard Bureau

Conclusions:

• The Abrams Doctrine is a valid notion which led to the creation of the right forces to be available to fight the Gulf War.

• Its implementation challenged bias and tradition in the Active Army and the National Guard.

• Its implementation challenged Guard soldiers to accomplish training beyond anything they had been called upon to do before.

• We are at a watershed moment in history. Doctrine of the past 50 years, including the Abrams Doctrine, has served us well but possesses strengths and weaknesses. Our nation needs a top-to-bottom look at our national security needs.

First Hand View of Implementing the Abrams Doctrine

Speaker: Ltg. Donald E. Rosenblum (ret.)
former Commander, First US Army

Conclusions:

• Integration of Guard and Reserve with Active Army was not an easy proposition and required the creation of readiness regions and groups to maintain as much integration as possible with the Active side of the house.

• Integration was enhanced with the development of Roundout.

• Guard and Reserve forces provide a great stability in our armed forces.

• Roundout/Roundup units must be utilized when parent units are called.

• Conditions should be created where the active Army has to learn about the Guard and Reserve to increase its appreciation of citizen-soldiers. Similar conditions must be created for the Guard and Reserve to learn more about how the active Army works.

The Abrams Doctrine: Blueprint for the Future

Moderator:	MG Francis S. Greenlief (ret.)
	former Chief, National Guard Bureau
Panelists:	GEN John R. Galvin (ret.)
	former Supreme Allied Commander
	Europe
	GEN Dennis J. Reimer
	CINC, US Forces Command
	LTG, Richard G. Trefry (ret.)
	former Inspector General, US Army

Conclusions:

•Mobilization for Desert Shield/Desert Storm was the best mobilization of Guard and Reserve forces to date. The mobilization processed helped generate great support from the American public even when the end-state was unknown.

•There is a need to standardize Total Army Authorization documents.

• Potential adversaries learned as much from Desert Shield/Desert Storm as we did.

•Volunteerism is a two-edged sword.

•CAPSTONE is a good program.

•Title XI initiatives, on the whole, are constructive efforts to improve the readiness of the Total Army.

•Simulation, computer assisted exercises and new innovative training programs must be taken advantage of to improve combat capabilities.

• At all times, but especially in times of change, a focus must be kept on people - those leaving and those staying.

•When we go to war, it is something we do as a people; the Guard and Reserve make sure that happens in the broadest sense.

Note:

The following abbreviations will identify speakers in the transcript, after the first reference:

MG Robert F. Ensslin, Jr. (ret.)	RFE
MG Bruce Jacobs (ret.)	BJ
GEN John W. Vessey, Jr. (ret.)	JWV
Dr. Lewis Sorley	LS

LTG Herbert R. Temple, Jr. (ret.) HRT
LTG Donald E. Rosenblum (ret.) DER
MG Francis S. Greenlief (ret.) FSG
GEN John R. Galvin (ret.) JRG
GEN Dennis J. Reimer DJR
LTG Richard G. Trefry (ret.) RGT

The Abrams Doctrine: Then, Now, And in the Future
July 16, 1993 • Morning Session
An Historical Perspective of the Abrams Doctrine

MG Robert F. Ennslin, Jr. (Ret.), Executive Director, National Guard Association of the United States:

We believe that one of Creighton Abrams' goals as Chief of Staff was to establish a nationally supportable army in the context of 1970s defense strategy. The development of any type of defense strategy, especially the conventional part of it, is subject to many outside influences. Among these are resources, technology and politics. Resources, from our perspective, equates to personnel availability, equipment and the money to train. Technology is a question of what is available to prosecute war and how it is applied. Political influences are a dichotomy, the people and the kind of national defense they want and the leaders we elect and their perception of what the people want. Within this context is a key variable, the ability of leaders to make the decisions that are in the best interests of the nation.

Creighton Abrams was a leader whose influence we still feel today. It's our view that General Creighton Abrams saw first-hand the stresses created on the Army when it was forced to expand in size for Vietnam. He was Vice Chief of Staff of the Army during the expansion period, and when it was forced to shrink, he was Chief of Staff of the Army. All this occurred within about a ten year period of time. It's also our view that Creighton Abrams was very cognizant of the change Americans underwent in their views toward the war in Vietnam.

It's been said that when Creighton Abrams became Chief of Staff of the Army he set out to fix the "problem" as he saw it. And I place the world "problem" in quotation marks for a reason. This has been interpreted by some to mean that Abrams set out to institutionalize and integrate the relationship between the active forces and the Guard and Reserve for three reasons. Number One, to make integration of the Active Forces and the Guard and Reserve structure so tight that no major commitment of American forces could be accomplished without a reliance on the Guard and Reserve. Number Two, to ensure that integration of the Active Forces, Guard and Reserve was so close that a future mobilization, to even be contemplated, would require public support to commit our nation's forces. And Number Three, to assure that maximum use is made of Guard and Reserve cost-efficiencies.

We believe that addressing the circumstances with which General Abrams was faced and how he approached solving his challenge is very appropriate today. And the first panel will be addressing this. We feel that General Abrams faced a situation that is similar in many respects to that which we are facing today and faced at the end of World War II and the end of the Korean War. Declining resources for the military, a changing political environment, and a changed perception of what the American public wants in the way of national defense, coupled with a change in the threat. It's a great tribute to the man that what he envisioned, and what he began to create, and the foundation that he established turned out to be exactly what this nation needed when we were faced with the Iraqi invasion of Kuwait.

We now want to generate discussions as to whether or not Abrams laid out a formula that has validity in a new American and world environment. Our first panel this morning is moderated by Major General Bruce Jacobs, Chief Historian of the National Guard Association. Joining him as panelists are General John W. Vessey, Jr., a former Chairman of the Joint Chiefs of Staff; Lt. General Herbert R. Temple, Jr., a former Chief of the National Guard Bureau and a Director of the Army Guard during the period of time when resources and standards for the National Guard were dramatically increased; and Dr. Lewis Sorley, historian and biographer of Creighton Abrams, whose biography *Thunderbolt* is must-reading for everyone who is interested in our Army.

We have asked our morning panel to focus on the circumstances that created the Abrams Doctrine, the political and military environment at that time, how it came to be implemented, and its impact on the nation. We've asked our luncheon speaker, whom I'll introduce later, to give us his personal views and experiences on implementing what Abrams set in motion. We have also asked him to take us up to the pre-Desert Shield/Desert Storm period.

Our afternoon panel, which our Moderator, Major General Francis Greenlief will introduce after lunch, has been asked to look into the future. Much has been said and written about the changes in the world. Arguments have been presented contending that it it such an uncertain future that all of our forces must be immediately available to respond to any threat to U.S. interests in the world. In our view, this implies a lessened reliance on the Guard and Reserve. Extending this argument might also imply removal of citizen involvement in defense, along with the removal of the ability to easily debate defense policy issues.

MG Bruce Jacobs (Ret.), Chief Historian, HSM & NG:

In the context of General Ensslin's opening remarks, we have defined an NGAUS view of an Abrams Doctrine which concerns, among other things, the critically of Active, Guard and Reserve integration as a major step towards ensuring national public support for action taken by an Administration to use military force when U.S. national interests are at stake. And to Bob Sorley, I would like to address the first question.

Bob, as you have looked so extensively, an intensively, into the life and times of Creighton W. Abrams, can we start by throwing the first question to you and asking, do you thing our postulation is a fair one? Do the actions and expressions we have identified constitute in effect an Abrams Doctrine?

Dr. Lewis Sorley - Historian and Author:

I have to begin by saying I think General Abrams would smile to hear his policies given so grand a title as "the Abrams Doctrine." During his service, he often made use of what others came to call his saying, pithy comments that he would use to illustrate a point, or quite often, to deflate somebody who was over-impressed with his own importance.

When a staffer would come in with a grandiose scheme that Abrams thought was too pretentious or was maybe promising more than the Army could deliver, he would predictably observe, "We are going to be stuck with living up to the rhetoric." And that's what he might tell us today as we propound an Abrams Doctrine. But I think that there is, nevertheless, justification for considering the sum total of what Abrams did and planned with respect to Reserve Forces as a unified doctrine.

Abrams was a very consistent man. Consistent in his values, consistent in his focus on readiness and the well-being of the soldier, and consistent in his insistence that everything the Army did should contribute to one or another of those priority concerns. His consistent approach to the role and importance of Reserve Forces, taken as a whole, does seem to me to constitute what might be formalized as a doctrine.

Thinking about our meeting here today, I consulted my source of first resort, Webster's Dictionary, and there I learned that a "doctrine" is something taught, or teachings; a second meaning, something taught as the principles or creed of a religion, political party, etc., tenet or tenets, belief, dogma. And then it said, "Doctrine refers to a theory based on carefully worked out principles and taught or advocated by its adherents." I think what General Abrams put together, in terms of the policies governing Reserve Forces on his watch, does amount to a carefully worked out set of principles, and certainly he taught and advocated those with great force in the limited time available to him during his truncated period as Chief of Staff.

I think that it could be useful to talk just for a minute or two about the background that led him to the formulation of those policies.

Everyone knows, of course, that he had served for five years in Vietnam, the last four as the commander there, during one of the most difficult periods our Army has ever undergone, a period of increasing drug abuse, racial disharmony, indiscipline and internal dissent, eroding public support, a virtually impossible mission as he tried to command a force that was progressively being withdrawn from under him, and so on.

And I think almost everyone knows that before he went to Vietnam, he spent three years as the Army's Vice Chief of Staff during the period of the build-up for Vietnam, a time when, because Lyndon Johnson would not mobilize the Reserve Forces, all the expansion had to come from made-up units and stripped units, and cadre units, and, as Abrams often described it, "all the new acquisitions were in private and second lieutenant." As a consequence, the maturity, the experience level of the Army was on a progressively declining slope.

I believe—I'm not a sociologist, but I believe that there is a casual relationship that could be identified between that progressive decline and the later great increase in the problems I've described before. And had we been able to draw on the experience and maturity of leaders from Reserve Components, instead of bringing in all privates and second lieutenants, some of that might have been averted.

So those are the key, most recent experiences that General Abrams had: Two assignments spanning eight years, during which he saw the support of the American people for the war in Vietnam and, I guess you could say its attitude towards the Army as well, decline precipitously. I think that the failure to mobilize the Reserve Forces had something to do with his outlook.

But I also think that judgment has to be approached with a little caution, so long with the Truth-in-Lending, I will say that I think we need to remember, too, that for quite a long time, in my view a significantly long time, the American people supported the effort of our Armed Forces in Vietnam and it was only when year after year after year went by without demonstrable progress toward a successful resolution of that enterprise that that support began to taper off quite precipitately.

Then, of course, we had the cataclysmic event of the Tet 1968 offensive, which is very complex, and we can talk about that.

I want to take you back just a little further into General Abrams' background because, while those eight years focused on Vietnam, I am sure his earlier experiences also had a lot to do with how he came to view the appropriate policies for the Reserve Forces.

He spent a period in the early 1960s as the Assistant Deputy Chief of Staff for Operations, and during that time spent most of his time going around on a sort of special assignment as the personal representative of the Chief of Staff on-site where civil rights crisis, had either erupted or were impending. And on many occasions, he either was involved with mobilized Reserve and National Guard forces, or they were planning for or contemplating such use, as well as in some cases Active Forces as well. That brought him into close contact with a lot of units and leaders in the Reserve Forces, especially the National Guard, and there were people, especially people in the media, who were raising questions at that time as to whether these forces could be relied upon, whether they were politically reliable, and whether they would remain disciplined and responsive to orders under the circumstances confronting them. General Abrams never reflected the slightest doubt of that, and to the credit of the units and the leaders, they performed as he had predicted that they would. But that was not an assured thing before the fact, I suggest, and I believe that he gained a great deal of respect for them in the course of that assignment.

Earlier, his first assignment as a Brigadier, he was a Deputy Special Assistant to the Chief of Staff for Reserve Affairs and worked for an interesting fellow, the result of which was that Abrams was often the man doing the testifying, often the man going to the field, and I believe it's fair to say that during that time not only did he get to know large numbers of the Reserve Force leadership and gained confidence in them and respect for them, but that they gained the same appreciation for him, building a relationship that went on over the years.

And now I'll tell you one more thing. I think this may be a little controversial, but I believe it to be true. In World War II General Abrams commanded a Regular Army tank battalion, but there weren't more than a handful of Regular Army soldiers of any rank in that battalion. The battalion was formed in the spring of 1941, and it was formed out of people who had been brought into the Army because we were about to go to war. These are the same kinds of people, I suggest, who make up the Reserve Forces. And Abrams served with them through that war, and when the war was over—with only a few exceptions, and those were people who had been influenced by Abrams and decided therefore to make military service their career—the vast majority of them went back to their civilian pursuits. They'd come to the colors when the nation needed them, and when they'd done their duty, and they did it brilliantly, they went back to where they had been before. And I suggest that that's very much the mold of the citizen-soldier as well.

So, even from his early days as a young officer in World War II, I believe that there was a building-up of an outlook and a confidence and a respect on the part of General Abrams for what reserve forces can do, and that we saw that reflected in the policies he put in place when he became Chief of Staff of the Army. Now, there were other factors involved there, budgetary factors, they had gone to a volunteer force, there were recruiting factors involved, there was the necessity to stop what he saw as the precipitate decline in end strength, and that was involved. So I don't want to over-simplify it, but I'm trying to give a little background of how I think he came to view Reserve Forces as he did.

General Ensslin suggested in his comments that we are at a period now which is similar in many respects to the period in which General Abrams propounded these policies. And I agree with that. But I'd like to agree with him by saying "Yes, but," because I think there are many things that are dissimilar today as well. So what we are going to try to work out ourselves by the end of the day is, given the similarities and given the dissimilarities, and weighing the respective impacts on what we ought to be doing, if there is an Abrams Doctrine, is that applicable under current circumstances?

BJ: Thanks, Bob. I wonder if either of our other panelists, let me start with General Vessey. Would you care to comment on the original question, which is the validity of our postulation that there is, in effect, a collection of expressions which can be defined as an Abrams Doctrine? How do you react to that, and anything that Dr. Sorley had to say?

GEN John W. Vessey, Jr. (Ret.), Former Chairman, Joint Chief of Staff:

Bruce, after listening to Dr. Sorley and to General Ensslin, I have so many comments to make about what's been said that we can't finish it this week. But let me say a little bit about the Abrams Doctrine, and I believe that we are justified in calling it an "Abrams Doctrine."

Let me preface my remarks by saying that, and perhaps give another little historical vignette and shed some light on how this all came about. I think that Dr. Sorley summed it up, but the important question for the nation today is, ""What do we take from the past that is right to move into an uncertain future?" Let's not try to rebuild the past because we will not be successful in doing that, and we will probably be successful only in defending the nation inadequately if we take everything from the past and try to move it into a future that is, clearly, remarkably different from the past. So the question at hand is, "What strengths and orientations do we take from the past to move us into a very uncertain future?" And I believe there are many things that we can take from the past, and among them, some of the lessons from Abrams, the period of the Abrams Doctrine.

I think it is important for us to understand that the fundamental question for General Abrams was how to get enough Army, total Army, to face the future that we faced. Bob, you cited the demonstration of the Force that Abrams built, and I really believe that that was a demonstration of the Abrams Force, in the Desert in Iraq, but the goal was the demolition of the Berlin Wall, the demise of the Soviet Union. That was really the culmination of the Abrams Doctrine. The question for General Abrams at a time when, as Bob pointed out, the end strengths were on the way down, the budgets were on the way down after the Vietnam War, is how to have enough Army to deal with the very real Soviet threat, the Warsaw Pact threat, our commitments in East Asia, and how to survive that and defend the nation. That was the overall goal.

And, clearly, he saw what Washington saw, when Washington wrote his thoughts on a peace establishment, a standing force. Washington, at that time said, to awe the Indians—George wouldn't say that today, but he would say to awe the bad guys, and protect our borders and our commerce and our overseas interests, and a Ready Force to deal with immediate problems. His second part was a standardized and well-regulated militia. The third was stores of military supplies. The fourth was a system of academies for instruction in the military arts. And the fifth was manufactories for arms, military arms and equipment, a defense industry, And, really, since George's time, we haven't supported all elements of that strategy but that's basically been the United States' strategy.

General Abrams could see that in a world in which the other fellow had the opportunity to attack, and attack suddenly, that we had to have a Ready Force that went through these five parts of Washington's Peace Establishment, yet he knew that the budgets would not support a Regular Army of the size needed. We were headed toward 730,000, 750,000 I guess it was, the number we were given. And the largest Army we had supported, at 750,000, was about ten divisions, before, under the conditions that existed. We had many people on the Army Staff and in the Office of the Secretary of Defense who were convinced that we could only have ten divisions. General Abrams put a study group together to look at the world, and that study group—as almost anyone with common sense would have said, ten divisions is simply not enough for the United States with the responsibilities it faces.

We had at that time the so-called OSD studies about how to integrate Guard and Reserve units with the Active Force, and General Abrams sent his immediate troops, his staff, to find a way not to have ten divisions, but to have sixteen divisions, with the budget and end strength that we had. There was no other way to do it, other than a far closer integration of the Guard and Reserve with the Active Force than we had experienced in the past.

Now, I want to say right now that I believe that is the important part of the model that we need to understand in moving into the future. That the question for us will be, "Will there be enough?" And there will be many voices in the United States who will say, "What you have is too much." And the inclination will be to cut more. Cut more from the Active Force, and cut more from the Guard and Reserve later on. So I think it is extremely important for us to see that model that General Abrams built, at that time, not as the carbon copy of what we need in the future but a guide for an action in the future. How do we tie Active Forces and Guard and Reserve Forces together to make the whole enough for what the nation faces, within the budgets that the people of the United States are willing to spend?

That's the challenge. There is clearly an Abrams Doctrine. And that Doctrine, a part of that Doctrine, was integrating the Guard and Reserve Forces closely with the Active Forces to build a large enough force to meet the nation's needs.

BJ: Thank you, General Vessey. General Temple, would you like to comment on this particular issue?

LTG Herbert R. Temple, Jr. (Ret.) - Former Chief, National Guard Bureau:

My response will probably be the briefest of all. For one thing, I did not know General Abrams. As a matter of fact, I don't recall that I had ever seen him. What was interesting was that, at the time he passed away, I was a student at the United States Army War College and the Commandant at the time was General Dee Smith, who held General Abrams in very high esteem. There were a great many ceremonies that took place at Carlisle, attendant to General Abrams' death. And I was impressed with one aspect of his life that sometimes is really not appreciated. The word that kept coming out of all of the events that were taking place was "integrity." Now, as I read Bob's book and other material relevant to General Abrams, that, again, seemed to be reinforced in everything I read.

You know, if you look back on those people who have probably had the greatest impact upon the United States Army, and maybe upon national security in general, I believe that most people would conclude that Gen. George Marshall fulfilled that role, because when George Marshall spoke, the United States Congress, and the people of America, took him as being absolutely forthright and honest, and his objectives were always for the best interests of the country. All that I can tell from my investigation of General Abrams—and Bob perhaps can deal with this better than anyone, was that that was the hallmark of his leadership of the Army. As he served as the Chief of Staff of the Army, I suspect that his integrity and his honesty were appreciated in the halls of this nation's leadership in the same way that General Marshall's was. And it was a tragic loss that we lost him when we did.

It's often been said that one of the failings of the United States Army is that they've never had the right Chief of Staff at the right time. I think they did have General Abrams as the Chief of Staff at the right time. There are a couple of other times in history we would have been well served had he been the Chief of Staff of the Army. He would have been the right man at any time.

In concluding my remarks, let me say that I really feel very humbled being on his panel. I didn't realize my antiquity until I found the panel that they put me on. It's a very startling realization to find that you are a principal in history, rather than being someone who's involved in the current issues. So I guess I feel my age today more than anytime.

BJ: But, Herb, being involved in history doesn't mean you are history. So take some heart in that.

JWV: Let me just add one thing, to what Herb said. And that's just that Abrams was once approached by a new political appointee who was about to testify at his confirmation hearings. This fellow said, "General Abrams, I'm going to testify to the Congress. Do you have any advice?"

And General Abrams, in his usual laconic fashion, said, "Yes, you should start by telling the truth." That's all the advice he gave him.

BJ: General Vessey, let me turn to you again with our next question. And you have already referred to the environment in which the Abrams

Doctrine began to emerge in terms of what the world was, in the world of the 1970s. It was a period in which many people felt very draconian steps were being taken. CONARC was replaced by TRADOC and FORSCOM. The STEADFAST reorganization. Affiliation, ROUNDOUT, the other new partnership-type programs to increase Guard and Reserve readiness through significantly increased Active Army support and participation. We were winding down and ending our combat role in Vietnam. Only a very, very small National Guard and Reserve presence had been there. General Harold K. Johnson had likened his situation to that of an owner of a string of race horses who was not allowed to take them out of the barn. General DePuy undertook to have FM 100-5 done over, I guess reflecting his feeling that rather than a call-up of units, you had to write it for the level of individual, largely untrained Reserve officers and draftees. At least, that's the conventional wisdom that comes out of it.

As you look back at this period, do you feel the Army was ready for a doctrine which would place such heavy reliance upon the Guard and Reserve that, to quote a passage from Bob Sorley's book, "the force could not function without them and, hence, could not be deployed without calling them up." What mindsets had to be overcome in the active Army to make such a drastic shift a success?

JWV: Well, it wasn't only mindsets in the Active Army. There were mindsets in the Guard and Reserve and in the civilian community as well, because, the Defense establishment itself, and the Army in particular, was aboil at that time. You cited some of the changes and most of those were believed by General Abrams to be necessary changes, that is, the reorganization of CONARC, and the movement toward a training command that would focus on training for the Army. General Abrams understood very clearly, probably better than any of the leaders that I ever served under, the importance of training, how important an ingredient that was in battlefield effectiveness.

And there were other changes under way. We were moving from a drafted Army to a volunteer Army. We were integrating women at a level never before experienced. So we had all sorts of matters to deal with. It was a hard time for those who were defenders of the status quo and an exciting time for those who wanted to induce change. Were we ready? I guess an institution as big and as bureaucratic as an army is always more comfortable with the status quo than it is with the change.

But we, fortunately, had some marvelous leaders both in the Active Force and in the Reserve Components, who could see the wisdom of what was being done and were enthusiastic supporters of that change. Some of us needed a kick in the shins, or a kick in the tail from time to time to make sure we were enthusiastic, but we all got enthusiastic about it.

The Headquarters cuts were huge. We slashed General Officers positions right and left and scarfed up Staff. I often told the story that, well, the next thing that General Abrams would tell us to do is hand out numbers to the Army people as they came into the Pentagon, and all Number 1's would report to their post, and all Number 2's would fall in in the North Parking Lot and draw muskets in the Eighth Corridor, because we were forming a new division. The change was that stark.

So, the answer is Yes and No.

BJ: Let me move along to General Temple. First, on the National Guard Bureau Joint Staff, then as Director of the Army National Guard, and for four years as Chief of the National Guard Bureau, General Temple had to work to create the kind of Army National Guard which could measure up to the force needed to sustain an Abrams Doctrine. During General Temple's tenure, the ROUNDOUT program flourished, as Guard brigades trained with their parents Active Army divisions. In addition, the Guard Force structure was increased by the reactivation of two divisions, the 35th and 29th. We talked a good deal in those days about the heavy percentage of Army combat and combat support which is to be found in the Guard, and which presumably had to be at a high state of readiness to support an Abrams Doctrine.

General Temple, would please address, Number One, what mindsets had to be overcome in the National Guard community, which is obviously a significant one, as General Vessey has alluded to it, and whether this rather new concept of the Active Army having such a major stake in the success of the Guard and Reserve challenged traditional responsibilities for the training of the Guard, and what this increased participation of the Army in what might have traditionally been called "the Guard's business" did in terms of the functions of the Chief of the National Guard Bureau in dealing with the Army, dealing with the States?

HRT: The period that I served as the Director of the Army Guard was more important in dealing with this matter. By the time I became the Chief, the relationships had reached their apex and maybe were beginning to decrement a bit. But keep in mind, it would be necessary to consider the environment that we were in at the time. Every morning when we woke up, we thought we were going to war that day, and that was driving everything. I you were privy to the war plans, and you were a National Guardsman and you could see the plans to employ National Guard units throughout the world to meet those war planes, you had to be struck with the fact that never before in the history of the National Guard was the nations dependence upon the Guard more critical than it was at that time. If you had parochial views, you had to submerge those to the best interests of the country, because the National Guard was being prepared to meet commitments that they had never faced before. If you didn't become energized about those matters, you were exercising a disservice to your country, but equally as important, a disservice to your soldiers, because the soldiers were not going to fight as part of the California National Guard or the Florida National Guard, but they were going to fight as part of the United States Army. There was already in place because of the work of General Greenlief, General

Weber, and General Walker, the framework for much of this relationship. However, there didn't appear to be a sense of urgency. And that, perhaps, best came to light at the time that one of the members of the audience here, General Dick Trefry, was the Assistant DCSPER of the Army.

General Trefry set aside about four or five days when he sat in his office and invited everyone who was involved in mobilization to come and tell him about mobilization. He invited me to sit with him, and it was remarkable expose of what had not been achieved in preparing to meet the nation's war plans. I think after about the third day, General Trefry sat back in his chair and as only he can do, raised his hands and said, "Christ, I'm frightened." That became a benchmark as I went back to the Army Directorate, to come to grips with the issues of how were we going to mobilize the Guard. To mobilize, deploy and fight as part of the Total Army.

Now, about of the mindset in the National Guard. Probably the most dominant one was fear, that fear manifested itself in several ways. At the upper levels, as Bruce indicated, the leadership of the National Guard was uncertain if they were going to lose control of what had been historically their purviews. We in the National Guard Bureau had been captured by some of those same fears. I recall an instance I asked the folks that were involved in the automation program to come in and talk about automation, and I was surprised to find that we had always acquired computers that were different from the Army's. We were then at the stage where we were beginning to go out and acquire new computers. I said, "Why don't we buy the same ones tht the Army has?" And the fellow who was talking to me said, "Well, if we do that, the data in our computers will be available to the Army Staff and there's no telling what mischief will come from that."

Well, we changed that policy. We went out and acquired computers that were compatible with the Army. I recall that during the mobilization exercises our units that were affiliated or rounding out Active units used to have to carry the punchcards down to the 24th Division and hand them to the computer folks in the 24th Division; and they spent all night transferring them to their cards so they could begin to account for our soldiers. That, it seemed to me, was a disconnect from what we were trying to achieve, the rapid mobilization of the Guard.

An interesting sideline to that, after we went ahead and got the computers, about four years later the Logistics Chief in the National Guard Bureau came in to see me in great excitement and anxiety, and he said, "I regret to inform you that the DCSLOG of the Army is redistributing our equipment." I said, "How can he do that?" He said, "He now has our data and is unilaterally redistributing Guard assets." So the fellow who warned me at the beginning, gave a legitimate warning. It simply meant I had to go up to the DCSLOG of the Army and, as General Vessey may recall, we had to take a lead pipe and say, "No, you won't do that any more." The practice stopped abruptly.

Although fear at the upper levels was one of control, at the lower levels, it become more related to a fear of not doing well. The National Guard had always trained in a relatively mundane, lethargic way. Now, maybe our National Guardsmen will take exception to that, but we never trained to our full potential in the National Guard that I grew up with. Much of the constraint was forced on us by the narrow perception by the Army of what you could expect in training National Guardsmen. My personal view, and the view of other National Guardsmen that I associated with during my development, was that the National Guard had never been challenged to do what it was capable of doing.

So the challenge was, how do we generate a greater sense of urgency and increase the output, the training output of a National Guard which was unaccustomed to training at the pace which was essential if the Army was going to be reinforced by a National Guard that will meet its wartime demands.

That was one of the reasons, or the genesis, I should say, for the expansion of the KPUP Program. KPUP was not invented here. It was a program which the Army Reserve had under the Title, I believe, of Counterpart Training, and the idea what that you took a Reservist or a National Guardsman and you put him or her with Active units so that they could improve their personal skills and their military skills working side by side with Active people. It is interesting to note that FORSCOM didn't fund the USAR's Counter part program. The Guard changed the name and secured separate funding from the Congress.

We had one hell of a time getting National Guard units to go out and participate in Army and joint exercises because they were afraid that they couldn't measure up to the standards. So, by taking our soldiers and puting them in with Active Component units, our theory was that they would see that they were not training in an environment with standards they could not achieve themselves. And that came to fruition very early when a Cavalry unit from the Army was down at Fort Bliss and was involved in an exercise. We sent National Guardsmen from Oregon and Idaho under KPUP to participate in the exercise. And the message that went to the soldiers was that General Temple was interested in their perceptions of the level of training which the Active Army unit was involved in and their ability to participate at that level in their own unit. And would they call me at that first opportunity and give me their observations.

My wife and I were sound asleep one night, but at one thirty or two o'clock in the morning the telephone rings, which was not unusual. Sometimes the Operations Center would call at that time. My wife reached over and got the phone and she says, "Who is this?" and she says, "Who?" And she says, "Herb, it's a Lieutenant So and So." And so I reached across and got the phone and the fellow said, "Hi, I'm Lieutenant So and So with the, "I think he was with the Idaho National Guard, and he said, "I'm here with this Cavalry outfit from the Army.

We've been exercising for about five and a half days in the desert, and this is the first time I could get near a telephone to call, and somebody said to call you. And I'm doing that to tell you that I am really impressed with the training. It is first class. But I want you to know that my unit can train this well, too."

I believe KPUP was the most successful means of integrating the Guard into the Army. It provided hands on experience that Guardsmen could transfer to their units at little cost.

It was worth being woke up for. So that was the mindset - fear. Getting the soldiers willing to train at an increased tempo and perhaps even at higher levels, which we eventually were able to achieve. There was a great deal of distrust in the National Guard about the motives of the Army, as they began to accept us into more of these activities. And the question then was, "Is this simply a cover for the Army assuming more control over the National Guard?"

From the perspective that I had, there was never any question in my mind that the Army would have enjoyed command authority over the National Guard, but for those of us who understood the system, the statutes and the responsibilities of each of the separate components, there was never really a threat. Of course there were intrusions during the course of events into what had been the prerogatives of the Guard, but these were resolved by the leadership of the Army, principally. And though there may be those of us who have been critical of Army leadership in their relationship with the Guard, I must tell you, from having over twelve years of experience in working with the leadership of the United States Army, the Guard today could not have achieved what it's achieved if it had not been for the Chiefs of Staff of the Army with whom I served, and that goes back all the way to General Rogers, to General Myer, to General Wickham, and General Vuono, and of course Secretary Marsh. He was absolutely key.

I must tell you that each of those chiefs of staff, within his ability, was absolutely committed to the National Guard meeting its wartime responsibilities. The difficulty we had at the time—and I don't know how it is today,— was that the mindsets of the Army, as General Vessey may have described them, and the mindsets of the Guard, with which NGB was dealing, were separated by a great gap of ignorance. Neither one knew very much about the other. As a National Guardsman, I can tell you most Guardsmen knew about the National Guard, and beyond their state knew even less about the Army. So it was important to us that if we were going to resolve these matters, we had to find a way to integrate the Guard into the Army, the Army they were going to fight with, and they had to get to know each other because they were going to have to live and fight together.

Those were our objectives: perhaps it's questionable how successful we were. I do believe the Guard attained unprecedented capability and readiness through a closer relationship with the Army and that was achieved without loss of control of the Guard.

BJ: That's a very, very interesting summation. I think we have now heard enough to launch us into a more public discussion. I'll just mention one little personal aside to General Temple. Knowing of your interest in General Marshall's management of the Army and the integration of the National Guard, and your mention of Keep-Up, it's interesting that we reflect back that the year before the National Guard divisions were mobilized, General Marshall got all the Division Staffs to run through a week with counterpart training with Regular Army Division Staffs. There's very little record of that, but we know that every National Guard Division Staff got a week on active duty doing the job that they would do on active duty with one of the few Regular Army Divisions then in the system.

But now the time has come to turn to you, the members of the Symposium, and who would like to shoot the first question to the panel? Do we have any? I see a few people edging around out there. Yes, Sir.

Q: I wonder whether the time that we were—I'm General John Lenhardt, from OSD Reserve Affairs. I wonder, and probably either General Temple or General Vessey might know the answer to this: When the Army and General Abrams in particular were beginning to take a look at the levels of integration in the ROUNDOUT concept, my information would tell me that it was done at two levels. There were ROUNDOUT battalions, the ten battalion divisions, and then there were the brigades. How much debate occurred on that? And did anybody take a look at going perhaps even lower than that? And did you have any feeling about where you were going to get the greatest level of utility and the greatest level of integration?

JWV: I think I can say something. I can probably say more than you want to hear about that. But many of you in the audience, Fran, others in the audience, will recall the so-called OSD Tests we ran in the early '70s on integration. We ran tests on various levels of integration.

The tests were questionable tests. I'd put "tests" in quotations, because what they were, were attempts at integration at various levels, and there wasn't a broad sampling. There were onesies and twosies around the country. Some were done very, very well. They were more dependent upon the capabilities and enthusiasm of the local commanders, both the Active and Guard and Reserve people, than they were on a concept. So we had some that did superbly and some that did poorly. The debates centered more on some of the fears that Herb raised earlier on the question of, what's going to happen if you integrate Guard and Reserve units at low levels; do you then automatically rule out the opportunity for this marvelous group of American patriots who give up their vacation time to serve the nation's defenses for the opportunities to rise to higher ranks? And that's a very legitimate question and fear.

I think that, overall, we know that with 38 training days a year, the lower the unit is, the [more the] readiness from that particular unit, and that in theory you could integrate at the level of one. You know, there are all sorts of positions, I believe, in the Active Force today that could be filled by Guardsmen and Reservists on the 38 training days a year, or perhaps two for the position or something like that, and the nation would never miss a beat. But what we don't want to have is a system that says if you are going to enlist in the National Guard you are doomed forever to rise no higher than the rank of squad leader or platoon sergeant or tank commander, or something like that. "That's a different problem to be solved.

So there were all sorts of debates and questions raised and finally, when there are debates and questions about things like that, it was decided by fiat. General Abrams decided where we would integrate and the recommendations were taken to him and he made the decision and we integrated it at that level. And, you know, it worked far better than the people in the Active Army, there were many people in the Active Army who thought this was a bummer. I, along with some of you in this room, were at the meeting of the Army Reserve Forces Policy Board when I presented the integration concept.

I stood up and, you know, I was very proud of my Guard beginning. I'd fought for three years with the National Guard Division in World War II and enlisted in the National Guard and am very proud of my National Guard heritage. Unfortunately, I didn't have my 34th Division patch on this day, but I got up and briefed the concept, the integration concept which was the heart of the Abrams Doctrine, to the Reserve Force Policy Board. John Baker stood up and said, "General, I don't know who you are or what your background is, but I can tell you one thing. You don't know a damn thing about the National Guard." So, it was a concept that was not enthusiastically embraced by either the Active or the Reserve Component Force.

It took great leadership. People like Fran Greenlief and Vern Weber in the Guard and leadership on the Active Force to make it works at the levels that we did. Now we know a lot more. I think it is time to examine other concept, but we have to keep in mind all the lessons, not just some of the lessons.

We have to keep in mind all the lessons that we know about what a militia is for, you know. What is the State's role? The very legitimate role of States to have a militia. How do we serve that? How do we build a larger force for the nation? How do we adequately reward both monetarily and pysically the people who enlist in the Guard and Reserve.

So, there are a lot of questions to answer. There aren't any simple answers to this thing. But we have a lot of information that we didn't have before General Abrams imposed what we are now—and I agreed with Bob, that he would be appalled to hear us call it "the Abrams Doctrine."

HRT: I'm going to invite General Vessey to correct me, because I was not privy to the level of discussion that he was during this time, but as I recall ROUNDOUT, it was designed to do something that was more strategic in nature in that the Soviets were counting divisions and we were striving to reach a prudent risk force. I don't recall, but 32, 33 divisions, something of that sort. And the idea was to raise division flags in the Army, not only for a fighting a capability but also a deterrent.

Because of dollar constraints the Army could increase the number of active divisions only through this method of integrating Guard units into their divisions. The brigade was the most effective level and though there were some battalions that were integrated into Active units, brigades seemed to achieve better results more clearly and more quickly than at the lower levels.

As General Vessey discussed, maybe it's time to begin to look at different techniques and different methods to achieve this integration, or is that kind of integration relevant today? If no one is counting divisions, do you really need ROUNDOUT as we've known it in the past?

I won't even discuss ROUNDUP because I'm not certain that I know what that is. The fact is ROUNDOUT had prove to be successful when the division commanders made the effort to make it successful. I can recall that many of the division commanders in the 24th Division though they were my shadow, from Jim Vaught to Don Rosenblum to General Galvin. These guys were on the phone frequently to the National Guard Bureau pounding the table and demanding that the National Guard Bureau meet its responsibilities to ROUNDOUT. These men made the program work.

But the question, I think, that we now need to ask, that General Vessey alluded to, was, "Is now the time to examine different courses and perhaps the National Guard ought to return to a more traditional role? But that's your afternoon question.

BJ: Yes, Sir.

JWV: In answer to your question, you are absolutely right that part of it was building divisions. We could not build 16 divisions without making the third brigade of a number of those divisions Guard brigades. But we also wanted—General Abrams made it clear that they were to be real fighting divisions, not just hollow divisions, we wanted big, tough, divisions, and that's why additional battalions were added to some of the divisions, to make the big, tough divisions.

MG Francis S. Greenlief (Ret.):

Perhaps I can add something to this discussion by relating an anecdote. General Vessey and I were members of a group called the Dance of the Pachyderms that developed the STEADFAST Plan. Part and parcel of this was the integration of the Guard into the Active Army through ROUNDOUT. A great debate occurred between General Vessey and myself, at that time both Major Generals. Jack proposed that battalions of Guard, organic to Guard Divisions be available for ROUNDOUT. I was utterly opposed, although I was very willing to integrate Guard separate battalions as ROUNDOUT. My argument was

I didn't want to destroy the ability of the Guard Division to be mobilized as a whole division.

General "Dutch" Kerwin was the Chairman of the group, as I recall, and after General Vessey and I had our discussion, at the end of the discussion General Vessey, having heard my diatribe, said, "Hey, Fran, if I were a Guard battalion commander"—and I knew General Vessey's background—"If I were a Guard battalion comander I would be absolutely delighted to have my battalion mobilized as part of an Active Army division, even if I ran a Guard division." I've said that wrong. What Jack said was, "If I were the division commander of a Guard division I would be delighted to have one of my battalions mobilized with an active division." And Dutch said, "Jack, it's pretty obvious you ain't going to command no Guard Division."

But considering those relative positions, then, I'd have to tell you that today I'm not sure I'd hold to that position. Considering the kind of environment we are involved in, the kind of mobilization that would occur. I'm inclined to believe that today I might agree that a Guard battalion of a Guard division, in the right time and place, could be mobilized as part of the Active Army. I agree. It's a new environment, and it's time to take new approaches. Thank you.

BJ: Thank you, General Greenlief. Just to refer back for a moment to the original question, I recall an initiative, a strong initiative, but I don't remember the exact year. But if you recall the Finsterle Study, that went in great depth into ROUNDOUT at below battalion level, and had a concept for rounding out artillery battalions with batteries from the Guard, as an example, and it got quite a lot of scrutiny during a specific period of time.

Q: I want to ask a question of General Temple. You were speaking about the mindset and you were speaking about the commitment during his time at the Bureau of Army leadership to the concept of integrating the Guard and Reserve. Is there the implication, perhaps, that that some commitment may not have existed then, or maybe even now, on lower levels toward integration of the Guard and Reserve?

What I'm asking, somewhat diplomatically, is that when you talk to Guard commanders who participate in foreign force deployments, or even the Persian Gulf War, and when they speak rather explicitly and vehemently about second-class treatment that they perceived that they received from their Regular Army counterparts, is there just a bureaucratic problem in trying to take the commitment from that leadership and reach down to lower levels? Because that is just something that has always existed in American history and it's difficult to deal with.

HRT: No. I never found a case of a soldier in the National Guard who wasn't proud and excited and wanted to participate as part of the Army, at the levels you are talking about. Again, back to my original comment, the fear and the anxiety was at the senior levels. The soldiers, as I said earlier, were in many cases uncertain about their own abilities because the Army had done a pretty fair job of convincing them that they could not do very much, and many of their own leaders who lacked the experience themselves to provide the leadership to train the levels and at the tempo that was necessary, had convinced them that perhaps they could not.

I never found a case of a Guardsman who wasn't fully committed to the United States Army. I often had a hell of a time sorting out the fact that every National Guardsman thought he was in the Army even though he only was in the Army a few days a month was irrelevant to him. He was in the Army and he wanted to be a part of it, and he wanted all the trappings that went with it, and perhaps the personal slights or insults that might have been leveled at him were off his back very quickly. I never found an instance where a National Guardsman was afraid of losing his Guard integrity because of his relationship in relationship to the Army. Just the opposite. They were always willing to soldier.

LS: I would like to say something about that. As I think you know, I'm working in a book—I've been working on it too long and it should be finished—a book about Reserve Forces in the Gulf War, and that's given me an opportunity to talk to an awful lot of people about the kinds of things your question addresses, at least in that limited conflict. And I will have to say the evidence is not homogeneous. It's quite differentiated in terms of how people, mobilized people, were treated by Active Forces that they served with. And it ranges all the way from people who thought that they really were treated very poorly to people who thought that they were treated better than the Active Forces that they joined, they were treated almost like VIPs. Neither of those extremes represents, in my view, the center of mass or reality.

A lot of times people described to me experiences where initially they might be treated—I think second-class citizens is too strong a term, but might be treated with some, I don't know quite what to say, suspicion is not the right term, either, but not fully accepted. Let me just put it like that. And after they'd worked a little while they found that they evaporated, and I really feel—this is a personal opinion—I really feel one of the sort of sad things in the aftermath of the Gulf War is the following: The relationships between the components in many respects had reached, I thought, an unprecedented level of mutual respect and comity and to a degree that was undercut by the later controversies that surrounded the performance, readiness and utilization of the ROUNDOUT units, which were after all not the main part of the story, although they are an important part of the story.

But I'll have to say, I'm even somewhat critical of some of the senior leadership of what we might call the Reserve Forces community, active and retired, for putting undue emphasis, I felt, on that aspect when so many of the other forces deserved so much credit. And you could tell anecdotes all day that would illustrate that, but one anecdote that I think almost everybody here has probably heard involves an armored division that was just about out of fuel, and into their CP late in the day, maybe early in the evening, walks a female captain. And they look at her and they say, "What are you doing here?" And she says, "I got fuel. Want some?"

And they did. And, believe me, it was accepted with more than open arms. So there are a lot of stories of that, I think, are true, are valid, and that help reflect a reality that is more differentiated than the experience of some individuals who maybe felt they weren't accepted in the beginning and never were. Undoubtedly there were cases like that, too. But that's not the center of the mass, at least as my research to this point identifies it.

JWV: Well, the issue has been, I think, very well discussed by both these two people. I just recall my own serving as a soldier in a National Guard division between two Regular Army divisions committed to combat in the early days of World War II, and how important we all believed it was that we look as good as the Regular Army did out there. We didn't. We took more casualties. It was harder for us simply because we did not have the totality of training and experience that the 1st Infantry Division and the 1st Armored Division had. And that should be no surprise to anyone. But we did all right.

That colored my later view of what to do. I later had the good fortune of commanding one of those heavy divisions that was rounded-out by a National Guard brigade. I want to tell you, I would have been very comfortable going to war with my National Guard brigades as the third brigade of that division. I recognized that there certain levels of training that they hadn't achieved, that you just couldn't do in 38 training days a year. If you could, there is no reason to have an Active Army. On the other hand, we had worked closely enough together to understand the strengths and weaknesses of each other and how we could accommodate to those, and I believe that the Doctrine was sound and that we could have done it.

In a way, I understand the decision that was made in the mobilization for the Gulf War with the ROUNDOUT brigades, but it is too bad that it happened the way it did. The way it turned out there was plenty of time to give them all the training that they ever would have needed before they fired the first shot, even if they had started at a lot lower level. But we shouldn't dwell a lot on that experience. What we should do is couple that into all of the things that we know about how to integrate the Guard and Reserve and deciding how we march on into the future.

Q: Sir, I'm Colonel Jack Mountcastle from the Army War College, and I've got a question for Dr. Sorley as General Abrams' biographer. I think all of us, given our experience in the '80s when the CAPSTONE Program involving the National Guard and the Army Reserve, and a program like the National Guard captains in Europe, was working and very aggressively. There was almost no time, in my experience while serving in Europe, when you could not find a National Guard commander and his staff or individual Guardsmen on duty in Europe. Did

General Abrams, during his short tenure as Chief—because I know he went to Europe, so, did he take any steps toward the formation that we would then later know as the program of CAPSTONE and aligning Reserve Components to directly with the active . . .

LS: I'm going to have to say, Jack, that I'm not sure of the answer to that, but let me speculate. And General Vessey may well know and can tell you.

As you know, General Abrams had a lot to do and little time to do it in. He died after just under two years in office as the Army Chief. One of the last and most significant things he did was to call his senior associates together and tell them that he had committed to a 16-division force with no increase in end strength and no budgetary impact, at a time when we had then maybe 13 and 1/3 divisions. In other words, we were going to take this out of our hide. He disestablished seven major headquarters and cut back drastically on many others, including his own, in order to try to get as many spaces as he could to underwrite that expansion of the division force.

He was able to do that because he reached agreement with Jim Schlesinger, then Secretary of Defense, that if he could make any savings of that kind he could keep them and apply them toward a greater combat force. And at this meeting shortly before he died, he said to them, "I'm committed to this course of action, unless anybody here knows of any reason why we shouldn't do that. And if anybody thinks that, they should have the courage to speak out now and tell me so." Now, you know, if you had been one of those people and had it put to you like that, I guess you would have to had really suck up your gut to say to General Abrams, under those circumstances, "We can't do this," or "We shouldn't do it." But the fact is no one did, and so he then said, "All right. That's what we are going to do."

And then it was only a matter of weeks before he died, and so it was left to others to carry that on. And so far I know, the manifestations of efforts to increase the capability of Reserve Forces, the step-up to this tougher, more demanding mission than they'd ever had before, (a mission that was in some ways tougher than what we had in the past asked of our Active Forces), the next half-generation of leadership, let's say, was left with that charge from him, which, in my view, they carried out, they executed brilliantly.

JWV: I would just add to that, that on the Active side, it was the triumphant effort of Kerwin, DePuy, and Fred Weyand, who were given this legacy, and then along with people like Frank and Vern and some of us lesser lights who were marching to the same tune because it was the only band in town, who were the foot soldiers in that exercise. Many of these other refinements came later.

The Guard captains to Europe, and CAPSTONE. CAPSTONE is Bob Shoemaker, we fortunately had a series of dedicated Active and Reserve Component people who made this work, and I think it's important that we understand that we had a good bunch of TAGs, a good bunch of

State Adjutant General, who were able to grasp the concept and make it work because it is out in that arena where these sorts of ideas work. You can have all sorts of grand ideas at the national headquarters, but if they don't work at the posts, camps, and stations in the Regular Army and in the States, in the Guard, they don't work.

LS: I think you might like to know one little vignette apropos of what we've been discussing, one that also occurred very late in General Abrams' life.

General Vessey mentioned that he commanded one of those heavy divisions and it had a ROUNDOUT brigade in it, and that he would have been very comfortable taking that unit to war with this ROUNDOUT brigade. There is a reason why he had that division.

Late in General Abrams' life, when he was mortally ill and able to do very little, he would do a little work on the veranda of Quarters 1 at Fort Myer. His associates would bring to him those things they knew he cared most about and viewed as most important. And on a given day, Colonel Bill Livesy, his Executive Officer, brought to him some such matters, including the proposed new slate of division commanders. The people who put those slates together knew General Abrams well, and they usually got those slates through without any change. On this occasion Abrams looked at the slate. Then he turned to Livesy and he said, "Have you got a pen?" Abrams took the pen, struck through one name on the list, we don't know whose, and wrote in, "Vessey" opposite that division. Then he gave the slate back to Livesy and said only, "He's a soldier."

Q: I'm Pat Garvey, from New York. This is kind of a follow-on to General Vessey's comments about integration on mobilization, and I wonder if (General Vessey) would like to comment on the role of the full-time cadre, the mix of the cadres, and what you think they might contribute to facilitate in the integration of the Guard and Reserve Forces on a, not only a day-to-day basis, but of course in terms of mobilization. Where do you see that whole business going?

JWV: Well, we are at a time when there's a great opportunity for us to examine what we've done in the past, what is good about that, and then look at the uncertain future that we see, and ask ourselves, what should we do in the future? I personally believe that it is time for a complete, top-to-bottom look at the way we mix Active and Reserve Forces. This will not be popular in much of any place. The Active Forces will have difficulty with this. Many Guardsmen and Reservists will have difficulty with it. Political leadership will have difficulty with it, when their plate is full of other problems, taking on something that obviously has great political overtones and the prospect of big debates and "why fix it when its isn't broken that badly?" will be raised. And that's a good question.

On the other hand, I would suggest that we are at a watershed of history. We have a model that has served us very well over the past 50 years, 50, 60, 75 years, and it has served us well. And we take, we gain from it enormous strengths. We also take from it knowledge of very clear weaknesses that need to be fixed. And I think that we have an opportunity to ask that question in the context that I have just raised. I think looking at bits and pieces is the wrong way to look at it now.

There are enormous problems with doing what I've suggested doing, but also, I think, enormous potential benefits for the country a few years ahead.

And there are great dangers to this country, and the greatest danger tht I see, on the Defense side of the house, is inadequate defenses for the years ahead. The population is growing; the percentage of population that's involved in defense activities is becoming ever smaller; compulsory military service has long since disappeared; the numbers of Congressmen and women who have served in the Armed Forces becomes an even smaller percentage.

National Guard Armories are being closed in communities that have had National Guard Armories since those particular states were states. How to tie any defense force with the population at large is a major question. How to get support for defense?

ROTCs are being folded up because "we don't need the officers that they produce." The ties between the citizens of this country and its defense forces are becoming increasingly weaker. So, what we have to look at is, how do we have enough? And the difference? There will be arguments about, well, you don't want too much because the nation needs its resources for other things. But if you have to choose between too much and too little for defense, the penalty for having too little is exponentially greater than the penalty for having too much.

Now, how do you do it? And I say, let's start with a look at how we tie the total force together, and that's not just Army, but Army, Navy, Air Force, Marine Corps, Coast Guard.

How do we build this nation's defenses from the roots of the nation and the histories and traditions that we have that are worth taking into the future? And how do we gracefully get rid of those things that have served well but aren't necessarily worth taking into the future?

That's a long-winded answer to your excellent question on a narrower subject.

BJ: Bob, in your research, what do you feel, looking at the keen sense that General Abrams had with respect to the values of this integration and the ability to build public understanding and support for military operations, do you feel that he had similar views with respect to the importance of a strong industrial base, with respect to manufacture, competition, and so forth? Certainly, in his Big Five Program he identified a certain level of interest. Would you comment on that?

LS: I will, But what I'm going to say is going to be speculative, because I don't have any detailed, factual knowledge of that.

I think you are right to look at the Big Five, and on an earlier occasion General Vessey had commented on the Abrams' legacy as we viewed it in the Gulf War, to which he also alluded briefly this morning. And he identified a number of different things.

The effective air support was one. The integration of the Reserve Forces was another. The training I think he identified as the most important, the great training which taught our soldiers how to stay alive on the battlefield. But he also talked about high technology that worked, and worked when he needed it. It was determined that the readiness of the force, which depended primarily on the soldier and his leaders, would also be enabled by the right kind of equipment. And, of course, this is one of the similarities between that period and what we are now seeing, the limited amount of resources, a lot of competition for those resources.

I think focusing on a few key systems was a very important aspect of that, and while many of those systems went through the kinds of growing pains that I guess is endemic to any high technology enterprise, I can't help but feel he would have been extremely gratified by how well those systems performed when the time came to have them tested in combat.

BJ: I'd like to give each of the panelists, starting with General Temple, an opportunity to take perhaps three or four minutes to summarize your thinking on the issues that we've discussed this morning, and orient them, if possible, towards a summation we might come out with before the noon break, to contribute toward a summary statement.

HRT: At the time, and of course this was during the Cold War era, the integration of the Guard into the Army was essential for the preparation for the nation to go to war. At that time the perception was that we'd be fighting outnumbered and outgunned in far off places, under very difficult circumstances, with very, very little time in the mobilization process, and very little time between mobilization and commitment to combat. That was the driving feature for everyone who was addressing the National Guard's preparation for war.

That concern for readiness convoluted how we trained the National Guard. We went from training from the bottom up sequentially, and we began to focus on the fact that we could not deploy divisions in 60 and 70 days if they had never trained Division Commanders and Staffs. We made a conscious decision that it was essential to focus training on the highest level of training that you could because that was the most difficult and complex level of training.

The difference between the National Guard of the 80's and the one which General Vessey related to when he was mobilized in World War II was the fact that the modern Guard was a totally different organization. Everyone had basic and advanced individual training as a requirement for service in the National Guard. Officers were already service school trained and many more officers C&GSC products.

We rejected out of hand the contention that 38 days of training was the training limit for the Guard. It was and is not. The stability in the Guard provided the opportunity to build on training over a period of years. You would go out and talk to National Guardsmen who were in training and ask them, "how long have you been in the Guard?" If he said ten years—and the average was running about seven, you were taking 38 days times seven, and then all of the additional training activities which were then incorporated into the Guard. And on top of that you had the basic and advanced individual training.

In many instances, you were now talking to peacetime National Guardsmen who were better prepared to go to war than many soldiers we sent to war in World War II, Korea and Vietnam. They had more actual training and experience.

So we were not dealing with novices, or recruits, in preparing them to meet their wartime commitments. It's just that we had to refocus on how we were going to train them with the view that you had to train divisions and brigades, and that the soldiers could be refreshed in basic skills after mobilization. You could do that in 28 or 30 days. You could not train divisions in 28 and 30 days. So what you found was in inverted approach to how we prepared the National Guard to go to war. But, if I could just take an additional moment.

Two people, in my experience, were key to achieving training success. One was General Bill Richardson, who was my next-door neighbor when I lived at Fort Myer. He had an opportunity to go up and evaluate the 38th Division of the Pennsylvania National Guard back in the late '70s, and came back and explained to me that, "You have very good soldiers in the National Guard, that I've seen" — he had never seen a National Guard unit before—he said, "But they are not very savvy. They can't put things together. They could not operate as a Division. They need practical experience." And he wrote a very lengthy report to General Jeff Smith, who was the First Army Commander, to whom he was reporting on his evaluation, and that report became the first training document the National Guard Bureau ever put out.

I regret to tell you I plagiarized most everything from General Richardson's report. But that was the genesis for our infusing a sense of urgency into the Guard. Train at the level organized, reinforce service schools with realistic experiences. Train units at an accelerated tempo oriented on CAPSTONE missions.

The second person that I thought played a very key role in permitting the Guard to expand beyond what it had ever envisioned for itself was General Sennewald.

When he became the Forces Command Commander those opportunities opened. I can recalled his telephone call to me at Fort Bliss where I was visiting. He said, "Look, I'm about to sign a policy that for every annual training period, a National Guard unit will train several days at the level it's organized. You've got any problem with that?" No, Sir. That's a good policy."

That was the impetus we needed to train units to accomplish their missions. This was proven in world-wide exercises and permitted the mobilization and deployment of large or organizations with little or no post-mobilization training for Desert Shield/Storm. It was now a new National Guard, ready and mission capable.

LS: I guess I'll just close by making an observation about then and now. It seems to me it's been established without question that the concept for the integration of the forces which stemmed from General Abrams' experience proved to be the right concept for the Gulf War. The working title of my book about reserve forces in the Gulf War conveys that, It's called, "Good To Go."

I would like to suggest that whether it proves to be the right policy for the future—and I would very much like to see the kind of top-to-bottom review of this issue that General Vessey advocated be done in the next year—depends in part on what role America decides to play in the international affairs of the future.

You hear, for example, people saying that the Cold War was an aberration, that the maintenance of a large standing Army during the period of the Cold War was an historical aberration. And the Cold War is over. And therefore, the implication is that we can go back to our historic primary reliance on Reserve Forces, with a small, almost a cadre of standing Army.

Now, I'm not prepared to say that's right or wrong, but I will just point out that the one major difference between the pre-Cold War period, as a model, and the post-Cold War period is we haven't decided to go back to being non-involved in world affairs the way we essentially were before World War II. So whatever determinations are made, I suggest they have to be made with that in view.

Now, if the United States continues to try to advance what some have called a "New World Order," and I'm not sure what that means, but what it means to me, or what I suggest it might mean, is a world in which aggressor nations and aggressor elements are not permitted by the world community to work their will through the use of illegitimate armed force. Any "New World Order" that is going to be imposed, because that's what we are talking about—imposing it, is going to have to see leadership by the United States in bringing that about. That seems to be unquestionable to me.

And under those circumstances, it seems to me that frequent resort to force in varying degrees will be a virtual certainty. So I close by raising a consideration that troubles me in this respect.

General Vessey pointed out quite eloquently how the budgets are going down, and how the percentage of the population under arms is going down, how the experience of our Congressmen with military affairs is going down, and a number of other factors, all contributing I think to the same drive in one direction. But if we are going to have frequent resort to armed force, Reserve Forces are inevitably going to be a part of that. And ought to be, in my view.

And yet in the Gulf War you saw some types of capabilities that reside in the Reserve Forces. Even such a mundane thing as line-haul trucking capability were used 100 percent, or close to 100 percent. The reason I mention that is that if we go back to some campaign like that again soon, we are going to have to go back to the same people and say,

"Come again." And the way to avoid that course is to have redundancy of a capability, so this time we can draw on these people, and then if we have to go again pretty soon, we can go and draw on some other people elsewhere. But redundancy of capability is costly, and I suggested probably not politically attainable — under current circumstances, anyway.

So if we did a review of the kind General Vessey advocates, which I strongly support, I would hope that we would look very carefully at not only discreet instances of the potential use of force, but the cumulative impact over time, if indeed we are going to try to impose a "New World Order," or play a role in world affairs which causes us at fairly frequent intervals to have to mobilize parts of our military capability.

JWV: Well, I'm not sure I'm capable of doing that, Bruce, but the very title of this Symposium here sort of says two things. One is it's sort of a tribute to General Abrams, and I think that's right and good that we should do that. But it also raises a huge question for what do we do in the future, and I gave my little speech about that. Bob has just reminded us of some of the things that we need to examine. There are some others.

General Abrams was a very human individual, among other things. He was a person who could find you in serious trouble but put you at ease by telling of some similar circumstances that he had once been in that was very akin to the kettle of fish that you now found yourself in. He understood soldiers wonderfully.

As we look at how to make the best defenses by using Active, Guard and Reserve Forces, we need to understand that it is in the strengths and weaknesses of those people that we call soldiers, whether they be Active or Reserve Component, that will decide the issue.

Many of you have heard me tell the story before, but I'll tell it again, about the enormous strengths that one finds in soldiers, that can be part-time soldiers.

I visited a tank battalion at Fort Drum, before Fort Drum was an Active Army post. A New England tank battalion (was) there in training, and it was far down the DAMPL. They had old turkeys for tanks. But I engaged in one of my favorite activities, which is riding the bustle rack of a tank as it's going down a Table 8, and I did that. Got the headsets on, and listened to the crew.

And this was absolutely a topnotch tank crew that would have compared very favorably with any tank crew any place in the world. It just went down that range, bang, bang, bang. The commands were right. The techniques were just absolutely top-notch. And they scored very high on that Table 8.

We got back to the start point and I dismounted, and I hadn't been introduced to the crew before I got on, and I introduced myself and talked to them and talked to the tank commander and asked him how long he had been tank commander.

He said, "It depends on how you count it, Sir." He said, "I was supposed to be a gunner in the Second Armored Division at Fort Hood, but I was, most of the time, the tank commander for three years. And then, "he says, "I was tank commander for three years or something like that in the Third Armored Division in Europe. And then I've been with this outfit"— I've forgotten the number, whether it was seven years, or eight years or whatever it was that he was a tank commander with his outfit. "So," he said, "I think you can probably say 13, 14 years." I asked him where he lived. And it turned out he lived about a four-hour drive from the Armory where his tank company drilled. And I said, "You drive that far for drill?" And he said, "Yes, Sir." I said, "Why do you do that, Sergeant?" He said, "General, it's the closest good outfit with tanks."

Now, therein is sort of the heart of the strength of the Reserve Components, and the Active Force. We understand that.

In our county seat back home in Minnesota is the 194th — was the 194th — Tank Battalion, before you dummies here in Washington took them off the rolls. But it was the first tank battalion to fire a shot in anger on the beaches of Luzon. It covered the withdrawal to Bataan. It made the last counterattack on Bataan, with the battalion commander and his three remaining tanks. All of them Guardsmen, who never fired a shot in anger out of the main gun of those tanks 'til they fired at the Japanese. And an outfit that maintained 110 percent strength all through the years because of its association with Bataan and those battles. And we took it off the rolls. We can't do those things.

Now, how we take those sorts of strengths and build for the future is the question. That model won't fit the future. Maybe the 194th ought not to be a tank battalion in the old form, but somehow there's an armory there with a unit there and guys reporting, and somehow the legacy of that battle has to be infused into those people. So, that's your problem. But we have to do it.

BJ: Thank you, General Vessey. I think General Vessey has made a very eloquent case for our large discussion of our intense desire to somehow hang on to our National Guard unit lineage during this great period of restructuring and turbulence.

In summary of this morning's discussion, an almost impossible task, there have been so many thoughts and ideas that have been thrown out at us. I think what we can say in retrospect about the morning session is that, "Yes, we can agree, from the panel's standpoint, there is a validity to our reference to the emergence of an Abrams Doctrine," albeit it was a doctrine that really forced the National Guard into a position of more prominence in the Defense structure, and really put it to a great test. To a test which I think one of our panelists said required National Guard soldiers to do more in the way of preparation and training than perhaps soldiers of even the Regular Army had had to do under normal conditions, under non-Cold War circumstances. But that even successful doctrine must be subject to reevaluation, as we look not only to the past as to the accomplishments, but to the future as to what needs to be done.

First Hand View of Implementing the Abrams Doctrine

RFE: Our luncheon speaker today, Lt. General Don Rosenblum, has had an awful lot of experience that relates to the subjects that we've been discussing this morning. He was one of the architects of STEADFAST when he was on the Army Staff. He was one of the earliest participants in ROUNDOUT brigades as they developed.

When I was appointed the Adjutant General of Florida, he was my CONUSA Commander, and I don't know whether he inherited me or I inherited him, but he was, let me say, vitally interested in the training of the National Guard units in the State of Florida and evidenced that by a lot of personal interests and attention.

We've asked him if he would reflect upon those steps that began to carry us up to the Desert Shield/Desert Storm arena. And it's with a great deal of pleasure that I introduce Don Rosenblum.

LTG Donald E. Rosenblum (Ret.), Former Commander, First U.S. Army:

Thank you. I am used to being a utility ball player, because when I was in high school I was a damn good baseball player.

When I went to college the curve balls were a little bit sharper and the fast balls were a little bit faster. So I became the utility infielder for my alma mater. I went in in the late innings, like Rafael Belliard does, and went to shortstop in the eighth and ninth or pinchran and everything. So pinch-hitting doesn't bother me. It probably bothers you because you are stuck with me for the next two hours and 38 minutes as I reflect on things.

And I would like to reflect. I probably, when I was on active duty, had as much experience with the Guard and Reserve as any other General Officer or maybe more. And so I think that I understood, in those days anyway, about the Guard and Reserve.

But my first brush with the National Guard was as a Second Lieutenant of Infantry, as I reported to my company in the Korean War. I reported to East Company, 224th Infantry Regtiment, 40th Infantry Division, California Army National Guard. Another Second Lieutenant who reported in at the same time, we came up through the Replacement chain together, took over the Weapons Platoon and I took over the First Platoon. His name was "Shy" Myer.

As a matter of fact, when Bob Ensslin asked me to speak here, I picked up the phone and called Shy and I said, "You ain't going to believe this, but I've got to speak to a bunch of guys, so give me some insights," which he said, and if you figure out what he told me to say, you will have figured out Shy Myer.

My battalion commander in those days was a fellow by the name of Alvin E. "Bulldog" Howell. Now, Herb Temple may know him. Bulldog Howell was a California Guardsman. He'd been a battalion commander in World War II, in the 40th Division in the Pacific. And they didn't call him "Bulldog" for any other reason except he was as tough as nails, and he taught me a lot. I'll never forget him.

I will not forget my regimental commander, who was "Walking Jim" Richardson, who'd been the Senior Army Advisor to the California Army National Guard was activated and sent to Korea for the war, he volunteered for it and was accepted as the Regimental Commander of the 224th Infantry Regiment.

Some twenty years later I got re-involved as I was assigned to the Pentagon, to the Office of the Deputy Chief of Staff for Operations, as it was called in those days. I was assigned to the Operations Directorate. And my assignment was the Special Assistant to the Director of Operations. My friends told me, "You are a Special Assistant for one of two reasons: You are either undergoing courtmartial charges or you didn't have a job." Mine was the latter.

A fellow by the name of Donnelly P. Bolton was the Operations Director, and he liked to stack up colonels just in case he needed them. Well, he needed me because I became the DCSOPS representative to STEADFAST, and it was a fascinating experience. STEADFAST, the reorganization was headed by a fellow by the name of Snapper Rattan, who was the Deputy Chief of CORC. You younger guys don't even know what CORC was. It was the Chief of Reserve Components, headed by a Regular Army lieutenant general, and his deputy was a Regular Army major general. I haven't figured that out, but that's what it was.

And my only claim to fame under STEADFAST was the fact that, when we were getting close to making decisions, the CONARC representative—and CONARC was then in the throes of becoming TRADOC and FORSCOM, which was another great thing during the Abrams era — the CONARC representative came up to the Pentagon at one of our final meetings, and he was a general and I was a colonel, and he got up and he said, "The CONARC position is we will test one Readiness Group on the West Coast and one Readiness Group or Region on the East Coast." And I jumped and said, "BS, It will take five years to implement and the DCSOPS position is we will do it now."

Now, hell, I didn't have a DCSOPS position. Neither did I have the authority to say it. But we did it. What we did in STEADFAST was probably one of the greatest things that ever happened in integrating the Regular Army and the National Guard and USAR.

Now, in case you've forgotten what happened in those days, the CONUS Armies, the CONUS as they are called, prior to STEADFAST, had responsibility for land masses, for commanding posts within their geographical area. That was changed to what it is today, or almost is today, where the CONUS Armies command the USAR and supervises the training and readiness of the Army National Guard.

Within each CONUS Army you had a certain number of what were called Army Readiness Regions, commanded by Regular Army major generals, with a staff of colonels and senior lieutenant colonels who were branch coordinators, depending on the branches within that geographic location. And under the Army Readiness regions were Readiness Groups commanded by Regular Army colonels, filled with very bright, dynamic, dedicated sergeants, captains, and majors. And then, within the Guard and Reserve, reduced to a very small number, were the advisory detachments.

Within the First Army area—we had four later on, and during that time, if you'll recall, the First Army stretched from Maine to Florida, east of the Mississippi to include Puerto Rico, Virgin Islands, District of Columbia.

We had four Readiness Regions, and each one of those major generals stationed at Devens, Dix, and Fort Meade, and in Atlanta, had "x" numbers of groups under them. It was a wonderful organization.

My only complain then and as it is today, and then then Vice Chief of Staff of the Army and the current Forces Command CINC has heard me say this to him on many occasions, the rest of the Regular Army never has understood what Readiness Group guys do and what Readiness Region guys do. So when the Regular Army guys who were out there, dedicated to cause of assisting, not advising, but assisting with hands-on, when the boards meet the guys sitting on the boards who have had no experienced with this say, "Gee, I don't know. What is a Readiness Group guy? What is a BAT? Some thing that flies?" No. It's a Branch Assistance Team, within that Readiness Group. A very dedicated young captain or major, who probably has more technical expertise in his field than his counterpart who is the S3 of the Third Battalion of the 505th Airborne, where he would rather be, but works harder and more hours, and probably accomplishes more, than his counterpart.

But nobody knows what he does, so when the boards come out and they don't select him for Leavenworth, or they don't make him a major, he doesn't understand that. And so that's my cross that I bear, that I've borne all these years.

But during the General Abrams era was when we had STEADFAST. If you look at what we have today, in addition to what General Reimer and his people are trying to do to increase and improve the readiness of the Guard and Reserve, STEADFAST, with the exception of no more Army Readiness Regions — which I think was a mistake to do away with, is in fact like it was twenty years ago. And if you think about that, you say, well, maybe Snapper Rattan, who headed STEADFAST, was pretty good. And so were the two guys from the USAR, CAR, and the National Guard. Joe Burke, who went on to bigger and better things in the Guard, and Rock Huddleston, who was the USAR guy, two colonels, did a superb job in attempting to meld the Regular Army and the National Guard. That was kind of my second look at the National Guard, USAR, and the Regular Army.

The next one was—and you've heard it this morning, when General

Abrams said, "We are going to increase the size of the Army from 13 Active Divisions to 16 Active Divisions, and it isn't going to cost five cents in more people, more spaces or anything of that nature." Nobody believed General Abrams could do that.

Now, one of the believers was the DCSOPS of the Army, who was an Abrams guy. He looked like him. Broad-shouldered, smoked cigars, Camel cigarettes. Most magnificent guy I've ever worked for. His name was Don Cowles, C-o-w-l-e-s. And that's another day for another story about General Cowles and General Abrams. But I'll relate one.

I used to say—I was General Cowles' Exec, and I'd say, "You meet with General Abrams three times a week. What in the hell do you do?" And he'd smile and say, "We run the Army." And they did. And the meeting that was talked about earlier this morning, when General Abrams said, "Does anybody have any objections?" I laughed. I sat in the back of the room there. I was a little colonel, you know, sitting there. My boss told me to go in. I'd learn something, which I did.

But anyway, take 13 U.S. Army Divisions, make 16 and not cost you any spaces or faces. But they were what we called Bobtail Divisions, two Regular Army brigades, two-thirds of a DISCOM, two-thirds of a Division Artillery, two-thirds of everything else, and to be filled out, or rounded-out as it was called, with a National Guard brigade plus their support, combat support, combat service support.

The 5th Division at Fort Polk, and Fort Polk was a training center. The 7th Division at Fort Ord, California. Fort Ord was a training center. The 5th Division would get a Louisiana Brigade. The 7th Division would get a brigade out of Oregon. And then, the 24th U.S. Infantry Division, to be activated at a place called Fort Stewart-Hunter Army Airfield, Georgia, in South Georgia, coastal Georgia, with the 48th Mechanized Infantry Brigade of the Georgia Army National Guard to be its ROUNDOUT brigade.

Well, I have personal knowledge of that because I went to Fort Stewart in January 1979 as the junior brigadier general in the Army, and I was assigned as the Commanding General of U.S. Army Garrison, Fort Stewart-Hunter Army Airfield, Georgia.

And I didn't like that title. I knew that my mission was to build the 24th Division. And so I made myself the CG of the First Brigade (Separate), 24th Infantry Division. Had the papers, you know, all the papers printed with this, signs up, and nobody gave me permission to do it, but, hell, I thought it was fun to do that.

When I first got to Fort Stewart I looked around and I talked to the people there, who were not very interested in seeing the Regular Army build up at Fort Stewart. Their biggest thing was to see who could get to the bar first, by 3:30 in the afternoon. And, seriously, their only mission at Fort Stewart in those days was the Reserve and Guard training. You know, training areas, ranges, officers clubs, things of this nature.

So when I got there I looked around and there were no barracks.

There were two permanent barracks but nothing else. I thought they'd have a bunch of wooden barracks. I remembered that from my days in the Pentagon. They were supposed to be there. And I said, "Where are all the wooden barracks?" And they said, "Well, we tore them down and we are waiting for the new barracks." And I said, "Hell, that's not going to be for another two years!"

So I called the Adjutant General of the great State of Georgia, in those days an Air Force Officer by the name of Billy Jones, and I said, "I am on my knees, I am either going to put my soldiers in tents or I am going to ask you if I can rent you National Guard barracks."

And he said, "Of course you can rent my National Guard barracks." And we worked out the agreement. And so the soldiers of the 24th Division, First Brigade (Separate), lived in the Georgia Army National Guard barracks.

Forty-man, cinder block barracks. Ron Harrison and Bob Ensslin and everybody else in the southeast knows what they looked like. No heat. No air-conditioning. Sergeants loved it because you could walk in the barracks, you could look down and see the bunks lined up, and the boots lined up. If you wanted to go to the bathroom or take a shower, you went outside. And that's where the 24th Division started.

Interestingly enough, they had the best reenlistment rate for two years of any division in the FORSCOM, and the best reenlistment rate of the posts in FORSCOM in those two years. I thought it was rather interesting when I looked, and I used to tell them, "You live in spartan conditions, so you are the toughest outfit around."

So we rented the barracks form the Adjutant General of Georgia. A year later we were told that the 48th Infantry Brigade of the Georgia Army National Guard was going to be our ROUNDOUT brigade. "Would you like to announce that?" And I said, "You are out of your mind. A fellow by the name of Sam Nunn and a Governor by the name of George Busby are going to announce that." I'm smarter than that. So we did.

The 48th Brigade came in and we had a meeting in the Officers Club, after a couple of drinks. We had a meeting of the leadership of the brigade, and we said to them, "Look, you all have a great history and I don't want you to take off you Gray Bonnet patch. But would you like to wear the 24th Division patch on your pocket?" I didn't have authority to do that, but I decided to do that anyway. And that weekend all the patches in the 24th Division were sold out. And then I said, "We wear "V"s on our helmet covers," which they still do today, "and you all might think about doing that." And that was on within a week.

And then we talked about being the Third Brigade of the 24th. And I said, "We all believe in that, and you are the Third Brigade of the 24th, and we will all meet the same standards." Well, the 24th Division didn't have too many standards because we were just new. But those standards that we did have, the 48th Brigade were part of it.

Now, it was a little difficult because the 24th Division was what I used to call a lightfoot division. It was an infantry division. The 48th Brigade was a mechanized brigade, had two mech infantry battalions and a tank battalion.

But regardless of that, the battalions of the 48th Brigade and the battalions of the First Brigade of the 24th and the DIVARTY in the support battalion, all became sister units, and each helped each other in whatever it needed to be helped on.

When we got tanks into the 24th Division later on, guess who taught us how to maintain them? Guess who taught us how to drive them? Guess who taught us, if you've ever been to Fort Stewart, how to retrieve them from the mud? The Georgia Guard.

So ROUNDOUT worked both ways, as far as I was concerned.

And every weekend and during annual training, soldiers of the 24th Division were with soldiers of the 48th Brigade. Now, whether it was at Fort Stewart or whether it was in Tifton, Georgia, made no difference. And whether our guys went there by helicopter or jeep or sedan or privately-owned vehicle made no difference. But they were out there assisting, in conjunction and coordination with the Readiness Group and the Readiness Region.

When we evaluated the 48th Brigade, the chief of staff of the 24th Division was the chief evaluator. I didn't have an assistant division commander because I was a brigadier general. I was the only guy that didn't have an assistant division commander, so I worked it all myself, which was a great hardship on me because I loved it.

But the point was that between the 24th Division and its ROUNDOUT was a great, close, professional camaraderie, and an almost love for each other. And so we started it out this way, and in talking to the current 24th Division commander, I think it's probably still that same way.

The 24th U.S. Infantry Division, Lightfoot, within a year went on a joint training readiness exercise, or training exercise called, I think it was called BOLD SHIELD or BRAVE SHIELD, in Florida. We were maneuvered against the 82nd Airborne Division. The Second Brigade of the 24th had just been activated. We had 13 guys in that brigade. And they CPXed along with members of the 48th, and our DISCOM along with members of the 48th Support Battalion, together went to Florida to support the 24th Division.

About that time, somebody said to me, "You know, the 24th Division, you might think about it being a mech division." And I said, "Well, I've never served in anything but infantry and airborne and air mobile divisions. I don't know anything about mechanization." And he said, "Well, you ought to look at it." And I said, "Okay." So I called them then DCSOPS of the Army, and I said, "Sir you ought to come to Fort Stewart because I know you are testifying in a little while."

And the DCSOPS of the Army came cown, and he said to me, "Rosie, we are in trouble. I've just looked at an engineer map and Fort Stewart can't take tanks or APCs or whatever we had in the Army in those days."

And I said, "General Vessey, I've got a G-2 and Assistant G-2 who've almost walked this whole grounds and you need to listen to the briefing." Part of that briefing came from the OSD tests, the Georgia units that had maneuvered tanks and other tracked vehicles at Fort Stewart, Georgia.

Well, General Vessey went back to Washington and obviously convinced those guys that the 24th could in fact be a mech division. And so, within a short period of time, we got a tank battalion in and, as I mentioned, the Guardsmen of Georgia taught us how to maintain and how to drive and how to do other things.

When I left Fort Stewart I became an Army Readiness Region Commander. And I went from Fort Stewart, Georgia to Fort Dix, New Jersey. And if you don't think that's a culture shock—with all due respect to you people from New York and New Jersey, it was a great culture shock to me.

But the Army Readiness Region, I learned, had a hell of a lot to offer to the training and readiness of the USAR and the Army National Guard. You've got to remember that the weekends of those young captains, sergeants, and lieutenants and majors was Tuesday and Wednesday. Lots of people don't understand that. It ain't Saturday and Sunday because they are working with the Guard and Reserve.

After that I did other things, but then I had the opportunity, as Bob mentioned, to command the First United States Army. And I remember the Adjutant General of Puerto Rico saying to me, "When are you coming to visit? I said, "I'm coming to visit you in the winter, because I'm going to Maine in the summer." And he allowed as how that—you may remember that, Billy—he allowed as how I probably wasn't very smart, but he understood why I was saying that.

Again, I'll go back and reemphasize for some people's memory, the Army Readiness Region was a great organization for the training and readiness and supervision of the Guard and Reserve. It was done away with because it "had no wartime mission." It ought to be looked at again.

I believe in that period of time that I was in the Army, we stopped paying lip service to the Guard and Reserve with reference to equipment and training readiness, although the Adjutant General of Florida always bitched to me about his Duster battalions which he wanted me to go about getting rid of. Now they are going to get Avengers, I understand.

On the other side of the coin, the Guard stopped looking at annual training as summer camp, where the guys could go and hava a hell of a good time for two weeks, and play cards, and drink beer, and maybe go to the range every so often. And I can recall very vividly the 48th Brigade going on their AT, going from home station to the field, which had never been done before. I also remember the middle weekends where they trained right on through, and continued to train until they had come in and maintain their equipment and get ready for perhaps the next unit or for themselves.

That was a great step forward for the Guard and Reserve. It was a struggle to do that. But we did that. And I think that is being done today, and it's something which has to continue to get done.

I think the Regular Army and the National Guard and the USAR started respecting each other, and seeing their capabilities from the PFC on up. Although Dr. Sorley has mentioned, and I agree with him, not to dwell on some things, but I think a terrible mistake was made, and maybe too much was made of it, by not calling the Roundout Brigades up and sending them with their Divisions.

Maybe I'm a little parochial about it because of my experiences with the 24th and the 48th Brigade, but I think that was a mistake, and I think what that did was open a chasm between the Reserve Components and the Regular Army, which had been probably closed very well before that time.

I don't know the reasons, and I don't know the rationale. But I think, from an outsider's viewpoint, we ought not to do that again.

I think that some people, youngsters, young people in the position of some authority forgot, when we talked about the draw-down of the Guard particularly the Guard, as we reduce our forces, have forgotten that the National Guard has state missions.

Now, many of you as I look out there, understand that. Many of you can understand it now, when you think about what South Carolina did, when we had Hurricane Hugo. When you think about Hurricane Andrew, when you think about the Los Angeles riots, when you think about what's going on right now in the middle west, and people ought to understand that there is a state mission as well as a federal mission for the National Guard.

Today, reconstituting the services with people and equipment, it doesn't appear to some that there is a firm policy on what to do with the Guard and Reserve. We all recognize that they cannot be as immediately deployable as the Regular Army, and as somebody, I think it was General Vessey mentioned this morning, if they were then we wouldn't need a Regular Army.

But when you talk about the Roundout brigades and the division commanders tell me it will be about ninety days, that's not a bad figure. And I don't know what it is for divisions, National Guard divisions or Reserve divisions, from that point on. But I think people have to understand that.

I think people also have to understand when you talk about 39 days of training, you are not talking about the first sergeant, company commanders, battalion commanders, brigade commanders, on up. Those guys go by the armory almost every day. They go and check in. They see what's going on. They work the papers. They check on training. And a lot of folks don't understand that. They think the guy jumps in there on Friday night and takes his company over to Fort Stewart, Georgia for training. That doesn't happen to a well-trained unit. And so the dedication of those young officers, and even old, and sergeants, is something that people have to remember.

I think the Guard and Reserve have to be looked at as our greatest stability in our Armed Forces. I go along with, again, General Vessey— I mean, I worked for him a couple of times, so, you know, it rubbed off on me, when he talks about an assessment—and that's what my notes say to me. An assessment as to what we want to do pertaining to the readiness of the Reserve Component.

And you have to understand, as you all know, it's a function of assets. There is a certain amount of uncertainty out there with the troops, and you have retention problems today in the Guard, and you have retention problems in the USAR. I believe, off the top of my head, with no facts to back it up with, that it's the basis of the instability and the unknown of the future. Let me give you an example.

A maintenance company in Georgia is told that it's going to be out of the system. They worked the issue very hard, turned in equipment, and just before it's to go off the book, they are told by "them," whoever "them" is, or "they" is, "We are going to keep you for a couple of more years." Now, there may be a good reason for it. I will not fight that.

But I would ask you who are in authority today to remember that every single decision that you make regarding these units affects people. These guys love the Guard. Let me tell you. These guys really like it. I've got a son that's a Guardsman today, and I'm very proud of him. He's a captain. He spent five years in the Regular Army. He's now in the South Carolina Army National Guard. But every decision you make affects people. And that's important.

I also think that we don't have enough officers. We've never had enough officers, at the Pentagon, FORSCOM, TRADOC, I don't care where, who are told what the Guard and Reserve really are. I'm talking about the Regular Army guys. They don't understand them. They do not understand what the Guard and Reserve is about.

Conversely, and just as true, you've got a lot of Guardsmen out there, and Reservists, who don't know what the Regular Army does and wht they are about. So that sometimes causes the head-knocking that we see, which I guess we can do away with at this point, because, in my view, with all the problems that we face today, you know, if we don't live together, then we'll perish together. As an Army, as a country, or whatever it may be.

In addition to all of that, and there are some here in the audience today, the contractors of the defense industries don't know what is going on, either, in the great struggle as we draw down the Armed Services. And so, I think we have to do a better job, or you all have to do a better job in keeping them advised and informed. I don't know how. I haven't figured that out. But it's an unknown. There are tough times out there. And if you talk to the Don Wilsons of NGAUS, or the Frank Eatons of the ROA, they'll tell you that the House and the Senate marks today are tough. We need to keep industry involved in what we are doing.

Well, what is it all about? I want to give you this background. We are talking about General Creighton Abrams, STEADFAST, taking an Army from 13 to 16 divisions with no increase in people, and the Roundout concept, which I think is a very sound, solid concept. I've seen it, I understand it, I think I know it works.

But we've got to be a little smarter on the Roundout-Roundup concept as to ensure that if you call the 24th Division, or if you call the 1st Infantry Division, by God, send that National Guard brigade with them. If you don't think they are up to snuff with them, keep them in Reserve, or whatever. And if we'd gone with the 48th Brigade to the Gulf, they would have gotten better training than they did at the NTC, anyway, but that's long past.

But don't forget the lesson that was learned.

I read a book, I'm a great reader. I don't read well, but I'm a great reader. I'm full of, among other things, quotes. And I love to quote from the book, "The Killer Angels," where Robert E. Lee is talking to Longstreet after the second day of the Battle of Gettysburg, supposedly. It's a historically correct novel. If you haven't read it, read it.

Lee knows that the battle is lost, the Confederacy has reached a high water mark. But what he says is as true today as it was 130 years ago this First, Second and Third of July. He says: "To be a good soldier, you must love the Army. But to be a good officer, you must be willing to order the death of the thing that you love. That is a very hard thing to do. No other profession requires it. And that's one reason why there are so very few good officers, although there are many good men."

And for you who sit out here with the Officer uniform on, it's something to consider as you go through your quest as to what to do with the National Guard and the Regular Army, and the USAR.

My last quote for you comes from Pat Buchanan's book, "Right from the Beginning."

This quote, it's right after Pat Buchanan's oldest brother dies, is a wonderful thing for life, as well as for those who serve this great country in the military. And it says: "You will learn there are only two important things in life, an old priest once said. "To live well, and to die well."

The old priest did not mean to die full of honors, surrounded by admirers, but to die bravely and in the Faith. And he did not mean to live successfully and comfortably, but to live truthfully and honorably and with courage. And that's what we need, courage, and courage of our conviction.

Thanks a lot for asking me. I appreciate it.

[APPLAUSE]

RFE: Do we have any questions for General Rosenblum? He's offered to comment on anything that you all would like to have him comment on or answer.

Q: You said in your talk that the Readiness Regions performed a really good function and you were sorry to see them go. If we did have a top-to-bottom, reaping experience from the integration reports and such (inaudible), what are some of the other things you'd like to see and what are the features of . . . (inaudible).

DER: I know someplaces they are talking readiness training detachments. I know in the 24th Division, because the division commander told me, he has 42 officers and NCOs living in the little cities where, the towns where the armories are located.

I'm not sure, to be very candid with you, what it is we ought to be looking at, but rather than do it piecemeal, as was said before and I agree with, let's really relook at the think. Let's not try to change things for the sake of changing them. Where did we, if we look back on history, where did we make our mistakes, and where did we have our triumphs in the dealings of the Regular Army and the USAR and the Army National Guard? Take a look at the Air Force. Take at look at the Marines. I'm not advocating inspector and instructor type things, or a division commanded by a Regular and a Reservist, but I'm saying to you, you have to look at those things that made the integration, the Total Force, the Total Army successful.

And that's the top-to-bottom thing that I think we ought to be looking at. But I am just an absolute believer in, I don't care if it's the Basic Course, the Advanced Course, Leavenworth, the War College, Regular Army Officers have to learn about the Reserve Components a lot more than they think they know. And Reserve Component Officers have got to understand how the Regular Army works.

And I think if we don't do anything else, we've got to do that education. And then you will have less "them" and "us" type things. And I think, six months ago it was pretty poor, pretty bad, "them" and "us." Or a year ago, whatever.

It's a great privilege to be here with you all.

[APPLAUSE]

Afternoon Session
The Abrams Doctrine: Blueprint for the Future

RFE: Our Moderator for the afternoon panel, Major General (Retired) Fran Greenlief, former Chief of the National Guard Bureau, is a Guardsman of great experience, who has been in leadership roles in the National Guard during much of the time of all the events that we have discussed thus far today, and we are privileged to have him as our moderator this afternoon. Fran.

MG Francis S. Greenlief (Ret.), Former Chief, National Guard Bureau:
Thank you, Bob. Good afternoon, ladies and gentlemen. General Jacobs has been good enough to provide me with a summary of the discussion this morning. I'd like to read that as the basis for the Afternoon Panel.

This morning the panel said the Abrams Doctrine is a valid notion. It led to the creation of the right forces to available to fight the Gulf War. Its implementation challenged bias and tradition in the Active Army and in the National Guard. It challenged National Guard soldiers to accomplish training beyond anything they had ever been called upon to do, and sometimes may have asked more of a Guardsman than had in earlier times been asked of a Regular.

And, finally— and this really sets the pace and the style for this afternoon's discussion, we are at a watershed moment in history. During the past half century we have followed doctrinal patterns which have served us well. The doctrine of the past fifty years, including the Abrams Doctrine, possesses strength, but also demonstrates weaknesses. We probably need a top-to-bottom look at our national security needs, even though this will trouble an institution, and by that we mean the military, which inherently favors the status quo.

With that as the starting point, I won't re-introduce the panel members because you have their bios in front of them, but they are uniquely qualified to discuss the subject at hand, including General Galvin, who will join us later.

General Dennis J. Reimer, as Commanding General U.S. Forces Command, is responsible for establishing the training requirements and standards of Army National Guard units. He assumes command of Army Guard units upon mobilization. As assistant executive officer and aide-de-camp for General Abrams, he has personal knowledge of General Abrams' philosophy and his actions while General Abrams was Chief of Staff.

General Galvin is today an author, an historian, a former Supreme Allied Commander, Europe, and is now the John M. Olin Distinguished Professor of National Security Studies at the U.S. Military Academy, West Point. While he commanded the 24th Infantry (Mech) Division, following Rosie, that Division was rounded-out, as you know, by the 48th Infantry Brigade (Mechanized) of the Georgia Army Guard.

General Trefry is a truly outstanding and timely member of the panel. General Trefry is a former DCSPER of the Army, and is a IG of the Army had a more in depth knowledge of the National Guard during my time than anybody else that I knew in the Active Army. He stayed current and he stayed abreast. As a matter of fact, General Reimer tells me that General Trefy has just completed a study for the Department of Army, a current study on force management and integration. Force management and integration is part and parcel of what we are talking about in the application of the Abrams Doctrine. Dick is a many-talented man. After he retired from active duty he served as Military Assistant to the President and as Director of the White House Military Office.

With that in mind, I have prepared several questions which we'll put to the panel, and we hope you will join in the discussion just as you did this morning.

I want to start with a question to, General Trefry. General Trefry, Desert Shield/Desert Storm, as this nation's most successful mobilization, clearly demonstrated that the Total Force is a policy that works and, it seems to me and to the morning panel, that it validated the

Abrams Doctrine. There were over 250,000 Guardsmen and Reservists mobilized. Of that number, 30,000 Guardsmen served in Southwest Asia. Thousands of others were deployed to Europe. Army National Guard Roundout units met the Army's readiness requirements before mobilization. And Georgia's 48th Brigade, although not mobilized until late November, was combat-certified to Southwest Asia before the ground war started.

And so, General Trefry, from your perspective, your past experience, your current role, what do the results of the Desert Storm mobilization portend for continued application for continued application of Abrams Doctrine, and what lessons should force planners learn from these results?

LTG Richard G. Trefry (Ret.), Former Inspector General, U.S. Army:

I think the results speak for themselves and I think that if you have any knowledge of history, this is probably one of the most successful mobilizations we've ever had. One of the interesting things that never really gets a lot of publicity, and you can probably substantiate, I think there are actually more volunteers from the units then we ever had before in the Guard and Reserve who have come on board.

I was invited down to Tennessee on the 24th of August 1990 to speak to the annual leadership conference that Carl Wallace had, and they were mad as hell because they hadn't been called up — they got called up about two weeks later. But it was amazing how well they did.

I can tell you, back in 1978, Bernie Rogers sent me down to Macon, Georgia, to the 48th, because there were a lot of allegations at that time that not only the Active Army and the Guard and the Reserve, but none of us could fight together, nor would we fight.

And he said, "Go down and take a look at the 48th." And I called Jim Vaught, and I called Billy Jones, and I went down there on a—I remember it was a Wednesday night, and I was there Thursday and Friday, when they started filing in and Saturday and Sunday. Jim Vaught came up.

And I came back and I told the Chief that there was no doubt in my mind that I thought those fellows could do the job. And you heard Rosie talking about the state of the 24th at that time. And he was exactly right, I think, in the way he portrayed that to you.

I had another very interesting experience with the 256th Brigade. When we started the force integration inspection in 1981, one of the first places I went to was down to Lafayette, Louisiana, and I spent the night before with Buddy Stroud, and we talked about the 256th. I went out to the 256th and I had had a team up there for about a week. When I got there the next day, I spent about an hour with my team, and then we brought in the leadership of the 256th, and I remember they put a series of charts around this room, and they said, "Now we are going to show you how the Regular Army screwed you." I'd heard about this for about an hour, and, boy, it was true.

That was one of the greatest educations that I think anybody could get, and I'll always remember, when it was over, Buddy Stroud came to me and said, "You have my permission to use this anywhere that you can if it will make it easier for the Active Army and the Guard."

Now, you hear that this business is touch-and-go, but I can tell you, back then, when there were some real problems, when they went mech from straight leg, the first tracks that were delivered to them, they didn't even know how to turn them on. And they told us, in one little place, they winched the, I think it was a 113, they winched it sideways on a lowboy, and the state cops went down the road because it wasn't wide enough for two cars to pass, until they got it to the armory and then winched it off.

Boy, have we come a long way since then! I think that was reflected in that mobilization.

Now, have we got a long way to go yet? Sure, we've got a long way to go. All the things that you heard here. This study that I just completed, about two-thirds to three-quarters of the Total Army is on the old series TOE, MTOE. The Guard is on G Series, L Series, H Series. I think that we make it very difficult for ourselves when we do that. One of the recommendations that we are making in the study is that. Where we no longer have a deployed Army or an Army that is going to deploy to a place, like the Fulda Gap, but we would, the battalion that was in, say, the 8th Division is now back in, hypothetically, Riley or Sill, they could go anywhere.

And the National Guard battalion that was designated to be part of III Corps Artillery or one of the groups that is gong to reinforce the 1st Cav or the 4th, that's not going to go where they went. They are going to go anywhere.

What we need to do is put everybody on a standard authorization document. The Guard has been part of this study, and so has the Reserve, and I think there's a lot of promise. And I think it will go a long way toward making the mobilization, as well as the training, as well as the relationships a lot easier than they've ever been before.

You can't help but realize that this is a shift. If you go back to NSC-68, that Harry Truman signed on the 15th of April, 1950, when he said, you know, we require large standing forces, mobilization-based, which meant a course a large Guard and a large Reserve, oriented toward this thing that we've called the Abrams Doctrine.

That wasn't even heard of in those days, but that's what it was, the forerunner of a draft supported Army, a large industrial base, large procurements, large R&D, short warning times. Then you go to the President's speech in Aspen on the 2nd of August 1990 and suddenly you have small standing forces, and a projected Army, a volunteer Army, but still the requirement, you see, for substantial assistance from the Guard and Reserve.

Some people will tell you that there is a long warning time, but, you know, you stop and think. Perhaps there was more stability with the monolithic threat than there is with idiots running loose in the world. Maybe the real fear is seven guys wrapped in sheets out here in Gainesville with a Ryder truck and some form of a launcher. How do you protect yourself against that threat?

And if you read the newspapers, they seemed to try to start something up in New York at the World Trade Center. Every day there's another target or something that they are working on. So our work is cut out for us. And, at the same time, the opportunities are there, and we ought to take advantage of them.

FSG: General Reimer, given the results of the Desert Storm mobilization, what do you think that does protend, from your point of view, for application of the Abrams Doctrine from this point on? In this changing environment and this changing Army.

GEN Dennis J. Reimer, CINC, U.S. Forces Command:

Well, I think you have to look at Operation Desert Storm and Desert Shield, to understand the totality of that mobilization. As we look back on it, I think people sometimes miss some of the decision gates we had to go through. When we started out, we did not realize that we were going to grow as fast as we grew. Nobody knew what the end-state was when we started out. The first authorization was for 25,000 Reservists. We worked with those numbers and it was kind of metered out because we were working the coalition issue at the same time. How big was the force going to be and what was going to be required? I don't think all of that was known at the very start, at least from my perspective.

I think there were some very valuable lessons learned from Operation Desert Storm. I think we've factored them in. I just wrote down a couple of them.

First of all, it was a window to the future for us, and I would certainly agree with General Trefry that warfare has changed just as the world we live in has changed. I think we've raised the level of warfare to the Ph.D level. The way we fight now is different than any other time in our history, and I think we do it much better than anybody else.

Desert Storm showed us the need for the Total Army. I was the DCSOPS of the Army at that particular time, and I made three trips over there with the Chief. Each time we would go into a session and talk to soldiers, they would tell us that everybody there was wearing "U.S. Army." You rolled up your sleeves and you got the job done under some very trying and austere conditions.

I think the great support we got from the American people was largely because of the fact that we went through a mobilization process. I just don't think you can over-emphasize how important that was to us. When you compare that with my experience in Vietnam, I think all of us would certainly agree that this is the way we want to go.

We certainly achieved "decisive victory," but I hope that we are never gauged by measure such as "can you win a war in so many hours, or so many days, and with so many casualties?" But, on the other hand, I think we have set out some expectations for the American people. "Decisive victory" to them is defined winning as quickly as possible with a minimum amount of casualties. I think that's one of the lessons learned.

I think the other things all of us realize is that the next time we may not have six months to build up the force. If I was on the other side looking in, I'd say, "Don't give those guys six months, because if they can get their act together, they'll clean your clock. You just can't allow them to have six months to build up."

I think the other lesson I would take out of Desert Storm if I was on the other side is that weapons of mass destruction cause a lot of concern for our troops and for our people. The Scud rockets were one of our great fears as we went through his mobilization. Just a few of them caused a lot of panic. And I so think those are some of the lessons learned that you have to factor in from the mobilization for Desert Storm, and I think those are the things we have to look at as we move to the future.

FSG: You know, General Reimer, you have raised a point, or made a point that I must admit I hadn't really considered, carefully at least, and that is that when you started that mobilization for Desert Storm, you did not know the end-state. There's a similarity there with the mobilization for Vietnam. Certainly, when we started that we had no idea of what the end-state was.

But the decision on how to do that even prolonged it. When you approached the Desert Storm end-state, you started by using some Guard and Reserve units as needed for your force at that time, and it grew, so I think that makes good sense and it's the best explanation I've heard of that subject at any time.

DJR: Someone might have known the end-state, but if they did, they didn't share it with me.

FSG: I don't think anybody did know it, and certainly nobody foresaw how successful the end-state would be, I don't believe.

General Trefry raised an interesting point to me. One that I'm not terribly comfortable with, I might say. You mentioned the volunteerism that occurred from the Guard for the mobilization of Desert Storm. In my day we fought for unit integrity. We viewed any volunteerism as weakening that unit back home that we had to have ready to mobilize as a unit. And yet I know that the National Guard Bureau encouraged volunteerism, and if it was very successful; it produced a lot of highly skilled individuals. General Reimer, what was your reaction to that volunteerism and what do you think about that as a method for the future?

DJR: I think, there was the volunteerism. Initially everybody was concerned about who was going and who was going to go, but as I mentioned, we were building up the Force. We were very hesitant to take soldiers out of one unit to build up another unit because we didn't know if we were going to have to use that other unit later. We might have been breaking good units that we were going to need later on in the fight.

You really have to work the volunteerism issue both ways. I mean, you are delighted about having them but you've got to look at the overall impact on the Total Army when you start taking volunteers from one unit and pulling them into other units.

I think, the other part of volunteerism that I would highlight, was the call-up of the IRR. We were told that, we were not going to get very many of those people to come back. When we called up the RT-12s we were very, very impressed with the number of people that actually came back. Some of them called and said, "Now I've got my orders to come, but three months ago you told me you didn't want me in the Army because I did such and such a thing. You really want me to come?" It was nice of them to call. We said, "Thank you very much, we don't need you to do that."

I think the volunteerism that we saw in the Total Force, was really good. But I think you have to always be careful about what you are doing for the readiness of the Total Force when you start taking volunteers out of one unit to beef up another. You want to take your must ready units initially. So those were the items we took into consideration when we went through the process.

There was a very detailed process for doing that. We had what we called a "sanity check," some of the people I see in this room were a part of that process. We would look at the requirement that was given to us by the war fighting CINC, we'd look at the readiness of units in terms of personnel, equipment and training, and we'd make decisions bases upon that, in terms of whether that unit was ready to be mobilized or not.

FSG: General Trefry, you mentioned the problem of the mix of TO&Es. That's certainly not a new problem. However, it's a problem we've lived with for a long time. How serious is that to the integration of Guard units into Active Army units?

RGT: Well, I think it varies. I think there are some units that have a very severe problem with that, particularly the units that have the old equipment. They are expected to be in support of units with comparatively new equipment, and not the newest equipment. Particularly if you have the newest equipment, you have problem. You have a particular problem with communications.

Now, just going on a TOE, or doing to a different document, is not going to help unless you are able to sort out the equipment. We have, I think, particularly with the reductions coming, a better chance to do that and if we go back into force packaging that General Thurman developed when he was the PA&E, the business of the first to go, the first to equip, I think we can do a lot to improve that.

We have a real problem in documentation, in that the system is so arcane I could spend the rest of the afternoon talking to you about it, and you'd just get more hopelessly confused as I went along. And it's the same with all of us.

What we have to do is simplify the system and have it so we understand it. We, I think, went too far in saying to young commanders at all levels, "If you don't like your TOE or you MTOE, tell us and we'll change it for you." And when we'd do that, it was usually changed all the way up, but when you reached the point of getting delivery, it was an unprogrammed cost, and there was nothing there to give.

But what happened? We changed the document and perhaps the best way to describe it to you is this: I am authorized four Humvees, I'm required four Humvees, and I've got four Humvees on hand. But I want to go eight. And so I submit a request up the chain, and as soon as it gets up there—everybody says yes, nobody says no, and it gets to the DCSOPS and suddenly the documents change to eight and eight, but I only have four on hand.

What have I just done to the readiness? The unit went from C-1 to C-4 with flick of a pen. And he's not going to get it next week, and he's not going to get it next year because it's an unprogrammed cost. Nothing in the form. And so the natural reaction for commanders is they don't post the requirement.

And then when you sit down and you try and figure out what is the wartime requirement, you've got a hell of a mess on your hands.

Now, that sounds very bureaucratic. But that's the way it works. And we have a real mess trying to sort that out. That's about the best way I can explain it to you. And I think if we get everybody on the same sheet of music, and we take a look at what the true wartime requirement is, I think we'll do a lot better than what we've been able to do because I'm not sure we really understand what the wartime requirements are.

FSG: Did that problem impede the mobilization, General Reimer, that you are aware of?

DJR: I think it's something that has to be taken into consideration and it was one of the primary factors of the sanity cell. In other words, they would take a look at the unit's equipment, as reported in the unit's status report, see what they had on hand, what they really needed to do the job, and then you could make a decision as to whether they needed some additional equipment or we'd send them as is. But it's a very complex issue, as General Trefry knows better than anybody.

I would just simply tell you that I think we are making progress in this area. As I go around, and look at the Roundout and the Roundup brigades, the equipment compatibility with their parent divisions is there. We've done a good job in that particular area.

When you get outside, the non-Roundout/Roundup category, you start to find it cuts both ways. I was in Salt Lake City just a little while ago and I looked at a National Guard Apache battalion, probably one of the best-equipped battalions that I've seen in the Total Army. I told the commanders over there, including the TAG, John Matthews, that the Active Component guys would kill for those facilities. I mean, those are just outstanding facilities, outstanding equipment, great pilots, great training area. That is a case where the Guard battalion is better equipped than probably a lot of our Active Component units.

Most of our units have the Apaches and they have them in the same quantity as the Guard battalion, but the facilities of that Guard battalion were just outstanding. And that's the way it should be. So I think you have to take into consideration the unit, and the specifics of that unit, when you make mobilization decisions.

We have a problem in terms of getting the rest of the force filled out. We have 500,000 short tons of equipment in Europe waiting to come back to the United States. We will take that equipment-and it's good equipment - and we'll replace some of the shortages that exist through the Total Army. So over time that's going to make things better. It just takes dollars, and it takes time to make that type of thing happen.

We have to plan to do it and we will continue to equip based upon the "first to fight" principle. The Contingency Force package will be equipped before the rest of the force. There's no other way you can do it. You can't make the Army well in five minutes, or five days, or five months. It's got to be a phased type of thing, and so we approach it from that standpoint.

The short answer is, yes, MTOE and equipment compatibility do impact upon your mobilization decisions.

FSG: I'd suggest that, in my experience, we have never fought the war that we planned to fight. Given that Guard and Reserve units were not mobilized for Panama, Grenada or Somalia, but Desert Storm required a very significant mobilization, and now we've got a military presence going in the Balkans with apparently no concern for mobilization.

Is there some way of defining a level of contingency that we might expect mobilization and that Guard and Reserve Commanders in the field can expect their role in the Abrams Doctrine to become very real like mobilization?

DJR: In terms of mobilization, I think you can make the argument that you mobilize based upon a situation. I think you do it through all spectrums of conflict. If we fight in a global war, we are certainly going to mobilize. It's the only way you can do it. You can't fight the major regional conflicts we have on the books without mobilization.

If you look at our Contingency Force package, we talk about being able to move five and a third divisions anywhere in the world in thirty days and being able to fight. You need the mobilization to move and sustain those particular units. So I think you can make the point for the major regional conflicts, and I think you can even make it in the military to support civilian authorities case that you need to mobilize. I think it's been demonstrated. We did it in (Hurricane) Andrew. We did it in Task Force LA.

It's a situation-dependent exercise. You go through and you do what you have to do with the Total Army. We probably will not have to mobilize based upon what I seen in the Mississippi River Valley. That's being handled very, very well by the National Guard, and I think they are doing a great job. They are providing some regional support and that type of thing. As I talk to the TAGs who are involved there, that's working out very, very well. I don't think, unless something happens differently than what we expect, that we will necessarily require a mobilization decision. I think it will be handled on state active duty.

FSG: The Fiscal 1993 Defense Authorization Act includes Title XI, Army National Guard Combat Reform Initiatives. Congressional intent was to ensure that Army National Guard units were combat-ready and available for use at all levels of the contingency, just as General Abrams intended. We will start with you, General Reimer. What are your views on Title XI, and other initiatives being taken by the Army itself to ensure the establishment of, and acceptance of, readiness and by that I mean acceptance by the Army establishments and acceptance by the Army of the readiness and accessibility of Army Guard units? The ability of the Army to get at them when they need them.

DJR: Let me go back and try and tie that together with what was said this morning. I though this morning's panel did a great job, and it was a very educational thing for me to hear; I learned a lot. But just from my experience, based upon the short time that I had the opportunity, and the good fortune, to work for General Abrams, there were a couple of impressions that I have of that particular time.

I think, first of all, the overriding theme of General Abrams' tenure as Chief of Staff of the Army was the terrible price we pay for unpreparedness. If you go back and look at his speeches, look at his testimony in Congress, and particularly his first AUSA speech, that's what he hit and he hit it so very, very, hard.

I can just close my eyes and see him saying, "Nobody wants war, especially those who have seen it. The pain and the human suffering are beyond telling." And he would pound the podium, and the powerful message was such that nobody could miss the point. I mean, you just couldn't possibly sit through and not understand what he was saying. And I think he made that point time and time again.

I would tell you that based upon the time that I worked with him from the time he was Chief of Staff until his death, I thought he was focused on turning the Army. He used to always talk about changing the direction of a large organization. He said, "To do that, to change it even one degree, is a tremendous, challenge."

What he was faced with was bringing the Army back from a rather bad experience in Vietnam and getting it focused on the main act in Europe. I think about the second or third trip after going to Vietnam, we went to Europe, and I can tell you that I think he was very, very concerned about what he saw. He knew he had a lot to do in that particular area. And he was very concerned about being able to deter the Russians threat, being able to build up the force, particularly the tooth-to-tail ratio which was important to him. It's already been talked about.

I think General Temple brought up the fact that he was going from 13 to 16 divisions, and keeping the end-strength of the Army constant at 780,000. I think he knew that he wouldn't have deploy, or couldn't deploy the Army all at one time, that some of them would have more training available to them.

He was one of the first to recognize that there were skills that were transferable from civilian life to military units, and that those particular units would be easier and faster to deploy.

He emphasized the strategy of containment and the deterence that has now been called the Abrams Doctrine, and I think it's a good name. I think the strategy of containment was very successful. Obviously, we won the Cold War and I think he deserves a lot of credit for that. That's the first thing I would say.

I would also say that the world has changed, and I think everybody here recognized that. That change I often talk about is that the Wall came down in November of '89.

I had the guys at Forces Command do a little bit of work on that other day, and I asked them to take a look at June of 1989 and compare it with a day in June of 1993. And what you find when you do that is that we are moving at an optempo that is about twice as fast in '93 as it was in '89. In other words, if I go back and look at the number of soldiers deployed out of Forces Command to various places in '89, it was about 4,500 on a given day in June. That same day in June of '93 we have over 9,000 deployed. They are deployed in Somalia. They are deployed in Saudia Arabai. They are deployed in South America. It's a Total Army perspective now. So the optempo is much faster. And at the same time, we are having to downsize and reshape the Army. A terrific challenge.

The other thing that makes it more difficult is that when General Abrams was going through this in the '72 to '74 time frame, there was a single threat. It was the Russian threat. We refocused on that.

Now, it is more difficult. What is the threat? We've never been good at predicting the threat. We've talked about CAPSTONE. A very, very good program and a very popular one. One that I believe very deeply in, and I'm trying to get reinstituted throughout Forces Command. But it's difficult because you don't have a single war plan driving the training right now. You have people who focused on one area, now you have those same people focusing on several different areas of the world. I mean, you've got people who look at different areas and it does not line up neat and tidy. We'll sort that one out. That one's solvable.

Those are some of the changes that have occurred. Now, let me talk about the specifics of your question because I think it's important.

You know, we've talked about mobilization and the fact that it can go on at any end of the spectrum, and I think we've got to be able to handle all ends of that spectrum with the Total Army. And, as I said, whether you mobilize or not is dependent upon the specific situation you face. I think as we continue to get smaller, we have to become more integrated, and it's going to require more mobilization decisions. We must learn how to do that.

If we are going to have a Total Army, we are going to have to have one that is capable, available, and affordable. Those are the three major challenges that we are working on.

In general terms Title XI moves in the right direction. It was primarily designed, to improve the readiness of the Army National Guard combat units but we've expanded that somewhat and we are now talking about the readiness of the Total Army. There are an awful lot of initiatives in this particular area that should help us with the readiness.

We've got the BOLD SHIFT initiative, that was started by Ed Burba before I can to Forces Command. That is doing very, very well. As I go around and check the training, I see a lot of good things happening. And I think that's a step in the right direction.

We've started what we call a Total Army Training Study that is being developed, it has not been approved, but I think it clearly gets at the Total Army readiness, issues such as the Tri-Component Division, and some things that we've talked about here today. We still need to flesh that out a little bit. There's a lot of people involved in that, and we haven't got total consensus yet but I think we are moving forward more of a Total Army that is ready to do whatever the nation wants us to do and we are moving to greater integration.

We are building a force that will meet the national military strategy. There's some exciting things going on right now in that particular area.

So I guess, from my standpoint, there's some goodness in Title XI.

FSG: General Reimer, let me include you in this, as well as General Trefry. Let me ask you a couple of specific questions about Title XI. First of all, Title XI requires the Army, or the Army Guard, to have a personnel mix by 1997, I believe, in which 65 percent of all the officers in the National Guard will have had two years Active Duty and 50 percent of all enlisted personnel in the Guard must have two had two years Active Duty. And the end date of that is September 30, 1997.

Now, I happen to believe that's a very desirable thing. But I've got some real questions about can that be achieved? And, if so, how, what are we going to do to achieve it? General Reimer.

DJR: As you suggest, it is a tough thing to achieve. And it depends upon the size of your forces. RAND has studied that, and basically concluded that, given the sizes we're looking at right now, you probably can't achieve that just through the normal course of events. In other words, if you go back historically and look at the number of people that have gone from the Active to the Reserve Components, you probably won't meet the 50 and 65 percent goals that have been established with the projected and strengths. You are probably going to have to do some special things.

I don't know what the size of the Army, the Total Army, is going to be, based upon the Bottom-Up Review, but I certainly share you concern about that goal being hard to achieve.

On the other hand, I think it's a very desirable goal. We need to give it a good shot to see if we can make it. I don't think we've looked at the innovations that we need to look at yet. At least, I'm not aware that we have. We probably need to do, more in this particular area, but it will still be tough to achieve.

FSG: Would you think that's a desirable enough goal that perhaps there'd be a payoff in providing either incentives to Active Army personnel to early-out into Army Guard combat units? Or incentives for Guard personnel to volunteer for the additional time on Active Duty?

DJR: I think it's a desirable goal, and I hesitate to say yes or no to that specific question until I know what the ramifications of the rest of that really are. I don't know how much turbulence that creates throughout the Total Army when you say something like that. I think turbulence has to be factored in.

My assumption is that those types of things are being looked at in the Bottom-Up Review going on here in Washington right now. I'm not a part of that, in Forces Command, so I cannot comment directly on it. But I think incentives to reach those objectives, the 50 and 65 percent, are important. We ought to look at initiatives that will help us achieve those goals without degrading readiness.

FSG: General Trefry, I'm going to ask you the next question because I know that you had experience with this problem sometime in the past. Let me go back to, I guess, General Rosemblum's statement, or remarks.

Before STEADFAST we had thousands of advisors in the Army Guard. They existed in every level down to battalion, and not just one, but there'd be several at many levels. They had both officer and enlisted advisors. Thousands of them.

One of the ways STEADFAST saved spaces to create new divisions was to eliminate most of those advisors and then, using the organization that General Rosenblum talked about, they provided the support services, the hands-on work with Guard units. The intent was to replace and do better what advisors had done.

Now, we are kind of going full circle. The Army Readiness Regions are gone, and the House Armed Services Committee in the Army-Guard Combat Reforms initiative has mandated 5,000 advisors to the Army National Guard. Now, it's always been a problem, it's been a quality problem. In a particular discussion with me, General Abrams promised that the advisors that did come to the Guard and the personnel that were assigned those Readiness Regions would be the cream of the Army.

I had pointed out to him that what we were getting were people, not bad officers, but they were officers at the end of their career, wanting to retire in place, we got no water walkers at all. And he promised that the Army would send their top talent. And for a while that occurred.

Now, I don't know if that occurs now or not. But given all of that, and your experience with the problems, what do you think, General Trefry, of the Army's ability to follow this mandate, and with quality personnel?

RGT: I think they are going to have a hell of a tough time. And I can't make it any plainer than that. You know, it's very hard to get where we are trying to go with what we've got now. And what am I talking about? When you take a look at the number of schools that an officer has to go to, he goes to the Basic Course, he goes to the Career Course, he goes to CAS[3], he goes to Leavenworth, and today everybody had to get a master's degree somewhere along the line. If the Army doesn't send them to school in association with some assignment that requires it, it then has to put him somewhere where they can get one on their own.

When you start mandating, you have to do this, or you have to do that, that's when, whether correct or not, you get into this ticket-punching syndrome. And that's bad.

The average Regular Army Officer spends about 23 years on Active Duty, and then he retires, and part of that is that a fellow gets to be a lieutenant colonel or colonel, 18, 19 years service, he doesn't get selected for a brigade command, or he doesn't get selected for brigadier general. He says, "Oh, what the hell, there's nothing here."

And it's a young man's game. Fighting is a young man's game. No question about it. And it's very more physical today than it ever was. And so you have a tendency for people to get out.

Now, how do you squeeze all that in twenty years? And now you say, if you look at Goldwater-Nichols, it says you've got to have certain Joint time if you want to be a general. You see, we could never have another George Marshall because Goldwater-Nichols says that the guy who's going to be Chairman must have been a commander of a unified, Specified Command, or a service chief. Well, by my count that's thirteen guys. And George Marshall came up 50 or 60 in from the pile.

So you limit choices, and when you start putting all these things on that and say. "This is what you have to do," then it gets very tough.

Now, it's extremely desirable that you get people who have experience, if they are Guard soldiers, that they have experience with the Active Army, and vice versa. But how do you do that, when you think of all the other things that you have to do? It gets very, very tough.

You can have a roomful of geniuses and put them on a bell curve and 50 percent will be above the line and 50 percent will be below. We bell curve everything, as you well know. And we grade on the curve. So no matter how you look at it, you are going to get some above and some below. I think we are going to have a very tough time, and I think it's going to take a lot of patience and understanding.

And the other part is, I don't think people who write these things really understand what they do. People want to do right by their people, and some people may not have the strength of character that other people do, and it opens the window to cheating. It opens the window to enervating reports, vitiating reports, because it's tough to tell a guy he hasn't been too impressive. And if you say, "Well, you've got to do this, or you've got to do that," then pretty soon you get people griping.

Now, all those kinds of things, unintentionally, attack the very core of what we stand for. As an institution. I'm not talking the Total Army. So I think we are going to have a tough time with that.

FSG: General Reimer, General Trefry, it seems to me has talked mostly about the quality issue, but numbers, it seems to me, is a very serious problem. How does the Army, with a declining force structure and a declining end strength, produces 5,000 advisors for the Army Guard?

DJR: Let me pick up on a couple of things General Trefry said, which I think he said very, very well. But I think the point that he made there is that it is going to be a tough challenge to meet the quality gates for most people in order to meet the criteria for basically promotion and selection for school.

And I think the point he made towards the end was very compelling, at least in my mind. And that is, when you look at that requirement individually, it's probably a pretty good requirement, but when you look at the totality of the other things we are doing, Goldwater-Nichols and that important things, it may be an almost impossible task, given the quality guidelines that we generally use. I mean, we are getting to the point that we are really getting boxed in in terms of being able to assign our officers and NCOs to the right jobs.

The other thing I would say is that the quality of the people out there in the field is good. I've talked to a number of them, and I have not found anyone who does not have the credentials to be an advisor or to participate in the job that he or she is doing. I haven't found a National Guard or USAR Officer whose not satisfied with their advisor or the full-time support which they are receiving from the Active Component.

We've got an awful lot of quality in the Total Army right now. The bench is very, very deep. Now, the issue is, how many of these people will be selected for promotion, and how many of them will be selected for school? And that's what we've got to watch very carefully.

We are committed to try and make that happen. I've talked the General Putnam, who heads up the Officer Personnel Directorate, and we've discussed this in great length, and we are trying to assign the right people. Just based upon the limited amount of checking that I've done, I'm convinced that we are.

I've seen battalion commanders from Europe that have been assigned there. I've seen some red hot captains that have been assigned there. We continue to work the Jump Start Program and I think we can expand that.

In the Jump Start Program you take a graduate out of Leavenworth and send him for two years to the 4th Division, for example, and then you send him two years to be an advisor or to work in what we call the Regional Training Detachment with the 116th Brigade, which is a Roundout brigade for the Fourth Division.

So, those are the types of things we are trying to do. I think we can do more of it. Most of the divisions, based upon what I've seen so far, are getting somewhere around 20 or 30 Leavenworth graduates that are coming to them this year. We'll take those people and put them in key jobs in the division like XO or an S3 and then assign them to the Regional Training Detachment.

We can do things like that and move them back and forth. That's going to cost some money because there are PCS moves. But if we are serious about this, those are the types of things we've got to do.

In numbers, we need some help. If we are held to the DOPMA criteria here, you are talking about 5,000 advisors or full-time assistors, as I call them. That's about a division's worth of leadership. And to the extent that we are not able to get the DOPMA relief, you are going to hollow out the Force in terms of leadership that's not going to be available in the divisions, or that's not going to be going through the requisite Officer Professional Development or the NCO Professional Development which is very important to our future.

We are going to take that one on, and were are going to need some help in terms of being able to convince Congress that they need to make change.

That's a winnable argument. They are the ones who have told us to do that, and they ought to be able to give us relief, if that's what they really want. Otherwise, we are talking about hollowing out in terms of readiness. And I don't think that's what they meant for us to do.

RGT: I don't think people really realized the impact of DOPMA and ROPMA and Goldwater-Nichols and some of these things that put these things on. And, believe me. I wasn't referring to just quality. I was referring to numbers, because as the end-strength goes down and the grade levels are reached, you don't have the people to play with.

Now, there's one other point that goes back to what we were talking about this morning, and that I think vitally affects this.

Up until about ten years ago, we had the experience from World War II and Korea and Vietnam in mobilizing and building armies. Most of that has now retired. The emphasis in the last ten years has been on unit training and so forth. And when we went into the accreditation problem in the schools, we went to electives and that type thing where we taught people how to mobilize and do that kind of stuff, and that's not there any more.

We don't have enough time now to teach people how to fight as much as we'd like, but we don't really teach in the school system how you raise, provision, sustain, maintain, train and resource the Army. And that is the meat of what we are doing here. That's why we have a problem in force management.

I can remember I came down to visit Jack Galvin one day and I said, I'm down here because the Chief tells me you've got a computer game on mobilization. I'd just written a scathing IG finding because there was no mobilization computer game in the Army. And Shy said, "Go down and see Jack Galvin. He's got one." I went down and I said, "Look, show me this mobilization game you've got. He says, "Hell, I don't have any game." And he didn't. And I think you've got one started now, but that's the first one. And this was, what, fourteen years ago, when I was writing those kinds of findings. So we need to look at this kind of thing.

FSG: Ladies and Gentlemen, General Galvin has arrived, as I'm sure you've all noticed. General Galvin, welcome. WE have introduced you briefly before. Your full bio is in the folder. And I did mention that you are the former Supreme Allied Commander, Europe; you are now the John M. Olin Distinguished Professor of National Security Studies at the U.S. Military Academy, West Point; and that you commanded the 24th Division, Mechanized Infantry Division when they were rounded-out by the 48th Infantry Brigade.

This morning we had a distinguished panel that discussed the Abrams Doctrine on the basis of then and now. They summarized that by saying that the Doctrine is valid, is a valid notion today, although Bob Sorley mentioned well that General Adams himself would have laughed at such a high-flung title. He made the point that it led to the creation of the right forces to be available to fight the Gulf War, that it's implementation challenged bias and tradition in the Active Army, and in the Guard. It challenged Guard soldiers to do more and better and harder trainign than they ever had before.

But even a successful doctrine must be subject to reevaluation, and that's really what we are doing today. He makes the point that we are, they made the point that we are at a watershed moment in history, that during the past half century we've followed doctrinal patterns which have served us well. That the doctrine of the past fifty years, including the Abrams Doctrine, possesses strength, but also demonstrates weaknesses.

And this afternoon we are doing really quite a lot of discussion about how do we address those weaknesses.

The participants here in the audience may wonder if I haven't gotten a little off the Abrams Doctrine, since I've been concentrating on Title XI. But when we talk about the Abrams Doctrine, General Abrams stood for a whole bunch of things.

And my impression was that he stood for training and readiness above all. And the facts of the matter are the Abrams Doctrine can't work unless the Army National Guard combat units can in fact attain and maintain the standards required by the Army, and that they can be as accessible to the Army as is possible.

So we've discussed a number of aspects of that question this afternoon, General Galvin. And at the moment we are talking some about the Title XI, but before I do that, you have long experience and you know the subject matter. Would you like to just make any sort of an opening statement?

I want to also say that this distinguished gentleman has made the maximum effort to be here. To start with, he's on leave at Fort Story. Now, when you compare Washington, D.C. and Fort Story, nobody makes that trip from there to here just for the fun of the drive. And they've been told about your difficulty en route. That you have come at all is a very real plus to us, and a very real tribute to the National Guard. We are delighted you are here.

Would you like to say a few words before we pick up the discussion?

GEN John R. Galvin (Ret.), Former Supreme Allied Commander Europe:

Thanks, I really don't want to try to jump into what's been going on without, you know, knowing a lot more about it than that. I would simply say that I do think we need to apply every effort to Guard readiness in order to still keep the Total Army concept, which is really, basically, very much what Abrams was talking about. Guard participation in whatever contingency that comes up is going to be important. I want to get in a little bit later as we go along on the how, but I think I'd rather not try to come in the way I have here and start off with a statement. I'll just go along here now, if I can.

FSG: Thank you, very much, Sir. About twenty years ago, in the Army Staff I propose a system of training our division and brigade staffs using simulators. I did that because, in my view, in my experience, Army leadership has always had a very real reluctance to accept the ability of National Guard division, and to a lesser extent brigade, commanders and staff to do their thing in combat. I don't have to tell you that a lot of Guardsmen here might wonder about my saying it, but I shared that view. And one of the reasons is that over the years, about the best we ever did for a Guard division commander and staff is, first of all, they had to be a Leavenworth graduate, —which might have been done by extension course-and then we had an annual refresher course at Leavenworth. I must have done that a half a dozen times myself.

But in my view, nowhere in the system did we have a way of providing National Guard division commanders and their staff the kind of training and experience, and I want to underline experience, in maneuvering battalions, management of fire power, and logistical and administrative support of units. You know, at that point in time all you could do is have a maneuver and we neither had space nor time nor money for maneuvers. And yet we required divisions in the structure.

And in my point of view, to make the Army comfortable with mobilizing them, we need to do something about the training. Well, with that in mind, I note that Title XI has some language in it that requires-I don't know if it's just exploration or development, but it talks about - the use of simulators in the conduct of training. I don't know if they are just talking about firing simulators to train commanders and staff in the maneuver, fire power, logistical and administrative support. I know you are all qualified to discuss the subject. General Reimer, would you like to start with that?

DJR: Yes, Let me take that one on, because I think it is one of the areas where real improvement has to take place.

I mentioned earlier the outstanding battalion I saw in Salt Lake City, the Apache battalion. The closest simulators that have are located at Fort Campbell and Fort hood. So it makes it a very, very tough situation to train that battalion if you have to go there to use the simulators. We will square that away. I've got the J3 at Forces Command laying out for me the current simulation, or simulator distribution, and then what's planned in the future. But, again, Apache simulators are not just small change, and it's something that's going to take a little bit of time to fix, but I think we are going to be able to fix that one.

If you go to Fort Knox, Kentucky, right now, and I'll start at a lower level, and then bring you up to the division level; you can bring a battalion's worth of tank crews, for example, and go through the SIMNET training. You can fly in on the weekend and conduct simulation training.

If you really want to be innovative, and any unit in the Total Army can do this, you can hook up with simulators at Fort Rucker, and start to work your air-ground team through simulation. You could do that for 48 hours, or whatever time you want to spend. So there are some exciting things that are on the horizon, and they will only grow.

In terms of training at the brigade level, part of the innovation that we have with the Total Army training study is something called the Battle Command Battalion Staff Training Program, where units go through staff training. For example, I was with a brigade of the 29th Division at Fort Dix, and they were doing a CPX that was driven by the 78th Division. The brigade commander indicated they were getting a lot out of it. It's a simulation exercise, just like we put our Active Component brigade commanders through.

The Battle Command Training Program has been a part of the Combat Training Center Experience in the Active Component for the last three of four years, and we require every Active Component division commander, and every corps commander and his staff to go through it, and it has now been expanded to the Reserve Component. I'm going out to see the 35th go through the training in August.

So, I think those programs are in place and they are moving. We understand the need to do that. It's going to take us a little time and a little money to do it, but I think it's terribly important. So, I would agree with you that we have not done well in the past, but I think we are moving in the right direction right now, and I think there's a lot of momentum.

The Battle Command Training Program that General Galvin and his people did such great work on over there in the Warrior Prep Center brought the Army into a new era in terms of simulation training. We are building on that right now, and trying to expand as fast as we can.

JRG: I would add to that by saying, we have seen this experience where the Active Army over the past several years, because of such things as the computer-assisted exercises and so forth, the simulations, and a lot of other things, too, the National Training Center and on and on, has taken a quantum jump in its own capabilities, its readiness capabilities, its ability to work with the other Services. The Gulf War is a good example.

There is a felling, I think, sometimes, that the Active Army is so far ahead of where the Guard is that, that there just is no way for the Guard to catch up. But the Active Army, in terms of that quantum jump, didn't increase the number of days it had at its disposal, which I think, some people put it at like 270 a year, or whatever that is. So that happens to be the same situation of the Guard. The Guard hasn't increased its number of days, either.

But, following along with what Denny Reimer just said, I think the challenge there is to see how far, with the kind of help that the Active Army is looking at providing, and with the legislation that we've seen here, what is the size of the jump in capability that the combat, as well as combat support and combat service support, units of the Guard can make? I don't think we know that. And I think it's something that we, that obviously the Congress is telling us to dedicate ourselves to looking at, and to supporting. And so I think it's probably premature to say that the vast majority of the Guard would be combat service support and combat support, especially for an early contingency, that is, a short-fuse contingency.

I think that what we really need to do is to look at that and see what level can the Guard reach, that is, unit organizational level? And, as I said before, I'm a little hesitant because maybe a lot of people talked about this already.

But I would see that as a parameter that will move over the next period of time, the short-range future. So I think it's very clear and the Army, the Active Army has been very clear, I think, on where we stand in terms of the capabilities that the CS and CSS can reach. Let's leave a little bit open here as to what the combat capabilities are until we see, given every way that we can improve that very few number of the activities, within the very few number of days the Guard has, let's see what it can do.

I think that it may be true that the Guard cannot field in a very short period of time a division. Maybe it can't field a brigade in a short period of time. But I think that it would be premature to pin down some particular point right now. I think that's the big question. That's the thing that nobody can answer except, give the Guard the opportunity to answer.

FSG: Let me pin you a little bit, Sir. Let's assume that Guard battalions, combat battalions, in fact can meet the Army's training requirement, meet their standard, pass the test. And now we've got all the maneuver elements and support elements that we need to fight. So then the requirement is, can the brigade commander and his staff use them to support the division?

In your experience, do you think that the use of sophisticated computer system could teach that to a Guard brigade and division since they don't have the opportunity to maneuver?

JRG: When I commanded the 24th and the Gray Bonnets were rounding-out the 24th at that time, I didn't know how it would turn out, what the 48th could do. I was very proud of the 48th, and we had a very close association with Joe Griffin and the others.

What I always felt was that, if we went, it would depend on how the 48th was at that moment. If we were going to go and if we were going to take the 48th, then there were all kinds of combinations and permutations that could be involved. For one thing, I looked at the tasks. If you can't train more than about 39 days a year with the 48th, then if you are not going to have much time—and that's a question, how much time are you going to have? We saw that in the Gulf War.

Then one of the things that we can do is limit the tasks under the conditions and standards that the units within the brigade are going to train to. Instead of trying to make sure that they could do everything, make sure they can do some things well, really well.

The next thing is that tailoring is part of the concept of combat in a division, anyway, and within brigades. And so we could have tailored across the division. If we felt the 48th wasn't as trained as we'd like to have it be, wasn't as trained as the level of the other brigades within the division, if the battalions weren't trained up to that, we could nevertheless cross-level, so the 48th would end up with other battalions from the division, and the division would have some battalions from the 48th.

How that would be tailored would depend, again, on the mission that the 48th was going to get. Maybe it would get limited missions for the first operations of the division in the field, in combat. Maybe it would be able, with the tailoring, to take on all the missions that the brigades were taking.

The point I'm making is that there is some flexibility in there, in terms of the use of the brigade. That flexibility, such as the tailoring and so forth, such as the tasking, such as the missions and the tasks within training, none of that violates anything that we would normally think of as the routine operations of a division. So, I would have to see. I think it's very hard to say what could the 48th have done at a given time in the past, just as it's going to be hard to say what can it do in the future.

But we now can pin that down pretty well. And we know we are going to be giving Guard units a lot more assistance, in a lot of different ways, in order to see what kind of a quantum jump they can actually make. It would be something, I'm sure, that in some ways parallels what the Army, the Active Army has been able to do.

FSG: Dick, you've got a lot of technological knowledge about computers and the level of performance they can accomplish. What's your view of this subject?

RGT: Well, I think, in the first place, that we, if you compare it to, let's go back to between 1975 and 1993, and if you compare that to going to kindergarten and graduating from high school, we are just graduating from kindergarten, from the standpoint of the understanding of what computers can do.

You know, you stop and think, in 1978, at the end of the Christmas season, the computer industry had sold its 38,000th PC. Ten years later, in 1988, they had sold their 39,000,000th PC. And the curve has continued to go up, although I read this morning Apple is in trouble.

Just before I left the White House, a guy came around with a thing about the size of a shoe box and he said by 1999 this will outdo a Cray. When you stop to think about that, you think of the potential of employing these things. I don't think we have even imagined it. We have SIMNET.

A little company I'm associated with has got contracts to run four of these centers but they are largely for the Reserve. I think the Guard could really get into this more than they are because I think the potential is there.

You see, my own experience is, I could take you to, when I was the IG, 105mm and 155mm Field Artillery battalions in the Guard that were just as good as anything on Active Duty. I could take you to aviation outfits that were just about as good as anything on Active Duty. The problem we had is when you try to put all this stuff together to maneuver, and it has nothing to do with anybody's intelligence, it has nothing to do with anybody's motivation or their patriotism, or anything else. What it has to do is what I call dexterity.

Understanding how you can change the frequencies on a radio. Understanding how you can get these people to do what you want them to do, just mechanically. That's where the problem is.

And if you can teach that to a guy on a simulator so that when you do put him in the field it doesn't take him three weeks in the field, it takes him three days, that's where you are going to make the gain. At least that's what I think, and maybe Denny and Jack could comment, if I'm wrong, but I think that's where it is.

DJR: I would agree with that.

FSG: Let me shift to another point. Title XI requires compatibility between Army Guard units and Active units. Now, given the disparity in the levels of field equipment, the numbers of equipment we have, and the disparity in the modernity, certainly in non-Roundout/Roundup units of the Guard, of their equipment with the Active, can those compatibility objectives be achieved? General Reimer.

DJR: Well, I think I touched on that a little bit earlier when I said that we've got about 500,000 short tons of Class VII to return from overseas. That will be a gigantic step forward in terms of modernizing the Total Force. We will take that equipment and we'll fill the holes that exist out there. We are not going to be able to make the whole Army modern all at once. We just don't have that amount of equipment, unless the Army gets terribly, terribly small, and I don't think anybody wants to see that.

FSG: Nor money to buy it.

DJR: More money to buy it, that would also be helpful. But I think we also have to be realistic. It's going to take us some time to do that.

We will fill based upon the "first to fight," and the Contingency Force will be filled before anybody else. Those members of the Reserve Component community that are part of the Contingency Force will get filled before those members of the Active Component that are not members of the Contingency Force.

We have always had a disparity of equipment in the Army. When I commanded the 4th Division, we were an M-60, M113 unit; then we went to M-1s and we still had M113s. So we've dealt with that throughout the Army basically because you cannot modernize a force as quickly as you would like. It takes time to do that. But I think that we are going to take a big step forward with the movement of equipment back from Europe.

I think we are doing some things to ensure that units are properly trained on equipment that they have to support in wartime. I think the CAPSTONE alignment will test us in terms of ensuring that we are compatible there. If we get the CAPSTONE program back to that we train with those units that we are going to fight with. I think that will help us in terms of ensuring that the force is compatible across the board.

Those are the things that have to be put in place and that we are doing right now. But, again, it's something that's just not going to occur overnight. Those are the initiatives that are in place. They are working. Once we get everything back from Europe, get settled and get an end-state that makes sense, I think we are going to probably be okay.

FSG: I probably owe an apology to the audience. This is such an interesting, knowledgeable panel to talk with, I really haven't given you in the audience a chance to ask some question and enter the discussion. So let's do that now. Are there some questions from the audience.

Q: I'd like to refer to a question, or a statement, General Trefry made relative to the possibility of cheating, the anxiety. I'd like somebody to address the subject.

You've been talking about technology. You've been talking about equipment. You've been talking about numbers. But you have the human element. What you have built-in right now, with the downsizing, the political implications are showing no humanitarian interests. What support do you have for that man or woman who has made a commitment to a career? He now has these problems, "Am I going to be surveyed out? Am I going to be promoted?" What implications does that have toward your readiness.

RGT: I think you have a heck of a problem. And I think it's there. And I think it's a tribute to the leadership that we have, all the way from sergeant level to the Chief of Staff of the Army, that they've been able to cope with it as well as they have.

We've got rid of damn near 200,000 people in the last two years, or since March of '91, not counting all the Guard and Reserve who went back to civilian life.

Q: Plus no jobs on the outside.

RGT: Right. And we don't know where it's going to stop right now. That puts a tremendous strain on people. It is a tremendous tribute to these young men that they are coping with it, and their families, that they are coping with it as best they are. I think that we've been remarkably free of the kind of thing that you are worried about, that we are all worried about, compared to what it might have been and was back in '73, and what it was in '54, when we went through these RIFs, we had all kinds of problems. I think we've been able to keep away from that to a great extent.

It's going to take a tremendous amount of leadership to keep upon that keel, and I think we are very fortunate that we are in as good shape as we are in today. We have to recognize it. And that's perhaps the most important thing, to be able to recognize it.

FSG: General Reimer, I suspect you are trying to cope with the humanitarian problem all the time.

Would you have a comment, then?

DJR: Yes, sir, I do. I think it probably is the most difficult thing that I've wrestled with in the past three or four years. It's not easy to take down an Army. It's not easy to reshape it, particularly when you are talking about an Army that's a volunteer Army, people want to be a part of it, this is a successful organization.

I have a brother that's an oilman in Indonesia, and I tell him, "Charles, what we are going through is like if you established certain goals for your company and you achieved those goals, and they are the highest goals that you have ever achieved, and then they said, 'Okay, because you are so successful we are going to cut you a third.' That's the type of challenge that we are facing right now." And it is terribly, terribly difficult.

I think we are doing some good things. We are not sitting on our hands. We are not fighting getting smaller. Basically, the country has made a decision and we are in the process of executing it.

The first thing that I would say is that we are a value-based organization, and we stress values, very, very much. It's terribly important to us. Go back and look at a document called FM 100-1. It's a very thin document, but it talks about the Army, and it talks about the values the Army has, the integrity, how we've always been under civilian control. I was fortunate enough to be able to speak to the graduating class from West Point at the graduation banquet this year. I asked them to go back and reread FM 100-1 before they go to their first assignment and to reread it on a regular basis, because I think it's terribly important, particularly during these times right now.

We've got to keep the integrity. We've got to keep the values that have been so much a part of our history. And we've got 218 years of distinguished history to guide us.

We went down to an army the size of 80 people, in 1784. We survived hardship, and we'll come back from this. I think we'll make it.

Now, what are we doing specifically because, as you mentioned, these are good people that we are letting go? It's terribly, terribly emotional when you deal with the people and you deal with the families involved. But I'll tell you we have fought hard for transition programs.

We've got SSI and SSB for soldiers and VSEP and VERA for civilians. These are programs to help people transition. We've got the Army Civilian Alumni Program, and I don't know whether you've ever been to one of our centers, but if you haven't, I invite you to go to any one. It is for the Total Army, somebody that's getting out and entering into civilian life.

We will go through and we ask them, "What are you interested in doing? Where do you want to work? Here's some of the things you need to know about writing resumes." For example, there's a truck company called Schneider Truck Company, in Green Bay, Wisconsin. I was at a National Guard Enlisted Association meeting one time and sat next to Schneider. Schneider said, "Look, I'll take any of the people that you've got that I have vacancies for, because you have a great product. You have a drug-free product, a disciplined product, they are ones you can count on."

We now have that in our computer based and when people say, "Hey, I'm interested in going to Wisconsin, I used to be a truck driver," Bill Schneider's name will pop up and it'll be a part of the information that we hand that particular soldier.

We have worked very, very hard to try and take care of our people. It is important to the people that are staying in the Army, and to those people that are leaving, and it's not easy. It is terribly, terribly difficult when you deal with human emotions. But, when you compare that with any of the reshaping efforts that we've done in our previous history, I think we are doing this one much, much better. But it doesn't take any of the pain away.

JRG: Well, Dick Trefry mentioned 1954. That was the year I was commissioned a second lieutenant. And it was also a year in which the Army was being very rapidly drawn down, because nuclear weapons were going to take the place of the ground forces, and that was going to solve the problem.

One of the things that I tell officers and NCOs is, especially young officers and NCOs, young soldiers for that matter, "When you look at your career in the Army, don't judge it by current events all the way. The Army changes over time, because the situation in the world, and America's reaction to that situation changes. And so there will be times when the Army is drawing down, and times when the Army is building up. And leadership is important to us, both drawing down and building up."

We need to be aware of all the help that we can give, that Denny mentioned, and many other things that I know he could mention about people who are getting out of the Army.

We also need to spend time with people who are staying in the

Army, to tell them what their future is going to look like in the Army. And it is going to go through a series of changes. And so we need people whose thinking is flexible, people who are able to react to vastly different situations, because one of our goals as we draw the Army down, is to keep the best people, the best people possible. And, as far as I can see it now, we are doing that. We still are challenging the good people, the people who realize that if you are good, the Army would have to get awful small before we'd let you go.

So, there are just so many aspects of this. Thank God, again, for the computer, because to try to draw down the way we've done with stubby pencil would have been awful. At least we have a lot more support for the kind of personnel actions we have to take than we've ever had before.

Q: There was a discussion this morning and General Temple made the point that there was a great chasm of understanding between the Active Components and the Guard and Reserve, and very little of a bridge across it.

I know that all of you have had experience in building that bridge, and in examining ways to make the three components of the Army all understand one another better. I think that's imperative and it's the root of our successful future. It's how we spread the understanding across the components.

I wonder if our panelists have some ideas that they might express about how we do that.

JRG: There are a lot of a decisions that have to be made at every level of the Reserve Components and the Active Components. One of the most important things is that when those decisions are being made, that everybody is involved.

I like very much what I see in terms of the working groups, the committees that have representation from the Reserve Components, the Reserve and the Guard and the Active, at the right levels. I think that one thing, to be sure, is that we do that to the nth degree so that we are able to keep the confidence of people that nothing is going on behind closed doors, that nothing is under the table. Everything is on the table as we go down the line. In fact, that's the only way to do it. The more that we can keep checking to make sure that everybody is in on every decision, I think the better off we are.

DJR: No. I'd just echo that, because I think that is terribly important, and as Bob knows, there are a number of different groups discussing these issues right now. They are not easy issues. There's no easy solution. If there was an easy solution, we'd have already arrived at it and gotten on with it. And so, they are painful, just like the emotions associated with downsizing the Army.

But, at the same time, it is very helpful that we are all meeting together, people are rolling up their sleeves, throwing the issues on the table, and we're discussing them in an open forum.

I'm trying very hard, as the FORSCOM Commander, to meet with as many of the leaders of the Total Army as I possibly can. I've had a couple of sessions with TAGs already, and have been to the ROA meeting in Nashville a couple of weekends ago. I will continue to go through the list of TAGs. I'm trying to get around to see as much as I possibly can.

Q: ... the hurdles here on the agenda, according to General Abrams and General Vessey, and then the press who was there, it seems as though a very essential—is that right?—a very essential point here is that by the Abrams Doctrine, at least it helps circumvent the Congress's Constitutional requirement to declare war, which, of course, many Presidents have participated in.

I'm a Vietnam Era veteran of the Marine Corps. And I noticed that on the news release it indicated that you all felt, or that somebody felt, that the mobilization of the Guard and Reserve in large numbers during Desert Storm throughout the country affected communities and forced the Congressional vote on whether to commit forces to Southwest Asia.

Is that a one-time shot, now that General Galvin is here? Do you think that was a one-time thing? Or do you think that this concept will be effective for the foreseeable future to force the Congress to at least partially do its duty to follow the Constitution on the declaration of war issue?

JRG: Well, of course, that's not an issue in which there is undivided approach right now. I mean, the powers of the President versus the powers of the Congress is something that could be discussed for a long time. And I know Bob Sorley was here this morning and he talked about his—were you here this morning, by the way?

Q: I wasn't.

JRG: I wasn't either. There was some discussion about Bob's chapter in his book on Abrams, in which the question that you've brought up comes up in there, and I think it's Schlesinger who comments in that chapter that these are decisions that political leaders will make, and I tend to agree with that. We in the military can configure ourselves so that we can most effectively carry out missions that we are given by our leadership. But we don't create those missions. That's a political decision.

Now, as to where that decision takes place I think we, all Americans, have not been able to be too clear about what is the President's prerogative and what is the Congress's prerogative when it comes to conflict.

And so I tend to feel that it was right and correct for Abrams—and he wasn't the only one, by any means, but we've used Abrams as the point man on this. There were lots of people, though, involved in how the Army, and the Armed Forces indeed, would be configured in order to carry out whatever mission that they are given.

It seems to me that we are correctly configured when we go to war as a people. That's my own view. I think that when we go to war, it is something we need to do as a people, and therefore our Reserve Components make sure that that happens in the broadest possible sense. And I think that's right. But I don't think that the debate was about the role of the Congress vis-avis the role of the President. I think that's a debate that belongs somewhere else.

RGT: I was just reviewing a book last night on the President as Commander-in-Chief, put out by the University of Kansas. If you haven't read it yet or looked at it, it starts with William McKinley and progresses through Richard Nixon. I was struck by a line in there that said Presidents have committed troops 170 times in the 200 years since 1787, 1789, and only five times has the Congress declared war. So, it just reiterates what General Galvin said, that's a political question.

But the point, I think, that General Abrams was talking about what we called the Doctrine this morning 1972-73, after roughly eleven years of war in Southeast Asia, (and that's a horse of another color altogether, and the monolithic threat at that time) was, "How do you keep the Russians out of Western Europe?" And, you know, there's a big difference between that and something like Grenada.

FSG: And, of course, as far as the National Guard is concerned, they played really no role in that except what they might play as a citizen, and their job is to be available for the Army when it's required, and when they are called under law.

Q: I'd like to pick up on this thing because it goes back to something that General Reimer talked about earlier in the game. One of the important and critical elements in the Readiness equation is the factor of how much training time will you have available between mobilization and deployment or commitment.

General Reimer touched on decision gates, the incremental force building, the necessity to build up a domestic consensus, and the international coalition part of the equation, which is also very important.

What I would like to ask of whomever on the panel would like to touch on that, and I think it relates to this last question as well: Why is that time getting shorter, or longer, in your view? The time between mobilization and deployment or commitment.

JRG: Well, first of all, I think that it would be wrong to say today that we are in a situation where we won't have the luxury of having Reserve units in the Reserve Components, the Guard, for example, that would have relatively long preparation times after some crisis came up.

I can think of a variety of times when long preparation times would be acceptable. For one thing, if we look at what can happen to us now, we can have all kinds of varieties of crises, everything from an outright heavy conflict to a light conflict to a humanitarian assistance effort to a counter-terrorist, counter-drug operation, to a wide variety of things that can happen. Crises within crises.

We could have a situation in which we sent forces to participate in a crisis and then we needed to rotate those forces at a later time. And we would recognize that if we were going to send in forces we might want to rotate them, so therefore we might, in that case, call up Guard units who might be farther down the line in terms of their readiness, and begin to bring them up.

But we might have other Guard units that were Roundup or Roundout units that had a shorter time and, based on that, we would figure out how are going to sustain our efforts in this crisis.

We reached, if you take the Gulf crisis for example, a point at which, when we committed the VII Corps to the Gulf, and if we had then not gone to war but had sat there for some time, simply keeping Saddam from doing anything further— that may sound far-fetched, but I can think of lots of things that sound far-fetched that have happened. But if for some reason we had committed the VII Corps and then had not gone to war, we would have had a question come up immediately about how long are we are going to sustain that force there, and is it for duration? Or is it for a year? Or is it for a year and a half, or two years? Or what is it?

And the answer to that would have been, "Well, what Reserve Components do we have that can be made ready and in what time frames?"

And so we, in some cases, have to configure ourselves to the realities. And in this case, in a case like that or resembling that, the force that was committed would have to stay there, obviously, until it could be replaced. And so this could mean a long time.

However, I think that the more likely thing to happen is a require-ments that is short-fused, and therefore I think we do need to make this effort, right now, that I think we are making to see how good the Guard can get. And I would tell you, as I said before, that we don't know the answer to that. But we know how to find out.

We have a lot of capability, everything from the computer support, the simulation, the brigade-level training for key commanders and staff officers, the equipment that Denny mentioned coming back from Eu-rope, and the equipping of the Contingency Force, all with the best everything before somebody else gets something, on and on. There are a wide variety of actions that can be taken. But I think that we need to continue to look at a spectrum of time, of early readiness Guard units, middle and late readiness Guard units.

Q: If I can address, sir, perhaps more to General Reimer, because the other two generals may not be aware of this legislation on the Hill. Certainly, what we call the General Abrams Doctrine really had its implementation, if you will, or impetus in mobilization legislation that went to what we call to day the Presidential Selective Reserve Call-Up, or the 200,000K Call-Up.

Currently, there is in the DOD '94 Authorization bill presented to the Hill, legislation to amend that, what we call 673b, or the Presidential Selective Reserve Call-Up, to extend that call-up time frame. Two important areas of the amendment: One to extend the call-up time frame from 90-90 to 180-180 and, additionally, to give a step-down, a secretarial level, a SECDEF level if you will, call-up authority for a limited number of Reserve Components, like the Reservists.

My question really, is how significant do you see this modification? And do you see this as somewhat of an unconscious enhancement, if you will, of what we are calling the Abrams Doctrine today?

DJR: Let me take the Abrams Doctrine first, because I'm not clear in my mind whether General Abrams was trying to solve the problem of how you go to 16 Division from 13, with a fixed-in strength of 780K, or whether he was trying to solve the problem of how you prevent the Army from being committed without calling up the Reserves.

My guess is he was trying to solve both. But I personally never heard him talk about anything other than the tooth-to-tail ratio. There are a lot of other people that have been in those sessions that I wasn't in, so I'm not sure in what terms of the application to the Abrams Doctrine you are talking about.

What I am convinced of, though, is that the two specific points that you mentioned are lessons learned from Operation Desert Storm.

The 90 plus 90 was basically a tough thing to work your way through because about the time you got people over there, you had to start bring them back because, as you know, you have to have them off Active Duty by the 180 days, (90 plus 90). So you had to bring them on back. They have to go through the demobilization, that type of thing. The 180 plus 180 will give you much, much greater flexibility, and I think will work much better.

The other point had to do with the fact that it was about two weeks into Operation Desert Shield before we got 673b, and we had some units that we'd brought up, under the only thing we could, the Secretary of the Army's Active Duty for Training program. Some of those units were USAR units that ran ports and some other things that were critical. The Air Force I think also had some issues with volunteers and we all needed 673b. So I think there's a realization that we cannot get the force out of CONUS without the Reserve Component. And I think that's what that 25K is designed to do.

I think that reflects changes required by the power projection strategy; it reflects a crisis response strategy, and I think it will help us do that, so I feel that those are good initiatives.

Now, the Constitutional question has go to be solved by somebody besides me, but I certainly think from a military war-fighting stand-point, both of those are good initiatives.

FSG: Gentlemen, you are such an erudite panel, and your discussion has ranged so far, I'm not going to attempt to sum up for each of you. I'd like to have each of you take a couple of minutes to sum up your views on that afternoon's discussion. General Reimer.

DJR: Well, I would say that, first of all, I appreciate the opportunity to participate in this discussion, and I guess I did it for a number of reasons.

One, I figured that anything that could bring General Vessey all they way from Minnesota to Washington had to be important, so I came.

But, secondly, as FORSCOM Commander I find this issue terribly, terribly important. The Total Army is important to me, it's important to the Chief, and it's important to everybody in the Active Component.

But, most importantly, I came because of the tremendous respect and admiration I have for General Abrams. I was very fortunate to have has the opportunity to work for him, and it was just a great experience in my lifetime. I've been fortunate in a lot of ways, but that's the reason I'm here.

If I had to talk about the Abrams Doctrine, and as I said, this is kind of the first time that I've heard it, I would say the Abrams Doctrine was associated with the readiness of the Total Force. And I would go back to the point that used to stress: the terrible price of unpreparedness. When we are unprepared, we pay that price in blood. And he used to talk about the cemeteries and the monuments and the things that we've built to soothe our conscience, and I think that's what drove him. It's what drove a lot of our decisions during Operation Desert Storm.

I would tell you, as the DCSOPS of the Army, that I would think very often about him describing the terrible, terrible pain and human sacrifice associated with war. And I was committed, as I know a lot of other people were committed, not to send people over there who weren't ready for that particular battle.

At that time we were going through that, it wasn't at all clear that we were going to win this in a hundred hours, and that we were going to have less than a hundred casualties. There were some tough decisions that had to be made, and that's what drove our decisions at that time.

I think the world has changed, obviously; we've talked about that, and I think everybody understands that and knows the Army is changing. I don't think we are given credit for the changes that we are making. When you look at all that we are doing right now, and the fact that we are reshaping the Army, I think we are managing that fairly well. So I'm not going to hang my head and apologize for what we've done. We have taken, as was mentioned already, over 250,000 people out of the Total Army. That's 150,000 Active Component, 50,000 Reserve Component, and 50,000 DA civilians, since Operation Desert Storm. And we still have a higher optempo in '93 than we had in '89.

So I think we are doing okay. There is uncertainty out there in the Total Force; we need to solve that. I think the Bottom-Up Review will help us in that particular area. I think it's obvious that we are going to get smaller. The challenge that all of us face here, I think, is how do we get smaller and still keep this great organization together? How do we keep the Total Army strong?

I really believe that we've got to leverage the strength of each component. I see that as I go around from place to place, each component bring a certain strength to the table. Our challenge is to talk to each other, to build that trust and confidence among each other so that we

342

do leverage that strength and we do keep the Army strong and we do continue that great history that we've had for over 218 years.

We can't do it overnight. As we've talked about, and as I've mentioned many times, there are initiatives on the board that are working. They haven't all matured, they haven't all been approved, but they are positive. We've got Total Army groups that meet and talk about these things. I think there's some great things on the table that have to be fleshed out and have to mature, and be approved. But I think we are moving in the right direction. I'm very comfortable that that is true.

I think the primary bottom line for me is that we've all got to resolve that we are going to do what's right for the nation. If everybody approaches it from that standpoint, I think we are going to be okay.

JRG: Well, I would start by saying that the Total Army is the only way. There is no other way in the United States, I don't think, that would be satisfactory to the people, that would be a continuation of our historical view, our tradition. And that's one of the reasons I wanted to be here today. And because, like Jack Vessey, I started out in the Guard and have always felt that that was a big advantage, and I always have felt that it formed a lot of my thinking, which you probably can see in what I have had to say, or what I'm saying now.

I don't know what was said this morning because of my absence here, on the state role of the Guard. But I think that we always have to think of that, also. I mean, there are certain things that are vitally important in terms of the Guard and the relationship it has to the state and to the governor as its commander. And therefore, I think that we have to consider the effect of that on the question of the balance of combat, combat support, and combat service support, because I think that the Guard still needs to be a well rounded force, a militarily capable force on its own. And, no, I don't necessarily mean it has to mirror somehow the Active Component. And I don't really think that it's necessarily so, that it should mirror it. But I do think it needs, and there's something that has to be constantly looked at, the combat element as well as the other elements.

In terms of the Abrams Doctrine, I think that it is important to see that what we are talking about there is war and the American people, and I don't know of a subject that could be more important than that.

We need to see, from the point of view of military people, what it is that we can do and how it is that we configure ourselves so that we are able to respond in the most effective ways possible, but also in ways that take that into account, and I think that was one of the purposes of today.

And so I think it needs to be emphasized, again and again, that when we go to war, we go to war as a Total Army, just as we train and configure ourselves as a Total Army.

We can take great pride in the way that the Army has changed for the better in the past couple of decades. I know that in the 24th Division I used to say sometimes, and actually I was quoting people who had talked to me, to soldiers and NCOs and Officers, "Do you feel ready for combat with the kind of training we've been getting?" And they would say, immediately, "Yes, Sir." And I'd say, "Are you ready for the National Training Center?" And they would say, "Well, we've got a few things we've got to work on here. We need a little time." We have built the National Training Center and the other things we've discussed.

I can remember, as you can, too, because it hasn't been long ago, that when we came out with a new tank table, everybody said, "This is impossible. How are we ever going to reach this? I said it, myself. I looked at that and gulped, and said, "This is what they want us to? This is how we are going to score, on these templates? Firing on the move, firing as a platoon, and so forth and so on? And I didn't think we could do it. And we did do it. We made great strides.

I think we have to be frank enough to say that the Guard didn't make the same great strides, proportionately, in that period. And it's clear what the Congress thinks about that. Probably we all in the Active Component, I should put myself in the past in that, but I think the Active Component realizes, too, that there's a support question there. There is a resourcing question. And I think the Active Component is dedicated to addressing that even more strongly than in the past.

Ground maneuver is extraordinarily complex. It's a big difference between what happened when Napoleon did his planning for Waterloo and he conducted that battle. He wasn't worried about air strikes and a lot of other things. Or, Nelson at Trafalgar wasn't worried about what was over the sea or under the sea, just what was on the surface. We operated on a map that was two-dimensional. It was a flat map.

But today, any soldier has to know that the map's not flat, It's a cube. It's three-dimensional. And this makes an enormous difference.

And trying to—I forget what you called it, Dick, but I call it "orchestrate." You called it—

RGT: Dexterity.

JRG: Dexterity. I call it the ability to orchestrate, or people call it "synchronizing." But whatever it really is, to try to pull all that together is a very, very difficult thing to learn. And the challenge there is for Guard leadership at the squad, platoon, company, and battery and so forth, squadron, battalion, brigade, division level, to work that.

Maybe it would be in the long run that the Guard would keep division flags but basically be brigades. This is true in many cases already. But I don't think that we would either say, the combat side is something that we could only use in very limited terms, or the combat side is something that could work only in terms of being ready, let's say, at platoon or company level. I still think battalion is a level that we can challenge the Guard with and a level they can reach if they get the right resources, because they already have the right spirit and dedication to do it. And I would end here.

RGT: Let me start by saying I was very privileged in 1951 to be the liaison officer from the 70th Armored Field Artillery in Merrill Barracks to what for one month was Lieutenant Colonel Abrams, and then Colonel Abrams when he was Commander of the 2nd Armored Cavalry Regiment.

If you want to have an education, you want to sit down beside him as his Field Artillery liaison officer when you are out in the field, which we spent a great deal of time doing. I got a great education, I can tell you that. And I say that because of the comments that have been made here on this emphasis on training. I remember one day. It rained like hell, lightning hit the OP, nothing went right, the mess truck got lost, battalions were wandering around in the wilderness, and at 5:00 a.m. he called the officers together. He stood under a tree, and I can see it and hear him now. He said, "Gentlemen, what does it all prove? God-damn it, we are not qualified!" That's what he said.

That's all he had to say. We knew it. because if we had been any good, we'd have done it whether it was raining or shining or any other damn thing. But that was his standard. And that's what he was trying to get across.

And, year, he wanted to make sure that when we went to war, we went as a Total Army.

Some of you have been privileged to spend the last thirty years as close to this as I have, and to see the difference now compared to thirty years ago. Unbelievable. If you think we've got problems now, sure we do; but when you think of what it was thirty years ago and what it is now, it's unbelievable.

But we are at a time to change. We are at a time, not change for change's sake, but because of technology, because of politics, because of education, because of all the things that make our world, externally and internally, all the dynamics that affect the Total Army, this is a time of opportunity.

But to do that you have to have a real inquisitive, questioning mind. And you have to ask yourself, "Why do we do this?" And if we do that, then I think we have nowhere to go but up.

FSG: Gentlemen, you've been a truly wonderful panel. It's been my very real privilege and pleasure to be associated with you. Thank you so much. General Ensslin.

[APPLAUSE]

RFE: We've been privileged today to have assembled here at the National Guard Memorial, I think, the greatest assortment of experience in the Reserve Component world that could be assembled. Certainly, the experience of the National Guard and the experience of the Army has been here with us, and I don't know how we could have added more experience to the two moderators and the six panelists and the luncheon speaker that we had today.

We have been greatly stimulated by these discussions. I think all of us have had an awful lot of ideas racing through our heads as a result of the things that were said here. I think we've been challenged by people of wisdom and experience in the world that means so much to us, and I think that, as we reflect further, some very positive and worthwhile things for the Total National Defense will come forth.

As General Temple said, the Guard does change. General Vessey said, you know, we have got to change. Obviously.

Well, we do change, and we have adapted over our 355-plus years of being. General Galvin has traced those early years of the Militia for us. I know I joined a National Guard artillery battery organized at 55 percent strength, and our challenge was that, if we were needed, we were going to have to be ready to deploy and fight in probably six to twelve months.

And the training year General Temple referred to had two events. One was the annual IG inspection, when the Army came to take a look. We spent six months getting ready for that. The other key event was the ATT, the Army Training Test that we took at annual training. We spent the other six months getting ready for that. It was a different world.

We've come a long way and, as several of our speakers have said, we've got to keep in mind how much progress we've made. But we also have to keep in mind what General Galvin said. We don't really know yet, with all of our experience, exactly what level we are capable of achieving. We haven't done enough or gone far-enough to have a very clear picture of just what the limits are in the National Guard. At least, I read that into General Galvin's remarks, and it's my feeling.

But, again, a round of applause for all of our participants today, and our thanks for being here with us.

[APPLAUSE]

MEMORANDUMS

The Secretary of Defense
Washington, D.C. 20301
August 21, 1970

MEMORANDUM FOR
Secretaries of the Military Departments
Chairman, Joint Chiefs of Staff
Director, Defense Research and Engineering
Assistant Secretaries of Defense
Department of Defense Agencies

SUBJECT: Support for Guard and Reserve Forces

The President has requested expenditures during Fiscal Year 1971 and extension of these economies into future budgets. Within the Department of Defense, these economics will require reductions in overall strengths and capabilities of the active forces, and increased reliance on the combat and combat support units of the Guard and Reserves. I am concerned with the readiness of Guard and Reserve units to respond to contingency requirement and with the lack of resources that have been made available to Guard and Reserve commanders to improve Guard and Reserve Readiness.

Public Law 90-168, an outgrowth of similar Congressional concern, places responsibility with the respective Secretaries of the Military Departments for recruiting, organizing, equipping and training of Guard and Reserve Forces. I desire that the Secretaries of the Military Departments provided in the FY 1972 and future budgets, the necessary resources to permit the appropriate balance in the development of Active, Guard and Reserve Forces.

Emphasis will be given to concurrent consideration of the total forces, active and reserve, to determine the most advantageous mix to support national strategy and meet the threat. A total force concept that will be applied in all aspects of planning, programming, manning, equipping and employing Guard and Reserve Forces. Application of the concept will be geared to recognition that in many instances the lower peacetime sustaining costs of reserve force units, compared to similar active units, can result in a larger total force for a given budget or the same size force for a lesser budget. In addition, attention will be given to the fact that Guard and Reserve Forces can perform peaceful missions as a by-product or adjunct of training with significant manpower and monetary savings.

Guard and Reserve units and individuals of the Selected Reserves will be prepared to be the initial and primary source for augmentation of the active forces in any future emergency requiring a rapid and substantial expansion of the active forces. Toward this end, the Assistant Secretary of Defense (Manpower and Reserve Affairs) is responsible for coordinating and monitoring actions to achieve the following objectives:

- Increase the readiness, reliability and timely responsiveness of the combat and combat support units of the Guard and Reserve and individuals of the Reserve.

- Support and maintain minimum average trained strengths of the Selected Reserve as mandated by Congress.

- Provide and maintain combat standard equipment for Guard and Reserve units in the necessary quantities; and provide the necessary controls to identify resources committed for Guard and Reserve logistic support through the planning, programming, budgeting, procurement and distribution cycle.

- Implement the approved ten-year construction programs for the Guard and Reserves, subject to their accommodation within the currently approved TOA, with priority to facilities that will provide the greatest improvement in readiness levels.

- Provide adequate support of individual and unit reserve training programs.

- Provide manning levels for technicians and training and administration reserve support personnel (TARS) equal to full authorization levels.

- Program adequate resources and establish necessary priorities to achieve readiness levels required by appropriate guidance documents as rapidly as possible.

The Secretary of Defense
Washington, D.C. 20201
August 23, 1973

MEMORANDUM FOR
Secretaries of the Military Departments
Chairman, Joint Chiefs of Staff
Director, Defense Research and Engineering
Assistant Secretaries of Defense
Director, Defense Program Analysis and Evaluation
Directors of Defense Agencies

SUBJECT: Readiness of the Selected Reserve

As integral part of the central purpose of this Department — to build and maintain the necessary forces to deter war and to defend our country — is the Total Force Policy as it pertains to the Guard and Reserve. It must be clearly understood that implicit in the Total Force

Policy, as emphasized by Presidential and National Security Council documents, the Congress and Secretary of Defense policy, is the fact that the Guard and Reserve forces will be used as the initial and primary augmentation of the Active forces.

Total Force is no longer a "concept." It is now the Total Force Policy which integrates the Active, Guard and Reserve forces into a homogenous whole.

As a result of this policy, the Selected Reserve has moved towards timely responsiveness and combat capability. Application of this policy has improved equipping, funding, facilities, construction, programming and some training areas.

I recognize and appreciate the great amount of effort that has been made to develop the Guard and Reserve. Progress has been made.

However, gross readiness measurements (which should be improved) indicate that we have not yet reached a level consistent with the objective response times. It is clear that we should move as much post-mobilization administration as possible to the pre-mobilization period and streamline all remaining post-mobilization administrative and training activities.

We must assure that the readiness gains in the Selected Reserves are maintained and they we move vigorously ahead to reach required readiness and deployment response times in areas still deficient.

I want each Service Secretary to approach affirmatively the goals of producing Selected Reserve units which will meet readiness standards required for wartime contingencies. Each Secretary will provide the manning, equipping, training, facilities, construction and maintenance necessary to assure that the Selected Reserve units meet deployment times and readiness required by contingency plans. You will have my support and personal interest in overcoming any obstacles in these areas.

The Assistant Secretary of Defense for Manpower and Reserve Affairs is charged by statute and by Defense policy and Directives with the responsibility for all matters concerning Reserve Affairs. It is my desire that the Assistant Secretary of Defense for Manpower and Reserve Affairs, as a matter of priority, take such actions as are necessary to bring the Selected Reserve to readiness goals. In this respect, the Services, the other Assistant Secretaries of Defense, the Joint Chiefs of Staff, the Director of Defense Program Analysis and Evaluation and other Defense Agencies will provide support on a priority basis. Particular emphasis will be placed on assistance in manning, equipping and training. The Deputy Assistant Secretary of Defense (Reserve Affairs) will continue to function in accord with current statutes and directives.

To emphasize and to strengthen Selected Reserve management, I suggest a civilian Deputy Assistant Secretary for Reserve Affairs in the office of each of the Assistant Secretaries of the Military Departments for the Manpower and Reserve Affairs. This Deputy should be supported by an adequate staff and be assigned responsibilities and functions similar to those assigned the Deputy Assistant Secretary of Defense for Reserve Affairs.

At the military level, the Navy has been given specific guidelines for developing the new office of Chief of Naval Reserve. The Air Force and Marine Corps management structure has produced combat readiness and that is the vital test. I expect that the Army's reorganization, with strong command emphasis and good selection of leaders will produce demonstrably visible improvement and I shall follow the results with interest.

The Chiefs of the National Guard and Reserve components will be the staff level managers of the Guard and Reserve programs, budgets, policy, funds, force structure, plans, etc. They will be provided the authority, responsibility and means with which to accomplish their functions effectively. The overall management responsibility of the Chiefs of the Selected Reserve, under the Service Chiefs, will be supported by all other appropriate staff agencies.

In addition to the foregoing emphasis on Reserve Force policy and management, I am asking my Deputy Assistant Secretary for Reserve Affairs, with your support, to manage a study covering the issues of availability, force mix, limitations and potential of Guard and Reserve Forces.

In summary, strong management with achievement of readiness levels in the Selected Reserve is among our highest priorities — we must and will accomplish this objective as soon as possible.

National Desert Storm Reservists Day, 1991
By the President of the United States of America

A Proclamation

On this occasion we gratefully salute the members of the National Guard and Reserve forces of the United States—dedicated and highly trained men and women who played a major role in the success of Operation Desert Shield/Desert Storm. Whether they served directly in the Persian Gulf or on military bases in the United States and elsewhere around the world, as member of our Nation's Total Force, these National Guardsmen and reservists made a vital contribution toward the liberation of Kuwait.

During the course of the war in the Persian Gulf, more than 228,000 members of the Ready Reserve were ordered to active duty. Thousands more volunteered in advance of being called to support the coalition effort. Members of the Army National Guard, the Army Reserve, the Naval Reserve, the Marine Corps Reserve, the Air National Guard, the Air Force Reserve, and the Coast Guard Reserve—these men and women were trained and ready to do their jobs. As they have done for all conflicts since colonial times, guardsmen and reservists responded quickly to the call. They promptly assumed a variety of combat missions such as armor, artillery, tactical fighter, tactical reconnaissance, and minesweeping. Their support missions included transportation, medical, airlift, service/supply, civil affairs, intelligence, military police, and communications.

When called to active duty, members of the Ready Reserve were suddenly required to leave behind their families and their careers. As we thank our Desert Storm reservists for the many sacrifices that they have made in behalf of our country, it is fitting that we also honor their loved ones. They too have shown the extraordinary degree of patriotism and courage that we have come to expect of the Nation's military families. National Guard and Reservist units worked in close cooperation with the Active Services to develop a broad-based family support network to assist these new military dependents.

The Nation's employers, educators, and other institutions throughout the private sector have provided strong support and assistance to their reservists employees and students who were called to duty on short notice. The National Committee for Employer Support of the Guard and Reserve, a 4,000-member network of business and civic leader volunteers, has put forth special efforts to help guardsmen and reservists, as well as their employers, to understand their job and responsibilities.

In recognition of their vital role in the liberation of Kuwait, the Congress, by Senate Joint Resolution 134, has designated May 22, 1991, as "National Desert Storm Reservists Day" and has authorized and requested the President to issue a proclamation in observance of this day.

NOW, THEREFORE, I, GEORGE BUSH, President of the United States of America, do hereby proclaim May 22, 1991, as National Desert Storm Reservists Day. I call upon all Americans to observe this day with appropriate ceremonies and activities in honor of the courageous men and women of the United States Ready Reserve.

IN WITNESS WHEREOF, I have hereunto set my hand this twenty-first day of May, in the year of our Lord nineteen hundred and ninety-one, and of the Independence of the United States of America the two hundred and fifteenth.

NATIONAL GUARD GOALS FOR THE 90'S

WE, THE NATIONAL GUARD-AMERICA'S TEAM

1. **The highest state of readiness commensurate with wartime tasking** - Attained and maintained through the efforts of satisfied, motivated, quality-equipped, quality-trained, quality-supported soldiers and airmen.

2. **Equal opportunities for career development** — Each man and woman must have equal opportunity for entry into the National Guard. Each National Guard soldier and airman must have equal opportunity to plan and develop a productive and personally rewarding military career.

3. **An increased role in counter-narcotics operations** — Expand National Guard support of local, state, and federal law enforcement agencies in the interdiction and eradication of illegal drugs.

4. **Effective response to natural and man-made state emergencies** — Increased emphasis on planning, equipping, training, and mobilizing for state missions.

5. **A cleaner environment** — Aggressively pursue a cleaner environment through identifying and correcting problems, and by developing preventive measures. Strict compliance to environmental protection laws is paramount.

6. **Strong community support for the National Guard** — Increase the public's knowledge and support of the purpose, goals, missions, and capabilities of their National Guard through increased emphasis on Public Affairs.

7. **Employers in partnership with the National Guard** — Create a "full partner" relationship with the employers of our National Guardsmen. This teamwork provides stability and continuity between the dual roles of citizen soldiers and airmen, and enhances retention.

8. **Improved quality of life for National Guard Families** — All commanders and leaders need to be active in organizing and supporting National Guard Family Program activities. Guard families are an important part of readiness, recruiting, and retention.

9. **Effective management of all resources** — Optimizing the use of National Guard resources through comprehensive planning and analysis linked to programming.

10. **Institutionalize Total Quality Management (TQM) within the National Guard** — TQM highlights teamwork and team structure. Teamwork aligns personal and organizational goals, objectives, and thought. Team activities build communication and cooperation, stimulate creative thinking, and provide an infrastructure for improving all National Guard processes. TQM also focuses on doing things right the first time — an effort that increases unit effectiveness and stops wasted resources.

BIOGRAPHIES

Lt. Gen. John B. Conaway

Lieutenant General John B. Conaway's military career spans five decades, from college ROTC during the Korean War to the triumph of his Guard forces in Desert Storm.

Upon graduation from the University of Evansville, he spent four years on active duty with the USAF flying continental air defense on the Distant Early Warning (DEW) line situated along the northern US border.

He joined the WVANG in 1960 and flew special operation missions for three years before transferring to the KYANG in 1963. He became a full-time Guardsman in 1965, rising in rank as a flight training instructor and test pilot. In January 1968, then-Maj. Conaway and the 123rd Tactical Reconnaissance Wing were mobilized in response to the North Korean seizure of the USS *Pueblo*. He spent the next 18 months flying on active duty in Korea, Japan, Panama and Alaska.

Deactivated in 1969, Conaway rose to the rank of Colonel and became vice-wing commander of the 123rd. Two years later, after a nationwide search, he was chosen Deputy Director of the ANG and transferred to the Pentagon in 1977. In 1981 he was appointed Director of the Air Guard and promoted to major general. Reappointed director in 1985, in 1988 he was selected to become the first-ever Vice-Chief of the National Guard. He was elevated to Chief of the National Guard by President George Bush in February 1990.

John Conaway's long-time experience as a field commander and his intimate knowledge of the Pentagon and Washington politics provide him with a rare military background. He has received numerous state, federal and foreign military decorations, is a command pilot with more than 8,500 hours of flying time, and has been recognized by organizations as varied as the National Association for the Advancement of Colored People and the Air Force Non-Commissioned Officers Association.

Known throughout the Pentagon as the "states' rights general", he is a familiar figure on Capitol Hill and in hundreds of cities and towns across the United States. In many ways, Gen. Conaway's tenure in the Guard, his visibility throughout the nation, and his advocacy of the citizen-soldier concept have led many to consider him a leading representative of the National Guard.

BIOGRAPHIES

JEFF P. NELLIGAN

Currently the Director of Communications for the U.S. House of Representatives' Tranportation and Infrastructure Committee, chaired by Congressman Bud Shuster (R-PA), Jeff Nelligan has spent the last decade in Washington working in a variety of goverment positions. He served as Press Secretary to Congressman Bill Thomas (R-CA), current Chairman of the House Oversight Committee, and then later worked as a speechwriter for the Deputy Secretary of State and Administrator, U.S. Agency for International Development. He also served as a legal aide to Commissioner Carol Crawford, a senior member of the U.S. International Trade Commission.

Nelligan has been an enlisted member of the U.S. Army Reserves and National Guard since 1988 and presently serves with the 629th Military Intelligence Battalion, 29th Infantry Division, in Laurel, Maryland. He is a graduate of the U.S. Army Air Assault School and the French Army's Brevet Commando School in Martinique.

Prior to coming to Washington, Nelligan was an editorialist at William F. Buckley, Jr.'s *National Review* magazine, the *Cincinnati Enquirer*, the *San Diego Union*, and the *Carteret County (N.C.) News-Times*.

Nelligan is a graduate of Williams College and Georgetown University Law School. He lives in Bethesda, Maryland with his wife, Beatrice, and two sons, Devlin, and Braden, both future E-1's in the National Guard.

INDEX